INTO THE LION'S MOUTH

THE TRUE STORY OF DUSKO POPOV: WORLD WAR II SPY, PATRIOT, AND THE REAL-LIFE INSPIRATION FOR JAMES BOND

»

LARRY LOFTIS

BERKLEY CALIBER, NEW YORK

An imprint of Penguin Random House LLC
375 Hudson Street, New York, New York 10014

This book is an original publication of Penguin Random House LLC.

Library of Congress Cataloging-in-Publication Data

Names: Loftis, Larry, author.
Title: Into the lion's mouth : the true story of Dusko Popov : World War II spy, patriot, and the real-life inspiration for James Bond / by Larry Loftis.
Other titles: True story of Dusko Popov, World War II spy, patriot, and the real-life inspiration for James Bond
Description: First edition. | New York, NY : Berkley Caliber, an imprint of Penguin Random House LLC, [2016] | Includes bibliographical references and index.
Identifiers: LCCN 2015039212 | ISBN 9780425281819
Subjects: LCSH: Popov, Dusko. | World War, 1939–1945—Secret service—Great Britain. | World War, 1939–1945—Secret service—Germany. | Spies—Great Britain—Biography. | Spies—Germany—Biography. | Espionage—Germany—History—20th century. | Espionage—Great Britain—History—20th century.
Classification: LCC D810.S8 P6 2016 | DDC 940.54/8641092—dc23
LC record available at https://lccn.loc.gov/2015039212

First edition: June 2016

PRINTED IN THE UNITED STATES OF AMERICA

10 9 8 7 6 5 4 3 2

Jacket design by Daniela Medina.
Front jacket photograph of man © Michael Dos Santos/Gallery Stock.
Illustration of swirl © Miloje / Shutterstock Images.

Interior text design by Kelly Lipovich.

Penguin
Random
House

[H]e had the steel within, the ruthlessness and the cold-blooded courage that enabled him to go back to the German Secret Service Headquarters in Lisbon and Madrid time and time again, when it was likely that he was blown; it was like putting his head into the lion's mouth.

—LIEUTENANT-COMMANDER EWEN MONTAGU
British Double-Cross Committee (1940–1945)

My own life is much less important to me than that of my family. . . . I hope to continue to be useful to our common cause and to be able to help within my modest means to bring the victory which alone will bring me happiness.

—DUSKO POPOV
Letter to Major Tar Robertson, August 9, 1941

CONTENTS

MAP ix

DRAMATIS PERSONAE xi

PREFACE 1

1 » FORGING THE ANVIL 3

2 » EXITING FEET FIRST 9

3 » SPYING FOR HITLER, KILLING FOR CHURCHILL 14

4 » MAGIC 21

5 » THE BEE HIVE 28

6 » TOO MANY DEVICES 39

7 » PASSION AND ADDICTION 46

8 » DEATH IN THE AFTERNOON 54

9 » "HE'S NOT DEAD" 61

10 » TARANTO AND THE TARGET 68

11 » CASINO ESTORIL 77

12 » PEARL HARBOR WARNING 88

13 » COVER-UP 99

14 » I'LL KILL HER 115

15 » BUTTERFLIES AND CARNAGE 123

16 » BLOWN 133

17 » INCOMPLETE CANVAS 146

18 » THE ART OF THE SILENT KILL 154

19 » "TURN AROUND SLOWLY" 165

20 » TICKING 174

21 » FIVE LIVES 182

22 » SHOTS RANG OUT 189

23 » TRUTH SERUM 198

24 » *AUF* 209

25 » D-DAY 221

26 » NAKED AND SHAVED 237

27 » ULLA 241

28 » PARTISAN POLITICS 247

29 » JOHNNY 254

EPILOGUE 259

SOURCES AND ACKNOWLEDGMENTS 267

APPENDIX 1: AUGUST 19, 1941, TRANSMITTAL LETTER FROM E. J. CONNELLEY TO J. EDGAR HOOVER WITH PEARL HARBOR QUESTIONNAIRE 273

APPENDIX 2: POPOV OPERATIONS 277

APPENDIX 3: IAN FLEMING'S BOND AND POTENTIAL MODELS 279

APPENDIX 4: LIVING *CASABLANCA* AND *DR. NO* 285

NOTES 287

BIBLIOGRAPHY 339

INDEX 351

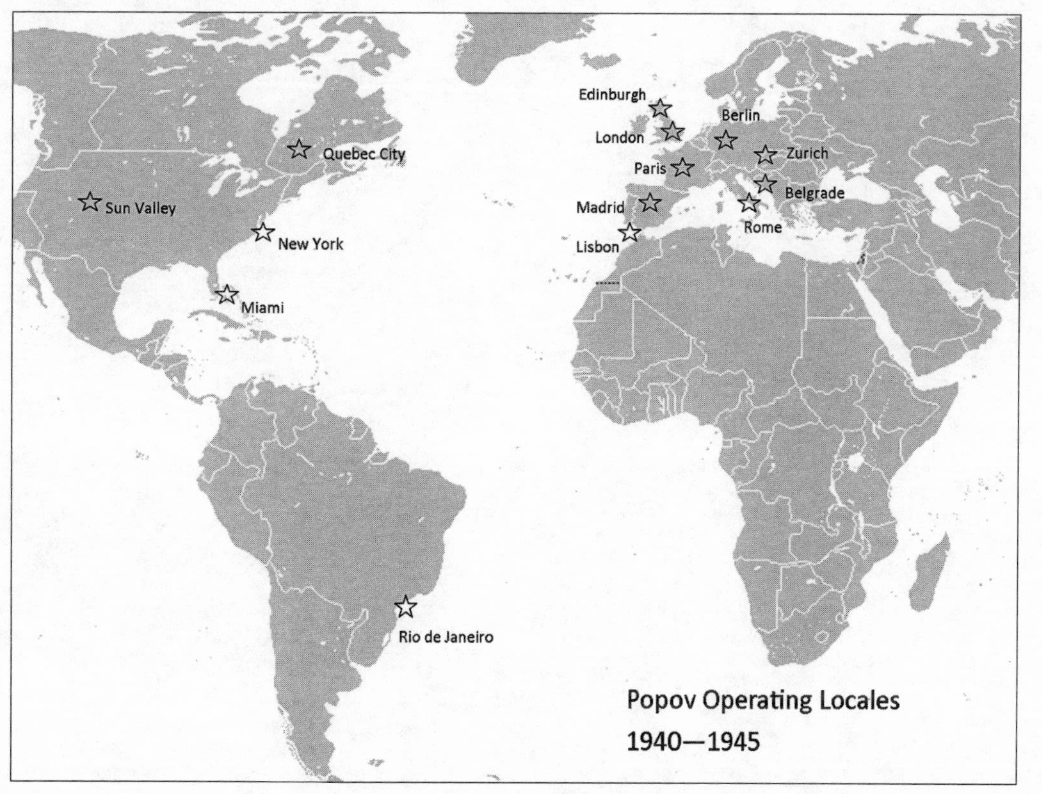
Edinburgh
Berlin
London
Quebec City
Zurich
Paris
Belgrade
Sun Valley
Madrid
Rome
New York
Lisbon
Miami
Rio de Janeiro
Popov Operating Locales
1940—1945

DRAMATIS PERSONAE

TRICYCLE NETWORK DOUBLE AGENTS

Marquis Frano de Bona » FREAK (Popov's radio operator; German, GUTTMANN)

Friedl Gaertner » GELATINE (German, IVONNE)

Johann Jebsen » ARTIST

Dickie Metcalfe » BALLOON (German, IVAN II)

Dusko Popov » TRICYCLE, SKOOT (German, IVAN)

Ivo Popov » DREADNOUGHT (German, PAULA)

Hans Ruser » JUNIOR

Eugen Sostaric » METEOR

Stefan Zeis » THE WORM

MI5 (SECURITY INTELLIGENCE SERVICE) STAFF

Guy Liddell » Section B chief

William Luke » Dusko Popov case officer (initial)

John Marriott » Assistant to Colonel Tar Robertson

Colonel T. A. "Tar" Robertson » Section B1A (Double Agents) chief

Ian Wilson » Dusko Popov case officer

MI6 (SECRET INTELLIGENCE SERVICE) STAFF AND AGENTS

Kenneth Benton » Agent, Madrid

Major Desmond Bristow » Agent, Lisbon

Colonel Felix Cowgill » Section V (Counterintelligence) chief

Major Frank Foley » Section V (Counterintelligence)

Cecil Gledhill » Lisbon station chief following Colonel Ralph Jarvis

Major Peter Hope » Agent, Paris

Colonel Ralph Jarvis » Lisbon station chief

Major-General Stewart Menzies » Director; "C"

Major Walter Wren » Trinidad station chief (and part of Popov's New York support team)

DOUBLE-CROSS COMMITTEE

Rear Admiral John Godfrey » Director of Naval Intelligence (boss of Montagu and Ian Fleming)

Professor J. C. Masterman » Chairman, Double-Cross Committee; Oxford don

Lieutenant-Commander Ewen Montagu » Naval Intelligence (working closely with Popov)

BRITISH SECURITY COORDINATION (NEW YORK)

Colonel C. H. "Dick" Ellis » Assistant to Director Stephenson (transfer from MI6)

Captain H. Montgomery Hyde » MI6 Security Officer, Bermuda Censorship

William Stephenson » Director (code name, INTREPID)

ABWEHR STAFF

Abwehr I » Foreign Intelligence (I H = Army)

Abwehr III » Counterespionage

Admiral Wilhelm Canaris » Director

Albrecht Engels » Agent, Rio de Janeiro station (code name, ALFREDO)

Colonel Georg Hansen » Replaced Pieckenbrock as head of Abwehr I

***Oberstleutnant* Hans Kammler** » I H West, Berlin, Spain, Portugal

Major Albert (Ludovico) von Karsthoff » Lisbon station chief

Lieutenant Fritz Kramer » Abwehr III, Lisbon

Colonel Gustav "Papa" Lenz » Madrid station chief

Colonel Ernst Munzinger » I H East chief, Balkans

Colonel Hans Pieckenbrock » Head of Abwehr I

Elisabeth Sahrbach » Secretary/mistress of Major von Karsthoff

Major Aloys Schreiber » Head of Abwehr I H West, Anglo-American Section

Lieutenant Colonel Martin Töppen » Financial supervisor

Major Helmut Wiegand » Paris station chief

SD AND GESTAPO STAFF

Major Adolf Nassenstein » SD agent, Lisbon
General Major Walter Schellenberg » Nazi Foreign Intelligence chief, head of SD
Major Erich Schroeder » SD agent, Lisbon chief following von Karsthoff
SD » *Sicherheitsdienst* (Nazi Security Service, branch of the Gestapo)
Dr. Warnecke » Gestapo specialist

FBI STAFF

E. J. Connelley » Assistant Director, New York (initial Popov supervisor)
Percy "Sam" Foxworth » Assistant Director, Security Division (Counterintelligence); Assistant Director in charge of New York Division, head of Special Intelligence Service (Popov supervisor)
J. Edgar Hoover » Director
Charles Lanman » Special Agent, New York (Popov case officer)

OTHERS

Victor Cavendish-Bentinck » British Foreign Office; Chairman, Joint Intelligence Committee
William "Wild Bill" Donovan » Director, Office of Strategic Services (forerunner of the CIA)
OKW » German Armed Forces Supreme Command
King Peter II » King of Yugoslavia
Terry Richardson » Popov girlfriend
Simone Simon » Hollywood actress, Popov girlfriend
SOE » Special Operations Executive (British commandos)

PREFACE

He knew he'd have to kill him.

It was late July 1943. In a luxury villa salon on Portugal's Riviera, British double agent Dusko Popov waited for his German controller, Major Ludovico von Karsthoff. By now his Abwehr minder had more than enough evidence to believe Dusko was doubling for the Allies.

British Colonel Tar Robertson had warned him not to return. How would Popov explain his complete failure to provide the Germans with anything useful in the last fourteen months? How would he answer for the FBI radio messages sent in his name? How would he justify not visiting the Pearl Harbor naval base as instructed? When Dusko replied that the Germans probably wouldn't kill him right away, his case officer, Ian Wilson, said, "You might wish they had."

The odds were good—far more than even—that von Karsthoff would have orders to arrest him on the spot. That wasn't going to happen. Popov was an expert marksman, and his Luger rested inside his coat with a chambered round.

Problem was, he might be outgunned. If a Gestapo agent came in with the major, he'd have no chance. They'd take his weapon and truss him up for a long night of interrogation and torture. Once the lemon was fully squeezed, they'd discard him in a Lumiar alley.

He nudged off the Luger's safety.

Glancing about the room, he saw two doorways, one to a dining hall and the other a set of French doors leading to a garden. He stepped to the window and peered outside. As he studied the escape route, his mind raced through the last three and a half years of intrigue and double dealing.

Suddenly, steps behind him—

"Turn around slowly, Popov, and don't make any sudden moves."

Von Karsthoff's tone was hard.

Dusko slipped his palm over the pistol.

1 »

FORGING THE ANVIL

The word *spy* carries with it a certain pejorative connotation. Soldiers serve with patriotism and courage. Admirals lead with brilliance and heavenly wisdom. Field marshals and generals attack gallantly and operate, as Rommel proved, within an ethical code of conduct. Spies, on the other hand, thrive between the shadows of deceit and skullduggery.

Spies lie with impunity and lie with the enemy. They double-cross without conscience and kill without confession. If a spy wasn't a criminal before the secret service, he became one in the process. As one intelligence officer put it, he "must be prepared to be a villain, to be ruthless and dishonest in one role while being honest and tolerant in another. Second, he must be, or try to be, a good showman."

Like none other, Dusko Popov was born for the role. With equal measure he could and did wear all masks: villain and hero, killer and lover, deceiver and patriot.

But above all, he was a showman.

»

Born July 10, 1912, in Titel, Serbia, Dusan "Dusko" Miladoroff Popov was the second of Milorad Popov's three sons—Ivan, Dusko, and Vladan—and the grandson of Omer Popov, a wealthy banker and industrialist who had built a sizeable empire of factories, mines, and retail businesses. Dusko's father continued the family business, adding residential real estate to their investments. Like many of Europe's aristocrats, the family divided their time between luxury homes—a winter residence in Belgrade and summer retreat in Dubrovnik.

The boys grew up sailing the Adriatic, playing water polo and tennis, and riding horses. Vladan, the youngest of Popov's sons, was not as personally close as his brothers and would spend the war years in college. Dusko's older brother, Ivan ("Ivo")—whom Dusko idolized—was six-foot-two and handsome. An instinctive leader, Ivo would become a surgeon and a courageous operative in the Yugoslav resistance. Like Dusko, Ivo was intelligent, charismatic, and intensely independent—traits which would endanger their lives in the years to come.

Milorad Popov desired a first-rate education for his boys. Vladan would attend the universities at Freiburg and Bologna, and later medical school in Paris. Ivo would receive an undergraduate degree at the Sorbonne, a medical degree at the University of Belgrade, and a surgery degree from the University of Naples. Dusko would travel to three countries before he finished. When he was sixteen, his father enrolled him at Ewell Castle, a well-respected preparatory school outside London. Housed in a castellated mansion on the former grounds of Henry VIII's Nonsuch Palace, the institution was the epitome of Gothic revival and pupil refinement. Dusko's refining, however, was not to be; at least not there. Three months after enrolling he confounded the staid establishment with a belligerent independence not seen before, or since. One day after missing a detention, Dusko was sentenced to a cane whipping. Objecting that the adjudication was inappropriate for the offense, Dusko snatched the cane from the teacher and snapped it in two—in front of the class.

He was expelled.

»

Popov transferred to the Lycée in Paris and managed to matriculate without incident. Upon graduation he enrolled at the University of Belgrade, where he received a law degree. Not particularly keen on commencing a demanding legal practice, he decided to pursue a doctorate in law at the University of Freiburg.

Graduate work in Germany seemed illogical; the country was politically unstable and German was his fourth language. But Germany dominated the cultural and economic realms of southeastern Europe, he felt, and anyone seeking business success would do well to learn its customs. Even now, some eighty years after Dusko's decision, Germany's economic hegemony continues. "Germany sits at the heart of this vast economic and demographic domain,*"

---

*European Union.

wrote one Wall Street expert in 2014. "Through its indirect control of the ECB* and the euro, it will dominate commerce, finance, and trade." With limited knowledge of Hitler's power and plans, Popov's decision in 1934 was nothing less than savvy.

Of the numerous options within the country, Freiburg offered charming allure. Beautiful and historic, the cozy town was nestled in the shadow of the Black Forest, was close to ski slopes, and was not too far from Belgrade. The school also offered an internationally renowned academic tradition. Founded in 1457, the University of Freiburg was one of the oldest colleges in Europe and was known for outstanding critical thinking. Philosopher Martin Heidegger taught here, and for two years had been rector. What few outside Germany knew, however, was that Heidegger was a committed Nazi.

Dusko was aware that going to school in Germany would entail certain disadvantages—Nazi propaganda, in particular—but he figured the advantages of Freiburg outweighed the negative political environment. Besides, he'd be in and out in two years. What he couldn't see from Belgrade, however, was the national system of indoctrination and terror being orchestrated and implemented from Berlin.

Hitler became Reich chancellor on January 30, 1933, and within a month passed the "Ordinance for the Protection of the People and the State." A month later, the first concentration camp was established and two months later the Gestapo was formed. Under Ernst Röhm, the *Sturmabteilung* (Storm Battalion, or SA) began arresting, beating, torturing—in some cases murdering—thousands of Berlin Communists, Social Democrats, and Jews. In 1934 henchman Reinhard Heydrich became Gestapo chief and Heinrich Himmler declared the SD (*Sicherheitsdienst*) the political intelligence and counterespionage service of the Nazi Party. To that end Himmler tasked the organization with discovering and stifling opponents of National Socialism.

On April 12 of that year the minister of the interior announced the principles for "preventive arrest" and *Schutzhaft* protective custody. Soon thereafter, the Gestapo consigned to concentration camps all treasonists, Communists, and members of the International Bible Research Association. In short order, those liable for preventive detention included "anti-social malefactors": beggars, homosexuals, prostitutes, drunkards, brawlers, and even

---

*European Central Bank.

grumblers. By the time Dusko entered the University of Freiburg in 1935, the term *malefactors* had been expanded to cover anyone who opposed Nazi rule.

At universities throughout Germany the SD formed "Working Associations," each having local leaders and an army of collaborators and informants. Those in associations included academics, judges, businessmen, and scientists. Some in academia served as "reporters." When Dusko graduated in 1937, the SD surveillance network had grown to three thousand full-time employees, with another fifty thousand serving as informants. At major universities like Freiburg, SD collaborators would have long since infiltrated faculty and student clubs. Future Secret Service chief Walter Schellenberg started with the SD in this fashion, having been recruited by two professors while a student at the University of Bonn.

The malediction of the system was significant and swift; once denounced by a Nazi collaborator, a victim was immediately arrested. And Dusko was mistaken in his belief that foreigners were exempt from prosecution and punishment. A thirty-one-year-old American physician, Joseph Schachno, was a prime example. One evening shortly after Hitler's rise to power a team of uniformed men visited Dr. Schachno's home in Berlin. They were responding to an anonymous tip that Schachno was a potential enemy of the state. Though the Gestapo found nothing incriminating in his home, the American was taken to headquarters, ordered to undress, and whipped mercilessly. His entire body was flayed, leaving a mass of raw, bleeding flesh.

But the danger was just beginning.

Two years after Hitler's election, the Reichstag passed the anti-Semitic Nuremberg Laws. When Freiburg stores were ordered to post signs forbidding the entrance of Jews, the owner of a favorite campus café—Mrs. Birlinger—refused. The Nazis responded by picketing the restaurant and posting soldiers to collect names of patrons. It was a less than subtle intimidation at which Dusko took umbrage. One day he and his two closest friends—Johann Jebsen and Alfred "Freddy" Graf von Kageneck—supported the recalcitrant café by giving their names to the guards and taking a table by the window for all to see.

Dusko Popov, the *foreign* student, had caught the watchful eye of the Reich.

As a handsome and charismatic doctoral student, he was also catching the eyes of co-eds. Women and trouble invariably commingled for Popov, and throughout his early years he was never far from either. Sunning with a girlfriend one afternoon, Dusko wrote in his memoirs, he was resting peacefully when another suitor—Karl Laub—approached to pester the girl for a date. A disagreement ensued and Laub challenged Dusko to Mensur—a saber duel sometimes called "academic fencing." Practiced in German universities since the sixteenth century, Mensur was thought to instill mettle and courage in young men. Hitler encouraged the practice as a means of building up fearless soldiers. German traditionalists, men like Walter Schellenberg, joined university student groups specifically *because* they had "a code of honor and duelling."

The tradition was not favored by handsome foreigners, however, since the object of the bout was to disfigure the opponent's face. Mensur contestants wore a protective vest, neck armor, and a small mask to protect the eyes and nose; the cheeks, forehead, and chin were the principal targets, and a quick flip of the wrist would lacerate anything the saber touched. The duel, which was officiated, allowed no ducking, flinching, or dodging of an opponent's blows.

Mark Twain described a bout he witnessed in Heidelberg:

> The instant the word was given, the two apparitions sprang forward and began to rain blows down upon each other with such lightning rapidity that I could not quite tell whether I saw the swords or only flashes they made. . . . I saw a handful of hair skip into the air as if it had lain loose on the victim's head and a breath of wind had suddenly puffed it away. . . . The surgeon came and turned back the hair from the wound—and revealed a crimson gash two or three inches long. . . . The duelists took position again; a small stream of blood was flowing down the side of the injured man's head, and over his shoulder and down his body to the floor, but he did not seem to mind this. The word was given, and they plunged at each other as fiercely as before; once more the blows rained and rattled and flashed. . . . The law is that the battle must continue fifteen minutes if the men can hold out. . . . At last it was decided that the men were too much wearied to do battle any longer. They were led away drenched with crimson from head to foot.

Gruesome Mensur scars, *Schmissen* ("smite") the Germans called them, adorned the faces of many World War II officers, including SA cofounder Ernst Röhm, head of the political police (later, Gestapo) Rudolf Diels, RSHA chief Ernst Kaltenbrunner, and legendary commando Otto Skorzeny. No less an authority than Otto von Bismarck was reported to have said that dueling scars were a sign of bravery, and that a man's courage could be determined by the number on his cheeks.

Dusko had neither the need for distorted courage nor the desire for a deformed face. When the time for the duel arrived, he demanded a different weapon.

Pistols.

Laub and his second objected. Pistols had never been used in student dueling, they complained to the referee. Johnny Jebsen, who was Dusko's second, countered that the one being challenged traditionally had choice of weapons, and that Dusko was duty bound by his Yugoslav cavalry regiment to duel only with pistols. Laub appealed to the student honor court, which found a middle ground: Dusko was allowed a choice of weapons, but pistols had never been used in a university duel.

The bout was canceled and Laub lived on.

»

On June 9, 1937, Dusko turned in his dissertation—"The Vivovdan and the September Constitution of Yugoslavia"—and began wrapping up his doctoral studies. By late summer he had finished his exams and made preparations for a celebratory excursion to Paris. He had been to the French capital many times and loved all that the city offered: endless cafés, exquisite wines and cuisine, and—most importantly—adventurous popsies. A few days before leaving he gave a pro-democracy speech at the foreign-student club.

He never made it to Paris.

EXITING FEET FIRST

A day or so after the speech Dusko was awakened by pounding at his door. A team of Gestapo guards, looming in the hall like black-and-gray gargoyles, ordered him to get dressed and follow them to an awaiting car.

He knew why.

From the day he stepped onto the Freiburg campus in the fall of 1935, he had either ignored or ridiculed the Nazis. Birlinger café. Articles for the *Politika*. Speeches at the foreign-student club. Naively, he had assumed the social setting would allow free speech. He also believed that his status as a foreigner would exempt him from *Kadavergehorsam*—the zombie-like obedience Hitler demanded. Dusko despised Nazism, and since he wasn't German, he believed he owed no allegiance to Hitler or the state.

He was wrong.

By 1937 Hitler had been Reich chancellor for four years and had spread Nazi doctrine and terror across Germany with fanatical resolve. Heinrich Himmler, as de facto head of the Gestapo in 1934 and as *Reichsführer-SS* in 1936, had begun implementing many reforms: Jewish professors were fired from university posts, church leaders were forced to embrace National Socialism or lose their parishes, and *Konzentrationslagers*—concentration camps—were ordered to full development.

Dusko Popov, a nonconformist foreigner, was another perfect target. As a Polish jurist later wrote, the Nazi scheme was a coordinated plan to pass laws "that attacked the political and social institutions of culture, language, national feelings, religion and the economic existence of national groups, and [that tended to] the destruction of personal security, liberty, health, dignity, and even the lives of individuals belonging to such groups."

Virtually around the clock, Gestapo agents interrogated him. The first agent charged him with an unthinkable crime—*dating a girl who worked in a factory*. Surely this was proof that Popov was a Communist. Another agent followed. And another. Eight days. The Gestapo questioned everyone he knew—students, professors, merchants—and only von Kageneck and Jebsen defended him.

Like Dusko, Freddy and Johnny had come from aristocratic backgrounds. The von Kagenecks were one of the oldest and most influential Catholic families in Germany; the Jebsens, one of the richest. Freddy's noble heritage could be traced back to the twelfth century, and Johnny's wealth, although invested largely in ships, was almost beyond measure.

Johnny's family was originally from Denmark, and his grandfather, Michael Jebsen, Jr., had established a shipping company there in 1871. To open an Asia trade route, he moved his operations to Hamburg, and the eldest son, Johnny's uncle Jacob, cofounded Jebsen & Co. in 1895 in Hong Kong. It appears that the youngest son, Michael III, was Johnny's father and had continued the Hamburg business after Johnny's grandfather died in 1899. The date of Michael III's death is unknown, but by the time Johnny enrolled at Freiburg in 1935, both of his parents were dead. By then Johnny had inherited not only a sizeable part of the shipping empire, but other assets as well. Part of Jebsen's loyalty to Germany, he would later say, was because he owned so much of it.

Johnny was Dusko's best friend and, as Popov would later reveal, the person who most affected his life. They had many things in common, including an addiction to "sports cars and sporting girls." Dusko drove a BMW and Johnny drove a supercharged Mercedes 540. Both were confident, well-spoken, and popular. Dusko, who himself had a short-term photographic memory and spoke five languages, wrote that Johnny's knowledge was "encyclopedic," his recall infallible. MI5 files repeatedly mention Jebsen as exceptionally intelligent, clever, and highly cultured. His English was also quite good.

Both men were complex, often aloof, and invariably charismatic. Popov's account that everyone was under Johnny's spell mirrored MI5's depiction of Dusko himself: "He is courageous, discreet, and has great charm of manner," Popov's case officer wrote. "In more senses than one he is rather an adventurer."

Hedonists and spendthrifts, the restless friends were also loyal to a fault; either, time would tell, was more than ready to give his life for the other. Not surprisingly, they shared a worldly wisdom—a *Weltanschauung* that espoused capitalism over socialism, liberty over safety, gumption over discipline, and rebellion over indoctrination. They were no men's fools and would little suffer ideologues.

Dusko Popov.
National Archives and Records Administration

In other ways, they could not have been more different. While Dusko had boyish good looks, Johnny was pale, weak of eyes, and had black, tobacco-stained teeth. Dusko was athletic and skilled at numerous sports: water polo, horsemanship, sailing, skiing, tennis, and marksmanship. As belligerents would later discover, he was also good with his hands.

Jebsen, conversely, played no sports and was thin and frail. Like Orwell's poor Winston, Johnny suffered from varicose veins and walked with a limp. Perhaps to compensate for his less than ideal features, he dressed impeccably. On one occasion, he told Dusko he was willing to pay $600—an exorbitant amount at the time—for a suit of English cloth. With intimidating intellect, wealth, and an enviable savoir faire, Jebsen conveyed unusual power and confidence.

Johnny idolized Dusko, who was five years older and seemed to excel at everything, especially women. Dusko, in turn, admired Johnny's independence and savvy worldliness. They also shared a common passion: hatred of the Nazis.

»

After the Gestapo investigation, Popov was transferred to Freiburg prison. It was a rude awakening, to say the least. Life in Nazi incarceration was largely

Johnny Jebsen.
The National Archives of the UK

the same across Germany—ghastly. No visitors. No correspondence. Minutes in the exercise yard once a day. Lutheran pastor Dietrich Bonhoeffer would later write: "The blankets . . . had such a foul smell that in spite of the cold it was impossible to use them. Next morning a piece of bread was thrown into my cell; I had to pick it up from the floor. . . . For the next twelve days the cell door was opened only for bringing food in and putting the bucket out. I was told nothing about the reason for my detention, or how long it would last."

An SOE operative captured in Vichy France had a similar tale: "In a very few weeks I lost over forty pounds. My jailer came three times a day: in the morning with a mug of hot water which he assured me was coffee, at noon with a slightly larger mug of so-called soup in which floated three or four beans . . . at night, another cup of soup and a lump of dark brown bread." On Wednesdays, he went on, "there was a small piece of meat—sometimes only a bone." One mug of cold water to drink each day. For weeks he did not wash or shave.

After some time in his new home Popov met another prisoner who explained that the Nazis would not pursue formal adjudication; Hitler's *Schutzhaft* allowed the Gestapo to imprison without proceedings. Courts were not allowed to investigate or intervene. Dusko would be secretly shipped to a concentration camp, the other prisoner said, listed as missing, and never heard from again. And the usual exit from these camps, he added—was "feet first."

Little did Dusko know then that the Nazis had already perfected their ideological cleansing; a dissident's mere existence was a palimpsest, neatly erased by an efficient concentration or forced-labor camp. By 1937 such camps had been established at Oranienburg, Esterwegen, Dachau, Sachsenhausen, Buchenwald, and Lichtenburg. More disturbingly, the Gestapo had official and unilateral authority for *Sonderbehandlung* ("special treatment")—execution. Because he had been snatched before dawn, Dusko's university friends would assume he had left for Paris. Within days he was scheduled for transfer to a camp and eventual extermination.

Mysteriously, he was suddenly released and told to be out of the country within twenty-four hours. He caught the first train to Switzerland.

He was followed.

SPYING FOR HITLER, KILLING FOR CHURCHILL

The telegram that would forever change Dusko Popov's life arrived February 4, 1940. Everything had been going so well. He had been practicing law in Dubrovnik with a business attorney, Dr. Jaksitch, since the fall of 1937 and had built an impressive stable of clients including Savska, a prominent Belgrade bank. Negotiating contracts for the import of machinery, he also conducted business with the German Embassy, meeting often with an undersecretary named von Stein.

Secretary Stein, who was about Popov's age, was much like the strident Nazis Dusko had gone to school with in Freiburg. In every respect he was Hitler's prototype: well built, short blond hair, clean-shaven with a good complexion, overbearing, and boasting that all-important credential—a dueling scar. Von Stein wasted no time recruiting; upon hearing that Popov knew Bozo Banac, one of the wealthiest men in Yugoslavia, the secretary suggested that Dusko might do more and better work for Germany.

When Popov visited the embassy again in January 1940, von Stein pursued the possibility: "You are well acquainted with Karlo Banac," he said, "the brother of Bozo Banac, and through this channel can get an easy entry into British circles." Dusko reminded the diplomat that Germany had expelled him from the country. Undeterred, von Stein said that they would forget the past.

Popov sidestepped, suggesting that he wasn't sure he could produce much from his contacts. Even if he could, he thought silently, Germany was hardly a client he would represent, and it had now been at war with Britain and France for four months. Besides, he had no need for additional business or money.

Although Popov worked at a leisurely pace—usually out of the office by 11:00 a.m.—he brought in over £3,000 a year, a considerable sum in 1940. He lived in a large home—complete with housekeepers and grounds servants—on an Adriatic peninsula. MI5 recorded his address simply as "Lapad, Dubrovnik."

At twenty-nine he was well connected, mingled in society circles, and vacationed annually a month or more in Paris. He owned a yacht—*Nina*—and as a member of the Dubrovnik sailing club was fond of saying that he was "born in the sun, and would die in the sun." Family, sailing, tennis, women—life was good.

»

The cable from Berlin threatened to spoil everything:

> NEED TO MEET YOU URGENTLY. PROPOSE 8 FEBRUARY, HOTEL SERBIAN KING, BELGRADE.

No greeting. No reminiscing. No reason. Johnny was in some sort of trouble.

It had been two and a half years since the Gestapo expelled Dusko from Germany, and he was deeply indebted to his friend. Concerned about Dusko's disappearance, Johnny had asked around and heard of the arrest. He called Dusko's father, who contacted the Yugoslav prime minister, who in turn contacted Hermann Goering. By the time Johnny heard of the release, Dusko was at the Freiburg train station. Prohibited from entering the platform, Jebsen assumed the route and raced Dusko's train to Basel. It was a rescue Popov would not soon forget.

He drove to Belgrade.

»

Johnny looked like hell, Dusko remembered. Unkempt hair, ragged mustache, sullen and apprehensive eyes, he was chain-smoking—100 to 150 cigarettes a day—and drinking heavily. In just three short years Jebsen had aged considerably.

After ranting about Hitler for a few minutes, Johnny came to the point of his visit. A number of German ships in the Norddeutche Lloyd fleet, he said, a company in which Jebsen was a director, were stranded in several neutral ports. He had obtained authorization to sell the lot—provided that they sailed under a neutral flag—but he needed help finding a buyer. The logical prospects were Britain and France, but if the SD got wind that he was selling war assets to an Allied country, he'd be executed. Popov would have to negotiate and consummate the deal without Jebsen's participation, and a neutral third party would have to be the first sale.

Dusko wondered aloud about the risk for Johnny, but his friend was stoic. Jebsen loved his country, he said, but felt no obligation to follow "a bloody tyrant." Popov appreciated his predicament. A wealthy aristocrat without a care in the world and seemingly overnight his estate and lifestyle were in jeopardy. Yet it was more than that. Independence, freedom of thought, resistance—even disobedience—were deeply rooted Prussian values that permeated German nobility. It was reported that a Prussian commanding officer once scolded a major for following orders to the letter, saying, "The King of Prussia made you a staff officer so that you would know when you ought *not* to carry out his orders."

Wehrmacht commanders of Prussian heritage regularly exhibited this independent thought and disobedience. Field Marshal Paul Ludwig von Kleist would lose his command in March 1944 when he disobeyed Hitler's order and allowed the Eighth Army to retreat when in danger of annihilation from the Russians. General Dietrich von Choltitz, military governor of Paris, also disobeyed Hitler's order by refusing to destroy the city in August 1944.

And such independence was not limited to the military. Historian Hans Schoeps described Prussia as "the home of thought." As later years of the war would reveal, most of the leaders of the resistance movement—Carl Goerdeler, Helmuth Graf von Moltke, Ulrich von Hassell, Adam von Trott zu Solzm, Peter Yorck von Wartenburg, Henning von Tresckow, Ernst von Harnack, Wolf-Heinrich Graf von Helldorf, and Johannes Popitz—were Prussians.

With an upbringing in a wealthy Hamburg family influenced by this tradition, Jebsen kept his own mind on politics and man's place in the world. He was no one's harlequin, especially Hitler's, and Nazis be damned he would orchestrate his own path through the war.

Popov agreed to help and took the list of ships to the British Embassy and met with a Mr. How, first secretary. While there, Dusko informed the secretary of the prior advances of von Stein, and inquired as to how he should move forward. Without mentioning a double agent role, How suggested that Popov indicate his willingness to work for the Germans. As for the ships, How passed Dusko to H. N. Sturrock, commercial secretary, who agreed to look into a possible purchase.

Days later Johnny informed Dusko that he had joined the Abwehr. At the time, most German aristocrats were enlisting in one of the two secret intelligence agencies—the Nazi Party's SD or the military's Abwehr. The latter, under legendary Admiral Wilhelm Canaris, was expanding rapidly. When

Hitler rose to power, the Abwehr maintained a staff of one hundred fifty; by 1937 the organization had expanded to more than nine hundred. A man of Jebsen's intellect and nobility was exactly what Canaris wanted for his spies. And for Johnny, joining a branch staffed almost exclusively with non-Nazis was exactly what *he* wanted.

Popov wasn't entirely surprised by the announcement; every German male who didn't join the service was considered a traitor, and treason was punishable by death. In his capacity as a *Forscher* (researcher), Johnny would avoid being cannon fodder on the front lines. But Jebsen had another reason for joining the Abwehr—freedom. Since his job entailed recruiting other spies, he was free to travel as he pleased, which would keep him in touch with what was happening in the world outside Germany. It was what opposition leaders like Carl Goerdeler referred to as ties to the "greater world."

For Dusko, the stakes were mounting. His best friend had joined the Abwehr, and von Stein—working independently of Jebsen—pressed Popov to throw his lot in with the Germans. At the same time, the British remained coy.

Soon after this St. George Lethbridge, SIS (MI6) Belgrade station chief, summoned Popov to Passport Control. Dusko told him about von Stein, Johnny, and the overall German recruitment. Without offering specifics, Lethbridge said to play along. Anxious to stoke the fire, Dusko suggested that he could fool the Germans by claiming that a friend in London—Mr. Ivanovitch, director of the Yugoslav Lloyd and nephew of Bozo Banac—would be able to assist with information; the Abwehr could readily confirm the source and Dusko's bona fides would be established. Ivanovitch had recently left for an extended stay in America, they soon discovered, and Popov suggested a second, fictional source who would be a staff member at the Yugoslav legation. Dusko would claim that the man refused to give his name, thus protecting the ruse.

Lethbridge agreed, but told Popov he couldn't mention their meeting to Jebsen. Dusko left with both feet planted firmly in midair—not quite a British agent, gagged with respect to Johnny, and about to become an Abwehr operative with unknown terms.

Dusko informed von Stein of his decision, and over the next few weeks Jebsen delivered three questionnaires to pass along to the London source. The documents requested information on British defensive measures along the south coast, location and sizes of divisions, officer names, anti-tank developments, armament factories, Churchill's enemies, and more. The answers would take considerable time, Dusko realized, since the "diplomat" providing the information would be a team of British intelligence officers.

While leading the Germans to believe he had sent the questionnaires on through the diplomatic bag, Dusko instead gave them to Lethbridge, who forwarded everything to SIS London. At once MI6 and MI5 recognized the difficulty in processing the questions. All answers would have to be meticulously researched, coordinated between both agencies and the military, and approved. One slip and Popov would be blown.

As British Intelligence worked on the questions, the Germans became impatient. Weeks went by and Popov had heard nothing back from Lethbridge or MI6. When Johnny inquired about the delay, Dusko told him that his embassy source was fearful of putting the classified information in the diplomatic bag. Popov, the Germans suggested, would have to go to London to personally collect the answers.

The shell game between Dusko and Johnny continued, neither knowing the full intentions of the other. At their next meeting Jebsen said that they were "now both in the same service," but probed as to Popov's motivation. Johnny said he had joined the Abwehr because his varicose veins prevented normal duties as a soldier, and because he fit in better as an export/import type of agent. But why would Popov—being a democrat—help the Germans? he asked.

Dusko bluffed. He said he wanted an easier living, and that he had been promised big positions after the war. Johnny made no mention of the fact that Dusko needed neither.

»

The first week of November Jebsen advised that a Major Ollschlager, head of the Abwehr's I. H. Ost (Army Intelligence East) and Johnny's supervisor, was in town. His real name, Popov learned, was Colonel Ernst Munzinger, and he also used aliases of "Hoeflinger" and "Anzueto." About fifty, Munzinger had a ruddy complexion, with graying hair and rimless spectacles. Precise in his dress, the colonel preferred dark suits but always wore a green hat—with a feather.

At a restaurant outside Belgrade, Munzinger made the formal offer and disclosures. Espionage had risks, he admitted, but the Abwehr paid agents well and Popov would be rewarded with a position of prominence in the new Yugoslavia. Dusko accepted and the following day met Munzinger at the

German Embassy to receive final instructions, a questionnaire for the London source, a vial of secret ink, and his code name: IVAN.

He was now a double agent.

Dusko's decision did not come lightly. Joining the Abwehr and MI6 meant he'd wear no uniform and have no protection; spies were excluded from the Geneva Convention. If the Abwehr or the Gestapo caught him doubling, they could do with him as they pleased. That was a risk he was willing to take, but what about Johnny? Granted, Jebsen was not a Nazi, but neither was Canaris or Oster, his chief of staff, yet they and others like them were loyal to their country. Did Johnny realize that Dusko's hatred of the Nazis would push him to the British? More importantly, would Jebsen look the other way?

»

Over the ensuing weeks Popov had to establish a legitimate cover—linking trade between Yugoslavia and England—as an import/export consultant. One day while drumming up business, his BMW broke down. Since Dusko's parents were in Dubrovnik, his father's chauffeur, Bozidar, agreed to drive him around. A few weeks later, Dusko recalled in his memoirs, Johnny burst into his bedroom waving a set of papers.

"You're being sold out by Bozidar!"

There were nine pages, Jebsen said, listing every appointment, every person Popov had seen in the last two weeks. Before he left for Vienna, Munzinger had hired Popov's family chauffeur to spy on Dusko. Bozidar had sabotaged the BMW.

Dusko glanced at the report and shrugged. It was mostly a record of where his girlfriends lived, he said.

"What about *this*?" Johnny pointed to multiple visits to the same address. Dusko said it was the Passport Control Office, where he applied for his visa to England.

"*Six times?* Come off it, Dusko. It is also the headquarters of British Intelligence."

Popov let the silence hang for a moment as he considered his predicament. He knew Johnny was anti-Nazi, but Jebsen was now a soldier in the German Army. He, Munzinger, and Bozidar were all on the same team, and Popov's multiple visits to British Intelligence all but proved Dusko was doubling for the enemy. Was Johnny's comment a shot across the bow?

He processed loyalties. If Johnny put the Abwehr first, he'd not have revealed the problem with Bozidar and the report. Patriotism aside, Dusko believed their brotherly bond was more secure than uniforms. He said he hoped this didn't change things.

Johnny bristled and said that it was liable to blow Popov and everyone connected with him.

After a few moments Dusko told Johnny he'd prepare a new, false report and deal with Bozidar. Jebsen left, and Dusko went to inform his brother Ivo, whose medical office was nearby, that he was going to send the chauffeur on a long trip. Ivo didn't like the solution. "Bozidar is a cancer now," he said. "There is nothing we can do that will alter him. As long as he lives, he always remains a threat to you."

Like a patriarchal brother, Ivo wanted to intercede and take care of Bozidar. It would be safer, he said, in case the Germans investigated. Dusko was touched but felt that it was his mess and his responsibility. He'd do it.

But not until nightfall.

4 »

MAGIC

Dusko wrestled with the decision all day. Years later, he would explain the dilemma: "[A] world at war is not sane. It has no rules. . . . Your weapons are lies, treachery, violence, murder. If you do not use them the result may be that you will lose a battle. You might lose thousands of lives which could have been saved. Or you might lose the whole war."

After sunset he met with two roughnecks he'd represented previously in a criminal case. Whispering his predicament, he slipped the men a sheaf of bills. Later that night he asked Bozidar to run an errand. Struggling with the finality of the action, Dusko wrote in his memoirs, he gave Bozidar an opportunity to come clean.

"Have I been running you around too much these past few weeks? You look tired. Or worried. Is there anything?" He offered to use taxis until the BMW was repaired.

"Oh, no, no, no," Bozidar said. "I'm glad to be of service."

Dusko nodded and retired to bed.

»

The following day police reported that Bozidar had been shot by railroad guards during an attempted theft. After the war, Dusko would have no regrets. Bozidar was working for the Nazis, he told an interviewer, and "could have caused death to me and many others."

Johnny arrived that afternoon and chastised Popov for the lethal action. "Would you kill me, too, if you discovered I was playing dirty?" The question was unnerving. Dusko could only wonder if the tension and the loyalty issue would persist throughout the war. Would he have to constantly look over his shoulder, even with his best friend?

Johnny let it go and moved on to Munzinger's questionnaire, telling Dusko to deliver something soon as the Abwehr would be watching closely. Dusko, however, was hamstrung—since the British were preparing the report, he'd have to hold Johnny off until MI5 delivered the goods.

The situation was precarious. He'd just started as an official Abwehr spy and already the whole thing was a mess. Jebsen knew he'd bumped off Bozidar, yet looked the other way. He knew of Dusko's multiple visits to British Intelligence, yet assisted in the falsified report. Johnny was protecting him, yet was dutifully performing his Abwehr assignments.

»

Sometime later, Popov wrote, he met Lethbridge at a secluded park outside Belgrade for final tutelage. "Act as if you are a real German spy," the spook said. "Forget you belong to us. While traveling, look as though you are worried that the English may suspect you. You can be sure the Germans will be observing you at every moment. Keep your eyes and your ears open and your mouth shut. Remember names and addresses and faces and every word you hear from or about the Germans, but put nothing in writing."

Lethbridge explained that British Intelligence was interested in anything Dusko might hear about Operation Sea Lion, Germany's planned invasion of Britain. He didn't know to which unit Dusko would be assigned, but explained that British Intelligence was comprised of two primary sections: the Secret Intelligence Service, better known as SIS or MI6, which handled intelligence abroad, and the Security Intelligence Service, MI5, which oversaw domestic counterintelligence and double agents.

Indeed, the British were learning the double-cross game on the fly. Their only other double agent with Abwehr contact—Arthur Owens (codenamed SNOW)—was believed to be a triple, and MI5 was perplexed with how to use him. A Welsh engineer, Owens had patented a special dry cell battery, which was sold in great quantities to the German Navy. In 1936, during one of his frequent trips to Hamburg, Owens met with an Abwehr controller. MI6 put him under surveillance, and it appeared that Arthur had been engaged as a German spy. When Owens returned to London, British Intelligence interrogated him at length. Through it all, Owens proclaimed his loyalty, and MI5 allowed him limited duties as a double agent. On August 18, 1939, however, SNOW's wife and son notified Scotland Yard that Arthur was a Nazi spy. Owens, who appeared to be playing both sides for money, continued to proclaim his innocence. In the ultimate game of double-cross, MI5 used Owens—by radio link from Wandsworth prison to Hamburg—to contact his Abwehr controller, Dr. Rantzau (whose real name was Nikolaus Ritter). It was the first wireless contact with the enemy.

Owens was allowed to visit Antwerp in 1940, but Major Robertson and Guy Liddell of MI5 continued to have serious doubts about his loyalty. The agency's other spies proved equally uninspiring. Sam McCarthy, codenamed BISCUIT, was a reformed criminal, con man, and drug dealer. Gösta Caroli, a turned Germany spy codenamed SUMMER, MI5 planned to execute. Walter Dicketts, codenamed CELERY, was an air intelligence officer during World War I who had been discharged from the RAF for dishonesty.

Popov, on the other hand, offered intriguing potential. MI6 chief Stewart Menzies, "C" as he was known in intelligence circles, sought to use him to find out everything he could about his own counterpart, Abwehr chief Admiral Wilhelm Canaris. Canaris had been a peculiar opponent, and Menzies was processing considerable evidence that the admiral was not a Nazi and did not support Hitler. Better still was information that Canaris had gone so far as to warn the Allies of Hitler's invasion date for Poland. But, to be sure, "C" needed confirmation from someone on the inside.

Major T. A. "Tar" Robertson, as head of MI5's section controlling double agents, also could use Popov's talents. Dusko spoke five languages, had a doctorate in law, and came from wealth; he could travel and mingle in the highest social circles. As Popov would say later, the Britons knew he "didn't drink out of the finger bowl" and could hold his knife and fork. Like SNOW, however, Dusko carried tremendous risk of being a triple: He wasn't British, had gone to school in Germany, and was recruited first by the Abwehr. MI5 would have to take significant precautions.

Within months Dusko would be working for MI5 *and* MI6. In the meantime, he was recorded on their books and given an initial code name of SKOOT.

»

Berlin's approval of Popov's visit to London finally came, but instead of sending him directly, Munzinger ordered him to go to Rome, where someone would contact him. The British, in turn, told Dusko that someone would approach him in England with the password "Rubicon." Since Popov was on a trial basis with both, he realized he might have two tails—one German, one British.

Hopefully, they'd not meet.

»

On November 17, 1940, he left by train for Rome and arrived two days later. Per instructions he went directly to Ala Littoria; Munzinger had said he'd have no trouble acquiring passage to Lisbon. The airline clerk had no ticket, however, or even a reservation, but gave Popov a note, typewritten in German:

> *Dear Dusko, do not go away before seeing me; I shall be in Rome at the Hotel Excelsior. Johann*

Returning downtown, Dusko checked into the Ambasciadore Hotel, called the number Munzinger had given in case of emergency—Rome 44168—and gave his name and hotel as the code. When Dusko mentioned his plane ticket, the man said there must be a mistake, that he had no idea what Popov was talking about. Dusko repeated his name and stated his business; the man said he'd heard of neither. Popov hung up and tried to find the Rome 44168 number in the phone book.

No trace.

Half an hour later two men showed up at the hotel. A small man, sixtyish with white hair and a pale, ill complexion, introduced himself as Dr. Campiagni. The second Italian, tall and about forty-five, said nothing. Campiagni asked a few questions, and Popov, who had been told nothing of a rendezvous by Munzinger, gave generic answers. After a few minutes the Italians admitted that Popov's business *was* known, and was "receiving attention." Giving Dusko his card, Campiagni said to visit in two days. It read: "Ardanghi–Lawyer, Via Torino 7, 4th Floor."

The following evening, November 20, Dusko met Johnny for drinks. Sea Lion was being delayed, Johnny said, due to disagreements between the different armed service branches. Unknown to Johnny or Dusko at the time, British Intelligence was intercepting Goering's messages to Luftwaffe commanders, enciphered in the ENIGMA machine, and Bletchley Park was breaking the code and passing to MI6 far more than Jebsen knew. By the end of July, ULTRA—the British code name for secret intelligence produced by the intercepted and decrypted messages—revealed that the German Army and

Navy disagreed over how the troop and supply demands for Sea Lion could be met by seaborne transport.

Johnny went through what he knew of the plans of General Franz Halder, Hitler's chief of the General Staff, and moved on to Dusko's assigned station—Lisbon. The Portuguese capital was the Abwehr's most important outpost, he said, and Dusko's spymaster would be Major Ludovico von Karsthoff, chief of the Lisbon desk. An Austrian from Trieste, von Karsthoff's real name was Kremer von Auenrode. Highly secretive, he was listed on the German Embassy staff as "Albert von Karsthof," wanted to be called Ludovico, and sometimes signed documents as Anzuweto.

Johnny warned that the major was quite charming and that Dusko would like him, itself a bit of a danger. If they became friends, Jebsen feared, Dusko would be more prone to making mistakes. They did become friends and Popov later lamented the situation. "He was a terribly likeable person," Dusko told an interviewer after the war. "I was very fond of him and I felt guilty all that time because he was the main instrument by which I deceived the Nazi government." Such the travails of double-cross.

Before leaving, Dusko recalled, Johnny gave him specific rendezvous instructions: Upon his arrival in Lisbon he was to call von Karsthoff from a pay phone and ask for Karl Schmidt, saying that his cousin from Stuttgart told him to call. Schmidt would come to the line and indicate a specified time and place to meet. Dusko was to arrive an hour before the scheduled time and linger. A woman would walk by, wink, and lead him to a waiting car, where he'd be driven to the meeting.

No words were to be spoken.

»

Systems of elaborate codes and clandestine meetings, even in neutral countries, were more than necessary. Hotels, cafés, and bars in Madrid, Estoril, and Lisbon were the principal battlefields of World War II espionage, and where one went, and with whom one spoke, often could be seen by the enemy. Surprisingly, each side possessed a startling amount of information on the other's secret agents, headquarters, and procedures.

In November 1939 the Germans had kidnapped two of Britain's most senior MI6 agents, Captain S. Payne Best and Major Richard Stevens, and acquired operative names and other classified information. Posing as members of the Nazi resistance movement, Walter Schellenberg and his assistants had lured

Best and Stevens to a restaurant in Venlo, on the Dutch–German border, and quickly subdued them. One man was killed in the encounter and the MI6 agents were hustled to Berlin, where they were interrogated and held until 1945.

For the duration of the war, each side made concerted efforts to learn the other's operations. Walter Schellenberg wrote in his memoirs that he had "full lists" of American and British personnel operating in Spain. On the British side, by the spring of 1940 the Radio Security Service was intercepting so many German radio signals that it was said the Bletchley Park code breakers knew of Hitler's orders before his generals. Further, all German spies dropped into England in 1940 and 1941 had been arrested, some executed, and four turned into double agents. From 1941 on, all German agents operating in England were controlled and run by the British.

None were more cautious about the value of their information than the chieftains of secrecy themselves. In his offices on the fourth floor of 54 Broadway, "C" had a secret passageway which led to his official residence at 21 Queen Anne's Gate. By slipping through concealed doors at both ends, he could move unobserved from his workplace to the drawing room of his apartment.

On the German side, Walter Schellenberg—who had numerous enemies inside the Third Reich—was less subtle. His office contained hidden microphones inside a lamp, his desk, and even the walls. Windows were covered with wire mesh and photoelectrically charged so that if anyone approached, an alarm sounded. The desk itself, he wrote, was like "a small fortress":

> Two automatic guns were built into it which could spray the whole room with bullets. These guns pointed at the visitor and followed his or her progress towards my desk. All I had to do in an emergency was to press a button and both guns would fire simultaneously. At the same time I could press another button and a siren would summon the guards to surround the building and block every exit.

When he traveled, Schellenberg guarded against revealing information if captured by carrying two cyanide capsules—one inserted inside an artificial tooth, another hidden under the stone of his ring.

And it wasn't just the Germans and British taking precautions. Dusko would say after the war that in every hotel, regardless of locale, his belongings would be searched again and again by everyone—German, British, American, Russian, Italian, Japanese. To survive, anything of intelligence value had to stay on his person at all times; he would operate, move, and live by codes and covers.

»

The following morning, November 21, Popov called on Dr. Campiagni at Via Torino 7. The doctor's real name, he said, was Major Conti, and the lawyer—Ardanghi—was the Italian chief of counterespionage. About forty-five, Ardanghi was tall, six feet or so, and spoke German like a native. Conti made the introduction, and together Popov and the chief contacted the Air Ministry.

No flights were available for Lisbon.

Dusko left, not knowing whether the Germans and Italians were testing him, or whether the Roman bureaucracy was worse than the Yugoslavian. He called Jebsen, and over lunch Johnny asked for the spy ink Munzinger had given him. Johnny poured it out and gave instructions on a better formula, pyramidon. Dusko would take one and a half pills of amidopyrin and dissolve them in a large spoon containing 75 percent clear alcohol, such as white gin. He was to wrap a pencil tip in cotton wool, dip it in the solution, and write in block letters between the lines of any correspondence. He'd then wait half an hour for the ink to dry and gently rub a sheet of the same paper across the secret message to smooth out any raised letters.

Johnny also told Dusko that any messages from Lisbon should be sent to Don Augustin Mutiozobal, Colon Larreategni 7, Armado, Bilboa. Any correspondence, he concluded, should state: "Still . . . waggons deliverable," the number of wagons to indicate the days Dusko intended to stay. When they finished their meal Johnny suggested that Dusko try Ala Littoria one more time.

Magically, a seat was available the next day.

THE BEE HIVE

"The most fascinating place in the world," one writer called it. "The hub of the western universe." The Duke and Duchess of Windsor, the Duke of Alba, the King of Romania, the Prince of Sweden, the Prince of Poland, and the Princess of Greece and Denmark were here. Affluent Parisians, including the Guggenheims, were here, too. The City of Light had become the City of Refuge, the "last of the gay capitals," and the "port of good hope."

The *New York Times* described the locale as a "veritable bee hive" of activity.

It was home to Europe's largest casino, a sixth-century castle, a twelfth-century cathedral, and the remnants of a Roman theater built by Emperor Augustus in the first century. Its cobbled streets and medieval villages reminded one of Naples or Sicily, and its Avenida da Liberdade was matched in grandeur only by Paris's Avenue des Champs-Elysées. Cafés were open all night and the languages heard in them included not only English, French, and German, but Romanian, Japanese, and Russian.

And no rationing here. Stores glistened with new typewriters and cameras, McVitie's petits beurres and clotted creams, fresh fish and sardines. Newsstands overflowed with the *New York Times*, *Der Spiegel*, the *London Daily Mail*, and Madrid's *Arriba*. *Time* magazine, *Harper's*, the *Saturday Evening Post*—all available.

British and German aircraft rested side by side on the Sintra tarmac, and propaganda shops of the two countries often occupied adjoining spaces. Allied and Axis spies shared hotels and sat next to each other in swanky bars. Wealthy Jews lounged leisurely on Tamariz Beach while tepid Gestapo agents looked on.

Lisbon.

City of peace on a continent at war. Harbor of last hope for refugees fleeing fascism. And, where Dusko was concerned, a shore ripe for Machiavellian machinations.

In 1940 only six European countries were neutral—Switzerland, Sweden, Ireland, Turkey, Spain, and Portugal. Switzerland, historically unaligned, landlocked, and small, was insignificant. Sweden, Ireland, and Turkey, not being contiguous with mainland Europe, played lesser roles in the war. Only Spain and Portugal, with their proximity to France and strategic islands and ports, were of critical importance.

Spain was only nominally neutral, however. Germany had supported Franco's fascist regime in the Spanish Civil War, augmenting his rise to power, and Madrid leaned heavily to Axis affiliation.

Portugal was a different matter. The country shared the oldest existing alliance treaty—signed in 1373—with England. British soldiers had helped Portugal gain independence in the twelfth century, and the country had maintained its empire largely due to the British Navy. Portugal fought with the Allies in the First World War.

Given historical precedent, the Allies expected Portugal to throw its lot in with Britain and France. The country's president, however, Dr. António de Oliveira Salazar, was a crafty and slippery leader. Weighing against Portugal's treaty and historical bond with Britain was Salazar's fear that Spain might attack to annex its small neighbor. While Portugal's relationship with Spain was good, rumors of Franco's intention to invade west constantly surfaced. In addition, Salazar assumed that Germany would support a Spanish invasion of Portugal, or might invade independently.

Throughout 1940 and 1941, Roosevelt and Hitler conducted a silent war over Portugal. While Lisbon provided a handy port for key shipping lanes, Portugal's colonial empire, which comprised a landmass twenty-five times larger than the mother country, had far greater military importance. From the African islands of Cape Verde to China's Macau and India's Goa, Portuguese territories provided tempting targets. The crown jewel, though, was Portugal's Azores archipelago. Located halfway between Lisbon and New York, it was the only refueling spot in the mid-Atlantic and allowed the only carrier with service, Pan American Airlines, to shuttle between the two continents. If the Allies or the Axis powers seized the Azores, Salazar feared, the islands would quickly be transformed into a naval and submarine base. It was the queen of the Atlantic military chessboard.

In a speech on May 27, 1940, President Roosevelt announced—largely for Hitler's ears—that the Azores were of such strategic importance that the United States could not permit them to fall into hostile hands. The comment terrified the Portuguese, who inferred that the U.S. would soon move to occupy the islands. If that occurred, Salazar knew, Hitler would invade Portugal to even the scales. Two days later, Portuguese troops—with helmets strikingly similar to the German model—left for the Azores to fend off *American* invaders.

It was a high-stakes game, and Portugal had no chance of thwarting Axis aggression on their homeland. The joke among those living in Lisbon was that if Hitler wanted Portugal, he could take it with a phone call. Salazar knew this and his concessions toward Berlin were less than subtle.

In 1936, for example, Salazar had created a "Youth Movement" to promote physical fitness, character, respect for law, and discipline. Modeled on the Hitler Youth, the participants wore paramilitary uniforms and marched in regimented order. Harvey Klemmer, in his August 1941 article for *National Geographic*, included a photo of the Portuguese Youth Movement boys parading before officials on Avenida da Liberdade—offering a fascist salute.

When war broke out in 1939 and escalated across the continent, Salazar continued his appeasement of the Third Reich. His position that the "question of the Jews" was an internal matter for Germany was well known and presumably well received in Berlin. In addition, he strictly limited the number of Jewish refugees landing in Lisbon. On November 13 he sent a notice to each embassy stating that Jews would require direct approval from the Foreign Ministry for temporary immigration visas.

Aristides de Sousa Mendes, Portugal's consul in Bordeaux, knew this procedure would cause impossible delays and would result in countless Jews being sent to concentration camps. In the summer of 1940, as the Wehrmacht marched across France, mobs of refugees inundated Mendes's office. His Christian conscience overriding his consular directives, Mendes disobeyed Salazar and began authorizing visas for thousands of Jewish refugees, saving their lives. Furious, Salazar recalled him to Lisbon and on July 4 began disciplinary proceedings. Within weeks, Mendes was fired. Hitler was surely pleased.

Yet appeasement on the Jewish question was not enough. Portugal and Spain—and especially their territories—provided too many military opportunities. In a meeting with his generals on November 4, 1940, the Führer announced Directive No. 18: Germany would attack and capture the Portuguese Cape Verde Islands, the Spanish Canary Islands, and Gibraltar in a plan codenamed "Felix." After that, in an operation called "Isabella," Hitler envisioned three German divisions moving in from the Spanish border to attack Portugal itself.

If Franco and Hitler didn't provide cause enough for neutrality, Salazar had another reason for remaining on good terms with Germany:

Gold.

The principal metal necessary for armoring Germany's tanks and machinery—tungsten—was produced from a raw ore called *wolfram* and was found almost entirely in Portugal and China. Since the Royal Navy had cut off the Chinese shipping lane, the Iberian Peninsula—Portugal holding some 90 percent of the deposits—was the only source. Salazar and Hitler knew the alternatives: Germany could purchase the wolfram or extract it by force.

Salazar opened the trade floodgates. In 1942 alone, Portugal shipped some 2,800 tons of wolfram to Germany. The Portuguese president knew the shipments would draw the ire of the Allies, but he had a ready counter—much of the production came from German-owned mines. Aside from nationalizing the operations, Salazar reasoned, he could scarcely object to trade with Germany, particularly given the benefits to Portugal's coffers. And because Salazar recognized the fragile and speculative value of German marks, much of which were now being counterfeited, he demanded payment in gold. The Third Reich agreed, and over the course of the war Germany would transfer some 124 tons of gold—much of it looted from occupied countries—to Portugal.

To preserve neutrality, Salazar granted an equal allocation of wolfram to the Allies, again demanding gold. His strategy produced staggering results. In 1939 Portugal's gold reserves were a mere 63 tons (Germany, by comparison, held 133 tons); by 1945 Salazar had more than doubled the country's holdings—from Germany alone. With another 169 tons from sales to other countries, Salazar had swelled Portugal's gold reserves to an astounding 356 tons.

And while wolfram was causing Portugal's wealth to burgeon, the refugee, diplomat, and spy influx was bursting its economy at the seams. Restaurants and cafés were packed. Casino Estoril pulsed all night, every night. Simply finding a bed in the city was a chore.

In December 1940 a Lisbon correspondent for the London *Times* stated that American generals slept in attics because they couldn't find hotel rooms. *New Horizons*, the Pan Am magazine, reported that between June and December 1940, more than eighty thousand refugees were in Lisbon awaiting transit overseas. By the time Dusko arrived in Lisbon in 1941, some forty thousand refugees were awaiting passage to the United States alone. It was, as one reporter wrote, the "bottleneck of freedom."

The transients were trapped. For these thousands of ex-politicians, ex-intellectuals, and ex-industrialists, only one ship a week left for New York—American Export Line's *Excaliber*, *Excambion*, or *Exeter*—and refugees waited months for a ticket. Pan Am's Clipper departed twice a week, but the few seats it carried were reserved for American legates and military brass.

Added to the influx of expatriates were hordes of government officials. Britain and Germany each sent hundreds of diplomats and spies to Lisbon. The Gestapo sent its agents, too, some alleged to be disguised as refugees and some at work on Operation Willi—the German plot to kidnap the Duke of Windsor. Others, while operating in civilian clothes, might as well have been in their SS uniforms. One American journalist reported that when the Gestapo chief for Portugal entered the casino, croupiers greeted him in German and SS officers left their tables to pump his hand.

Rumors circulated about the less amiable tactics of Gestapo and SD agents operating in the city. In late 1939 the Germans were said to have discovered an MI6 operative who was meeting regularly with an Abwehr agent. That operative, in turn, was leaking information. One night German agents kidnapped the man and demanded to know the source of the Abwehr leak. The British spy remained silent.

To encourage their captive to cooperate, the story went, the Germans placed him inside a refrigerated meat locker. Placing a fragmentation grenade in his hand, they told him to hold down the detonator, and pulled the pin. When he was ready to talk, they'd re-pin the explosive. The Germans left, locking the door behind them. The refrigerated cell expedited the man's predicament—he not only couldn't sleep or nap, the chill would quickly cripple his grip. The Germans expected a hasty change of heart. The man allegedly lasted seventy-five hours. When his fingers could squeeze no more, he dropped the grenade and was eviscerated.

Another Lisbon officer was said to have died more swiftly. Supposedly stumbling while boarding a DC-3, the man had fallen into a spinning propeller. A witness testifying later claimed that three men had *thrown* him into the arc.

And German operatives were not the only hazard. America, France, Italy, Japan, and countless other countries sent their agents as well. Many hired locals as informers. Lisbon was a swarm of refugees and spies, rumors and lies.

Don't worry about them, came the remark at the Palácio lounge one evening. *They're just a bunch of leg men. The one on the left tells Musso who's here. The big fellow does the same for Himmler. The little guy keeps Goebbels supplied with English newspapers.*

And on it went. Information was Portugal's priceless commodity and bellmen, clerks, valets—anyone—could be on a country's payroll. Even in the Allied-friendly Palácio the head waiter was Italian and thought to be working for the Italians or Germans.

Added to this incestuous nest was the local secret police. Like *Casablanca*'s Captain Renault, Lisbon's Captain Agostinho Lourenço supervised an aggressive force—the Polícia de Vigilância e Defesa do Estado (PVDE). Desmond Bristow, an MI6 officer who described them as "over-zealous Germanophiles," reported that they could be found at the airport, tram stops, and most hotel lobbies. While he was on assignment in Lisbon, Bristow recalled, an officer at Passport Control warned him about these "devils."

One day, Bristow wrote in his memoirs, he was conversing on a tram island with Jona von Ustinov,* a Russian-German MI5 agent. Ustinov had offered a Black Russian cigarette and Bristow was attempting to light it between gusts of wind. Suddenly, he felt two hands grab him at the shoulders. "Senhor," a secret policeman said, "please show me the license for your lighter. Here in Portugal, gentlemen, you have to have a license for a cigarette lighter."

The British agents shrugged.

"Passports please, senhores; you are obviously foreign."

From that moment on, Bristow remembered, the secret police followed them everywhere. For several days they would have up to five PVDE agents watching them as they dined, walked, and traveled about Lisbon and Estoril. When the agents suddenly disappeared, Ustinov was worried. "Better we see them seeing us," he said, "because then we can all see together, but when not seeing them seeing us we might not see them seeing us doing what we are doing."

Such attention compounded Dusko's apprehension. On any given night he might be shadowed by a German or British agent, who himself was being tailed by PVDE. It was possible that Popov might have *three* tails, all watching as he entertained a female companion—who also might be a German spy.

---

*Father of actor Peter Ustinov.

Aviz Hotel, Lisbon, 1940. *Gulbenkian Foundation*

But the PVDE controlled the music of the dance. Lourenço's men filed extensive reports and based on what he read, the secret police chief decided which espionage activities he would allow, and which he would prohibit. In many instances—as several German and British spies and journalists discovered—a run-in with Lourenço resulted in a quick trip home.

It was from this hive of refugees, diplomats, spies, informers, and secret police that Dusko would collect his honey.

And implant his stinger.

»

On November 22, 1940, he flew to Barcelona, spent the night at the Ritz, and the following day caught a Lufthansa flight to Lisbon. Per Abwehr instructions he checked in at the Aviz, the city's most luxurious hotel and home to Calouste Gulbenkian, the world's richest man.

Napoléon himself would have approved. The seventeenth-century French furniture, intricate ironwork, and mural entryways exuded aristocracy. The ominous crest looming on the building's exterior, however—which was strikingly similar to the Imperial Coat of Arms of the German Empire—hinted at why Berlin had instructed Dusko to stay there: The Germans controlled it.

According to Popov's memoirs, he called von Karsthoff and followed the "Schmidt" code; he was at the pickup spot on the Rua Augustus an hour early. The winking blonde appeared and moments later he ducked into an Opel. A few blocks later the driver let the girl out and then pointed the sedan west, toward Estoril.

Situated between the bustle of Lisbon and the cliffs of Cascais, Estoril was Portugal's Riviera. As early as the turn of the century local officials had begun initiatives to transform the charming fishing village into a commercially viable resort. In 1910 a Portuguese physician had published in London a medical report espousing the therapeutic advantages of Estoril's thermal springs and mild climate. Four years later Fausto de Figueiredo, the former president of Portuguese Railways, announced his vision of establishing Estoril as a tourist destination akin to the French Côte d'Azur. Although delayed in his work until the conclusion of World War I, Figueiredo set about his task vigorously, obtaining a betting license and overseeing construction. By 1930 his dream had been realized and Estoril boasted a world-class hotel (Palácio), an international casino, a glistening beach, gardens, a golf course, a thermal spa, and a complex of high-end restaurants, shops, and promenades. Advertising campaigns followed, and almost immediately Estoril was on the short list of "must visit" destinations.

»

At the outbreak of World War II, German, British, and American diplomats and military attachés stationed in Lisbon saw no harm in enjoying all that Estoril offered, including its luxury hotels. While Axis personnel preferred Lisbon's Aviz and Estoril's Atlântico and Parque, the Allies preferred the Palácio. Those with considerable means and extended stays rented lavish villas in Estoril and Cascais, estates originally constructed to house visiting royalty.

Popov's car was headed to one such estate, the Villa Toki-Ona. As the sedan crept into the garage, Dusko rose from his crouched position in the backseat as an attendant was closing the door behind them. Von Karsthoff was an imposing figure, not so much due to his physical presence, but because of his stature. Forty to forty-five years old, he was just under six feet, had dark

Palácio Estoril Hotel.

hair and eyes, and looked more Italian or Spanish than Austrian. Well dressed and well educated, he spoke Italian, French, and some Portuguese. He also could read English and, as Johnny had warned, was very much Dusko's equal—handsome, intelligent, charming.

And dangerous. Dusko would later describe his time with the major as "being in the company of a domesticated panther." Slim and lithe, the major's movements resembled those of a big cat, he recalled. At every moment, even in relaxed settings, the slightest mistake might rouse the creature to devour him.

Ludovico offered a drink and introduced a young woman, Elisabeth Sahrbach, his secretary. About twenty-five and with a good figure, Elisabeth was professional but cool. A fair-complected blonde, she wore no makeup but was nevertheless attractive. Dusko assumed she was the major's mistress and made a mental note to win her over early.

Von Karsthoff's villa, Dusko remembered, was Moorish, opulent, and boasted features necessary for any active spymaster: an enclosed garage, an interior stairwell, a high stone border, and within walking distance to the Palácio, the casino, and Estoril entertainment. Popov identified the property to MI5 as the "Villa Toki-Ona" and the "Villa Toki-Ana." Cascais land records, however, contain no properties called "Toki-Ana." A "Chalet Toki-Ona" on Bicesse, later identified as the "Vivenda Toki-Ona," was most certainly von Karsthoff's residence.

Not surprisingly, the property had a colorful history.

In 1923 a Luís Teixeira Beltrão filed with the authorities plans for a luxurious home at Estrada de Bicesse, Nº 31, a location which comports with the parcel later known as the Toki-Ona. The blueprints match Popov's description of von Karsthoff's residence in every detail: Moorish architecture, large—likely exceeding eight thousand square feet—and having an enclosed garage and interior stairwell. In May 1928 Beltrão notified the city that construction had been completed.

In 1936 an ad appeared in *O Estoril* for a property known as the Bom Refúgio, also on Estrada de Bicesse, which matched the construction plans filed by Beltrão. The property was sublet for a time as apartments, and the ad revealed the appeal: two hundred yards from the casino, luxurious accommodations, a spacious garden and garage. In all probability, the Beltrão property, the Bom Refúgio, and the Villa Toki-Ona were all one and the same.

In 1937 Beltrão sold the property to a Ms. Margot Seco de Topete, who appears to have returned it to single-family use. Margot de Topete, however, was not a Lisbon local; hotel registrations reveal that, although born in Paris, she was a Venezuelan national. She also was not living in the Bom Refúgio in 1939. On April 16 of that year she checked into the Palácio. The next day she was across the border, gambling at the French casino in Biarritz.

The day after that she was escorted from the country.

Ms. Topete, it seemed, was doing her part in the war—*for Germany.* An Associated Press release on April 18 carried the story:

FASCIST AXIS EMBLEM TORN FROM CLOTHING

> Politically-minded patrons of a Biarritz casino ripped the jewel-embroidered letters, "R-O-M-E, B-E-R-L-I-N, T-O-K-Y-O," from the gown of a stylishly dressed Venezuelan last night. . . . Intervention of a police commissioner enabled her and her companions to leave. The woman identified herself as Senora Margot Topete, widow of a Venezuelan general. With her were a group of young Spanish women and a German.

In addition to the gown letters, she was also wearing a belt with the three Axis powers prominently displayed. The story didn't identify the German, but he may well have been von Karsthoff, or one of the major's lieutenants. From May 25, 1940, to December 26, 1942, while Ludovico was renting the Toki-Ona, Ms. Topete lived at the Palácio. The Venezuelan evidently enjoyed gambling, and Casino Estoril patrons apparently were more tolerant of politically themed fashions.

In the meantime, von Karsthoff kept a low profile. Other than his listing with the German Embassy, his name—itself an alias—appeared nowhere, even though he rented several properties. He would expect Popov to observe the same level of secrecy; they would meet only after dark, and only after a car ushered Dusko inside the garage.

When they finished their drinks, the major concluded the meeting and Dusko left the way he'd come—hiding in the back of the sedan. The driver returned to Lisbon and dropped him off several blocks from the Aviz. Darting between moon-cast shadows, steps echoing down cobbled streets, Dusko hustled to the hotel. It was a scene reminiscent of a John Buchan novel.

What happened a few nights later, however, could only have been replicated in the sybaritic mind of Ian Fleming.

TOO MANY DEVICES

His second or third night in Lisbon, Dusko recalled, he emerged from the shower to find a beautiful girl in his room—in a silk negligee. He had seen her earlier at the Aviz but knew nothing about her other than her name—Ilena Fodor—which he had acquired from the front desk.

Somehow Ilena knew his name, and commencing with a kiss, she began asking questions about his origins, opinions, and why he was in Portugal. She was clearly a spy; Dusko's only decision was whether to partake in the forbidden fruit. He made up stories about his origins and opinions, and told her he was in town for a client who had lost a Gaugin and two post-impressionist paintings. Ilena nodded, seemingly disappointed. Reclining, she opened her negligee, exposing half of Gibraltar. The ruse was so blatant it was annoying. Dusko sent her on her way.

Bem-vindo à Lisbon.

The Germans had upped their game and Popov would have to follow suit. A few days later he discovered that he had been right about Ilena. While he was visiting von Karsthoff and going over codes and questions, the major dryly suggested that Dusko "stop trying to find those post-impressionist paintings." Ludovico had heard all about it, he said, and claimed that it was the work of Abwehr III, counterintelligence.

What he didn't mention was the mind-boggling level of Axis infiltration in Portugal. Graham Greene, the English novelist who served with MI6, saw firsthand the daunting task facing the Allies. As head of the Portuguese desk in 1943, Greene assembled a notebook providing the names and activities of known Axis agents operating in the country. Greene's report listed *two thousand* names. In addition, no less than forty-six companies doing business in the Iberian peninsula were considered covers for German espionage.

For his entire tenure in Portugal, then, Popov could be tailed, tested, or trapped by agents of Abwehr I, Abwehr III, the Gestapo, the SD, the PVDE, or informants of any.

The tightrope was long, taut . . . and invisible.

»

Dusko knew he had to leave the Aviz, and on November 28, 1940, he transferred to Estoril's Allied-friendly Palácio. His excuse was that the Aviz was too staid for his tastes; the fact that the Palácio was adjacent the casino and beach was merely incidental. Knowing of Popov's penchant for entertainment, von Karsthoff made nothing of the transfer.

On December 5 Dusko received his visa for England but was unable to secure a seat on the KLM flight. He was also beginning to run short of funds. A few days later he cabled Johnny: "Still 5–15 waggons deliverable—send letter of credit immediately." The number of wagons indicated his estimated days before departure. Hearing nothing back, he pressed von Karsthoff, who gave him $400. The major also delivered a questionnaire—*verbally*—for Popov's trip to London. Dusko was to find out:

1. The people opposed to Churchill who were working for peace with Germany, and how to get in touch with them. He was to ascertain their hobbies and weaknesses—money, drink, women, etc.
2. The type of bombing attack most affecting the morale of the population.
3. The most effective kind of propaganda.
4. The class of the population most affected by propaganda and how they could best be approached.
5. The circle of people surrounding Vice-Admiral Sir John Tovey, Commander-in-Chief of the Home Fleet. Once identified, Dusko was to ingratiate himself with as many as possible.

The answers were to be sent, von Karsthoff said, via a new secret ink formula. In a wineglass three-quarters full of non-chlorinated water, Dusko would dissolve a few crystals. Dipping a steel nib into the solution, he was to write on a postcard to one of three cover addresses in Lisbon. Once received, Ludovico could read the message by placing a hot iron on the card. Once the paper turned brown, the secret writing would suddenly appear in black.

The major added that if the invasion came while Popov was still on the island, Dusko was not to be afraid. "When our troops are there, just ask to be taken to the Commander, tell him who you are, mention my name and everything will be all right. The Commander might give you new orders, just do what he tells you to do."

If Dusko ran into difficulties or needed money, he was to telegraph a woman who would pass for his girlfriend: Maria Helena Barreto de S. Anna, Rua Donna Stephania 7b—4°, Lisboa. Maria was about twenty-two, he said, beautiful, and had a good figure. Von Karsthoff still had much to learn about his new spy; given Ludovico's description, there was a good chance Dusko would contact her even if he didn't need money.

»

On December 20 Popov finally acquired a KLM ticket, the plane arriving at Felton Airport, near Bristol, around 6:00 p.m. At Immigration he informed the agent that he was visiting England on business for the Savska Bank of Belgrade. The officer stamped his passport, and Dusko made his way through Customs, where he was met by a wiry young man with jet-black hair and a pencil-thin mustache. The man whispered that his name was Jock and that he would be Popov's driver. At the car Dusko met his MI5 escort, a Mr. Andrew.

Jock drove skillfully, Dusko remembered, but exceedingly fast. The Security Service, it turned out, had recruited well. The man's name was St. John Horsfall, a professional race car driver and winner of the 1938 Leinster Trophy.

Driving an Aston Martin.

They arrived at the Savoy around ten o'clock, just as the Luftwaffe was setting the city aglow. Like Lisbon's Aviz, Estoril's Palácio, and Rome's Ambasciadore, the Savoy was England's best, famous for its French chefs and favorite guest—Winston Churchill.

The clerk handed Dusko the key to room 430 and someone from behind whispered Popov's name. It was Major Tar Robertson, MI5's B1A section chief and the man who would directly run him.

Trained at Royal Military Academy Sandhurst, Tar had been commissioned in the Scottish Seaforth Highlanders before joining Intelligence and often could be found in the office sporting his tartan trews. Winsome, Tar had twinkling eyes which were at once disarming and engaging—the kind that partied with you before words were spoken. "A born leader," a colleague would say of him, Robertson possessed uncanny and perceptive judgment, traits critical for running enemy agents. Just three years older than Dusko, Tar was already an intelligence veteran, having joined MI5 in 1933.

Robertson introduced himself and over drinks explained what Dusko needed to know about B1A, and the overlap between MI5 and MI6. Since Dusko had not been vetted and remained a security risk, Tar did not reveal the puppet masters pulling the double-cross strings.

In the summer of 1940, MI5 and MI6, together with the military intelligence directors, had formed the Wireless Board (aka, W Board) to oversee all intelligence and counterintelligence. The members of the board were: Major General Stewart Menzies (head of MI6), Guy Liddell (director of MI5's B Division, Tar Robertson's boss), Admiral John Godfrey (director of Naval Intelligence), Air Commodore Archie Boyle, Major General F. C. Beaumont-Nesbitt (director of Military Intelligence), and the intelligence officer of the Home Forces. Before the end of September, however, the work of the W Board became too burdensome and Beaumont-Nesbitt suggested that the Board limit itself only to supervision of a subcommittee that could perform the daily chores.

That body, appropriately named the Twenty Committee for its XX (Double-Cross) abbreviation, held its first meeting on January 2, 1941. The committee was comprised of representatives of MI6 (Menzies), MI5 (J. C. Masterman, Tar Robertson, and John Marriott, Robertson's deputy), Naval Intelligence (Godfrey and Commander Ewen Montagu), the War Office, the Air Ministry, the Home Forces, and the Home Defense Executive. The Double-Cross Committee would be chaired by the tactful and even-tempered J. C. Masterman, a history scholar and Oxford don at Christ Church College.* Masterman, like his military counterparts, saw the unique potential of Popov. "We had in him a new agent of high quality who could plausibly meet persons in any social stratum," he wrote after the war, "who was well established with the Germans . . . and who had an excellent business cover." But in December 1940, Dusko's potential and plausibility were yet to be determined.

Over the next several days, Masterman, Robertson, Marriott, and Montagu interviewed and vetted Popov. He passed with flying colors and was invited to a New Year's Eve party at a Georgian mansion in Surrey. There, Dusko wrote, an austere gentleman with piercing blue eyes introduced himself and

---

*Later, vice-chancellor of Oxford University.

Registration Certificate No. 1022652

Issued at Piccadilly Place. W1

on 5th February 1941

Name (Surname first in Roman Capitals) POPOV Douchan

Alias Dusan

Left Thumb Print (if unable to sign name in English Characters).

Aliens Registration Office Metropolitan Police Piccadilly Place 7.2.41

Signature of Holder.

Nationality Jugo Slavian

Born on 10/7/12 in Titel Serbia

Previous Nationality (if any) Serbian

Profession or Occupation Representative

Single or Married Single

Address of Residence Cumberland Hotel W.1.

Arrival in United Kingdom on 22/8/1928

Address of last Residence outside U.K. 98, Boulevard Sevastopol

Government Service

Passport or other papers as to Nationality and Identity. Jugo Slav 4822 Issued Belgrade 16/11/40.

Dusko's English alien registration card. *The National Archives of the UK*

ushered Popov to a private study. The man was Major General Stewart Menzies—"C" as he was known in intelligence circles—head of MI6.

The ideogram had been inherited from the first director, Sir Mansfield Cumming, who had signed all documents with his last initial. Cummings's successor, Admiral Hugh Sinclair, continued the tradition, and Menzies followed suit. The moniker was almost universally known; Malcolm Muggeridge, who worked for MI6 during the war, noted that the agency's internal phone directory listed the SIS director with just the initial. The sobriquet was so well established that Menzies reputedly could draw checks on the Royal Bank of Scotland with it as his signature. The office and appellation even traveled in international intelligence circles; none other than Reinhard Heydrich, chief of the SD, began to use "C" in envious imitation, stamp and all.

That Menzies was one of the most powerful men in all of Britain was evident during the war, and after. He reported directly to, and *only* to, Winston Churchill. During the 2,064 days of World War II, Menzies met with Churchill no less than fifteen hundred times, often while the prime minister was in his bed or bath. "C" was perhaps the only person who, at any hour of the day, had access to the king, the prime minister, and the foreign secretary. Indeed, many foreign powers believed that "C" was the power behind the throne. Over time, "C" took on legendary status; years after the war Menzies would tell his biographer that Ian Fleming told him that he, Menzies, was James Bond's "M."

Stewart Graham Menzies's background was quite similar to Dusko's. Both men had come from wealthy families and their grandfathers had built vast estates, Graham Menzies as the owner of the second largest distillery in Europe, Omer Popov as the owner of a bank and various businesses. The fathers of Stewart and Dusko were also similar, neither working much and both squandering vast sums of money. Like Dusko, Stewart received a first-class education, graduating in 1909 from Eton, a fifteenth-century college founded by Henry VI. The school's curriculum included Greek, Latin, Plato, Thucydides, Lysias, poetry, music, and history, particularly *military* history. Menzies's housemaster, Edward Impey, also insisted that his boys master the Gospels, contending that only in them could a young man acquire courage, truth, honor, courtesy, chivalry, and manliness. Eton groomed young men to lead, after all, and Menzies would demonstrate leadership in every circle. He won the Consort's Prize in French and German, was captain of his house, master of the Eton Beagles, and president of the "Pop," the prestigious Eton College Society whose members were selected for their beauty, elegance, charm, and "power to amuse and dazzle." He also excelled in athletics, captaining the Eton cricket team and winning the Eton Steeplechase.

Upon graduation, instead of taking the typical route to Oxford or Cambridge, Menzies enlisted in the Brigadier Guards. Shortly thereafter he transferred to the exclusive Life Guards, the gentlemen soldiers charged with protecting the king. Two years into his service, Stewart's regiment was sent into one of the bloodiest campaigns of World War I, the First Battle of Ypres. Of 12,000 soldiers and 400 officers sent to the conflict, only 2,336 men and 44 officers survived. Menzies distinguished himself in battle and was later presented a Distinguished Service Order by the king, having shown "the greatest coolness" during the German attack. The following summer, in May 1915, at the Second Battle of Ypres, Menzies again distinguished himself in combat, this time receiving a Military Cross, Britain's decoration for acts of exemplary gallantry.

Little did Popov know, he was about to be dissected by a distinguished Etonian, war hero, spymaster, and the second most powerful man in Britain. Dusko recalled that "C" minced few words: "One man out of a thousand has the talent to play the fiddle," Menzies began. "One out of a hundred thousand has the capacity to be a virtuoso, and one out of a million actually becomes one. My capacity is to assess values and measure them. If I do that properly, I have fulfilled half my duty."

Menzies had led men in sports, society, hunting, and battle. He knew Popov was that one in a million virtuoso but, like the eccentric musician, Dusko carried considerable baggage.

"You are honest but without scruples," the general went on. "Your instincts and intuition are stronger than your intelligence, which is far above average. Your conscience never bothers you and you are mentally short-sighted and long-sighted at the same time. You are ambitious and ruthless and you can be cruel. But when you are cruel, it is with an animal cruelty, not a sick cruelty. You like to hit back but you are not in a hurry to do so. When you are frightened, you don't panic. Danger is a stimulant for you. You think more clearly and make better decisions when pushed by the instinct of self-preservation than by contemplation."

Dusko sat in shocked silence at the insightful evaluation from a man he'd just met. "C" knew him better than he knew himself.

"You have too many devices on your banner," Menzies concluded. "You have the makings of a very good spy, except that you don't like to obey orders. You had better learn or you will be a very dead spy."

Dusko did have many devices, but most of them required living. Boldly, almost prophetically, he would stretch his banner over the next four years to the limits of disobedience and death; yet, almost despite himself, his devil-may-care attitude would somehow protect him.

Devices notwithstanding.

PASSION AND ADDICTION

JANUARY 1, 1941

The blitz of September 1940 had brought a surprising windfall to MI5. When the headquarters at Wormwood Scrubs* was severely damaged, the agency relocated to Blenheim Palace, eight miles north of Oxford. A gift in 1704 from Queen Anne to John Churchill following his victory over the French, Blenheim was a fortress surrounded by two thousand acres, adorned with soaring gardens and water terraces. MI5 staffers were well aware of the significance of their new home—Winston Churchill had been born and raised at Blenheim, and had proposed to his wife Clementine at the estate's arboretum.

Yet the noble refuge provided no sanctuary against the trials within. As Major Robertson sat in his office on New Year's Day, he was faced with a problem not atypical for supervisors of double agents: Was one of his men a triple? While Dusko had sailed through vetting, three of Popov's initial evaluators had significant reservations about agent SKOOT. Mr. How, whom Dusko had met at the British Embassy in Belgrade, distrusted Popov and later described him as "an absolute crook."

Lieutenant-Commander Ewen Montagu of the Double-Cross Committee also had second thoughts. At their initial meeting in the Savoy, Ewen said, Dusko claimed to be an experienced yachtsman, yet seemed to know no technical terms of sailing. As a member of Dubrovnik's Orsan Yacht Club, Montagu thought, Dusko's ignorance was inexplicable. Popov's MI5 case officer, William Luke (whom Dusko knew as William Matthews), had even greater suspicions. In a report to the Double-Cross Committee, he wrote: "I

*A Victorian prison in West London.

cannot help regarding him with a good deal of suspicion. . . . I have just the general feeling that he may be a most accomplished liar."

The information couldn't be worse for Tar, but there was more. Popov had been expelled from a London prep school, had received a doctorate in Germany, and had been recruited into the Abwehr by his best friend. If Dusko was tripling, the damage he could do would be immense. Britain routinely executed spies and with Germany winning the war, killing a rogue double agent was not out of the question. Popov had star potential, the major knew, but MI5 could take no chances. He called Montagu and asked him to meet with Popov again, at six that evening at the Savoy. Ewen was to go up to Popov's room, Tar said, visit for a while, and then take Dusko to the hotel bar, where Montagu's brother would join them for drinks. Together they would try to get a feel for agent SKOOT and otherwise work out details for explaining to the Germans how they met.

When Montagu met Popov in his room, Dusko immediately calmed the suspicions. "I found him a most charming person," Ewen wrote in his report, "and I should be most surprised if he is not playing straight with us." They spoke again of their mutual interest in sailing, and decided that they'd tell the Germans they met through a mutual friend in the Royal Ocean Racing Club. Montagu also gave him a name to satisfy the Germans' request for someone close to Admiral Tovey. Foster Brown, Ewen said, had been a fleet signal officer in Nelson and was now liaising at the Admiralty for Tovey. As for naval information to take to Lisbon, Dusko was to tell the Germans that Ewen had, in a moment of indiscretion, mentioned that almost every Atlantic convoy was having an escort of one or more submarines. In addition, the larger ships would be fit with aircraft which might carry torpedoes.

Business covered, Dusko told Ewen that he had a college friend who owned some ships in the Norddeutche Lloyd fleet, which were in neutral ports, and which Popov had been asked to sell. Dusko explained the neutral flag hurdle and how they would need an intermediary. Montagu had another idea. Just tell us when and from where they are sailing, he said, and the Royal Navy would intercept and "capture" them.

Later that night Popov met with Robertson and Marriott for final instructions. The MI5 officers went through the questionnaire and told him to tell the Germans that he couldn't get all of the answers due to his friend's work responsibilities at the legation. He was to add that his friend was a bit nervous with the work and suggested that Dusko return, establish his own contacts, and collect the information himself. In the meantime, they gave him information for a few of the questions, and Dusko had the Admiralty names of Ewen Montagu and Foster Brown, together with Montagu's indiscretions about convoys. Tar also mentioned that Dusko could offer three lords who sought peace with Germany: Brocket, Lymington, and Londonderry.

What Robertson recorded the next day had to come as a mild surprise: "Over the question of money, SKOOT is absolutely insistant that he should receive nothing from us."

»

Dusko returned to Lisbon on January 3. Per instructions, he recalled in his memoirs, he rang von Karsthoff and told the woman answering, presumably Elisabeth, that he was "a friend of the major's cousin from Italy." Moments later von Karsthoff came on and provided the second part of the code: "A friend of my Italian cousin? You must come to visit. You'll bring some laughter to my house." Dusko continued: "It's rather urgent. Can we make it for Wednesday?"

Dusko's reference to Wednesday was a diversion; "urgent" meant a meeting that same day. The time of appointment was determined by the day of the week mentioned. All meetings would be in the evening, and pickups would be at ten after the hour. If Dusko mentioned Monday, the first possible hour, this meant he wanted to be picked up at 6:10 p.m. Tuesday meant 7:10 p.m., Wednesday, 8:10 p.m., and on through the days until the last schedule slot, Sunday, 12:10 a.m. If Dusko said that he would "come by train," this meant that he wanted to be picked up at a prearranged spot on the Avenida da Liberdade, in downtown Lisbon. If he said he was taking a taxi, it meant that he wanted to be picked up on the main road one mile east of Estoril. If von Karsthoff called Popov at the hotel and instructed Dusko to come "to the legation," it meant the major's villa.

Ludovico acknowledged the request and Dusko ended with "I shall come by train." At ten after eight an Abwehr sedan picked him up on the Avenida da Liberdade and chauffeured him to von Karsthoff's villa. After dinner and drinks, von Karsthoff asked him to spend the following day with him and Elisabeth at the major's country house in Cascais.

It was no picnic, Dusko remembered; Ludovico grilled him for hours on end, inquiring about every detail, time of activity, circumstance, and person involved. Like a seasoned barrister, he cross-examined every story, attacking from different angles and seeking additional facts. Dusko supplied the Double-Cross chicken feed, as false or harmless information was called, but von Karsthoff consistently probed further, requiring Dusko to improvise.

The following day the major left for Paris, and on January 7 Popov transferred to the Palácio. As Dusko had noticed with the Aviz, hotel registration was cumbersome. For the duration of the war, Portuguese lodging facilities were required to document on a special form every foreign guest, and to give these registrations to the PVDE. When the clerk asked Popov his occupation, Dusko gave one of his many identities—lawyer.

Another British Intelligence officer would soon check into the Palácio with less discretion.

»

On January 14 von Karsthoff returned from Paris. IVAN's information was considered too general, Ludovico's superiors felt, and Dusko would need to return to England for additional details. In addition, the major said, they wanted him to travel to America and then to Egypt for further assignments. Von Karsthoff showed him a questionnaire—some fifty questions over nine pages—which Popov was to memorize.

Ludovico then dropped another code: If Dusko received a call at his hotel from a girl saying, "I'm sorry I behaved so stupidly the other night," the major was calling a meeting. The girl would suggest that Dusko meet her at a nightclub later that evening; instead, he was to go to the casino. Elisabeth would show up at the roulette table and play three times. The numbers she picked would indicate the date, hour, and minute of the rendezvous, consecutively. She would then play zero or 36, the former indicating a Lisbon pickup, the latter Estoril.

The intrigue wasn't limited to Portugal, however.

Dusko returned to London on February 4 and stayed where the Germans had asked him, the Commodore Hotel. He assumed the reason was the same as for the Aviz—so that they could watch him. Four days later, Robertson and Masterman met with a Major Lennox and Sergeant Lewis for the same purpose—keeping tabs on Popov. Could the military provide a savvy and attractive female, Tar asked, who could "entertain SKOOT and keep him out of mischief," while at the same time keeping MI5 apprised of the "curious associations which he is making in this country?" Lennox and Lewis agreed to work on it.

On February 10, while lunching with Robertson and Luke, Popov mentioned that he was possibly being watched by the Germans. On the other hand, he told them, it was also possible that the shadows were MI5 agents. Tar and Bill gave no reply. Unruffled, Dusko said that the more British Intelligence tested his bona fides, the more pleased he would be.

As Tar schemed on how to keep tabs on agent SKOOT, Dusko was putting much of British Intelligence to work. He requested navicerts*—which MI5 would have to acquire from the Royal Navy—for sending two thousand tons of cotton from Portugal to Yugoslavia. The Double-Cross Committee, in the meantime, had to work on Popov's questionnaire, a copy of which Dusko had taken from von Karsthoff.

Most of the requests were to be expected: Where are planes of the Botha type stationed? Has the RAF in the Eastern Mediterranean been strengthened in recent months? How many fighter squadrons are equipped with Spitfires and Hurricanes? When will the five battleships of the King George V class be ready? Other instructions, even for a seasoned, full-time spy, were beyond the scope of what Popov could reasonably accomplish: sketches of military factories at Weybridge, Crayford, and Datford; detailed methods of fire direction for London anti-aircraft guns; position of division staffs with sketches; and a copy of the Circular of the British Ministry of Supply showing military depots.

Dusko and the Double-Cross gang would have to focus on those questions most suitable for misinformation, and Major Robertson saw one item with a double benefit: coastal defenses. The Germans wanted overall data, including details of naval bases in Scotland. Dusko would make the trip with Bill Luke tagging along; while the men toured Scottish towns, ports, and pubs, Tar planned, Luke would probe Popov's loyalties.

During this time, Commander Montagu concocted more chicken feed. During Germany's Operation Sea Lion, Ewen knew, channels of attack would be critical. Assuming that Popov could sell the information as legitimate, Montagu planned to waylay German warships. The Royal Navy had set up minefields along Britain's east coast, he knew, but a number of large gaps existed due to limited resources. Ewen's idea, dubbed Plan Machiavelli, was to pass to the Abwehr charts of minefields marked in "slightly wrong positions"; mines would be in place where gaps were shown, and vice versa. Dusko

---

*Navy certificates, which were needed for cargo coming to Europe through British-controlled waters.

would claim that he had obtained the charts from a Jewish barrister who had joined the navy but feared a German victory. Thinking he could buy insurance against a concentration camp, the man was to have given Dusko the charts to trade for the Jew's protection once England succumbed.

Remembering Munzinger's and von Karsthoff's penchant for sources, Popov pointed out to Montagu that he'd need an identity of the traitor—a real name. "I thought you had realized," Ewen said, "Lieutenant Commander Montagu. They can look me up in the *Law List* and any of the Jewish Year Books."

On February 14 Popov sent the bait. Writing as "John Danvers" from a cover address of 18 Queens Gate Place, Dusko addressed the letter to von Karsthoff's cover: Paulo Brimoes, Esq., Largo Santar Antoninho, Lisboa. On the front was an innocuous message written in English. On the back, in French with the secret ink, Dusko detailed Montagu's offer.

The following day he and Luke left for Scotland. They would embark on an imaginary tour of naval bases, but a real tour of quaint towns, friendly pubs, and fine restaurants. In the span of four days, Dusko visited Glasgow, Strathblane, Lennoxtown, Drymen, Balloch, Loch Lomond, Gare Loch, Helensburgh, Dumbarton, and Edinburgh. While glimpsing coastal ports, he also found time to enjoy cocktails at the American Bar, the Central Hotel, and the Piccadilly. In addition, he visited the Edinburgh Castle, Hollyroodhouse Palace, the Scot Monument, and the War Memorial. He even took in the theater.

When they returned to London on the twenty-first, Luke summarized his thoughts about Popov:

> I have come to the conclusion that he is definitely working for us and not for the Germans. . . . He is clever, versatile and firm of purpose. He knows what he wants and it will not be his fault if he does not get it. . . . He is fond of the society of attractive women [and] . . . his amorous exploits would provide good material for Maurice Dekobra.* . . . He has personality and charm and would feel at home . . . in society circles in any European or American capital, being much the usual type of international playboy. . . . SKOOT is an ingenious, cheerful and amusing companion of whose sincerity and loyalty I, personally, am satisfied.

---

*French writer of erotic thrillers.

»

With Luke's confirmation, Dusko was cleared as a full-time double agent, and Robertson and Marriott recorded for the MI5 file Popov's physical attributes: light gray eyes; receded and brushed back hair; high cheekbones; white even teeth; full lips; loose, sensual mouth; broad shoulders; athletic carriage; long-strided gait; and well-manicured hands. His complexion, Tar noted, depended upon the previous night's activity.

Even with Luke's assurances, however, Robertson continued to monitor Popov's daily movement. Within days Tar discovered that the Scotland tour was just a foretaste of Dusko's lifestyle; in London, MI5 tags shadowed him on the bachelor treadmill. Between meetings with Luke and Montagu, and appointments at the American, Portuguese, Spanish, and Yugoslav embassies, Dusko dined at the Berkeley, Haslemere, Savoy, Mirabel, L'Ecu de France, Claridge's, Dorchester, Hyde Park, and the Bachelors' Club. Before or after dinner, depending on the company, he enjoyed cocktails at the 400 Club, Grosvenor Square, the Mayfair, and the Coconut Grove.

Running at a frenetic pace, however, was when Popov's mind was sharpest; he suggested to Luke a bold idea for an Allied escape route. On February 27 he and Bill lunched with a Major Isham of MI9, the SIS section charged with aiding resistance fighters and POWs in occupied territories, and rescuing Allied soldiers trapped behind enemy lines. Isham mentioned that most British prisoners were held in Salzburg, and Popov said he could orchestrate—through his brother—an escape line through Yugoslavia. There was a hotel in Austria near the frontier, Dusko explained, which was owned by a Jew. So long as he was compensated for the rooms, the proprietor was sure to cooperate. Ivo, who was pro-British and had probably guessed what Dusko was doing, could bribe officials at the Yugoslav border.

Isham liked the idea, Luke noted, but did not know that Popov was a double agent. What Bill Luke didn't know was that Dusko was going to tell the Germans.

»

The following day Tar introduced Dusko to Friedl Gaertner, a striking thirty-four-year-old Austrian, with thoughts of having Popov pitch her to von Karsthoff as a sub-agent. Gaertner was perfectly suited to double because her mother and sister lived in Germany, and her father had been a member of the Nazi

Copy

1st. III. 1941.

Dearest Dusko,

Many thanks for the lovely flowers and our most charming evening. I did enjoy myself very much indeed.

If you can manage to give me a ring and we could arrange to dine

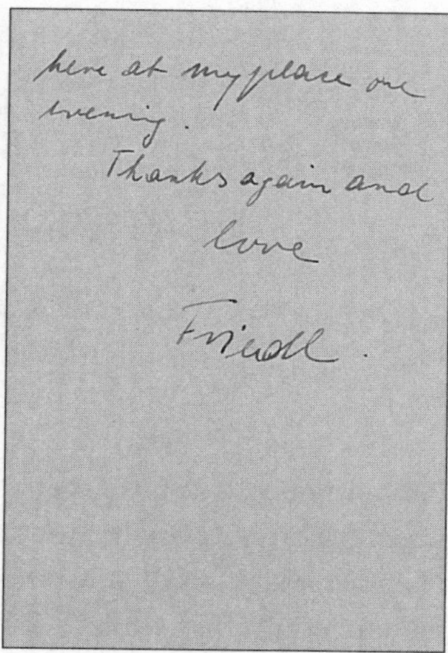

here at my place one evening.

Thanks again and love

Friedl.

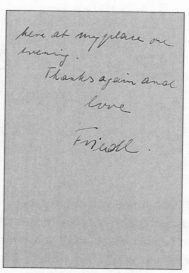

Friedl Gaertner's note of March 1, 1941, thanking Dusko for flowers and a "charming evening."

The National Archives of the UK

Party. In addition, after the Anschluss in 1938, MI5 had had her send the German Embassy a note of congratulations. Most importantly, as Menzies's brother's sister-in-law, she was considered safe.

Dusko was smitten by Friedl and immediately set sparks to the kindling. They went out that night and again on March 4, 5, 7, 8, 9, and 10. Mixing business with pleasure, they dined and drank about town in service to His Majesty's Secret Service. One day, Popov recalled, he and Friedl had a busy schedule: a lunch appointment, a cocktail party in the afternoon, and a dinner engagement that evening. Driven by a passion that had become addiction, Dusko admitted, he showed up at Friedl's cottage early. It went largely as planned. Gaertner had just emerged from her bath and answered the door in a short terry-cloth robe.

They missed the luncheon.

And the cocktail party.

And the dinner.

8 DEATH IN THE AFTERNOON

On March 4 Popov and Luke met again so that Bill could get a full understanding of the escape plan. In the afternoon, Luke met with Major Robertson, Major Lennox, and Captain Masterman to go over details. It would be expensive and dangerous, they realized, but the payoff was tremendous. Popov was to move forward.

That evening Dusko met Bill again to help evaluate a potential spy MI5 was considering for the operation. He said he thought the candidate was an excellent choice if Luke was confident the man was absolutely loyal; Bill confirmed that he was. Taking his leave to make a dinner date at the Mayfair, Dusko quietly reminded Luke that he still needed help sneaking something back to Lisbon.

A revolver.

»

Over the next two weeks Dusko met with Major Robertson several times to discuss overall strategy with von Karsthoff, and how to lead the major to accept sub-agents. Assuming Popov could sell it, Friedl would join Dusko's network as his source for political information, and Dickie Metcalfe, an MI5 officer, would be pitched as Popov's source for technical and military information. Friedl would be code named GELATINE—because Luke thought her a "jolly little thing"—and Metcalfe would be BALLOON, due to his ample girth. With a network of three, Dusko's code name was changed from SKOOT to TRICYCLE.*

Before leaving, Popov requested a meeting with J. C. Masterman. As chair-

---

*Despite MI5 files KV 2/845 and 2/862 indicating that the change of code names occurred when Popov acquired two sub-agents, two authors have promoted a racy and fictitious version of why Dusko's code name was changed—that he fancied "three-in-a-bed" sex. See Notes.

man of the Double-Cross Committee, the Oxford don was Dusko's ultimate supervisor, but it was more than that. Masterman possessed a temperance, objectiveness, and fatherly wisdom that Popov knew counterbalanced his own alacrity and adventurism.

Dusko, it turned out, was having second thoughts about his game of deceit. As Johnny had warned, Popov was developing a genuine friendship with von Karsthoff, and Dusko's conscience was gnawing at him. Ludovico was charming, and, in spite of the shadow clouding their consanguinity, Dusko much enjoyed his company.

"TRICYCLE . . . had some slight moral scruples about the part which he was playing," Masterman recorded at the time. "I tried to explain to him, I think with success, that the strictest moral censor 'having regard to his motives' would not cavil his conduct."

Dusko was relieved. With his moral sextant at peace, he returned to Lisbon on Saturday, March 15, anxious to expand his network. The following evening he met with von Karsthoff and Elisabeth at the Estoril villa. Ludovico was all business. Before delving into Dusko's answers to the questionnaire, however, he checked bona fides: At what London station had Popov arrived? At what hotel had he stayed? What did the wallpaper in his suite look like?

Dusko responded accordingly and von Karsthoff moved on to the written answers, after which he asked Popov to recount every day in England—where he went, people he saw, topics discussed. When Ludovico asked about sources, Dusko parroted the Double-Cross crafted stories for Gaertner and Metcalfe. Von Karsthoff appeared to know about Friedl and inquired about the origin of military information. His source, Popov told the major, was a former army officer who had been bounced for passing bad checks. The man was terrible with money, Dusko said, always spending more than he made. He was bitter about his army experience and desired a playboy lifestyle, which he couldn't afford.

The major nibbled at the bait and told Dusko to sound them out. As Ludovico continued with the questionnaire answers, Dusko filled in gaps with whatever seemed plausible. The major nodded. Everything looked fine, and he asked Popov to return on Tuesday, March 18.

When Dusko arrived, Elisabeth had already typed out his verbal responses, which they had sent to the Tirpitzufer* with his written answers. Abwehr

---

*Abwehr headquarters in Berlin.

headquarters had cabled back, Ludovico said, stating that Dusko was to go to Madrid to meet "some gentlemen from Berlin." Dusko agreed, having no idea what the meeting was for, or why he needed to see them. The important thing was that he and Johnny had planned to meet in Madrid about this time, and the trip would allow a discreet rendezvous.

As critical as Lisbon was, Madrid was the Abwehr's largest post. Admiral Canaris had been very close to Franco during the Spanish Civil War, and to some extent had influenced Hitler to back the general. At the outbreak of World War II, Germany expected Franco to return the favor. When Hitler and Franco met at Hendaye in October 1940, the Spanish leader signed a protocol pledging Spain's entry into the war—fighting for the Axis alliance—at an undetermined future date. The slippery general, however, delayed his formal affiliation by coyly asking for significant German armaments, and adding as a prerequisite that Spain would independently seize control of the Iberian Peninsula. Undaunted, Hitler sent Canaris to meet with Franco on December 7, and to tell the general that Hitler wanted to move German forces into Spain on January 10. Franco again demurred. For now Spain would remain neutral, albeit with a wink and a nod to Berlin. In the meantime, the Spanish Air Force would regularly train in Germany.

»

Von Karsthoff warned that the Abwehr's Madrid chief, Gustav Wilhelm Lenz*—"Papa" as he was known—might try to contact Dusko if for no other reason than to prevent Popov from encroaching on his territory. If possible, the major instructed, Dusko should try to stay clear of him. Ludovico knew as well as anyone that every German organization competed for power, prestige, control, and assets. This was particularly true between the Abwehr and the SD, the Gestapo and the SD, and Abwehr I and III: Canaris competed against Heydrich, Goering against Himmler, Schellenberg against Mueller, and on down the institutional line. At the station level, von Karsthoff's Lisbon competed with Lenz's Madrid.

As with Lisbon, Madrid had two luxury hotels—the Palace and the Ritz—Germans controlling the former, Allies the latter. On March 22 Dusko checked into the Ritz and a day or so later, as von Karsthoff had warned, Lenz called.

---

*His real name was Wilhelm Leisner.

The Madrid chief simply wanted to pass along a Berlin cable, however, stating that Jebsen would arrive in a few days.

While Dusko waited, on March 27, Serbian army officers staged a coup d'état and deposed Prince Paul, the pro-Nazi regent of Yugoslavia. In retaliation, Hitler launched Operation Punishment, a three-day bombardment of Belgrade. Since the capital had no anti-aircraft guns, the Luftwaffe dropped their loads at rooftop level, killing seventeen thousand civilians and wounding tens of thousands more. When Dusko heard the news, he was beside himself; if his parents had been at their winter residence, they were likely dead. The ensuing German invasion posed a second problem—the destruction of Dusko's cover business. Since Germany would now block imports from England to Yugoslavia, he would have to find another excuse for travel between Lisbon and London.

Days came and went and he heard nothing of Jebsen. Finally, on Sunday, April 6, Johnny arrived and came up to Dusko's room. A Dr. Warnecke and perhaps two other "specialists," he said, would be coming from Berlin on the ninth. Popov's report had been well received in Berlin, Jebsen said, and Johnny was instructed to be "very diplomatic" with him. He added that von Karsthoff was impressed with the mine chart, but Berlin thought it was out of date. Calling Dusko Germany's top agent, Johnny gave him $10,000, courtesy of Colonel Pieckenbrock. In addition, he said, the Abwehr had agreed to free any of Dusko's friends or family that were imprisoned in Yugoslavia.

They continued the discussion in the hotel lounge, where Johnny suddenly slipped into a melancholy languor. There was a flip side to the Abwehr's courting, he explained. Berlin would work carrot and stick, reward and threat, simultaneously. Johnny's supervisors had mentioned in passing that they could pressure Dusko by threatening to denounce him to the English, or by imprisoning him. For the time being, Johnny said, he could provide protection.

"I am not cruel enough, but now I am in a position to get rid of anyone I hate." Recalling a Freiburg professor that he and Dusko despised, Johnny said: "If I want to get rid of that man all I have to do is to say that Professor Miller said that and that and they will kill him at once without questioning."

And yet there was long-term risk which Jebsen couldn't control, and he grieved over having thrust Dusko into the crucible. "You're my closest friend," he said somberly. "If you want to analyze it, you're an ersatz brother and I wish you were a real one." He reached for a nut from the bar dish and cracked it in his hands. "You can be crushed like that."

Dusko shrugged off the warning. He was a big boy and knew what he had bargained for. Johnny brooded for a moment and then went on to say that Lenz had brought 120 agents to the city, and had another 400 paid informants. Any porter, waiter, or bellman could be his eyes and ears, he said; Dusko would have to be on his toes.

In all probability, Jebsen's estimate of Madrid agents was conservative. Walter Schellenberg, SD intelligence chief, reported after the war that apart from staff for active espionage and counterespionage, the German Secret Service had posted seventy to one hundred individuals in Madrid solely for decoding intelligence messages. The city was crawling with German agents, operatives, and informants. Once again, Dusko could be followed anywhere, and probably was. Even Samuel Hoare, British ambassador to Spain, was convinced that the Gestapo had bugged his telephone at the Ritz. The hotel, Hoare contended, was swarming with Germans and teeming with espionage.

»

On April 9 the "specialist" from Berlin—Dr. Warnecke—arrived. Short and sallow, he was a strident Nazi with sinister credentials—a saber scar on his right cheek, running parallel with his mouth, and a missing front tooth. The German was no lout, however; he held doctorates in chemistry and law, owned a chemical factory, and spoke French and English. Most importantly, Dusko found out, Warnecke was Gestapo.

Meeting Popov at the Ritz, the German grilled him for three and a half hours. Dusko had a doctorate in law, too, but Warnecke was well seasoned in carefully and methodically extracting information. Popov parried, postured, and otherwise played the opportunist spy. It worked. When Warnecke concluded his examination, he announced that IVAN was well suited for a new mission—setting up an espionage network in the United States.

Dusko wondered aloud about German spies already in America; surely the Abwehr had a network in place. Warnecke explained that they *had* a net, but that it had been broken up by the FBI. The details he didn't provide were significant.

On March 17 Germany's U.S. spymaster, Captain Ulrich von der Osten, a native-born American, had been hit by a taxi while crossing Broadway near Times Square. As he lay on the ground, a second car struck him. He was taken to St. Vincent's Hospital but died from his injuries the following day. Since he had registered at the Taft Hotel as a Spaniard—Julio Lopez Lido—police had little reason to suspect foul play.

Two days later Bermuda Censorship,* operating in conjunction with British Security Coordination (BSC), intercepted a letter from a "Joe" to a "Manuel Alonso" in Madrid. At this point "Joe" was well known as a German spy. As early as December 1940 BSC had intercepted a letter from him to a Lothar Frederick in Berlin. In it Joe had detailed Allied ships—movements and armaments—operating in New York harbor. From that point on, H. Montgomery Hyde, the security officer at the Bermuda station, asked his censors to keep a lookout for envelopes with the same handwriting. All letters to or from Joe were given to Hyde's best censor, Nadya Gardner, for deciphering.

After intercepting more than thirty such letters, Bermuda determined that the name "Lothar Frederick"—and ones like it—were covers for Nazi Secret Service and Gestapo Chief Heinrich Himmler. Ms. Gardner also determined that "Joe" often wrote of being in touch with "Konrad," whom he sometimes called "Phil" or "Junio."

In early spring 1941, however, neither the BSC nor the FBI knew the identities of Joe or Konrad/Phil/Junio. Osten's death and Joe's letter of March 20 would unravel the mystery. On the reverse side of the correspondence, in secret ink, Joe detailed Phil's death. Providing the tag number of the second car—SU57-35—Joe warned of a problem: "Phil's things are still at the Hotel Taft."

Bermuda forwarded the information to BSC chief William Stephenson, who passed it on to the FBI. Stephenson's biographer, William Stevenson, inferred cryptically that the BSC was behind the hit: "Rather reluctantly, BSC indicated [to the FBI] that Lido was known as a German agent using the cover name 'Phil.' The spy had been 'removed from circulation' . . . Someone had disposed of von der Osten. . . . In this period of neutrality, however, deeper FBI probing would have led to an embarrassment."

When the FBI searched Lido's hotel room, they found a letter addressed to a Carl Wilhem von der Osten in Denver. Carl, who was not involved in the war, acknowledged that Ulrich was his brother and that he had been working for the Abwehr. Following up on other names found among Ulrich's belongings, the FBI and the BSC determined that "Joe" was Kurt Frederick Ludwig,

*During World War II, all mail between the U.S. and Europe was processed through British-owned Bermuda.

a forty-eight-year-old American who had grown up in Germany, and whom Osten was running to set up a spy ring. The FBI put Ludwig under surveillance and soon rounded up his entire network—nine men and one woman. All were tried, found guilty of espionage, and imprisoned, Ludwig in Alcatraz.

Dr. Warnecke wanted Popov to replace the entire network: Osten, Ludwig, and the team of spies. The U.S. mission had advantages, Dusko knew, but from New York it would be harder to look after his parents—if they were alive.

That Sunday, fretting for his family and nervous about his new assignment, Dusko remembered, he decided to take in a bullfight at Plaza de Toros de Las Ventas. It was the action here that a decade earlier had inspired Ernest Hemingway to write *Death in the Afternoon*. Although the stadium held over twenty thousand, it would be packed. Dusko purchased a ticket and went in. A death in the afternoon would at least transfer his tension elsewhere.

Finding his seat, he watched the ceremony and pomp as the matadors, bandilleros, and picadors marched in procession. Moments later the bull entered and the ring erupted into a gladiatorial ballet: beast charging the horses in Act I, multicolored banderillas piercing the air and animal in Act II, matador orchestrating the symphony of death in Act III. The fight was a tragedy, slow-played and cruel, but the danger was no drama. And the analogy was unmistakable. Like the matador, Dusko had to draw the enemy bull so close that, as Hemingway said of Villalta, blood stained his belly. To do this, Popov would have to work the cape flawlessly—hiding here, turning there, flashing his counterfeit wares in centrifugal harmony. If he failed, even by inches, he would die face to the dust.

As Dusko's eyes and mind wandered, the crowd suddenly cheered. The torero had landed a banderilla and the bull stumbled.

"He's collapsing like Yugoslavia," shouted a man behind him.

Popov snapped. Jumping to his feet, he turned and slapped the man, knocking him backward across the bleacher. Immediately, Dusko realized his mistake. In a packed arena the odds of Gestapo being within earshot were great. He bolted for the exit.

He would have to leave Madrid.

Soon.

"HE'S NOT DEAD"

Madrid, Dusko would soon learn, would have cascading consequences in two directions. On April 23 he returned to Estoril to a chilly reception. Almost overnight word had spread about the bullfight incident and von Karsthoff wasted no time in bringing up Yugoslavia.

"Popov, are you a Serb or a Croat?"

Dusko stirred. It had finally come. The question he feared most allowed no suitable answers. If he admitted being a Serb, it amounted to a death sentence. All Serbs were pro-Allied, most affiliated with the pro-British royalists, some fighting with Tito's Communist Partisans. Croats, on the other hand, sympathized with Ante Pavelić's Ustaše government in Zagreb, which had essentially become a German vassal. But if Dusko said he was Croat, even the slightest checking would reveal his true heritage and he'd be caught in the lie.

"My city," Popov replied, "Ragusa, or Dubrovnik as it is now known, was the bright star of Dalmatia. It was allowed by the Pope to trade with the infidel Turks, and that way it remained free and became rich and independent." Dusko carried on with his encyclopedic answer for several minutes, until von Karsthoff stopped him.

"Thank you for that brief and clear historical treatise. But it doesn't answer my question. Are you a Serb or a Croat?"

Undaunted, Dusko charged on, stating that Ragusans were neither Serb nor Croat. Von Karstoff mulled the answer a few moments, and then seemed satisfied. Who was going to debate the issue with a native Ragusan? Besides, the major just needed a believable explanation to give to Berlin. To assure that Ludovico didn't lose his star spy, Dusko later found out, von Karsthoff wrote a fifteen-page report explaining Popov's political indifference.

Yet Dusko was not off the hook. The *British* were again questioning his loyalty. When he met with Johnny in Madrid, the two had worked on the sale of Norddeutche Lloyd ships in South America. It was a massive deal—$14 million—whereby the German ships would be sold to a Spanish consortium but registered under the flag of Peru. The funds would settle in the U.S., where they would be used to purchase NDL stock—a cash reserve to reconstitute the company after the war. While Popov had told MI5 in December of his interest in helping Johnny sell German ships in neutral ports, neither they nor MI6 knew anything of this transaction.

On April 19 Felix Cowgill, MI6 counterintelligence chief, notified Tar Robertson that he had received a report from a "reliable source" (ULTRA) that TRICYCLE was working with Johnny Jebsen and the Peruvian commercial attaché in Madrid—intermediary between the Spanish consortium and the Peruvian government—to consummate the deal. Germany had approved it with the condition that the ships not be resold to Great Britain. Felix had sent the report on to the Ministry of Economic Warfare, he told Tar, with the request that MEW let him know as soon as possible if TRICYCLE "is still on our side."

»

When Dusko next met with von Karsthoff, Ludovico revisited the idea of having Friedl Gaertner and Dickie Metcalfe as sub-agents. Dusko parroted the Double-Cross stories and the major ran with it, saying he was recommending both to Berlin. Assuming the meeting was over, von Karsthoff gave him a few thousand pounds to take to England.

Dusko took the money but seized the opening. As soon as he landed, he told the major, British Customs would record serial numbers of the bills he brought into the country. If Berlin approved Gaertner and Metcalfe, and Dusko had given them money, he pointed out, the money would be traceable to him if they were caught. Von Karsthoff appreciated the risk and said he'd figure something out.

Dusko was going to help him.

»

While in Lisbon and Madrid, Popov never lacked for female companionship. Unfortunately, his dating life was not off-limits to German or British Intelligence, and MI5 kept tabs on two of his girlfriends, Maria Elera and Martha Castello. Elera, a beautiful Brazilian, was elegant and a dead ringer for a São

Casino Estoril, 1941. *Cascais Archive*

Paulo model. Castello, on the other hand, MI5 believed to be a "high-class procuress."

That Dusko often had an audience for his amorous adventures was beyond an annoyance; he better than anyone knew that a single slip might doom him. Nevertheless, he would not be denied his favorite penchants—drinks, damsels, and danger—which brooded over him as stalking clouds. Occasionally, lightning would strike.

One night, Popov wrote, he asked a "French popsie" to join him at the Casino Estoril nightclub. Among the patrons that evening was a large contingent from London's *Daily Mail.* When the band took their break, Dusko recalled, a correspondent's companion—a drunk American girl—clambered onstage to showcase her a cappella skills. Finding the entertainment less than romantic, Dusko summoned a waiter, placed a champagne cork on his tray, and asked him to deliver it. The woman was offended and her friends were outraged. A brawl ensued and two men began pushing through the crowd to get their hands on the instigator.

In Popov's pocket was an envelope containing notes for the British and the Germans. If he was arrested in the melee, Dusko knew, the contents would travel from the PVDE to the Germans within hours. He jammed the packet into his date's purse and shouted for her to run for it; he'd meet her back at the Palácio. "I had to," he said later, "although I had never seen her before in my life."

View of the gardens from Casino Estoril. Hotels Parque and Palácio on the left, Estoril Castle in the distant center. *Cascais Archives*

As his date raced away, Dusko fought off the singer's friends and then escaped. Outside, he heard a scream and sprinted toward the voice. It was his girl, grappling with a man over her purse in the casino gardens. Without breaking stride Dusko kicked the man in the face, punting his head like a football. Spewing blood and teeth, the assailant fell unconscious.

"He's not dead," someone said, rushing up. It was the Palácio manager, George Black.

Popov helped his date up and retrieved the envelope. Black, whom Dusko had befriended, said he'd tell the police that the girl was attacked by two thugs. The following day he gave Dusko the full story: When the police came, Black had recited his line about thugs. Black also inadvertently confirmed that the assailant was a German operative; the man's testimony to the police at the hospital—that his injuries were from thugs who disappeared—matched the manager's.

»

At the end of April Popov returned to London. Catching up with his legitimate business, he notified MI5 that he had two pending export deals—sixty-five tons of turpentine—on behalf of Savska Bank. For an undisclosed reason, he had a shipment of fifteen tons—scheduled for transport to Yugoslavia—stopped at the Portugal–Spain border. The British asked no questions.

After his debriefing, Dusko presented Bill Luke with another idea. It started with a problem faced by all spymasters: paying agents on enemy soil. At Customs, all currency had to be converted to pounds, and someone exchanging German marks would be suspect. Even if the courier was traveling with sterling or dollars, any sizeable amounts would draw attention.

About this time, Guy Liddell recorded in his MI5 diary two accounts of how the Germans were desperately trying to pass money to their man, British double agent TATE. On May 15 Liddell wrote: "The man from the Phoenix who was to bring TATE his money has been picked up by a War Reserve policeman at Colney." The man was carrying £500 and $1,400. "The Supt.," Liddell added, "having had his instructions from our R.S.L.O. about suspicious persons carrying large sums of money, immediately came to the conclusion that the man was a spy."

On May 23 Liddell described another attempt: "He [TATE] is to take a bus No. 16 at 4 o'clock on a certain date from Victoria Station. There will be on board a Jap. TATE and the Jap would get off at the first stop and get into the next 16 bus. The Jap would carry the Times and a book in his left hand. TATE would get alongside him and ask whether there is any news in the paper. The Jap will then hand him the paper which will contain the money."

On the date of the rendezvous, however, the "Jap" didn't show. Intercepts revealed that he had received the message late. The Germans then decided to have him hide money inside four hollowed birch branches, follow behind the explosions of two 200-pound bombs to be dropped in a certain area, and place the branches amid the debris. But on the night of the planned bombing, the plane was unavailable.

On May 29 the Germans finally passed £200 to TATE, but that transfer too almost failed. Returning to the original plan, the two men had boarded bus No. 16, but before the first stop policemen abruptly held it. The Japanese agent exited, TATE followed, and the men made their exchange.

Still worse for the Germans, as Popov had mentioned to von Karsthoff, was that serial numbers of all bills over one pound were recorded at Customs. Even later in the war, when Schellenberg was counterfeiting currency, the Abwehr ran the risk of censors, serials, and transfers. Since the Double-Cross Committee was running a large number of turned spies, often more than ten, it was impossible for the Abwehr to effectively disburse funds. If the committee would approve it, Dusko told Bill Luke, he had a scheme to steal the Germans blind.

Money laundering.

Luke was intrigued and they presented it to Tar, who thought it worth a try. Naming the plot Plan Midas, Robertson pitched it to the Double-Cross Committee. They rejected it. Too far-fetched, they said. Tar and Bill were flummoxed; it was a case officer's dream, Luke thought, tricking the Nazis into funding their enemy. The MI5 officers pressed the committee again the following week, explaining the benefits and how they already had an intermediary in place, a London theatrical agent. This time the committee approved, authorizing £20,000 for priming the laundering pump.

Before Dusko's departure, MI6 gave him a code for contacting British Intelligence in Lisbon: From a public telephone he was to call 52346. If the Germans suspected nothing and everything was fine, he was to mention that it was a lovely day and he was enjoying the sunshine. If he thought the Germans suspected him and he was unhappy about his position, he was to say that he thought a storm was breaking and it was likely to rain. If the Germans had found him out and he was blown, he was to say "the party is over." And if he wanted to meet, he would make an appointment for the following day. He would rendezvous at the tennis pavilion on Tapada Ajuda an hour before the time stated. The appointments were only to be made during the week and he was advised to speak over the telephone in French.

»

On June 28, 1941, Popov returned to Lisbon to pitch Midas and went directly to the Estoril villa. Von Karsthoff was in a jovial mood and happily announced that Berlin had approved Gaertner and Metcalfe as sub-agents. As they spoke, Dusko uncovered the bait, telling von Karsthoff that he had a wealthy business associate in London who wanted to get some money out of England. The man was a theatrical agent, Dusko said, and had asked about a bank or exchange agent abroad who would be willing to accept pounds in England for U.S. dollars deposited in New York. The man was willing to lose some money on the exchange rate, of course. Did the major know of such a bank or agent?

Von Karsthoff nibbled at the edge of the idea. As SD Lisbon chief Erich Schroeder testified after the war, Ludovico enjoyed the pleasures of money and was known to skim off the top whatever Berlin sent for agent IVAN. All of this boded well for Popov's plan; the opportunity to make a commission was too appealing for von Karsthoff to miss.

"Don't do anything for a few days," he said. "I'm sure I can have a better deal for you than any bank."

Seeds planted, Popov returned to the Palácio. It was a lovely day and he was enjoying the Lisbon sunshine.

10 »

TARANTO AND THE TARGET

A few days later Johnny arrived and updated Dusko on his family. Part of their Belgrade home had been destoyed by bombing, he said, but Dusko's parents were safe in Dubrovnik. Ivo had a close call as well, going to ground when the Germans arrived.

Jebsen didn't know the half of it. In early July, Ivo had been condemned to death by Ante Pavelić's Ustaše. A Croat lawyer and former member of Parliament, Dr. Ante Pavelić was a psychopath who had been arrested for organizing the assassination of Yugoslav king Alexander in Marseilles in 1934. Pavelić somehow escaped and slipped into Italy, where he was protected by Mussolini. There he founded the Ustaše, with the goal of creating an independent Croatian state. When Germany invaded Yugoslavia in April 1941, Pavelić assumed power as head of Croatia and began a campaign of genocide. In his first year alone, the Ustaše murdered some three hundred thousand Serbs, Jews, and Gypsies.

As a Serb, a Nationalist, and the official doctor charged with overseeing Dubrovnik health matters, Dr. Popov was high on their list. Because Ivo treated countless patients free of charge, however, he was beloved in the community. When the death warrant was announced, Ivo's friends warned him. Disguised as a monk, he slipped away to Belgrade.

The atrocities reported across Yugoslavia were so outrageous that they seemed hard to believe. But they were true. British SAS operative Fitzroy Maclean, who had parachuted into Bosnia to assist the group most effectively fighting the Germans—the Partisans—saw with his own eyes the anarchy that was the Balkans. Four groups, he explained, vied for control of the country: the occupying Germans, Tito's Partisans, Mihailović's Četniks, and Pavelić's Ustaše. While the Partisans and Četniks had originally fought the Germans side by side, in short order each claimed the other had betrayed them to their occupiers, and by the end of 1941 they would be fighting each other.

In Bosnia, Maclean explained:

> Pavelić's accession to power had been followed by a reign of terror unprecedented even in the Balkans. . . . There were widespread massacres and atrocities. . . . Racial and political persecution was accompanied by equally ferocious religious persecution. The Ustaše were fervent Roman Catholics . . . [and] set about liquidating the Greek Orthodox church in their domains. Orthodox villages were sacked and pillaged and their inhabitants massacred, old and young, men, women and children alike. Orthodox clergy were tortured and killed, Orthodox churches were desecrated and destroyed, or burned down with the screaming congregation inside them (an Ustaše specialty, this). The Bosnian Moslems, equally fanatical and organized in special units by Pavelić and the Germans . . . joined in with gusto and a refined cruelty all of their own, delighted at the opportunity of massacring Christians of whatever denomination.

In Serbia, Maclean went on, the Germans had installed a puppet government, which sent large numbers of Serbs to concentration camps and massacred untold thousands of others.

The mayhem would hit the Popov family soon enough.

»

Johnny went on to say that he had been in Taranto, Italy, working with Baron Wolfgang von Gronau, Germany's air attaché in Tokyo. Jebsen's assignment—unknown to him or anyone—would later affect the lives of thousands.

In March Japan's foreign minister, Yosuke Matsuoka, had gone to Berlin with a contingent of army and navy officers to flesh out the Tripartite Pact. Months before, Japan had requested that Germany supply details of a British raid at Taranto, Italy, but little had come forth. Matsuoka repeated the request during the Tripartite meetings, and someone figured Johann Jebsen would be ideal for the assignment.

The Jebsen shipping empire was well known, even in Japan. By 1941 the family had offices throughout much of the world, and the Jebsen & Co. Shanghai office had been providing Abwehr agents cover in the Far East. The tandem of Gronau and the shipping magnate would, Japan hoped, finally provide a comprehensive report on Taranto. Their instructions, presumably from Hermann Goering and in concert with Japanese intelligence, were to ascertain attack procedures and damage results.

The raid was worthy of emulation. On November 11, 1940, the Royal Air Force and Navy had made history, forever changing the future of war. Under cover of darkness, the RAF launched twenty-one aircraft from two carriers against the Taranto naval base. A surprise, preemptive strike from fifty miles out, it was the first aerial assault against a defended port. The aging and ugly Fairey Swordfish, a lumbering and virtually defenseless aircraft designated as a torpedo-spotter-reconnaissance seaplane, was tasked for the mission. Designed in the early 1930s, it was outdated by the time the war began. With box-kite wings and legs that resembled an oil rig, it bore the unbecoming nickname "Stringbag."

Launched in two waves from the *Illustrious* and the *Eagle*, the Stringbags proved capable attack craft. The damage to the Taranto base was considerable, if not devastating. Three battleships were put out of action. The *Littorio*, Italy's finest and less than three years old, was hit by three torpedoes and took months to repair. The *Caio Diulio*, which was a step above all British counterparts save one, had to be dry-docked for half a year. The *Conti di Cavour*, which carried catapult aircraft, was damaged beyond repair. Two other ships—cruiser *Trento* and destroyer *Libeccio*—had suffered direct hits but the bombs failed to explode. The Stringbags also demolished Taranto's seaplane base and damaged its oil tanks. In the span of two hours, the raid had bloodied and significantly weakened the Italian Navy, securing for the British control of the Mediterranean.

What the Germans needed to know—and pass to the Japanese—was how the RAF did it. Taranto was heavily defended. Three walls of twenty-seven barrage balloons—a frightening array of lethal steel cables—hovered before the ships like a giant spiderweb. Under water, three rows of netting waited to snag torpedoes. Around the base a legion of anti-aircraft guns pointed to the sky. Enemy pilots attempting to drop a bomb or torpedo would have to run a gauntlet of twenty AA batteries.

The British did, and they did it *at night*.

Dusko asked the obvious: Why would the Japanese be interested in a British attack on an Italian naval base? Von Gronau, Johnny answered, thought the Japanese would enter the war and would do so by attacking the United States.

Taranto would provide the blueprint.

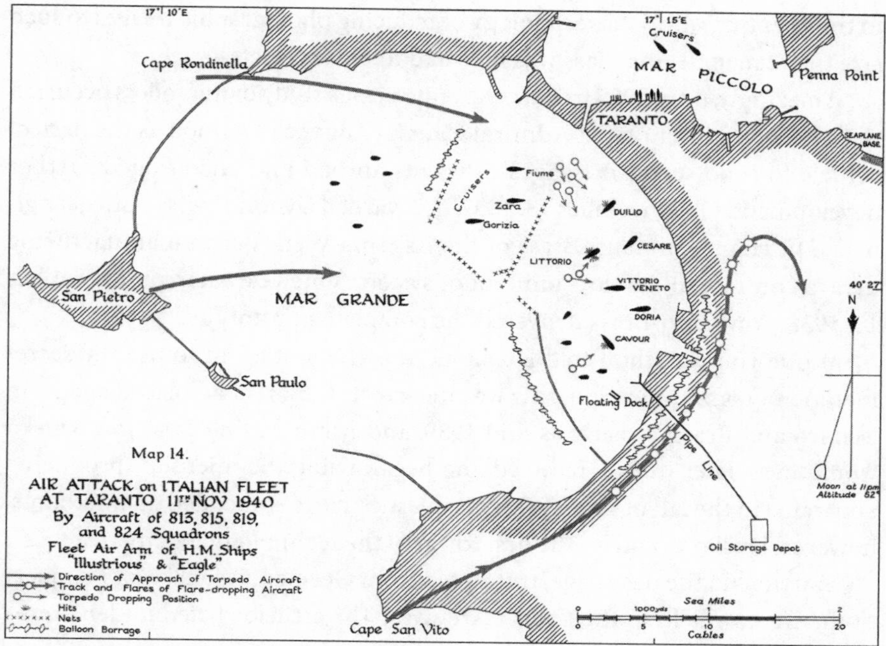

British raid at Taranto, November 11, 1940.

Days later, Dusko wrote, he visited von Karsthoff for details of the U.S. assignment. Ludovico gave him a questionnaire but directed Popov to peer inside a microscope on his desk. Dusko did, and he could see the first page of questions. Removing the slide, the major revealed a black dot, no larger than a period. The *mikropunkt*, von Karsthoff said, was what Dusko was examining. With this revolutionary element of spycraft, the Germans could take any document, reduce it in size by a factor of 450:1 to 750:1, and embed it in processed collodion* no larger than 0.1 mm in diameter.

While microphotography had been invented in 1853 by Englishman John Dancer, and patented in 1859 by Frenchman René Dagron, it would be decades before the invention offered espionage utility. Not until 1925, at the International Congress of Photography, would microdots† be revealed. At this Congress Dr. Emanual Goldberg, a Russian-born German from Dresden, introduced

---

*A flammable substance used in the manufacture of photographic film.

†*Mikrats,* Goldberg called them. See Notes regarding J. Edgar Hoover's allegation in 1946 that a "Professor Zapp" of the Technical High School in Dresden had invented them.

to the scientific world the technology of reducing photographic images to such size that a magnifying glass was required to observe details.

Amazingly, from 1925 to 1937, the only serious study of microdots occurred in Germany. Abwehr chief Admiral Canaris saw the invention as the perfect vehicle to send secret messages to agents abroad and encouraged further development. On November 18, 1937, he awarded a young Swiss optical engineer, Dr. Hans Ammann-Brass of the Askania-Werk Berlin manufacturing firm, a contract to develop a microdot system. One year later, on November 18, 1938, Ammann-Brass delivered the completed prototype.

While von Karsthoff told Dusko he was the first agent to use the secret method of communication, this was incorrect. Canaris had placed agents in Mexico and Brazil as early as mid-1939, and Albrecht Engels, whom Dusko would meet later in Rio, received and began using the microdot-producing apparatus in the fall of 1940. With his questionnaire embedded on microdots, however, Dusko would be the first to carry the technology to America.

Starting on the next page, translated from German, is Dusko's 1941 questionnaire now held in the British Archives. The airfields listed under "Aerodromes" are Pearl Harbor air bases.

Due to secret classification by the U.S. and Britain, the public would not see this questionnaire until 1972, when J. C. Masterman included it as Appendix 2 ("Tricycle's American Questionnaire") in *The Double-Cross System*. The book, written in the summer of 1945 as a report for MI5, included only agent code names and had never been intended for publication. Some twenty-seven years after compilation, and over considerable consternation from the Security Service,* however, Masterman published the report with Yale University Press. In his discussion of the questionnaire, Masterman stated that he received it from MI6 on August 19, 1941 (nine days after Dusko's departure for New York), and that it was translated and read to the Double-Cross Committee, copies being sent to appropriate service members.

Unknown to Dusko, the Germans already had a spy in Hawaii, a Dr. Kuehn. The Japanese had reported to the Germans, however, that the man was an amateur and that his information was useless. He was clumsy and a security risk, they said. As a result, Japanese Intelligence asked Goebbels to replace Kuehn, and Popov was given the nod.

---

*But with approval of Her Majesty's Government.

TRICYCLE QUESTIONNAIRE

Taken by agent to U.S.A. in microphotographs Aug. 1941

Circulated to Twenty Committee 21.8.41.

Translation

Naval Information. Reports on enemy shipments (material foodstuffs - combination of convoys, if possible with names of ships and speeds).

Assembly of troops for oversea transports in U.S.A. and Canada. Strength - number of ships - ports of assembly - reports on ship building (naval and merchant ships) - wharves (dockyards) - state and privately owned wharves - new works - list of ships being built or resp. having been ordered - times of building.

Reports regarding U.S.A. strong points of all descriptions especially in Florida - organisation of strong points for fast boats (E-boats) and their depot ships - coastal defense - organisation districts -

Hawai: Ammunition dumps and mine depots.

1) Details about the naval ammunition and mine depot on the Isle of Kushua (Pearl Harbor). If possible sketch.
2) Naval ammunition depot Lualuelei. Exact position? Is there a railway line (junction)?
3) The total ammunition reserve of the army is supposed to be in the rock of the Crater Aliamanu. Position?
4) Is the Crater Punckbowl (Honolulu) being used as ammunition dump? If not, are there other military works?

Aerodromes:

1) Aerodrome Lukefield: Details (sketch if possible) regarding the situation of the hangars (number?), workshops, bomb depots and petrol depots. Are there underground petrol installations? Exact position of the seaplane station? Occupation?
2) Naval air arm strong point Kaneohe: Exact report regarding position, number of hangars, depots and workshops (sketch). Occupation?
3) Army aerodromes Wicham Field and Wheeler Field. Exact position? Reports regarding number of hangars, depots and workshops. Underground installations? (Sketch).
4) Rodger's Airport: In case of war, will this place be taken over by the army or the navy? What preparations have been made? Number of hangars? Are there landing possibilities for seaplanes?
5) Airport of the Panamerican Airways: Exact position? (If possible sketch). Is this airport possibly identical with Rodger's Airport or a part thereof? (A wireless station of the Panamerican Airways is on the Peninsula Mohapuu).

Naval strong point Pearl Harbor:

1) Exact details and sketch about the situation of the state wharf, of the pier installations, workshops, petrol installations, situation of dry dock No. 1 and of the new dry dock which is being built?
2) Details about the submarine station (plan of situation). What land installations are in existence?

Dusko's Pearl Harbor Questionnaire in MI5 archives.

The National Archives of the UK

Naval strong point Pearl Harbor:

3) Where is the station for mine search formations (Minensuchverbaende)? How far has the dredger work progressed at the entrance and in the East and South-East lock? Depths of water?

4) Number of anchorages (Liegeplaetze)?

5) Is there a floating dock in Pearl Harbor or is the transfer of such a dock to this place intended?

Special tasks. Reports about torpedo protection nets newly introduced in the British and U.S.A. navy. How far are they already in existence in the merchant and naval fleet? Use during voyage? Average speed reduction when in use. Details of construction and others.

1. Urgently required are exact details about the armoured strengths of American armoured cars, especially of the types which have lately been delivered from the U.S.A. to the Middle East. Also all other reports on armoured cars and the composition of armoured (tank) formations are of greatest interest.

2. Required are the Tables of Organisation (TO) of the American infantry divisions and their individual units (infantry regiments, artillery "Abteilung", and so forth) as well as of the American armoured divisions and their individual units (armoured(tank) regiments, reconnaissance section and so forth). These T O are lists showing strength, which are published by the American War Department and are of a confidential nature.

3. How is the new light armoured car (tank)? Which type is going to be finally introduced? Weight? Armament? Armour?

1. Position of British participations and credits in U.S.A. in June 1940. - What are England's payment obligations from the orderssince the coming into force of the Land Lease Bill? What payments has England made to U.S.A. since the outbreak of war for good supplied, for establishment of works for the production of war material and for the building of new or for the enlargement of existing wharves?

2. Amount of state expenditure in the budget years 1939/40, 1940/41, 1941/42, 1942/43 altogether and in particular for the Army and the re-armament.

3. Financing of the armament programme of the U.S.A. through taxes, loans and tax credit coupons. Participation of the Refico and the companies founded by it (Metal Reserve Corp., Rubber Reserve Corp., Defence Plant Corp., Defence Supplies Corp., Defence Housing Corp) in the financing of the re-armament.

4. Increase of state debt and possibilities to cover this debt.

All reports on American air re-armament of of greatest importance. The answers to the following questions are of special urgency:

I. How large is:

a) the total monthly production of aeroplanes?
b) the monthly production of bombers (Kampfflugzeuge)?
c) " " " " fighter planes?
d) " " " " training planes(Schulflugzeuge)?
e " " " " civil aeroplanes (Zivilflugzeuge

II. How many and which of these aeroplanes were supplied to the British Empire, that is to say:

a) to Great Britain?
b) to Canada?
c) to Africa?
d) to the Near East?
e) to the Far East and Australia?

III. How many U.S.A. pilots finish their training monthly?

IV. How many U.S.A. pilots are entering the R.A.F.?

Reports on Canadian Air Force are of great value.

All information about number and type (pattern) of front aeroplanes (Frontflugzeuge).Quantity, numbers and and position of the echelons (Staffeln) are of interest. Of special importance is to get details about the current ~~training~~ air training plan in Canada, that is to say: place and capacity of the individual schools and if possible also their numbers. According to reports received every type of school (beginners'- advanced- and observer school) is numbered beginning with 1.

»

As von Karsthoff worked his way through the questions, Dusko noticed that the next section—"Hawaii"—asked about ammunition dumps and mine depots. Johnny's investigation at Taranto came to mind and the picture was complete.

The Japanese were going to attack Pearl Harbor.

Another maelstrom, however, would hit home first. Twenty days after Ivo's escape in early July, the Ustaše transferred the death sentence to his wife and child. Dragica was twenty-one and their child, Milorad ("Misha"), was three months old.

They were to be publicly hanged.

11»

CASINO ESTORIL

By mid-summer Midas was in full swing. That the plan was complicated and involved unknown players may have contributed to its success. Guy Liddell's July 16, 1941, diary entry reveals his confused understanding of the scheme:

> The Twenty Committee have got a plan known as Midas. The idea is to get the Germans to send over a large sum of money which will be held here by some selected individual who will make the necessary payments to agents in the U.K. Tricycle has succeeded in getting the Germans to bite but they propose to send over their own representative who will effect the disbursements. He will get the money from our agent who will be reimbursed by the opening of a credit which Tricycle will take with him to America.

J. C. Masterman, having heard details during Double-Cross meetings, recorded a more lucid understanding:

> In Lisbon Tricycle represented to the Germans that he knew a rich Jewish theatrical agent who was anxious to build up a reserve of dollars in America as he was afraid England might lose the war. The arrangement made, therefore, was that TRICYCLE should receive dollars in Lisbon or America from the Germans and that the Jew should pay over £20,000 in sterling to TRICYCLE's nominee in England. The nominee was, of course, to be a person chosen by the Germans.

Major von Karsthoff wasted no time pursuing the opportunity. Soon after the agreement was in place, Ludovico summoned Dusko to the villa and introduced Lieutenant Colonel Martin Töppen, Abwehr financial supervisor, who had flown in specifically to arrange details. Berlin had approved the exchange, he said; Popov would cable the theatrical agent with the exchange terms and tell him to expect a German contact to come by his London office to pick up the sterling. Once the courier notified Berlin that he had retrieved the funds, the Abwehr would notify von Karsthoff of approval to disburse the exchange dollars to Dusko. Popov would then deposit the money in the theatrical agent's account in New York.

Agreeing to the deal, Töppen asked for the man's name and address where his agent would collect the sterling and Dusko said his name was Erik Sand and gave the address. Töppen jotted it down and they were in business. Structured into the deal was a 5 percent commission for von Karsthoff. Unknown to the Germans, MI5 had incentivized Popov with a 10 percent commission.

No sooner than he had left, however, Dusko realized he had made a terrible mistake. The theatrical agent's name was Eric *Glass*, but he had mistakenly told Töppen the name was Erik *Sand*, sand being the main ingredient in glass. Dusko's mind—mixing contacts, codes, and cocktails—was playing dangerous tricks on him. If the German agent arrived at the address looking for someone who didn't exist, the scheme would collapse. When Dusko returned to England, MI5 had to implement immediate changes to Mr. Glass's office: a new name plate, an MI5 receptionist, and instructions for Glass to become "Erik Sand" until further notice.

Sand and Glass. Dusko was juggling too many balls.

»

In London, Mr. Glass assumed his new identity and welcomed a new receptionist, Miss Susan Barton (whose real name was Gisela Ashley). MI5's plan was simple: If the Germans sent an unknown agent for the pickup, Scotland Yard could follow and later arrest him; if the Germans sent an agent the British were running, so much the better.

On July 31, 1941, Dusko sent the telegram to Mr. Sand, informing him of the exchange rate:

```
TILLY HAD YESTERDAY A DAUGHTER WEIGHING 3 KILOS
PLEASE INFORM HARRY WHEN YOU MEET HIM = MARIA
GONCALVES
```

According to the arranged code, the first letter of the new mother's name ("T") would correspond to the number of pounds to be disbursed, in thousands, per the place of that letter in the alphabet, or £20,000. As a double check, the infant would be a boy if the amount was up to £10,000, a girl if it was over. The weight of the child was to indicate the exchange rate according to a table, 3 kilos indicating an exchange of $2 per pound, or $40,000.

Dusko sent a second telegram to Berlin confirming the dispatch to Sand and saying that "HARRY should confirm" by cable that he had received the money so that dollars could be paid to Dusko before he left for America. To make sure that he received the funds from von Karsthoff, Dusko delayed his departure for New York until August 10.

To MI5's pleasure the Abwehr contacted Wulf Schmidt, the turned German spy codenamed TATE, for the pickup. MI6, which had agreed to put up the initial £20,000, kept its money, but TATE notified Berlin that he had picked up the sterling. Detailing the charade, the Double-Cross Committee recorded the exact number and denomination of supposed pounds given to Schmidt—increments of £5, £10, £20, £50, and £100 notes. The Abwehr, thrilled that they had finally delivered money to Schmidt, told him to use all of it for operations.

Midas was golden, and over the next three years MI5 would launder some £85,000—almost the entire war budget for the Double-Cross Committee—through the Sandman.

»

Several days later von Karsthoff received word from Berlin and disbursed the $40,000, minus Ludovico's commission, to Popov. Thinking the bundle might draw too much attention in the Palácio safe, Dusko opted to keep it on him until he could deliver it to MI6 the next day. That evening—with the Midas money and another $30,000 or so he was carrying—he could paint the town twice over. Other eyes would watch to make sure he didn't.

When Dusko exited the hotel lift, a British officer was secretly waiting.

It is unclear whether Popov knew Ian Fleming personally, but he knew *of* Fleming, knew that Ian was with Naval Intelligence, and Fleming knew of him. "I had in my possession eighty thousand dollars in cash," Dusko later told an interviewer. "I was supposed to turn it over to British Intelligence. But I had the money on me for an entire evening which I spent in the Estoril Casino. . . . Fleming was detailed to keep an eye on me and the eighty thousand."*

---

*Popov sometimes mistakenly remembered that he received $80,000, or a $4/£ rate; MI5 files, however, reveal an exchange rate of $2/£, or $40,000. See Notes.

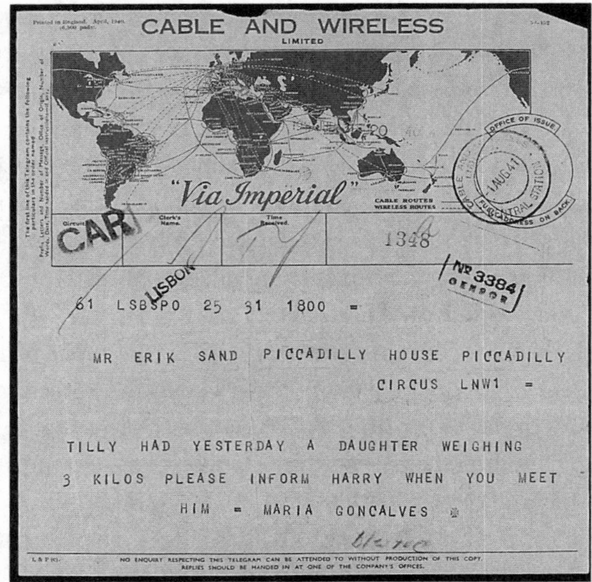

CABLE AND WIRELESS
LIMITED

"Via Imperial"

CAR

LISBOA

1348

Nº 3384 CENSOR

61 LSBSPO 25 31 1800 =

MR ERIK SAND PICCADILLY HOUSE PICCADILLY
CIRCUS LNW1 =

TILLY HAD YESTERDAY A DAUGHTER WEIGHING
3 KILOS PLEASE INFORM HARRY WHEN YOU MEET
HIM = MARIA GONCALVES

NO ENQUIRY RESPECTING THIS TELEGRAM CAN BE ATTENDED TO WITHOUT PRODUCTION OF THIS COPY.
REPLIES SHOULD BE HANDED IN AT ONE OF THE COMPANY'S OFFICES.

Telegram Dusko sent to Erik Sand on July 31, 1941.
The National Archives of the UK

Dusko's assumption that Fleming got wind of the deal was logical. Since Fleming's boss, Rear Admiral John Godfrey, sat on the W Board and the Double-Cross Committee, Fleming likely was well aware of Popov and Plan Midas. Godfrey had direct oversight of Dusko's activities and, as a member of the committee, had to approve the financial scheme. What Popov didn't know was that Fleming and Godfrey were returning from a visit to the U.S. The sequence of events is noteworthy.

In early May 1941 Godfrey and Fleming scheduled a trip to Washington to promote British-American intelligence collaboration, and to provide assistance with the development of the Office of Strategic Services (forerunner to the CIA) to be headed by William "Wild Bill" Donovan. In his foreword to H. Montgomery Hyde's *Room 3603*, Ian Fleming refers to this all-important mission: "In 1941 . . . I was on a plainclothes mission to Washington with my chief, Rear-Admiral J. H. Godfrey." Meeting J. Edgar Hoover, Fleming recalled that the FBI director "expressed himself firmly but politely as being uninterested in our mission."

On their stopover in Lisbon, Fleming stayed at the Palácio, checking in

BOLETIM INDIVIDUAL

Para os efeitos do art.º 1.º do Decreto N.º 16.386 de 18 de Janeiro de 1929

(Aprovado pelo Decreto lei N.º 26.327)

Nome completo / Nom et prénom: Ian Lancaster Fleming

Nacionalidade / Nationalité: Inglesa

Nascimento / Naissance — local / lieu: Londres

data / date: 28 de Maio de 1908

Profissão / Profession: Governmente Official

Domicilio habitual / Domicile habituel: England

(a) Indicar se é passaporte, cédula pessoal ou certificado de nacionalidade. / Indiquer s'il s'agit de passeport, carte d'identité ou autorisation de résidence.

Documentos de viagem / Documents de voyage — Passaporte / Passeport: (a) Passaporte N.º 193543

Expedido em / Delivré à: Foreign Office

Data / Date: 23 de Fevereiro de 1

Auto. N.º

Data–Date: 20 / 5 / 1941

Assignatura–Signature

Ian Fleming's Palácio registration, May 20, 1941. *Cascais Archive*

on May 20. Traveling under a diplomatic passport, he told the registration clerk that his occupation was "government official."

According to Fleming's biographer, John Pearson, Godfrey and Fleming visited the Casino Estoril on their second night in Lisbon, and it was here that Fleming cast a red herring about the inspiration for his famous casino scene in *Casino Royale*. In a Canadian Broadcasting Company interview shortly before his death, Fleming stated that he went to the casino to play Nazis, hoping to take their money. Fleming stated that he met and gambled with the enemy, but after three bets the Germans emptied his bankroll and his gaming night was over. Pearson explained Ian's imagination:

> Fleming himself has described how it all happened: how he got the idea of James Bond's baccarat battle with LeChiffre from a game he himself played here in deadly earnest against a group of Nazis. . . . The reality seems to have been rather different. It was a decidedly dismal evening at the casino—only a handful of Portuguese were present, the stakes were

> low, the croupiers were bored. The Admiral was not impressed. Fleming, however, refused to submit to the depressing atmosphere. . . . The game progressed. Then Fleming whispered to Godfrey, "Just suppose those fellows were German agents—what a coup it would be if we cleaned them out entirely!" It was not a thought that particularly appealed to the Admiral—he found it impossible to translate those somber Portuguese in their dark suits into Nazi agents. But Fleming liked the idea and played a long, unsuccessful game until he was completely cleaned out. Next day he and the Admiral boarded the flying boat in the estuary of the Tagus and left for the United States.

Fleming didn't garner a theatrical casino scene that night but he would have opportunity soon enough.

»

Around May 23 Godfrey and Fleming took the Pan Am Clipper to New York. The trip was significant as British Intelligence deemed it vitally important that the U.S. have one intelligence security boss—Colonel William Donovan. Upon arrival, Admiral Godfrey met first with the U.S. Intelligence heads, and then on the evening of June 10 he met with FDR to urge the appointment. The President agreed that "Wild Bill" was the appropriate choice, and on June 18 Donovan assumed the innocuous title of Coordinator of Information.

According to letters from Ian Fleming to Colonel Rex Applegate and Cornelius Ryan, Fleming was instrumental in the transformation of Donovan's COI to the OSS. In his letter to Applegate years after the war, Fleming wrote: "General Donovan was a close personal friend and . . . in 1941 I spent some time with him in his house in Washington writing the original charter of the OSS." As thanks for his contribution, Donovan presented Fleming with a .38 Police Positive Colt revolver inscribed, "For Special Services."

David Eccles, advisor to the OSS as an officer with Britain's Ministry of Economic Warfare, confirmed that Fleming stayed in Donovan's house during this trip. In a letter to Roger Makins at the Foreign Office on June 24, Eccles wrote: "I enclose a memorandum on the new agency which the President is setting up to co-ordinate strategic information. You will see that Bill Donovan is the co-ordinator. . . . I have installed Ian Fleming in my bed at Bill's house."

»

While Fleming was busy with Admiral Godfrey in the U.S., Dusko returned to Lisbon. On June 29 he checked in at the Palácio, staying until August 10. Fleming's schedule was almost identical. In mid-July, he completed his Washington duties and also returned, sending memo updates (from Lisbon) to Admiral Godfrey on July 18, July 30, August 1, August 10, and August 11. This time, however, he didn't stay at the Palácio but with his friend, David Eccles. On July 29 Eccles wrote from Lisbon to his wife: "My darling love—Ian Fleming is here and I am trying to arrange that he should go to Tangier. He came straight from Washington." Fleming left Lisbon for London on August 12, two days after Popov.

From mid-July to August 10, then, Popov and Fleming were together in Lisbon/Estoril. Following Popov's hotel registration and the memos of Fleming, their encounter would have occurred during these three or four weeks.

From the hotel, Popov wrote, Fleming followed him to a local bar, a restaurant, and then to Casino Estoril. At the time, Dusko was unsure why Ian was shadowing him. Had Ian heard of the success of Plan Midas? Had Godfrey asked him to watch over after the cash? If so, perhaps Fleming was following, and in his mind protecting, a king's ransom. *His Majesty's* money, to be precise.

"The scent and smoke and sweat of a casino are nauseating at three in the morning," Ian Fleming wrote for the opening line of *Casino Royale*. He was remembering Casino Estoril, which, unlike his prior visit, was bustling this night. Estoril's casino was "grand," one MI6 agent wrote, "with red velvet curtains and sparkling chandeliers everywhere." It would provide a suitable backdrop for the drama that followed.

With his shadow in tow, Popov made his way to the baccarat area, pausing at one table. The man holding the bank* was an annoying gambler whom he'd seen previously. Writing some thirty-two years after the event, Dusko recalled him as a wealthy Lithuanian named Bloch. During this time, however, Estoril hotels show no registrations for a Bloch from Lithuania. In all probability, the man was one of two brothers from Liechtenstein—Dr. Lippmann Bloch or Dr. Albert Bloch—and Popov confused the countries. Wealthy Jews who were co-owners of an Amsterdam trading company, the Bloch brothers had

---

*Dealer position.

BOLETIM INDIVIDUAL 16

Para os efeitos do art.º 1.º do Decreto N.º 16.386 de 18 de Janeiro de 1929

(Aprovado pelo Decreto lei N.º 20.327)

Nome completo / Nom et prénom	Dusan M. Popov
Nacionalidade / Nationalité	Jugoslaveg
Nascimento / Naissance — local / lieu	
data / date	10 de 7 de 1 912
Profissão / Profession	Advogado
Domicilio habitual / Domicile habituel	Beograd
Documentos de viagem / Documents de voyage — Passaporte / Passeport (a)	Passeport N.º 160 / 121
Expedido em / Delivré à	London
Data / Date	6 de 6 de 1 941
Auto.	N.º

(a) Indicar se é passaporte, cédula pessoal ou certificado de nacionalidade. Indiquer s'il s'agit de passeport, carte d'identité ou autorisation de résidence.

Data—Date 29/6/1941 Assignatura—Signature D. M. Popov

Recebi a declaração de alojamento do estrangeiro: Dusan M. Popov jugoslav

29-6-1941 (a) O Funcionário

N. B. – Este talão deve ser devolvido à Repartição que o passou, quando o estrangeiro deixar esse alojamento, com a data da saída.

data da saída do estrangeiro 10-8-1941

Dusko checked into the Palácio on June 29 and departed August 10, 1941. *Cascais Archive*

fled to Lisbon when Germany invaded Holland. Upon arrival, they had lodged at the Palácio.

Whether Lippmann or Albert, the Bloch gambling this night loudly and arrogantly proclaimed unlimited stakes. The gesture was an ostentatious disregard of accepted custom—discreetly providing the croupier with a stated limit—and out of place. Popov took exception to the man's boorishness.

Dusko was a Dostoyevsky gambler—gentlemanly and above passions of the game. A gentleman, the great Russian had said, plays for love of the sport and never because of any vulgar desire to win. The true aristocrat, he wrote, "must look upon the gaming table . . . as mere relaxations which have been arranged solely for his amusement." Even if he were to lose his entire substance, Dostoyevsky said, the gentleman "must never give way to annoyance. Money must be so subservient to gentility as never to be worth a thought."

Bloch, while rich, was no gentleman, and Dusko saw a double opportunity. "I don't know what prompted me," he said later, "perhaps I just wanted to shake Fleming up." He took a seat and reached into his pocket.

"Fifty thousand dollars."

Dusko spread the cash on the felt for recognition by the croupier. Players and onlookers gasped. The amount was more than ten times what most people made in a year. The casino fell silent. Dusko glanced at Fleming, thinking he might be pale. He wasn't. His face was *green*.

Bloch squirmed, unable to meet the bet, and Popov asked the croupier if the casino was backing him. The croupier said, no. Feigning irritation, Dusko swept the money off the table.

"I hope the management will not permit such irresponsible play in the future. It is a disgrace and an annoyance to the serious players."

Bloch cowered and Dusko peeked back at Fleming.

A smile creased his lips.

»

Years later Ian Fleming would re-create the scene in *Casino Royale*, his first novel. In the fictional version, Casino Estoril became Casino Royale. The Palácio and Parque hotels became the Splendide and Hermitage, complete with gardens, palms, and fountains identical to those seen by Fleming and Popov in 1941. In both the Estoril reality and the novel re-creation, the game is baccarat and the villains are "holding the bank." In both scenarios the villains are fleeing ruthless enemies (Bloch the Nazis in 1941, LeChiffre the Russians in 1953). In both cases, the hero is a charming and courageous British secret agent (Popov in 1941, Bond in 1953)—who happens to be a gallivanting playboy. In both instances, the hero throws down an outrageous bet with MI6 money. Even the *amount* of the bets is roughly identical, adjusting for currency exchange rates and inflation. Finally, in both scenes, a second intelligence officer is watching with keen interest (Fleming from British Naval Intelligence in 1941, Mathis from the Deuxième Bureau—French Intelligence—in 1953).

Fleming's description of Bond in *Casino Royale* also seems to match Dusko—blue-gray eyes, bon vivant disdain, and a likeness to Hoagy Carmichael. In 1957, three years after the release of *Casino Royale*, the *Daily Express* approached Fleming about creating a James Bond comic strip. While initially reluctant, Fleming agreed and commissioned an artist to sketch James Bond as Fleming saw him. Ian's authorized sketch bears a striking resemblance to the MI6 man he watched at the Estoril tables in 1941.

Like Fleming's hero, Dusko was an incorrigible playboy who dated enough women to make even Bond blush. In virtually every city visited he had girlfriends. In Lisbon, his female companions were Maria Elera and Ljiljana Bailoni; in Madrid, Martha Castello; in London, Friedl Gaertner, Gwennie, and Nani; in New York, Terry Richardson and Simone Simon.

One might wonder if Popov fashioned his memoirs in 1974 to match Fleming's story of 1954; after all, the comparison to Bond would have boosted book sales. That possibility, however, must be discounted based on dates and available information. If Popov had not seen Fleming in 1941, as he wrote and testified in interviews, how did Dusko know that Fleming was in Lisbon that summer? If Popov fabricated the story, numerous individuals from Naval Intelligence could have exposed him by reporting that Fleming was with Admiral Godfrey on assignment in the United States, or back in London, at the time Dusko suggested.

Fleming was in Lisbon only twice during the war: his outbound trip to the U.S. in May 1941 and his return trip in July/August. Fleming's cables to his boss, Admiral Godfrey, reveal that Ian was in Lisbon on this return trip from July 18 to August 12. MI5 records and Palácio Hotel registrations show that Popov was in Lisbon from June 29 to August 10. Writing thirty-two years after the event, how would Dusko have known that he and Fleming were in Lisbon together during the twenty-three days of overlapping schedules?

Yet the question looms: Why would Fleming follow him? Fleming worked for Naval Intelligence, not MI5 or MI6. But Admiral Godfrey would have been intimately aware of Plan Midas and the money Dusko would be receiving from von Karsthoff, possibly even knowing the date. Godfrey could have assigned Fleming to watch after the money or, as Dusko believed, simply informed Ian of the deal. The director of Naval Intelligence and his personal assistant were so close that Patrick Beesly, Godfrey's biographer and a fellow Room 39* staffer, stated that Godfrey saw Fleming as "the son he never had. He even remarked after the war that Ian should have been the DNI and I his naval adviser."

If Godfrey was not the link between Popov and Fleming, there is another reason Ian could have been in the Palácio that evening: The hotel was Estoril's finest and Fleming had stayed there on his outbound trip. He would have been well acquainted with the popular lounge and may have gone to the hotel for

---

*Office of Naval Intelligence.

drinks, seen Popov in the lobby, and then decided to see for himself what a secret agent did in the hotbed of espionage.

The money, too, is significant. It is unlikely that Popov wrote of making an outlandish bet in Casino Estoril based on Bond's bets in *Casino Royale*. The Plan Midas cash that Dusko personally carried—and apparently used to cover most of his bet—was documented at the time by correspondence and memos of several MI5 officers. Likewise, one could hold out that Popov made up his gambling scene but for one lingering detail—Bloch. How, one must ask, if Dusko made up the story when writing his memoirs in 1973, did he come up with the name and details of someone at the casino thirty-two years prior? Popov's wealthy Lithuanian named Bloch was almost certainly either Lippmann or Albert Bloch, documented to have traveled from Liechtenstein to Estoril at this time.

Finally, Dusko's playboy lifestyle wasn't invented to match that of James Bond; MI5 and FBI records from 1940 to 1945 confirmed Popov's lifestyle long before Fleming penned the first words of *Casino Royale*. The similarities and record of co-agent flings is also noteworthy: Ian Fleming wrote of Bond's affair with co-agent Vesper Lynd in 1953; Guy Liddell wrote of Popov's romance with co-agent Friedl Gaertner in 1941.

Ironically, it was Fleming's boss, Admiral Godfrey, who may have said it best: "World War II offers us far more interesting, amusing and subtle examples of intelligence work than any writer of spy stories can devise."

PEARL HARBOR WARNING

On December 13, 1940, Winston Churchill sent a letter to Sir Archibald Wavell congratulating the general on his victory at Sidi Barrani. Quoting Walt Whitman, Churchill tempered the cheer with a warning: "From every fruition of success, however full, comes forth something to make a greater struggle necessary."

Dusko's success with the Germans in Lisbon would come at a cost—a greater struggle in the United States. Hearing of the Abwehr's desire to send Popov to New York, MI5, MI6, and the Double-Cross Committee considered the implications of sending their star spy across the Atlantic. Dusko was having tremendous results with von Karsthoff, and the feedback from German intercepts was that IVAN was highly regarded in Berlin. *Why upset a good thing?* Yet, as MI6 chief Menzies pointed out, sending the FBI a ready-made counterespionage network would greatly enhance British-American relations. Besides, Popov had no excuse for objecting to the German reassignment.

Lieutenant-Commander Ewen Montagu, Double-Cross member and special envoy to the BSC, wrote of Popov's transfer: "After discussions between 'C' himself and J. Edgar Hoover, the head of the F.B.I., it was decided that Tricycle should agree to the Germans' wishes." The British made clear to Hoover the kind of spy they would be receiving. Montagu explained:

> When the offer of Tricycle's services had been made to Hoover, "C" had briefed him fully and given him a complete picture of Dusko Popov's background character and way of life—and how he would have to continue to live a 'playboy' type of life if the Germans were not to deduce immediately that he had been caught and was operating under control, but that this would not cost the American taxpayer a cent as the Germans were providing him with $40,000 and could be made to continue providing more. He was told how we completely trusted Dusko Popov.

During this time the British courted Hoover through BSC's William Stephenson,* and the personal visits of Godfrey and Fleming in July. MI5 B Section chief Guy Liddell, who had a good relationship with Hoover, also spoke with the director about Dusko and the possibility of expanding operations in the U.S. Not surprisingly, Hoover insisted that the FBI run Popov; any counterespionage on American turf would be controlled by a U.S. agency, he said. Knowing of Hoover's policeman mentality and lack of espionage experience, Stephenson and the Double-Cross Committee had strong reservations about relinquishing control. Nevertheless, the British acquiesced; Dusko would have a third set of controllers.

Behind closed doors, however, J. Edgar and his allies were maneuvering to stifle the BSC, OSS, and everything they offered. Kim Philby,† the MI6 administrator who oversaw Section V's Iberian Peninsula, summarized the problem:

> Stephenson's activity in the United States was regarded sourly enough by J. Edgar Hoover. The implication that the FBI was not capable of dealing with sabotage on American soil was wounding to a man of his raging vanity. . . . He foresaw that the creation of OSS would involve him in endless jurisdictional disputes. The new office would compete with the FBI for Federal funds. It would destroy his monopoly of the investigative field.

»

Hoover biographer Curt Gentry noted that J. Edgar secretly backed a bill "which would have greatly restricted the operation of foreign agents—friendly or otherwise—in the United States. Moreover, it would have transferred the monitoring of their activities from the State Department to the Department of Justice, and made them open all their records to the FBI. Donovan, acting on behalf of Stephenson, went directly to FDR and persuaded him to veto the bill."

In addition, Adolf Berle, assistant secretary of state and a Hoover ally, proposed that the BSC deal exclusively with the FBI. "No one has given us any effective reason why there should be a British espionage system in the United States," he wrote in his diary.

---

*Who had opened offices on the thirty-sixth and thirty-seventh floors of Rockefeller Center, just below the FBI offices on the forty-fourth.

†Later discovered to be a Soviet double agent.

On his U.S. trip with Godfrey, Ian Fleming experienced firsthand what Dusko was about to encounter: "Hoover's negative response was as soft as a cat's paw," Fleming wrote. "With the air of doing us a favor he had us piloted through the FBI laboratory and record department and down to the basement shooting range. . . . Then with a firm, dry handclasp we were shown the door."

The cat's claws would be reserved for Popov himself.

»

In Estoril, days before his departure for New York, Dusko received partial news about Ivo's family. When the death sentence fell on Dragica and baby Misha, Ustaše troops stormed the Popov Dubrovnik home. Dusko and Ivo's parents, Milorad and Zora, together with Dragica and Misha, fled from a back door, through a garden, and onto a parallel street. Racing to Hotel Zagreb, which was located within the Italian Consulate, they could hear gunfire at their home. Within an hour the Ustaše had surrounded the embassy. Despite diplomatic sanctuary, consular officials told the Popovs they could not be assured protection. If they left, however, the death sentence for Dragica and Misha would have been enacted immediately, and surely extended to Milorad and Zora.

The family waited. Somewhat miraculously, one of their friends contacted Mirko Ucovic, a Croatian who was friends with Ivo and Dusko, and who had been Ivo's best man at his wedding. Mirko slipped them out the night of August 5–6—under cover of a storm—and had a boat and sailor waiting for their escape. The sailor said he had been instructed to take them to Mljet, a Dalmatian island under sole control of the Italians.

Once on the island, however, they were informed that it was far from safe. They moved several times, eventually finding refuge in a large house occupied by three sibling families. While the hosts were kind, food was scarce and that posed an urgent problem.

Due to stress from the flight Dragica had lost her milk; she had no way to feed Misha. One of the brothers who lived in the house, however, a peasant fisherman named Antun, worked with Zora to keep Misha alive. As Antun brought in his catch—the little food available—Zora would boil it, chew it into a mash, and feed Misha from her lips.

In Belgrade, Ivo heard of the escape but had no idea where the family finally lodged. From Dubrovnik to Zadar, the Dalmatian coast is a series of archipelagos and they could have landed anywhere. Finding a high-ranking

German officer, Dr. Popov paid him one million dinars to find them. The officer dispatched Lance Corporal Gustav Richter to conduct the search. With the assistance of the Italian military, Richter found Vlado, Dusko and Ivo's brother, and together, after a five-week search, they located the Popov family. Richter requisitioned a boat for a return to Dubrovnik and supervised transit by train to Belgrade.

Surmising details of the limited information he had, Dusko penned a letter to Tar Robertson:

> *The news from Yugoslavia is very very bad, millions of people are being persecuted and massacred. . . . My family has not been spared, the youngest brother is a refugee at Zara where he is staying with a friend . . . and the oldest with my father has probably gone to Belgrade. The rest of the family is still at Dubrovnik. . . . Jebsen has himself left for Yugoslavia in order to organize the protection of my family. . . . My own life is much less important to me than that of my family. . . . I hope to continue to be useful to our common cause and to be able to help within my modest means to bring the victory which alone will bring me happiness.*
>
> *All the best, Dusko*

»

On Sunday morning, August 10, 1941, President Franklin D. Roosevelt stepped aboard the HMS *Prince of Wales* to offer British Prime Minister Winston Churchill his steadfast support. As he did, British double agent Dusko Popov stepped aboard a Pan American Clipper to offer FBI Director J. Edgar Hoover his counterespionage support. In Popov's briefcase was a treasure trove worthy of an international spy: a German questionnaire with an English translation, a vial of white crystals for making secret ink, special paper for sending secret correspondence, a copy of Virginia Woolf's *Night and Day* for coding messages, a torn half of a business card (the opposite to be presented by a German contact), addresses of mail drops in Portugal and South America, a paper bearing the name and address—in secret ink—for Elisabeth Sahrbach, instructions for operating a wireless radio set, and several files of letters and telegrams, four of which contained eight microdots. In addition, he had a letter, which had been forwarded from the Savoy, written by a girl who claimed to know him but whom he couldn't place; he suspected she was a German spy.

He was also carrying a considerable sum of money: $70,000. If he needed more, he was to contact a phony Portuguese company set up by the Germans; the funds would be forwarded as part of a sham transaction involving tin purchased in Spain and shipped to Yugoslavia.

On the layover in Bermuda, Hamish Mitchell, an MI6 agent stationed on the island, joined Dusko's flight to supervise Popov's transfer to the FBI. Dick Ellis, MI6 station chief for New York (whose staff had been absorbed by the BSC), would supervise the Bureau's running of TRICYCLE. While Dusko was en route, Dick called FBI Assistant Director for Counterintelligence, Percy "Sam" Foxworth. Popov might have been watched by the Germans when he left Portugal, Ellis advised, and might also be watched when he landed at LaGuardia.

Four groups, in fact, were candidates to shadow him: the Germans, the FBI, the Military Intelligence Division (MID), and the Office of Naval Intelligence (ONI). At least three did.

»

Dusko arrived in New York on August 12, 1941, and had luxury accommodation awaiting—courtesy of MI5 and the FBI—at the Waldorf-Astoria. He and Mitchell shared a taxi to town.

They were followed.

During the drive, Dusko silently slipped Mitchell a document and then jumped out at the Waldorf; Mitchell carried on to the Hotel Westover. After checking in, Dusko set out to explore the amenities of the Big Apple. Park Avenue was bustling, he remembered, and he found the grandeur of shimmering glass and soaring towers invigorating. He opened a bank account and, after a short walk, turned onto Broadway. A gleaming red Buick coupe—complete with sliding roof—beckoned behind polished windows. Within minutes, he purchased the car. New York might live up to its billing, after all. When he returned to the hotel, he noticed something strange—his belongings had been searched.

The following day he waited for the Americans to contact him but heard nothing.

On August 14, Washington-based Sam Foxworth sent an update to Hoover, advising the director that Dick Ellis had stopped by to see him that afternoon. Foxworth recapped for J. Edgar what Ellis had said of Dusko's background and, without using the term, explained how Popov was working as a successful double agent. "The British say that since he is to operate here," Sam wrote, "their only interest is to turn him over to us." Sam also mentioned that Popov had arrived and, based on what Ellis had said, was "bringing with him a set of instructions; a questionnaire, *a copy of which is attached*." [emphasis added] Adjacent to the "Attachment" reference at the bottom, however, was a handwritten note: "attached to memo for director 8/26 P.F."

Foxworth also informed of his initiative: "Without the knowledge of Popov or of Stott's organization [BSC], I have asked the New York office to discreetly cover any telegraphic messages which may be received by Popov and, if possible, to arrange to know of any other contacts made with him."

It was the start of a scandalously dysfunctional relationship.

Around nine o'clock that evening, Washington agent C. H. Carson notified Foxworth that he had spoken with Earl Connelley in New York, informing the FBI assistant director that Popov "should not be contacted at the present time, but his office should discreetly obtain any possible information about Popov, any messages he might send and any contacts he might make." Carson also told Earl that "the British have indicated that Popov is waiting to be contacted by the FBI . . . however, the Bureau thinks it advisable to obtain any possible information before contacting him."

Unknown to the FBI, two military intelligence officers, Captain Murray from MID and Lieutenant Chambers from the Office of Naval Intelligence, had called on Popov at the hotel that very day to discuss conditions in Yugoslavia. Dusko, thinking these were his American contacts, revealed that he was a counterespionage agent working for the British, and that he had in his possession $70,000 "for special purposes." The following day, August 15, Lieutenant Colonel Frederick Sharp of MID copied FBI Special Agent in Charge E. A. Soucy on a memo of the prior day's contact with Popov. Immediately, the FBI notified MID to "lay strictly off" Popov as the Bureau was handling him.

The British, however, remained in the dark. Popov had not been able to reach Ellis by phone, and Dick began to worry. He called Agent Soucy and said he wanted to set up an introductory meeting with someone from BSC, the FBI, and Popov. Three days later, on Monday, August 18, Dusko met with New York Assistant Director Earl J. Connelley, Special Agent Charles Lanman, and BSC's Dick Ellis at the Commodore Hotel. For three hours, Dusko testified to his background and German assignment.

In his memoirs Popov misremembered the details of the meeting,* recalling by memory an event more than thirty years prior and confusing Earl Connelley with Foxworth, who later replaced Connelley as assistant director, New York. But what Dusko shared during the meeting—that the German investigation of Taranto and his assignment to investigate Pearl Harbor warned of a similar attack by the Japanese—Popov swore to until his death. Unless the Japanese-American negotiations reached a resolution, he recalled saying, the U.S. could expect an attack by the end of the year. To be sure, Popov was guessing on timing, but the Taranto investigation verified the seriousness of Dusko's questionnaire.

At this meeting Dick Ellis gave Connelley an English version of Popov's questionnaire, stating that he'd supply a copy of the German original later. The following day, August 19, Connelley sent to Hoover a twelve-page letter recapping the discussion. Providing J. Edgar with a full account of Dusko's work as a double agent, Earl wrote: "Mr. Popov was furnished with a letter of instructions in German, which letter was turned over to the British authorities here, and Mr. Ellis furnished me with an English translation of these instructions, a copy of which is attached hereto as Exhibit C. Reference to these instructions indicates considerable information as to what the German authorities already have . . . and . . . indicates the detailed information which they expect him to obtain while in the United States."

Exhibit C was Popov's questionnaire.† As of August 19, 1941, then, almost four months before the Pearl Harbor attack, J. Edgar Hoover and the FBI were on notice of the German/Japanese interest in the Hawaiian naval base, and Dusko's assignment to investigate its defenses.

That same day Lanman met again with Popov, this time at the Lincoln Hotel. At this meeting Dusko turned over the materials from his briefcase: secret ink, code book, papers, addresses, instructions regarding setup of a radio, and the file of telegrams, including four with microdots reproducing the questionnaire. He also provided a typewritten copy of the German original.

As J. Edgar Hoover reviewed Connelley's Exhibit C, and Lanman received

---

*Popov stated that he first met with Lanman and Foxworth on August 13, 1941, in Foxworth's office in Rockefeller Center. Foxworth's office at this time, however, was in Washington.

†The pertinent pages of Connelley's transmittal letter and Exhibit C are included herein as Appendix 1.

Popov's microdots, Britain's Double-Cross Committee received copies of the questionnaire from MI6. "It will be remembered," J. C. Masterman wrote after the war, "that the full stops [microdots] were photographed and enlarged by the F.B.I. in America, who were therefore in possession of all the information contained in the questionnaire." And, for Masterman and British Intelligence, the purpose of the questionnaire could not have been more evident:

> The whole questionnaire covers approximately three quarto sheets typed, and of this one-third deals with Hawaii and in particular with Pearl Harbour. It is noticeable that, whereas all the other questions are more or less general . . . those connected with Hawaii are specialised and detailed. . . . It is therefore surely a fair deduction that the questionnaire indicated very clearly that in the event of the United States being at war, Pearl Harbour would be the first point to be attacked, and that plans for this attack had reached an advanced stage by August 1941.

»

On August 25 Lanman personally delivered the microdots and other items to the FBI laboratory in Washington. Nine days later, on September 3, the lab released an eight-page report, three of which reproduced the questionnaire as hidden in the four microdots. The following day Hoover forwarded a copy of the report to Connelley. J. Edgar had now seen the Pearl Harbor questionnaire twice, and would see it a third time when Special Agent Lanman submitted a full report on September 17.

Hoover submitted no copies or warning to the U.S. military.

»

After surveillance and the introductory meetings, the FBI-Popov relationship was anything but stable. On August 21 Hoover sent Assistant Director Connelley correspondence setting forth the British transfer of MI5/MI6 agent Popov and his bona fides: "The American Embassy in London advised the State Department that there was no question concerning Popov's honesty," J. Edgar wrote, "his reliability and his loyalty, further advising that Popov was being sponsored by Sir Walter Monckton, Director General of Information of the British Government." Seemingly averse to using the term "double agent," Hoover went on: "Through a confidential source [MI6 or BSC] the Bureau ascertained that Popov had been furnishing information to the British in

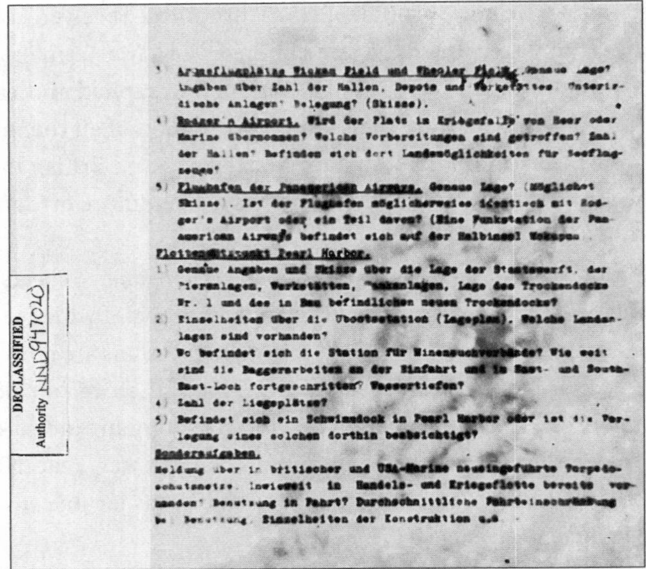

DECLASSIFIED
Authority NND947020

3) Armeeflugplätze Wickam Field und Wheeler Field. Genaue Lage? Angaben über Zahl der Hallen, Depots und Werkstätten. Unterirdische Anlagen? Belegung? (Skizze).
4) Rodger's Airport. Wird der Platz im Kriegsfalle von Heer oder Marine übernommen? Welche Vorbereitungen sind getroffen? Zahl der Hallen? Befinden sich dort Landemöglichkeiten für Seeflugzeuge?
5) Flughafen der Panamerican Airways. Genaue Lage? (Möglichst Skizze). Ist der Flughafen möglicherweise identisch mit Rodger's Airport oder ein Teil davon? (Eine Funkstation der Panamerican Airways befindet sich auf der Halbinsel Mokapuu.)

Flottenstützpunkt Pearl Harbor.

1) Genaue Angaben und Skizze über die Lage der Staatswerft, der Pieranlagen, Werkstätten, Tankanlagen, Lage des Trockendocks Nr. 1 und des in Bau befindlichen neuen Trockendocks?
2) Einzelheiten über die Ubootsstation (Lageplan). Welche Landanlagen sind vorhanden?
3) Wo befindet sich die Station für Minensuchverbände? Wie weit sind die Baggerarbeiten an der Einfahrt und im East- und Southeast-Loch fortgeschritten? Wassertiefen?
4) Zahl der Liegeplätze?
5) Befindet sich ein Schwimmdock in Pearl Harbor oder ist die Verlegung eines solchen dorthin beabsichtigt?

Sonderaufgaben.

Meldung über in britischer und USA-Marine neueingeführte Torpedoschutznetze. Inwieweit in Handels- und Kriegsflotte bereits vorhanden? Benutzung in Fahrt? Durchschnittliche Fahrteinschränkung bei Benutzung. Einzelheiten der Konstruktion u.a.

One of four microdots containing Popov's German questionnaire. "Pearl Harbor" can be easily seen in the text.

National Archives and Records Administration

London for some time although he had been actually working for the German Government." Even with assurances from the British and the American Embassy in London, however, J. Edgar instructed: "The Bureau desires to be kept closely advised of developments in this investigation."

Connelley assured the director that henceforth the New York office would refer to Dusan Popov—British double agent on loan to the FBI—as "Confidential Informant ND-63." What was weeks prior a planned *collaboration with* MI6 agent Popov was now being recorded in FBI files as *an investigation of* agent Popov.

»

Even without the questionnaire, Popov's warning from Jebsen and von Gronau about the German/Japanese interest in the Royal Navy's Taranto raid should have been sufficient. The Japanese did, in fact, use Taranto as a blueprint. On January 7, 1941, Admiral Isoroku Yamamoto, commander in chief of the Japanese Fleet, had submitted a nine-page outline to Navy Minister Koshiro Oikawa entitled, "Views on Preparations for War." The admiral also gave a copy to Rear Admiral Takijiro Ohnishi, a naval aviation strategist, for tactical

Left to right: FBI Assistant Director Earl J. Connelley, Special Agent Charles Lanman, Assistant Director Percy "Sam" Foxworth.
Federal Bureau of Investigation

evaluation. The report, bolstered by the British success at Taranto, suggested a preemptive strike on Pearl Harbor.

More importantly, Dusko's questionnaire and report constituted the FBI's *second* warning about Pearl Harbor. Just before Ulrich von der Osten's death at Times Square, BSC had tipped off the FBI about a German spy using the aliases of "Konrad" and "Phil." In early March 1941, the FBI intercepted a report from Konrad to "Mr. Smith of China." The package contained maps and photographs of Hawaii—*including details of the defenses at Pearl Harbor*—and a letter which concluded: "This will be of interest mostly to our yellow allies." Since Admiral Kimmel's* record of intelligence received did not include this intercept, it appears that neither the FBI nor the Office of Naval Intelligence forwarded it to Honolulu; if the FBI passed it to ONI, it stopped there.

The contents and interception of this letter could not have been more important to the Abwehr, and to the Allies. Since the details of Pearl Harbor's defenses never reached Berlin, the Germans needed someone else to collect it. From the FBI standpoint, the Konrad report would corroborate the questionnaire and warning the Bureau would later receive from Popov. When the connection was made between "Konrad"/"Phil" and the man killed on Broadway, later identified as Ulrich von der Osten, it was clear that Germany was gathering intelligence on Pearl Harbor as a target for the Japanese.

The dots should have been easy for the FBI to connect: Since the original

*Commander, U.S. Pacific Fleet.

Pearl Harbor report had been intercepted, Osten had been killed, and the German net in the U.S. dismantled, Popov was dispatched to replace Osten, recruit a new espionage ring, and acquire the Pearl Harbor information personally.

The FBI, then, had *two* indications of the enemy's interest in Pearl Harbor. With Hoover's bureaucratic infighting against the OSS and BSC, however, Osten's letter and Popov's questionnaire were buried on the intelligence beach.

»

Popov, meanwhile, settled into Manhattan. On September 2 he moved into a penthouse two blocks from Central Park, on the twenty-second floor of a new building at 530 Park Avenue. Since he could not provide the landlord with references, he paid a year's rent—$3,600—in advance. He had the apartment lavishly furnished—artwork, books, hi-fi equipment—but there would be no housewarming celebration. The next day he received a letter from home bringing news about the ongoing Ustaše genocide in Belgrade. Tragically, his uncle Jovan had refused to run away. He was killed, along with Dusko's aunt and two cousins. One cousin, Bata—a world champion water polo player—was crucified on a barn door.

He took four days to die.

13»

COVER-UP

When J. Edgar Hoover received the FBI laboratory report on September 3, he fired off a letter to Major General Edwin Watson, FDR's secretary. The correspondence was not a warning about Pearl Harbor, however, but a curiosity piece informing the President of the German method of sending secret messages via "microphotographs."

Hoover included an enclosure—a copy of a telegram containing two microdots. He did not mention:

1. how he came into possession of the telegram,
2. whose telegram it was,
3. how he learned of the microdots, or
4. the purpose of these particular microdots.

The telegram was Popov's, as can be seen from the two places where he wrote his name, and was given to the FBI upon Dusko's arrival in New York. The telegram was apparently legitimate, having been sent from Dusko's cover business address in Lisbon—Rue Bartholomew Dias (seen at the bottom of the image). Cleverly, Dusko did not include a street number, which could have been checked by the PVDE. The note, which Popov wrote in French, provides:

> *Please notice on this last packing list (lit. mode packed reference), your last request [of] gunny sacks (stop)*
>
> *Push back, urgent. (stop) Continue to try to send you tin/pewter despite suspension [of] licenses. POPOV*

Tin was one of the commodities Dusko handled in his export/import business, and the shipping referenced may have been genuine. The microdots,

906

not recorded

JOHN EDGAR HOOVER
DIRECTOR

Federal Bureau of Investigation
United States Department of Justice
Washington, D. C.

September 3, 1941

STRICTLY [redacted]

Major General Edwin M. Watson
Secretary to the President
The White House
Washington, D. C.

DECLASSIFIED
E.O. 11652, Sec. 5(E)(2)
Justice Dept. letter, 9-21-72
By DBS, NLR, Date JUL 8 1975

Dear General Watson:

I thought the President and you might be interested in the attached photographs which show one of the methods used by the German espionage system in transmitting messages to its agents.

There is attached a photograph of a message written on a form of the Eastern Telegraph Company Limited which has two microphotographs placed on the left side and which are marked 1 and 2. These microphotographs are on photographic film which is pasted on an otherwise innocent document in such a way as not to be discernible upon casual glance at the document.

Each microphotograph contains two small dots marked 1 and 2 on the telegram form, each of which is made up of a paragraph of written material. The Technical Laboratory of the Bureau by magnifying this material four hundred times was able to develop its contents. I am transmitting herewith enlargements of these microphotographs, showing the printed material contained in them in German. There is also attached a translation of this material in English. You will note that the two microphotographs contain the same substance.

The microphotographs referred to above were secured in connection with a current investigation being made by the FBI.

With assurances of my highest regards,

Sincerely,

J. Edgar Hoover

Enclosure

J. Edgar Hoover's September 3, 1941, letter to Major General Edwin Watson. *Franklin D. Roosevelt Library*

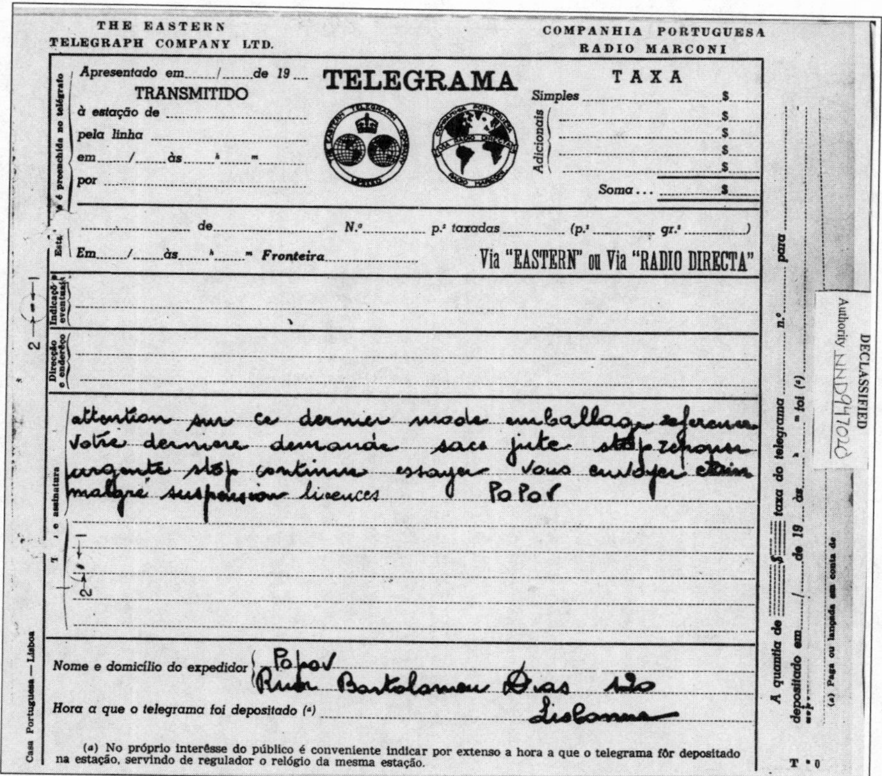

THE EASTERN TELEGRAPH COMPANY LTD.

COMPANHIA PORTUGUESA RADIO MARCONI

TELEGRAMA

Apresentado em....../......de 19....

TRANSMITIDO

à estação de

pela linha

em....../......às......h......m

por

TAXA

Simples ....$

Adicionais ....$ ....$ ....$ ....$

Soma ... .$

.... de .... N.º .... p.s taxadas .... (p.s .... gr.s ....)

Em....../......às......h......m Fronteira........

Via "EASTERN" ou Via "RADIO DIRECTA"

Indicações eventuais

Direcção e endereço

Texto e assinatura

attention sur ce dernier mode emballage reference votre dernière demande sacs jute stop renouvelle urgente stop continue essayer vous envoyer etain malgré suspension licences Popov

Nome e domicílio do expedidor: Popov Rua Bartolomeu Dias 120 Lisbonne

Hora a que o telegrama foi depositado (a)

(a) No próprio interêsse do público é conveniente indicar por extenso a hora a que o telegrama fôr depositado na estação, servindo de regulador o relógio da mesma estação.

Casa Portuguesa — Lisboa

A quantia de ....$ .... taxa do telegrama .... n.º .... para .... depositado em ....../......de 19......às......h......m foi (a)

(a) Paga ou lançada em conta de

T-0

DECLASSIFIED Authority NND947020

Popov's Lisbon telegram, including two microdots (circled by the FBI), which Hoover included with his September 3, 1941, letter to Major General Watson. *Franklin D. Roosevelt Library*

circled by the FBI, were given by Popov to Charles Lanman at the Lincoln Hotel meeting on August 19. Hoover stated in his letter to Major General Watson, however, that the dots were "secured in connection with a current investigation," suggesting that discovery had been made through astute police work.

While Hoover provided translation and enlargement of partial text from one of the dots, he did not mention that they were part of a German questionnaire given to double agent Popov, or that a third of the questions pertained to the defenses at Pearl Harbor. Seemingly intent on hiding the Hawaii information altogether, Hoover sent only the *last* two paragraphs of the questionnaire, which included none of the Pearl Harbor text, and not any of the eleven Pearl Harbor, Hawaii, or Honolulu references.

file
Confidential

TRANSLATION OF MICROPHOTOGRAPHIC MATERIAL

1.

All information regarding the American air-defense is of great importance. The answering of the following questions is urgent.

I. How large is a. the total monthly production of airplanes?
b. the monthly production of fighter-planes?
c. the monthly production of pursuit-planes?
d. the monthly production of training-planes?
e. the monthly production of civilian-planes?

II. How many and which of these airplanes were delivered to the British Empire, namely
a. to Great Britain?
b. to Canada?
c. to Africa?
d. to the Near East?
e. to the Far East and Australia?

III. How many USA pilots complete their training each month?

IV. How many USA pilots are joining the RAF?

2.

Reports regarding the Canadian Air-force is of great value. All news of number and type of the front-airplanes, number, location and numbers of squadrons is of interest. It is of special importance to learn in detail of the air-training plan being followed in Canada, namely the type, location and capacity of the individual schools, and if possible, also their numbers. According to the reports in question, each type of school (Beginner-, Advanced-, and Observer-) is numbered from 1 on.

The FBI's English translation of one of Popov's microdots, and the only part of Popov's questionnaire given by Hoover to FDR (via General Watson).

Franklin D. Roosevelt Library

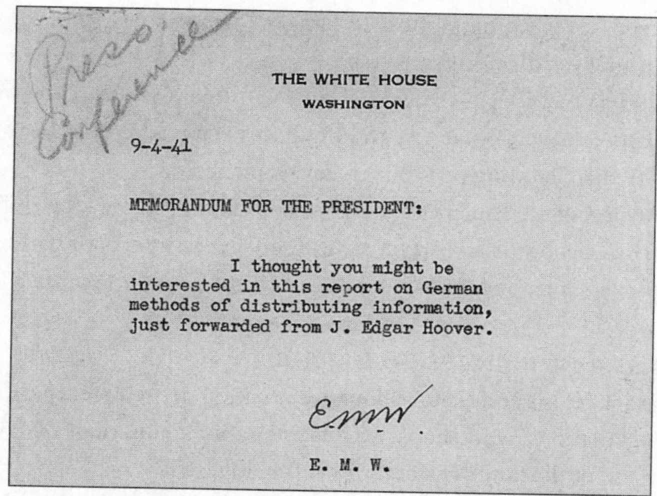
Press Conference

THE WHITE HOUSE
WASHINGTON

9-4-41

MEMORANDUM FOR THE PRESIDENT:

I thought you might be interested in this report on German methods of distributing information, just forwarded from J. Edgar Hoover.

E.M.W.

E. M. W.

General Watson's transmittal letter to FDR. *Franklin D. Roosevelt library*

The pertinent portion of the translated questionnaire omitted by Hoover is set forth below:

HAWAII.—AMMUNITION DUMPS AND MINE DEPOTS.

1. Details about naval ammunition and mine depot on the Isle of Kushua (Pearl Harbor). If possible sketch.
2. Naval ammunition depot Lualuelei. Exact position? Is there a railway line (junction)?
3. The total ammunition reserve of the army is supposed to be in the rock of the Crater Aliamanu. Position?
4. Is the Crater Punchbowl (Honolulu) being used as ammunition dump? If not, are there other military works?

AERODROMES.

1. Aerodrome Lukefield.—Details (sketch if possible) regarding the situation of the hangars (number?), workshops, bomb depots, and petrol depots. Are there underground petrol installations?—Exact position of the sea-plane station? Occupation?
2. Naval air arm strong point Kaneche.—Exact report regarding position, number of hangars, depots, and workshops (sketch). Occupation?
3. Army aerodromes Wicham Field and Wheeler Field.—Exact position?

Reports regarding number of hangars, depots and workshops. Underground installations? (Sketch).

4. Rodger's Airport.—In case of war, will this place be taken over by the army or navy? What preparations have been made? Number of hangars? Are there landing possibilities for seaplanes?
5. Airport of the Panamerican Airways.—Exact position? (If possible sketch.) Is this airport possibly identical with Rodger's Airport or a part thereof? (A wireless station of the Panamerican Airways is on the Peninsula Mohapuu.)

NAVAL STRONG POINT PEARL HARBOR.

1. Exact details and sketch about the situation of the state wharf, of the pier installations, workshops, petrol installations, situations of dry dock No. 1 and of the new dry dock which is being built.
2. Details about the submarine station (plan of situation). What land installations are in existence?
3. Where is the station for mine search formations [Minensuchverbaende]? How far has the dredger work progressed at the entrance and in the east and southeast lock? Depths of water?
4. Number of anchorages [Liegeplaetze]?
5. Is there a floating dock in Pearl Harbor or is the transfer of such a dock to this place intended?

SPECIAL TASKS.—Reports about torpedo protection nets newly introduced in the British and U.S.A. navy. How far are they already in existence in the merchant and naval fleet? Use during voyage? Average speed reduction when in use. Details of construction and others.

That same day the President had a forty-five-minute meeting with Japanese ambassador Admiral Kichisaburo Nomura and Secretary of State Cordell Hull. The full German questionnaire, together with Popov's and Jebsen's reports, likely would have been relevant to the discussion. The following day, September 4, Secretary Watson delivered Hoover's letter to the President: "I thought you might be interested in this report on German methods of distributing information," his note read, "just forwarded from J. Edgar Hoover."

At 2:45 p.m. that afternoon, Hoover had a meeting with the President and Attorney General Francis Biddle. Given the FBI director's correspondence, and the presence of Biddle, it is doubtful that Pearl Harbor was mentioned.

»

Dusko, meanwhile, waited for instruction and tended to personal affairs. He hired a Chinese manservant, Chen-Yen, took some flying lessons at Mitchel Field, and otherwise preoccupied himself with a new girlfriend, Terry Richardson.

Early in September he met again with Lanman and told Charlie that he'd like to take Richardson on his trip to Hawaii. Without explanation, Popov recalled, Lanman replied that Hawaii was off. Dusko was shocked. If the Germans found out he never went to Hawaii—his most important task—his cover would be blown. He pleaded with Lanman, but the case officer said Dusko would have to take it up with Hoover when the director came to town in two weeks.

About this time, J. Edgar sent a note to Foxworth: "Sam: see Connelley in N.Y. and get this Popov thing settled." Sam didn't get it settled, and Hoover and Popov left town—Hoover with his partner Clyde for vacation, Popov with Richardson to Miami. If Dusko couldn't luxuriate in the luaus of Honolulu, he'd settle for the sands of South Beach.

He notified Lanman of the trip and offered that they would stay at any hotel the FBI wished. Richardson was looking for a house to rent, he said, and if Terry found something they might transfer after a few days. Charlie arranged for daily contact, and Dusko and Terry left New York on September 14. Three days later they checked into separate rooms at the Pancoast Hotel on Miami Beach. Lanman, who had flown to Miami in anticipation of Dusko's arrival, reported the details to Connelley, who passed them on to Hoover. While Charlie would check in periodically with Popov, the FBI would secretly monitor Dusko's and Terry's calls from the hotel.

Dusko spent the seventeenth swimming, and the next day he and Terry went deep-sea fishing. That evening they went to Jack Dempsey's Club and Bar at the Dempsey Vanderbilt Hotel.* What happened next is disputed. Popov wrote that on Saturday, September 20, while sunning on the beach with Richardson, his attention "was drawn to a man who stuck out like a fur-clad Eskimo in a nudist colony." The man was an FBI agent, who motioned him for private conversation at the beach bar. There, a second agent waited and the G-men informed Dusko that he was in violation of the Mann Act. Officially titled the White-Slave Traffic Act, the 1910 law made it a felony to transport

---

* Currently the site of the Setai on Collins Avenue.

Terry Richardson by the pool at Pancoast Hotel, Miami Beach, September 17, 1941.

National Archives and Records Administration

across state lines "any woman or girl for the purpose of prostitution or debauchery, or for any other immoral purpose." Thinking the interruption was a shakedown, Dusko offered to fetch his wallet to clear things up. The G-men responded that they were on orders from Washington, and if Dusko didn't put Richardson on a plane that day, they'd arrest him and he'd spend a year in prison, minimum. Realizing that the agents meant business, Dusko complied and Terry caught the next flight out.

The FBI version of the story was that the agents merely kept surveillance. They knew when he was leaving, where he was staying, and what he would be doing each day. Bureau records state that Richardson flew to New York of her own accord on Saturday evening, September 20. Popov, meanwhile, returned by car on the twenty-first and arrived in New York at 4:00 a.m. the morning of the twenty-third.

Back in Manhattan, Dusko was fit to be tied. Hoover had blocked the Hawaii trip, seriously jeopardizing Popov's cover, and—if his story was true—had spoiled his Florida vacation. By Popov's account, Foxworth called about ten days later and summoned him to Rockefeller Center. Behind Sam's desk,* Dusko wrote—"looking like a sledgehammer in search of an anvil"—sat Hoover. There was no introduction or greeting, and the director wasted no time expressing his displeasure. "You're like all double agents," Hoover said, bristling. "You're begging for information to sell to your German friends so you can make a lot of money and be a playboy."

"Hoover had no use for me," Dusko later told an interviewer. "He detested my life style, my whole playboy reputation—the fact that I enjoyed going out with beautiful models and actresses, like Simone Simon. I explained to him that my personal life was my own affair, and that, besides, the Germans would become suspicious if I didn't live up to my reputation as a capricious millionaire's son. I told him I would gladly live in a slum if that would really help the war effort—but he just wouldn't listen to anything I had to say."

According to Popov, he reminded Hoover of the purpose of his mission and reiterated his warning of where, when, how, and by whom America was going to be attacked. The director would hear none of it, and later that day Dusko called Colonel Ellis to complain. Ellis said that he'd discuss the matter with William Stephenson, who had FDR's ear. In the meantime, Dusko would have to bide his time and work with Lanman as the FBI saw fit.

»

Some challenge the veracity of Popov's story. Clarence Kelley, the FBI director who succeeded J. Edgar, stated categorically that Popov and Hoover never met, pointing out that FBI files show no record of a meeting. Yet the absence of internal memos proves little. If they did meet, the lack of such records could readily be explained by Hoover's "Do Not File" system, formally established in 1942 for FBI "Black Bag" jobs. Hoover biographer Anthony Summers explained:

> Edgar made an art form of concealing information in alternate filing systems, or simply not recording it at all. Edgar's office records, released only in 1991, show that he was indeed in New York in late September 1941, the approximate time of the meeting alleged by Popov—a fact Popov could not have known when he wrote his memoirs. Popov did not concoct his

* Foxworth moved from Washington to Manhattan about this time to assume his new role as Assistant Director, New York.

story in the seventies to create a publishing sensation, as detractors suggest. He reported the episode to his superiors at the time.

William Stephenson, BSC director and liaison between Popov and the FBI, confirmed the meeting. "He [Stephenson] said Popov had indeed met Hoover—he knew all about it," said Stephenson's biographer. "He thought it was a terrible failing in Hoover." Anthony Summers, who interviewed Colonel Tar Robertson and the widows of two of Popov's closest associates, Ewen Montagu and William Luke, found consistent testimony: "He [Popov] was debriefed when he got back to London," Tar stated in 1990, "and he certainly reported that he'd seen Hoover. He was not going to make up a story of the nature he reported to us, that he and Hoover had had an awful row. I can't see any reason for him to make up such a story." Mrs. Montagu and Mrs. Luke agreed, stating that their husbands "had no doubt Popov saw Hoover."

The evidence of the Popov-Hoover meeting seems compelling, but even if Popov never personally spoke with the director, Dusko's delivery in August 1941 of the German questionnaire—which revealed technical planning for a Pearl Harbor attack—is verified by countless reports, letters, and documents now housed in the Franklin D. Roosevelt Library, the British Archives, and the U.S. National Archives. An additional document at the FDR Library, dated October 1, 1941, sheds light on Hoover's motives. In a letter to the President, care of Secretary Watson, Hoover boasted that the FBI had one-upped the Germans: "As a matter of fact," he wrote, "the Bureau's technicians have been able to reduce the photograph to an even smaller size than that used by the Germans. I am attaching three charts which illustrate the extent of the photographic reduction and the appearance of the dot as it is later viewed through the microscope." Hoover, who was now competing with Donovan's OSS for intelligence jurisdiction, was parading the FBI's lab in an effort to sway the balance of power.

On October 5, 1943, the FBI sent MI5 a twenty-four-page summary of Popov's activities, which stated: "Tricycle was furnished with a letter of instructions in German, which letter was turned over to British authorities [Dick Ellis of BSC] upon his arrival in the United States, who in turn handed it to our representatives [Earl Connelley and Charles Lanman]. These instructions were in the form of eleven microphotographic points and contained the following information." The memorandum continued, setting forth much of Popov's German questionnaire but omitting seven paragraphs. Ironically, it included all sections pertaining to Pearl Harbor and Honolulu.

»

There were eight investigations concerning the intelligence failure at Pearl Harbor:

- The Roberts Commission (December 18, 1941–January 23, 1942)
- The Hart Inquiry (February 15, 1944–June 15, 1944)
- The Army Pearl Harbor Board (July 20, 1944–October 20, 1944)
- The Naval Court of Inquiry (July 24, 1944–October 19, 1944)
- The Clausen Investigation (November 23, 1944–September 12, 1945)
- The Hewitt Inquiry (May 14, 1945–July 11, 1945)
- The Clarke Investigation (September 14–16, 1944, and July 13–August 4, 1945)
- The Joint Congressional Committee (November 15, 1945–May 31, 1946).

None of them mention Dusko Popov or the German questionnaire. Dusko was never called to testify before any commission or other fact-finding committee. "There have been official inquiries and courts-martial," he stated in 1973, "but in none of them have I ever read or heard mention of the documented evidence of the Japanese plans that I brought to the United States."

Admiral Kimmel, Commander of the U.S. Pacific Fleet, became the Pearl Harbor scapegoat. In his memoirs Kimmel stated that he had been given none of the "Magic" intercepts (which began September 24 when the Japanese failed to receive the results of Dusko's questionnaire) of Japanese messages pertaining to the December 7, 1941, attack. He also was not given Popov's questionnaire or the Taranto information from Jebsen and von Gronau.

Hoover biographer Curt Gentry summarized the information quarantine: "As far as the FBI's role was concerned, the Pearl Harbor cover-up was completely successful, with one exception. The British knew." Unfortunately, however, Popov, Stephenson, Montagu, Ellis, and the entire staffs of British Security Coordination, MI5, MI6, and the Double-Cross Committee were gagged by Britain's Official Secrets Act. The German questionnaire and Popov's warning would remain a secret until the release of Masterman's *Double-Cross System* in 1972. Since then, both have been revealed by countless sources, including Popov himself, Lieutenant-Commander Ewen Montagu, British Security Coordination Director William Stephenson, BSC staffer H. Montgomery Hyde, and biographers of Hoover, Donovan, Stephenson, and Menzies.

After the war, in the April 1946 issue of *Reader's Digest*, Hoover put a creative spin on how the FBI acquired the microdots. In an article entitled "The Enemy's Masterpiece of Espionage," J. Edgar set forth a masterpiece of subterfuge. Rather than explain how MI6 and BSC loaned double agent Popov to the FBI as part of a joint effort in counterespionage, Hoover stated that the FBI had discovered a "Balkan playboy" who was a German agent. To compound the ruse, Hoover also wrote that his men had *discovered* the microdots.

Incredibly, Hoover wrote:

> One day in August 1941 we met a youngish traveler from the Balkans on his arrival in the United States. We knew he was a playboy son of a millionaire. There was reason to believe he was a German agent. With meticulous care, we examined his possessions. . . . While a labratory agent was holding an envelope so that the light slanted obliquely across its surface, he saw a sudden tiny gleam. A dot had reflected the light. A dot—a punctuation period . . . a black particle no bigger than a fly speck. . . . Under the microscope it was magnified 200 times. And then we could see that it was an image on a film of a full-sized typewritten letter; a spy letter with blood-chilling text. . . . We now knew that the Balkan playboy had orders to investigate not only our atomic energy project but also to report on monthly production of planes, how many were delivered to Great Britain, Canada, Australia, and how many American pilots were being trained. Under questioning, he was bland, affable, and, seeing that we knew about the dots, he began to gush information. He had studied under the famous Professor Zapp, inventor of the micro-dot process, at the Technical High School in Dresden. . . . Through the constant scrutiny of micro-dots we got a daily insight into the doings of various gangs. They were viciously active, acquiring information on . . . the extent of destruction of our oil stores in the attack on Pearl Harbor. . . . On one spy we found what seemed an innocent telephone message on a crumpled memo form from a hotel switchboard. But the printing of that blank contained two periods which when enlarged contained several messages.

The article included significant misstatements, some intentional, some perhaps innocent. To date, the FBI contends that Popov and Hoover never met. Yet in 1946 Hoover wrote that "in August 1941 *we met* a youngish traveler from the Balkans." [emphasis added]. The context would indicate that the FBI director is including himself in the pronoun "we."

More importantly, Hoover's statement that "there was reason to believe he was a German agent" was knowingly false and intentionally misleading. The FBI director knew that Dusko was a British double agent and had insisted that the FBI, rather than the BSC, run him. Discussions between British Intelligence and the FBI about Popov had begun as early as the spring of 1941. On March 15 that year Guy Liddell entered in his diary: "Arrangements have been made for him [Popov] to obtain an American visa from Portugal and an Egyptian visa from New York. He can get into touch with us in Lisbon and will be contacted both by us and by the F.B.I. in America. In America he will stay at the Waldorf Astoria."

On June 5, 1941, J. Edgar himself had assisted in securing Popov's visa, writing to Assistant Secretary of State Adolf Berle, Jr., to clear Dusko's entrance. Perhaps couching his interest as part of an "investigation" to protect Popov's identity, Hoover wrote: "It would be of value to the Federal Bureau of Investigation, in connection with its current investigations pertaining to the national defense if we were afforded the opportunity of talking with Mr. Duchan [*sic*] M. Popov in the United States. We will, therefore, appreciate anything that may be done to make him available here."

While Hoover led the American public in 1946 to believe that Popov was an enemy agent, on August 21, 1941, he had advised Assistant Director Earl Connelley that Dusko had been operating as a British counterespionage agent, that the British government was sponsoring him to the U.S., and that the American Embassy in London had vouched for Popov's "honesty, his reliability, and his loyalty." Yet J. Edgar's article painted an entirely different picture. "With meticulous care, we examined his possessions," Hoover wrote, falsely claiming that the FBI discovered the microdots through investigation. As with his self-promotion to FDR, Hoover was now soliciting accolades from the American public.

It is noteworthy that Hoover mentioned the Balkan playboy's duties "to report on monthly production of planes, how many were delivered to Great Britain, Canada, Australia, and how many American pilots were being trained." The director was quoting from the last part of Popov's German questionnaire, yet he omits the section just above it: "Naval Base at Pearl Harbor."

The **Reader's Digest**

VOLUME 48 — APRIL 1946

An article a day of enduring significance, in condensed permanent booklet form

The mystery of the little dots, which a German spy-master boasted could never be solved

The Enemy's Masterpiece of Espionage

By J. Edgar Hoover

Director, Federal Bureau of Investigation

One morning early in January 1940, a traveler stood at the rail of a ship as it entered New York Harbor. The pilot had just come aboard with the usual officials. No one else was near as one of the boarding party whispered to the man at the rail:

"You are to be S. T. Jenkins. As soon as we land, go to the Belvoir Hotel. Wait in your room!"

That evening after hours of waiting, Jenkins heard a key turn in a lock; the door to the next suite quietly opened and two special agents of the Federal Bureau of Investigation marched in. Jenkins, who was on the FBI payroll, shook hands with the agents and plunged into a disturbing report:

"I have been a student at the Nazi Espionage School, Klopstock Pension, Hamburg. My class was graduated two weeks ago. In a farewell speech, the principal, Dr. Hugo Sebold, said:

"'The greatest problem of *der Führer's* agents in North and South America is keeping in touch with us. The Americans have given us a great deal of trouble. But before long we shall be communicating back and forth throughout the world with impunity. I cannot explain the method now but watch out for the dots—*lots and lots of little dots!*'

"I have been sent to America with my orders—and was told nothing more," our secret agent said.

Until this time, we had kept German and Japanese espionage backed into a corner by constantly uncovering every new enemy communica-

1

J. Edgar Hoover's article for *Reader's Digest*, April 1946.

Reader's Digest

Hoover continued the sham, suggesting that Popov "began to gush information" under FBI questioning. J. Edgar's statement that Dusko "had studied under the famous Professor Zapp, inventor of the micro-dot process, at the Technical High School in Dresden" is also erroneous; Dusko never studied in Dresden, never had a professor named Zapp, and Zapp did not invent the microdot.

Dr. William White, a microdot expert and technology historian, commented in 1992 on Hoover's statement: "Since the names of all German instructors in photographic science are well documented, it seemed strange to us that there was not a single reference to this 'famous Professor Zapp' anywhere in the vast and well-ordered German bibliography of photography." Walter Zapp, White points out, invented the Minox 9.5 mm subminiature camera but had no involvement with microdots, as Zapp himself admitted in 1981.

"On one spy we found what seemed an innocent telephone message," Hoover continued, not revealing that the spy was the same "Balkan playboy" he had just mentioned. By implying that this spy was *in addition to* the playboy, Hoover led the reader to believe the FBI was harvesting a litany of enemy agents.

»

Why such unscrupulous sleight of hand by the FBI director? Hoover's vehement opposition to the OSS and anyone threatening his turf—namely Donovan and BSC chief Stephenson—led to his ongoing efforts to publicize and exaggerate FBI efficacy. The *Reader's Digest* article was an attempt, like Hoover's letter to FDR, to position himself and the FBI in the best possible light. That Hoover thought the article would somehow escape the eyes of MI5, MI6, the BSC, Stephenson, and Popov is mystifying.

What Hoover included to highlight his agency's brilliant "discovery" of a microdot, like the telegram sent to the President for the same purpose, Popov gave to the FBI. The "innocent telephone message" Hoover referred to was the "scrap of paper" cited by FBI Special Agent Charles Lanman in his December 24, 1941, report on Popov's trip to Rio. As Lanman wrote, Dusko met with Albrecht Engels and Captain Hermann Bohny on December 1 and the Germans placed two microdots on a small piece of paper for him to carry in his pocket back to the United States.

Hoover included in the *Reader's Digest* article a copy of the message. What he didn't disclose was that it was from the Copacabana, notifying Dusko on November 29, 1941, that a Minister Alves de Sousa, Brazil's ambassador to the Yugoslavian government-in-exile, had called. The message, translated from the Portuguese, reads: "Minister Alves de Sousa asks your Exa. to call him at hotel Luxor—27-00-95."

Did Hoover assume that neither Ambassador Sousa nor Popov would see the image in the article? Sousa did see it, and phoned Popov to complain about the unwanted publicity. Since Hoover had portrayed Popov as a genuine German spy, and Sousa's name was clearly legible on the image, the ambassador likely feared political (if not criminal) repercussions. Angered, Popov later wrote, he called Hoover's office and left a message. He received no response. After a second call went unanswered, he flew to Washington and marched into FBI headquarters. When Dusko told an assistant that he wanted to speak to the director about the *Reader's Digest* article, the man said that the director would not see him. Exasperated, Popov told the aide to tell J. Edgar that if the director didn't speak to him, he would hold an immediate press conference and expose the whole matter. The director had time to see him after all. When he went in, Hoover exploded and threatened to throw him out of the country.

Popov called Hoover's bluff with his own, threatening to go public. "Truth to tell," Dusko later acknowledged, "it would have been a delicate matter to have exposed Hoover. I was bound to silence by the British Official Secrets Act." Nevertheless, the bluff worked. The director calmed down, and Dusko explained the problem facing Sousa. Hoover said he'd contact the magazine and try to stop publication of the Spanish and Portuguese editions. J. Edgar made the request, Dusko wrote, and apparently arranged the gag.

The FBI version of events is slightly different, and pertinent documents only raise further questions. On September 6, 1946, Popov sent a letter to J. Edgar requesting a meeting, reminding the director of his prior work with the Bureau. But if Dusko had spoken with Hoover in April, as he alleged in his memoirs, why would he request a meeting five months later? The correspondence seems to corroborate the assertion of Director Clarence Kelley in 1973 that the April 1946 meeting never occurred. Kelley acknowledged, however, that on October 24, 1946, Popov appeared in Mr. Hoover's reception and that Dusko spoke with two aides.

That same day FBI agent C. H. Carson sent a memo to D. M. Ladd, confirming that Popov had arrived to discuss the *Reader's Digest* article and the problem it had caused for Sousa. According to Carson, it was agreed that Dusko would personally handle the matter with Sousa, pointing out "that he, Popov . . . obviously was cooperating with the Allies during the war." Strangely, Carson's conclusion adds credence to Popov's original version of the story: "Popov was affable and seemed satisfied with the results of the discussion. He was advised that as far as we know, Mr. Sousa was satisfied *since the Director had written to him and the article had not appeared in the Spanish and Portuguese editions*." [emphasis added]

Which begs the question: If Popov had not met with Hoover in April as he alleged, why would the director write to Sousa, and why would the Spanish and Portuguese editions of the April 1946 *Reader's Digest* issue omit the Hoover article, the lead story in the issue?

Perhaps more important than the details of how Sousa's complaint was resolved, however, was Hoover's response to Popov's September 6, 1946, correspondence. Despite having just written about Popov in great detail five months earlier, J. Edgar penned a strange note at the bottom of the letter:

"Just who is this?"

14 »

I'LL KILL HER

NEW YORK
AUGUST 1941

As weeks passed, it became clear to Dusko that J. Edgar Hoover's sole motive for running him was to catch German spies. That goal explained the intense FBI surveillance, which Popov had unwittingly invited.

Not long after his arrival in the U.S., Dusko had cabled an Austrian named Stefan Otto Feldmann, a man MI6 had warned Popov about prior to his departure. Feldmann, whom the British suspected to be a German agent, was living in New York and apparently worked at American Express. Being transparent with his activities, Popov shared this information with the FBI, which, unknown to Dusko, had already contacted the cable companies to trace anything Popov sent or received. Soon thereafter, Lanman asked that Popov assist in trapping Feldmann.

Dusko agreed, allowing the FBI to install a microphone in his study. The plan was that Dusko would invite the man to his apartment, flip a switch in the cupboard to signal the FBI to start taping, and then get Feldmann to talk. Dusko mentioned to Lanman that there would be times when he was entertaining that he would want the microphone inactive. Charlie agreed, and the bug was installed.

FBI New York Assistant Director Earl Connelley gave J. Edgar Hoover a slightly different explanation:

> The informant has frequently advised us that we are at liberty to conduct any investigation we desire into his activities. . . . In this connection it was believed desirable to install a microphone in the informant's apartment, not only to cover the informant but also to cover any meetings which he

> might have in the future with any of his German associates. The matter was suggested . . . as a means of protection for him. . . . In connection with the idea that the microphone might be of protection to him . . . if . . . the Germans might trap him in the apartment with the intent to do bodily harm he could . . . bring the Agents to his apartment for his protection. Informant considered this proposal and stated that it would be satisfactory to him, provided a cut-off switch could be arranged so he could control the microphone. . . . Steps will be taken by us very shortly to perfect an arrangement of this sort.

Connelley, it appeared, viewed a microphone as a more effective "protection" device than an alarm. The setup, in any case, proved unfruitful. Feldmann came by a few times—per Popov's invitation to play cards—but never said anything of significance.

One day, Dusko wrote, he noticed that he had left the switch on and realized the FBI agents were taping needlessly. He flipped it off but out of curiosity followed the wire down the cabinet to the rug. A few feet later the wire stopped. It went to nothing. The switch was a dummy. The FBI was not bugging Feldmann, he realized, they were bugging *him*. Within minutes, he found a second microphone in the living room, and a third in the bedroom. The FBI had heard every conversation he'd had since moving in.

Popov protested with Dick Ellis at BSC, but it was useless; the colonel advised that his intervention would do more harm than good. "Hoover is very jealous about any interference with his organization," Ellis said, "especially from the British."

»

Around October 13 Popov met again with Lanman. The Bureau was nervous, Charlie said, about the girl Dusko had been seeing, Terry Richardson. She had moved into Dusko's building the prior week, Lanman knew, and the circumstances seemed dubitable. Popov's residence was one of the most expensive in Manhattan, and yet somehow Richardson couldn't pay her first month's rent; Dusko paid it. Lanman said that suspected German spy Stefan Feldmann appeared to have been "planted" on Popov, and that Feldmann had hired Richardson to spy on him.

Dusko scoffed at the notion. If the FBI could prove Terry Richardson was a German spy, he said, he'd kill her. Unamused, Charlie replied that Dusko could not do such things in the U.S., and if he did, he would be tried as any other murderer.

Dusko saw no hurdle. "I'll take her to South America."

»

When he next met with Foxworth, Popov wrote, he tried to remove the FBI stinger. He reminded Sam that British Intelligence had consulted the FBI about his coming and that the organizations were in full agreement. If the FBI would cooperate, he said, the British system could be duplicated in the U.S., with the Bureau controlling the agents. Foxworth acknowledged the reasonableness of the idea and suggested that a radio be set up where false messages could be sent to Berlin. Dusko agreed, but where could they get an Abwehr radio and appropriate codes?

He cabled von Karsthoff and requested a transmitter, noting that he had an operator and would soon have a house for installation. Ludovico didn't respond. There was an alternative source, Dusko knew, but it would require von Karsthoff's approval. Almost all German radio traffic coming from Berlin or Hamburg to the western hemisphere was routed through Rio de Janeiro, where Albrecht Gustav Engels—codenamed ALFREDO—ran a powerful shortwave radio transmitter. A 1942 FBI report would later show that Engels received or transmitted messages to Buenos Aires, Mexico City, Quito, Valparaiso, Los Angeles, New York, and Baltimore.

A native of Hamburg, Engels had left in 1923 to take a job with Siemens in Rio. The move seemed prudent; Brazil had a sizeable German community and close economic ties with Germany. In 1930 Engels transferred to Allgemeine Elektrizitäts Gesellschaft (AEG), a German electrical manufacturer. He moved up the corporate ladder and by 1932, at age thirty-two, was a director. Two years later he became a naturalized Brazilian citizen.

When war broke out in 1939, Albrecht was recruited to the Abwehr while vacationing that summer in Genoa. Technically adept, administratively skilled, and integrated into the Rio culture and business community, Engels was the perfect spy. While he was principally called to collect data on U.S. industrial and military production, he soon became the Abwehr's paymaster for South America. In 1941 alone the Abwehr had given him $100,000 to distribute as he saw fit. The agent Engels had heard about in New York—IVAN—would soon receive a sizeable chunk.

The story Dusko cooked up for the Abwehr, he explained to Sam, was that he had significant U.S. military information, too much to mail in secret ink, and that he would deliver it personally to an Abwehr officer; that person, he hoped, would be Engels. Foxworth went along and said he'd see what the FBI could supply.

Over the next few days Popov and Lanman conjured up bait. The Germans had asked for army tables of organization, Dusko told Charlie, and various updates on military production. Contacting army and navy sources, Lanman received a variety of information, including tables of organization for countless army sectors—armored companies, infantry divisions, engineer battalions, and more.

On October 15 they were ready. In a secret letter to one of Ludovico's drop addresses—Jose Nunes, Rua Conseileiro Arantes Pedrosa 26, Lisboa—Dusko set the trap:

> *It would be impossible to send you by letter all of them because it would take nearly a month to write them all down. Arranging to photograph them. Suggest following solutions:*
>
> *a) You tell me to whom to deliver the films or you send somebody very sure to take them from me. In that case, the password would be your secretary's first name.*
>
> *b) I could fly to a Central or South American capital, taking films with me. I could arrange trip under cover of diplomatic courier there and back. This solution is more convenient because it would enable me to take out other material I have. In case you take solution (b) send at once a cable . . . because I should take steps to obtain my diplomatic visa as soon as possible. Insert in a cable city to which I should go. Immediately after my arrival in designated city, I will send you my address by cable so your man can contact me. I should use same password as in solution (a).*
>
> *In case you take solution (b), send me at once the expenses for my trip or have man who contacts me reimburse me. . . .*
>
> *Why don't you communicate with me? Have heard nothing from you since my arrival here.*
>
> *Ivan*

The bait was tricky. Dusko didn't want von Karsthoff to think he'd orchestrated a trip to see Engels, so he would let the major pick the city. In theory, Ludovico could pick any location where the Abwehr was active, including Mexico City, but Rio was the western hemisphere hub and Engels was the South American driver. Dusko was confident Ludovico would select it.

Two weeks later, von Karsthoff cabled back:

ELIZABETH DEPARTED FOR RIO. FRANCISCO.

Dusko booked a Clipper flight and, rather than carry copies, prepared notes on various production numbers supplied by the War Department and the navy. The reasoning was that if he merely handed over materials, he'd lose an opportunity to see inside the German operation. By carrying only the tables of organization, a few documents, and notes, he could inform Engels that he'd need to dictate the full information to a secretary. In all likelihood, Dusko assumed, Albrecht would have a typist at the embassy take the dictation, thus requiring a longer stay and more opportunity to inspect facilities and espionage personnel.

On Wednesday, November 19, Dusko arrived in the Marvelous City and checked into the the Copacabana Palace. A telegram was waiting:

ELIZABETH WILL VISIT YOU THERE. GREETINGS. FRANCISCO.

Dusko assumed someone would call or come by the hotel, so he remained close, enjoying the beach and the pool. After three days, however, he had yet to hear from anyone, so on Saturday, November 22, he cabled von Karsthoff:

HAVING TO LEAVE RIO SOON. WONDER IF WILL BE ABLE TO CONTACT ELIZABETH.

Ludovico cabled back:

EVERYTHING POSSIBLE IS ORDERED. FRANCISCO.

Mindreading wasn't Popov's forte, and by Monday, having heard nothing, he was growing impatient. He located the address of the German naval and military attaché in the telephone directory, but what he found was a bit unusual: The building—some five or six stories—appeared to be the embassy, yet there was no marking. He introduced himself as Ivan to the receptionist. Minutes later an austere man with heavy, puffy eyes came out. Mid-fifties, he was small and very pale, sick-looking. Surely this was not ALFREDO, Dusko thought. The man ushered him to a private office and asked for a password.

"Elizabeth."

The official, Captain Hermann Bohny, nodded and introduced himself. Dusko gave him the tables of organization and other materials and said he'd have to dictate more from his notes to the attaché's secretary. Bohny gave him an address—156 Atlanticia, Manhattan Building, Apartment 84—and told him that someone would type the dictation there in the afternoon. Dusko also mentioned that he could build a radio transmitter for future correspondence but would need technical assistance. Bohny said he'd pass it along.

Hoping to kill two birds with one stone, Dusko told the captain that he had given von Karsthoff $10,000 to be delivered to Popov's family in Belgrade, but it seemed the money had disappeared. Bohny agreed to look into it and said they would talk again. As they walked out, Hermann escorted him through a room where a number of Germans were secretly working.

Dusko glanced at the items they were working on and then looked away.

It made no sense.

»

That afternoon he stopped by the apartment on Atlanticia and was met by a tall woman, about twenty-eight, who appeared to be German—blond hair, blue eyes, fair complexion. Her name was Simon. Dusko dictated his information, and Simon informed him that another woman would later show up at his hotel, pretend to be a friend, and advise of the time and place of his next meeting. No one showed, but on Wednesday Dusko received a call from a "Mrs. Dubois," who advised that he should return to the address of his prior meeting that night at half past seven. He returned to the Atlanticia apartment, but there was no meeting; instead, Simon told him to be at another address, 91 Rua Bulhoes de Carvalho, in Ipanema, the following evening at eight. The attaché would be there, she said, along with another man. Dusko was not to take a taxi, but should walk, she said, coming in the front entrance.

Per instructions, Dusko hiked to Ipanema, where Bohny introduced Engels. Late thirties, Albrecht appeared to be an accomplished athlete—six foot, 190 pounds, well built—and seemed, Dusko thought, to be in the mold of a Prussian General Staff officer. He was tanned, well groomed, and wore expensive clothes. With dark hair and complexion, his light, clear eyes conveyed a serious, sinister look; wearing his fedora, he looked like a gangster.

Engels said he'd seen Popov's suggestion to build a radio and confirmed that Dusko should acquire the parts and do so. Engels could place on microdots—which Popov would carry in his baggage—a list of parts to purchase, frequencies to use, and codes. In the meantime, Dusko was to continue sending letters to his contact in Lisbon.

After a few minutes the German switched gears and asked if Popov would help with some information Engels needed from the States—research on what the U.S. was doing with uranium. Albrecht showed him a questionnaire which asked how it was being processed, to what degree of purity, and how much had been stockpiled. Uranium ore, Dusko would later discover, was a key ingredient necessary to produce an atomic bomb.

He agreed, and suggested that Albrecht put the details of the request on microdots. Redirecting, he told the German that he had been promised a machine to produce the dots, and asked if Albrecht had any idea when Dusko would get one. Engels said he could help. If Berlin sent him the materials, he said, he'd forward them to Canada.

Engels said that he employed a Portuguese captain, and that the materials could be hidden on his ship. The material would take a month to reach Canada, and from there Dusko would have to transport it across the border. When the captain weighed anchor, he'd send a message saying that he had given the money to a bald-headed doctor. Thirty days later, Popov was to go to Quebec and check in at the Château Frontenac. The bald-headed doctor, Engels said, would stop by Dusko's room and drop off a prescription, which would explain where to pick up the machine.

On December 1 Dusko met again with Bohny and Engels. The Germans handed him $10,000,* courtesy of the Tirpitzufer, along with further instructions concealed on two microdots they affixed to one of Dusko's hotel phone messages.† One dot contained questions about U.S. production of destroyers, torpedo boats, escorts, submarines, and rapid-fire cannons for planes and tanks; the other provided new cover addresses, radio frequencies, codes, and times for contacting Engels once Popov's radio was up.

When Dusko returned to the Copacabana, he realized that if he had to wait a month for Engels's shipment, there was no need to hurry back. He had accomplished his goal regarding the radio, had seen the Rio operations, and had been given a nice payment. He canceled his airline reservation and cabled Lanman to let him know that he'd be leaving on December 3 aboard the

---

* Engels would later send him another $8,500.

† Which subsequently appeared in J. Edgar Hoover's April 1946 *Reader's Digest* article.

S.S. *Uruguay*, a Moore-McCormack luxury cruise liner. With ports of call in Trinidad and the Bahamas, he and the *Uruguay* would arrive in New York on December 15, Dusko well rested and restored.

When the *Uruguay* moored in Port of Spain, Dusko remembered, he and a girl he'd met on board were standing at the rails, basking in the sun. As the staff hustled for disembarking, a small pilot boat approached. Suddenly, the driver lashed his craft to the cruise ship and jumped aboard. Moments later, the man was at their side.

He wanted to speak with Mr. Popov—*privately.*

15 »

BUTTERFLIES AND CARNAGE

The man escorted Dusko off the ship and hustled him to a nearby beach house. His name was Colonel Walter Wren, head of the MI6 Trinidad station. He had been advised of Dusko's coming, he said, and wanted to get a recap of Popov's activities in Rio, particularly the operations of ALFREDO. Over lunch and drinks, Dusko recounted his entire agenda and the colonel saw him back to the ship.

When the *Uruguay* weighed anchor a few hours later, it did so with fewer persons on board than had been there upon arrival.

Several crew members disappeared on the stopover.

»

As Dusko sat for dinner that night, he stared at a familiar site: *butterflies*. The *Uruguay* menu had an art deco design featuring prominently in the foreground two butterflies. Not long thereafter, he noticed a passenger carrying a butterfly serving tray. A unique souvenir, the item was spectacular: Set within an inlaid hardwood frame and beneath protective glass, hundreds of delicate butterfly wings were arranged in intricate, iridescent designs. Not long after that he saw a crew member with a similar tray. And then another.

Sleep would be fleeting, but his insomnia was just beginning.

»

On December 7, Dusko remembered, the ship captain called everyone to the first-class lounge and announced that the Japanese had attacked Pearl Harbor. Dusko was elated. With the advance notice he had given the FBI, the Americans surely had vanquished the enemy. "I was very, very proud," he later wrote, "that I had been able to give warning to the Americans four months in advance." For once he had accomplished something totally unselfish, something unmotivated by business or lifestyle.

Cover of the dinner menu on 1941's S.S. *Uruguay*.
Larry Loftis collection

Then came the reports that Pearl Harbor had been annihilated. Dusko was stunned. *How was this possible?* The Americans knew the Japanese were coming. They knew *how* they were coming—like Taranto—dive and torpedo bombers. Exactly as Jebsen's investigation with von Gronau had suggested. Word then came that battleships had been sunk. Dusko was sick.

By the time it was over, the Japanese attack had killed 2,388 persons—roughly half sailors and marines aboard the *Arizona*—with another 1,178 wounded. Almost 400 sailors perished in an iron coffin when the *Oklahoma* capsized. Eighteen warships were put out of action: battleships, cruisers, destroyers, and auxiliary craft sunk or damaged beyond repair. Seventy-two fighter aircraft, forty-three bombers, and forty-six patrol planes were demolished. Airfields and installations—the very ones highlighted in Dusko's questionnaire—crippled.

It was Taranto times ten.

The disaster devastated Dusko, miring him in a deep depression. All his efforts in the U.S. had been for naught, it seemed. Hell, all his efforts in *espionage* had been for naught. Thousands of American lives had been lost, needlessly. Naval superiority in the Pacific had shifted from America to Japan in a matter of hours. *What had he done wrong?* His questionnaire *had* to have been turned over to military intelligence. President Roosevelt *had* to have seen the information.

But FDR did not see Dusko's information, at least not the part pertaining to Pearl Harbor. The true story would be buried for decades, entombed in boxes of secret files and obscured by shallow investigations. Soon after the disclosure of Dusko's questionnaire by Masterman in 1972, Popov's memoirs in 1974, and the declassification of Hoover's September 3, 1941, letter to the President in 1975, however, scholars began to dig.

Pulitzer Prize–winning historian John Toland wrote to the FBI in 1978, he stated, requesting all information regarding potential foreknowledge of the Pearl Harbor attack. Receiving nothing, Toland wrote again on October 11, 1979, requesting documents pertaining to Hoover's dealings with Popov. On January 10, 1980, he received from the FBI "750 pages of useless material." A week later Toland wrote again. The FBI's David Flanders responded February 4, Toland recalled, stating that the agency was still searching. Hearing no reply, Toland requested again on June 6. Nothing.

On January 25, 1981, Toland wrote to Flanders yet again. A Thomas Bresson of the FBI responded on February 4, stating that due to the volume of materials, more time was needed. On April 22 the FBI requested that Toland pay for copies, which he did, and the FBI sent him "yet another pile of almost useless material." On March 11, 1982, when Toland's book on Pearl Harbor was already printed and about to be published, he stated, "the FBI sent me 228 pages, which contained not one word of what I wanted."

Finally, on March 17, 1983, five years after his initial request, the FBI contacted Toland, requested further payment for copies, and sent an additional 324 pages. Only one document in the batch, Toland wrote, revealed anything about the FBI's handling of the Popov questionnaire—"a 4-page 'laboratory report' dated September 3, 1941, telling of the microdots and giving a translation of their contents. Most of the rest were denunciations by the FBI of Popov's claims that he had warned the FBI of an imminent Japanese attack."

As the FBI was sandbagging Toland, two Michigan State professors—John F. Bratzel and Leslie B. Rout, Jr.—were having similar problems. In a 1982 article for *American Historical Review*, they detailed their findings. Roger S.

Young, FBI Assistant Director in Charge,* Bratzel and Rout wrote, communicated on November 13, 1981, that the only information the FBI sent to army and naval intelligence was a duplicate of that sent to the President. If this was true, the admission was monumental. Since what FDR received had all portions referring to Pearl Harbor deleted, the Military Intelligence Division and the Office of Naval Intelligence would have had no reason to link Hawaii with the questionnaire or microdots. Bratzel and Rout further stated that "neither the Naval Historical Center nor the military records section of the National Archives has been able to locate the letter of September 3 with its edited questionnaire. The full text of Popov's [original] questionnaire still rests in the files of the FBI, where it has been for over forty years."

On March 30, 1983, Roger Young sent to the *American Historical Review* what he claimed to be an FBI rebuttal to the Bratzel-Rout article. Notwithstanding his November 13 statement to the professors, Young wrote: "The FBI had sent similar communications to the assistant secretary of war and the undersecretary of the navy" and had been "in contact with both the military and naval intelligence offices concerning the substantive messages in the questionnaire." As documentary evidence, Young included a memorandum dated September 30, 1941, from R. G. Fletcher to Charles Lanman, Dusko's case officer, stating that the "questionnaire . . . had been paraphrased and furnished to the representatives of ONI and G-2 [MID] by Special Agent Thurston."

The professors countered that the information "paraphrased and furnished" by Thurston, supposedly documented in an October 1, 1941, internal memo, was the special agent's statement that he had met with Colonel J. T. Bissell of MID and "*requested* detailed information of the type indicated in the attached questionnaire." [emphasis added] The attachment was not Popov's questionnaire, Bratzel and Rout wrote, but a paraphrased and abbreviated version which dealt "solely with army matters, and only the first four of twenty lines refer to Hawaii, specifically the dispositions at 'Wicham [*sic*] Field and Wheeler Field.'"

Young had provided a second document, the professors acknowledged—another file memo—as additional evidence. On October 20, 1941, over two months after Popov's warning and delivery of his questionnaire, R. G. Fletcher had sent a memo to Mr. D. M. Ladd informing him that Special Agent Thurston "rephrased and discussed . . . the entire questionnaire furnished [by]

* Office of Congressional and Public Affairs.

Popov concerning Naval matters" with the ONI. The attachment was a shortened, paraphrased version of the questionnaire, "half of which deals with naval installations in Hawaii, including Pearl Harbor," the professors admitted.

After reviewing the material, however, Bratzel and Rout concluded that Young's argument and documents only solidified their point—"that J. Edgar Hoover, Special Agent Thurston, and the other agents involved in handling Popov did not conclude from the contents of the double agent's questionnaire that the Germans were showing an extraordinary interest in Hawaii and its defenses. . . . Instead of providing ONI and MID with the original questionnaire, the FBI contented itself with two paraphrases, one of which (that sent to NID) seriously obscured the document's particular interest in Hawaii and Pearl Harbor. To our mind, not even the paraphrase sent to ONI carries the full force and impact of the orginal document with its repeated requests for information on and, if possible, sketches showing the 'exact' location of specific facilities at Pearl Harbor and in Hawaii."

The Bratzel-Rout conclusion is bolstered by a number of looming questions. Why did J. Edgar Hoover conceal the Pearl Harbor references in what he sent to the President on September 3, 1941? Why did the FBI wait so long to begin communication with other agencies when the subject matter involved imminent national security? Further, the documents involved reveal significant delays running across the agency, from Hoover himself down to mid-level staffers. Dusko gave the questionnaire and his warning to Connelley and Lanman on August 18, 1941. Why did J. Edgar Hoover wait over two weeks before sending anything to FDR? Why did two months pass before FBI agents sent *partial* information to the ONI and the MID? Why did no one in the FBI send *anyone* the full questionnaire? Why did neither Popov's personal warning nor Jebsen's testimony regarding von Gronau and the Taranto investigation grace any memoranda or letters of the FBI? Why did Hoover lie about Popov and the "discovery" of the microdots in his *Reader's Digest* article? Why do the FBI's Popov files in the National Archives not contain a sample of the April 1946 *Reader's Digest* or even a copy of Hoover's article? Why the unrelenting FBI objection to releasing documents to Toland, Bratzel, and Rout?

To date, the FBI has addressed none of these questions.

Perhaps realizing the fragility of his refutation of Bratzel and Rout, Roger Young attempted to redirect the intelligence failure to the military: "It should also be pointed out," he wrote, "that the report of the commission to investigate the Pearl Harbor disaster, headed by Associate Justice Owen J. Roberts, contains a wealth of detailed information on Japanese interest in Pearl Harbor available to military and naval officials well before December 7, 1941."

It remains unclear whether Bratzel and Rout pointed out to Agent Young that the wealth of information contained in the Roberts Commission report did not include a single reference to Dusko Popov or the German questionnaire requesting information on Pearl Harbor.

The professors did point out, however, that it took the FBI eighteen months to produce the two memoranda cited.

Rear Admiral Edwin T. Layton, Pacific Fleet intelligence officer at the time of the Pearl Harbor attack, summarized the intelligence breakdown:

> Hoover was to drop the ball completely when the British sent over to the United States their double agent known as Tricycle. . . . Hoover and his aides . . . failed to see any special significance in the [questionnaire] document. They were more concerned with claiming credit for uncovering the microdot technique. . . . Hoover did not communicate the entire Popov microdot document to either naval or army intelligence, despite a 1940 agreement by which the FBI pledged to cooperate with the military intelligence to counter Axis espionage. His failure represented another American fumble on the road to Pearl Harbor.

While Layton, like the FBI's Young, had a vested interest in pointing blame elsewhere, former CIA Director William Casey had no dog in the fight. As a young OSS agent working with William Donovan in Washington during the war, and later as director of American intelligence, he was as close to the classified information as one could be without personal involvement. "Hoover had shown his total incompetence for sophisticated war-time intelligence activity early on," Casey wrote in *The Secret War Against Hitler*. "His handling of the 'Popov Affair' might well have been a tip-off for his future legendary secretiveness and over-simplified way of thinking. Popov was a Yugoslav who . . . would prove one of the best and most effective double agents of the war. . . . Even when the Yugoslav gave Hoover a list of questions the Germans had asked him to answer, the FBI director did not react, although one of the questions asked for detailed information about installations and defenses at Pearl Harbor. Hoover failed to find this line inquiry important enough to pass on to the Army and Navy."

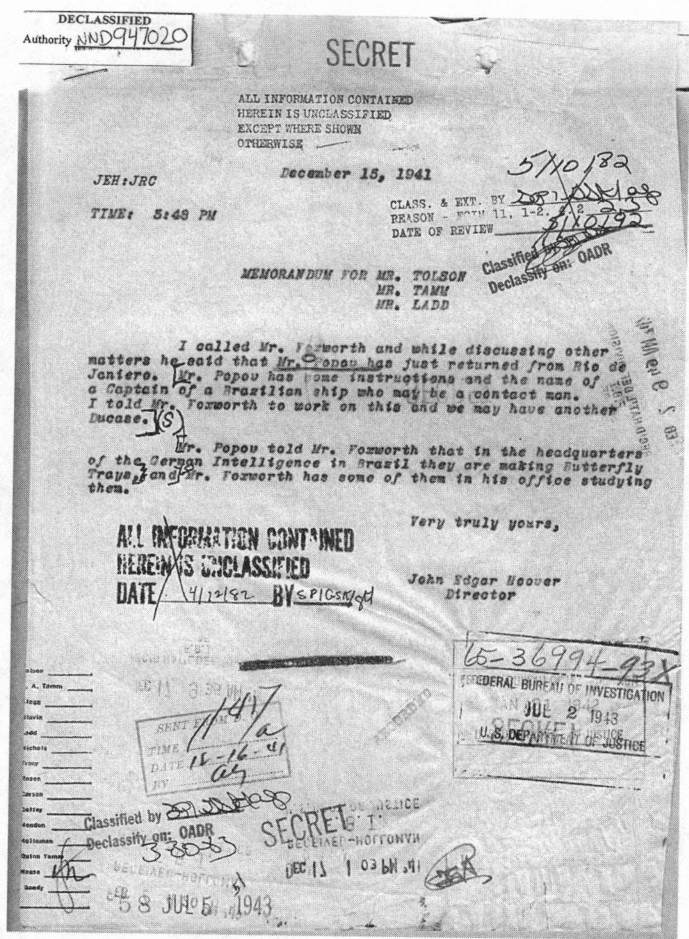

DECLASSIFIED
Authority NND947020

SECRET

ALL INFORMATION CONTAINED
HEREIN IS UNCLASSIFIED
EXCEPT WHERE SHOWN
OTHERWISE

JEH:JRC

December 15, 1941

TIME: 5:48 PM

CLASS. & EXT. BY
REASON - FCIM 11, 1-2.
DATE OF REVIEW

Classified by
Declassify on: OADR

MEMORANDUM FOR MR. TOLSON
MR. TAMM
MR. LADD

I called Mr. Foxworth and while discussing other matters he said that Mr. Popov has just returned from Rio de Janiero. Mr. Popov has some instructions and the name of a Captain of a Brazilian ship who may be a contact man. I told Mr. Foxworth to work on this and we may have another Ducase. (S)

Mr. Popov told Mr. Foxworth that in the headquarters of the German Intelligence in Brazil they are making Butterfly Trays, and Mr. Foxworth has some of them in his office studying them.

Very truly yours,

John Edgar Hoover
Director

ALL INFORMATION CONTAINED
HEREIN IS UNCLASSIFIED
DATE 4/12/82 BY SPICSK/gd

65-36994-93X

FEDERAL BUREAU OF INVESTIGATION
JUL 2 1943
U.S. DEPARTMENT OF JUSTICE

SENT FROM D.
TIME
DATE 12-16-41
BY

Classified by
Declassify on: OADR

SECRET

58 JUL 5 1943

J. Edgar Hoover's December 15, 1941, memorandum regarding butterfly trays aboard the S.S. *Uruguay*. *National Archives and Records Administration*

»

On December 15, 1941, the S.S. *Uruguay* steamed into the Port of New York. When the ship temporarily moored at quarantine, Charles Lanman boarded and began secretly shadowing Popov. Charlie watched from a distance, but before the ship docked at Pier 32 on North (Hudson) River, Dusko spotted him. Discreetly, he made his way over and whispered to Lanman that there were a number of butterfly trays aboard the ship, and that Charlie should not let them off. He would explain later, Dusko said.

Butterfly tray from Rio's Atelier Elizabeth (manufactured early 1940s). Workers in the German Embassy were removing the back panels and believed to be inserting secret messages. *Larry Loftis collection*

Unknown to Popov, there was another FBI agent aboard the ship, H. G. Foster. Charlie slipped away and told Foster, who raced to Customs before the passengers disembarked. Per arrangement with Gregory O'Keefe, port collector of Customs, the FBI confiscated all trays found on the ship. The FBI men rushed the items to Rockefeller Center, where Sam Foxworth sent ten samples to Washington for inspection by the lab. Within hours, at 5:48 p.m., J. Edgar Hoover fired off a memo to not one, but three assistant directors, advising them that: "Mr. Popov told Mr. Foxworth that in the headquarters of German Intelligence in Brazil they are making Butterfly Trays, and Mr. Foxworth has some of them in his office studying them."

The FBI, it turned out, had been tipped off in September on the possibility of secret messages being sent within butterfly trays, but inspection of four samples had revealed nothing; the Bureau had no leads or details as to which ship, which manufacturer, which trays, who was involved, or why. What Popov had seen in the Rio embassy—men disassembling the trays—confirmed that the Germans were apparently inserting coded messages inside the back panel, or within the butterflies themselves. Unknown to Dusko or the FBI, MI6 had removed the selected crew members in Trinidad for interrogation.

In his report on Popov's activities on December 24, 1941, Charles Lanman described the lab's findings: All of the trays were purchased from the

Bureau, were removed from the S.S. URUGUAY by the British at Trinidad. It has also been learned that these crew members are to be brought to New York City at a later date where they will be interviewed by Agents of the New York Office concerning the butterfly trays. (S)

These trays bore a black and gold label inscribed as follows: "Industra Brasileira Atelier Elizabeth, R. D. Gerardo 44-1° Rio de Janeiro." [The Atelier Elizabeth is a shop which, according to a highly confidential source known to the Bureau, is the place from which suspected German couriers are obtaining the butterfly trays which allegedly contain secret messages.] (S)

- 3 -

SECRET

FBI Agent Lanman's notation of the tray retailer—Atelier Elizabeth—from his December 24, 1941, memo.

National Archives and Records Administration

Atelier Elizabeth seal from the tray shown on page 130.

Larry Loftis collection.

same business—Industria Brasileira Atelier Elizabeth, R. D. Gerardo, 44-1°, Rio de Janeiro.

»

The next day or so Dusko met with Foxworth to give him a rundown on Rio. Hearing of Popov's discussion with Engels, Sam didn't attach importance to the German questions about uranium, but expressed significant interest in the microdot apparatus and the Portuguese captain who would be shipping it to Canada. Since MI6 had instructed Dusko not to mention the Portuguese captain to the FBI, Dusko played dumb. Sitting back, he wrote in his memoirs, he suddenly changed the topic and asked Sam what had happened with Pearl Harbor. Foxworth feigned ignorance, but Dusko pressed: "Did everyone have a lapse of memory? A *convenient* lapse of memory? I brought you the warning four months ago. It would appear that nothing was done about it."

Foxworth glared at him as one who had crossed the line. "You had better learn," he said, "to walk in step with us."

Dusko returned a steely stare and the G-man glared back, unflinching.

After several moments, Foxworth finally smiled. "Forget all that, Dusko. Searching for truth beyond your reach may be dangerous. It may stir up an idea in Mr. Hoover's head."

16 »

BLOWN

Popov languished in his role as a quarantined leper. The FBI wouldn't allow him to establish a network of double agents, which, after Pearl Harbor, was his primary mission. They didn't want him dating Terry Richardson, or anyone else for that matter. His sole duty now was to sit in his apartment as flypaper to catch German spies. Anything else, it seemed, and he might "stir up an idea" in Hoover's head.

Dusko brooded over Pearl Harbor and itched to get back in the game, yet he was stuck in unfamiliar territory—idleness. After seeing Sonja Henie in *Sun Valley Serenade*, he decided that if the Bureau wouldn't let him do his job, he'd at least clear his mind on the German nickel. He booked a flight to snow-drenched Idaho.

Under the vision of Count Felix Schaffgotsch and industrialist Averell Harriman, the Sun Valley Resort had opened with great fanfare in 1936. Harriman spared no expense on the amenities, and Schaffgotsch brought in six world-class Austrian skiers to offer America's first ski school. The resort also was the first to utilize a new invention—the chairlift. Within a year it was the favorite winter getaway for celebrities like Bing Crosby, Clark Gable, Errol Flynn, Lucille Ball, and Ernest Hemingway, who worked on *For Whom the Bell Tolls* at the lodge in 1939.

The distraction was helpful, but not the philosopher's stone for which Dusko had hoped. He skied by day and partied by night, yet, amid glistening snow and giddy girls, his heart was in turmoil. "My family was in occupied territory," he wrote, "my friends were under the bombs in London, Johnny's neck was in the noose of an Abwehr uniform, and I could only rust in America at the whim of a despotic bureaucrat." He knew he had to get back. He was having the time of his life, on and off the slopes, but the lives of his loved ones were hanging by a thin Nazi thread.

On New Year's Eve he sent a telegram to J. C. Masterman at the United University Club: "Wishing you and all our friends a Happy New Year." Masterman and MI5, he believed, would see the greeting as a sign of the locked loneliness in which he lived. Efforts by Ewen Montagu and BSC had done little to ameliorate Hoover's xenophobia, and everyone in British Intelligence knew that Popov was wasting away in his persona non grata status.

Five days later Lanman called and Popov returned to New York. That night they met to strategize a new plan, and Charlie said the FBI would begin transmitting to the Germans the following day. Urging Lanman to send enough material to compensate for his long silence, Dusko suggested a meeting with the radio operator. Lanman shunted the notion, saying that per Washington, Dusko was not to go near the radio or the operator. The danger was obvious; if the Germans asked about information sent in his name, or about the operator—which was almost a certainty—Popov wouldn't have the answers.

"You know what that means," Dusko said, "finished, curtains. . . . Washington is putting a bullet in the back of my neck."

Lanman had his orders, Popov knew, but the situation was maddening. The Bureau was working a double standard—Dusko could not speak with the radio operator or even see the messages the FBI was sending in his name, yet they wanted his help in doing so. To his credit, Popov complied. And all the while, the FBI continued surveillance, tapping his phone and keeping files on his girlfriends.

The only one that counted, at least as far as Dusko was concerned—the one who had captured his heart in 1939—was Simone Simon. They had dated briefly in Paris before the war, when Simone was an up-and-coming actress and he a budding lawyer, but 1940 called her to Hollywood and him to London. When Dusko arrived in the U.S., he contacted her and they connected in Sun Valley or New York as work permitted. When Simone finished shooting, she moved to Manhattan and took an apartment close to Dusko's on Park Avenue.

It all started for Simon in June 1931. She had been sipping coffee on the terrace of Café de la Paix, a favorite haunt of Oscar Wilde's decades earlier, when a well-dressed man noticed the twenty-one-year-old's sparkling blue eyes and angelic face. The man was Viktor Tourjansky, Russian director of over twenty silent films and for the past three years a director at MGM. Tourjansky launched Simon's career in France, which led to her breakout movie in 1936 for Twentieth Century Fox, *Girls' Dormitory*. The following year she costarred with Jimmy Stewart in *Seventh Heaven*, and with Walter Winchell in *Love and Hisses*. After two movies in 1938 she took a year off, perhaps because of the war, perhaps because she had met a real-life leading man—Dusko Popov.

Aside from missing Simone, Dusko also had to consider his dwindling bank account. In addition to his Park Avenue penthouse, he had rented a house on the Gold Coast of Long Island. With two properties to maintain, domestic servants, ski vacations, and expensive girlfriends, he had burned through the money the Germans had given him and was now tapping into personal reserves. While living in London and Lisbon, his overhead had been well within what the Germans were paying him. Now, however, things had changed. Because the FBI hadn't allowed him to send anything useful—bogus or otherwise—the Abwehr had shut off the spigot.

Lanman agreed to help, perhaps because the FBI wanted to catch a courier, and they cooked up a message from agent IVAN: "Please remember to send for first of March money for next three months. A. Me and Ralph – six thousand. B. Me, special American, three thousand. C. Radio operator and house, three thousand. D. Radio equipment, six hundred. Being out of resources, need urgently. Thank you."

Lanman radioed it to von Karsthoff on February 25 and they waited. Two weeks later, on March 11, the German responded: "Keep main attention on preparation for action of expeditionary corps and shipping of troops. Give exact details of embarkation, destination and kind of troops."

Von Karsthoff suggested that Popov return to Lisbon but made no mention of money.

Dusko was worried. Had the Abwehr given up on him or were they testing?

Without telling Popov, the FBI sent a reply: "Difficult to obtain diplomatic courier status and difficult to secure passage on Clipper due to war. Could you help me?" The Germans gave no reply, which Dusko later considered a logical result of the poor quality of information they were receiving.

Around this time, Dusko remembered Lanman coming out to the Long Island house. A message had come in, Charlie said, stating that money had been forwarded to the hairless doctor. Engels had apparently sent money with the microdot apparatus, Dusko assumed, and he was to pick up both per the Rio instructions. Charlie asked who the doctor was and Dusko said he didn't know, only that the man was to meet him in Quebec. Two days later, Popov wrote, Lanman was back, saying that Hoover wanted the doctor's name.

"Blindfold me. Maybe I can pin a tail on the donkey."

Lanman didn't laugh. "We sent a message to Germany suggesting that the hairless doctor come to New York."

Charlie's words confirmed Dusko's worst fears. By sending messages without consulting him, the FBI was bound to botch a code or otherwise suggest that IVAN was under American control. The FBI knew nothing of the hairless doctor, only that they might catch him so that Hoover could post it on his public report card. Given Engels's specific instructions, IVAN's request for the mysterious man to come across the border had to raise a red flag in Berlin.

It did.

»

Meanwhile, Popov's relationship with Simon flourished. Simone's mother lived with her, but that was no obstacle. Dusko and Madame Simon (Monique Ciorcelli) got along well, in part because he was the perfect gentleman, and in part because Mother often chaperoned. Their relationship was "very proper," Simone would say later. Not surprisingly, Simone's mother shared her likeness. "Her mother is a sensationally beautiful woman," a reporter noted, "extremely young looking. They are roughing it on Park Avenue."

Amid the FBI turmoil, Simon blessed Popov with distraction and joy. She was "enthusiastic about everything," he wrote later, "the most agreeable girl in the world." Without disclosing that he would be attending an air conference in Ottawa, he invited her to Canada. Simone had recently received an invitation to perform in Quebec City as part of a war bond drive and readily accepted. They planned the trip, and Simon flew out early for her appearance. A day or so later, as Dusko awaited departure, a U.S. Immigration officer appeared on his plane and asked for his exit permit. Popov was stumped. Simone had crossed the border days earlier without one, he was sure. The officer removed him from the plane, and Dusko's complaint to Lanman was useless. The FBI agent was either unable or unwilling to resolve the matter, and Popov's trip to Ottawa was canceled.

But Dusko's troubles with the Americans were the least of his worries. On March 20 Station X* intercepted a German radio message from Berlin to Rio:

* Code name for the radio interception station connected with the Government Code and Cypher School at Bletchley Park.

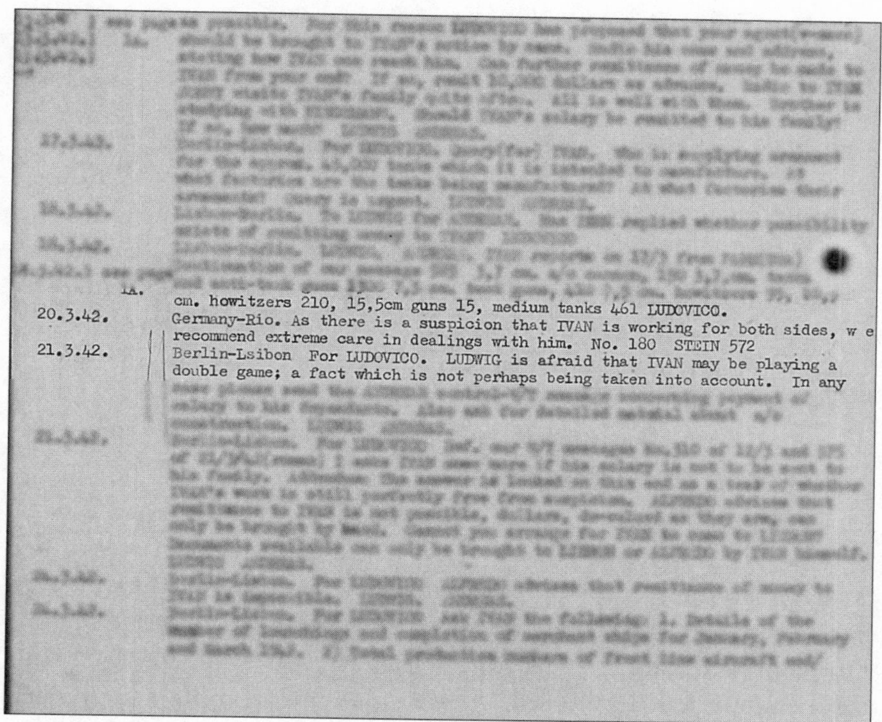

cm. howitzers 210, 15,5cm guns 15, medium tanks 461 LUDOVICO.

20.3.42. Germany-Rio. As there is a suspicion that IVAN is working for both sides, w e recommend extreme care in dealings with him. No. 180 STEIN 572

21.3.42. Berlin-Lsibon For LUDOVICO. LUDWIG is afraid that IVAN may be playing a double game; a fact which is not perhaps being taken into account. In any

Station X intercepts of Abwehr messages between Rio, Lisbon, and Berlin on March 20 and 21, 1942.

National Archives of the UK

```
As there is a suspicion that IVAN is working for
both sides, we recommend extreme care in dealing
with him.
```

The following day Berlin also notified von Karsthoff, telling him that:

```
IVAN may be playing a double game.
```

Unfortunately, Dusko couldn't be told of the intercepts without revealing that the British had broken the Enigma code. If MI5 told Popov of ULTRA and he was later arrested by the Gestapo, they feared, he'd disclose the breakthrough during torture and all future German messages would be lost. If it came to sacrificing a spy—even their best—the British would have no hesitation in protecting Bletchley's baby.

Instead, William Stott of British Security Coordination notified Sam

Foxworth and shortly thereafter sent him a scathing memo, criticizing the FBI over their handling of TRICYCLE:

> Before he left England . . . Popov was regarded, as he still is by my colleagues in London, as an agent of supreme importance and the very highest of value. The work which he did in England was of the utmost consequence in the revelation of enemy espionage network. . . . From that date until the present time we have not received, with one exception, any communication from you on the subject. . . . Furthermore we have never been informed by you what members of your staff are handling the case, nor any suggestion . . . that your agents in charge of the case should work with us; nor have we received copies of any messages dispatched or received since the W/T station commenced operation.

Meanwhile, pressure ratcheted. Near the end of March Dusko had exhausted his funds and asked the FBI for a loan. At the same time, the Germans increased their demands. On March 26 he received two letters and seven microdots from von Karsthoff. A week later, he received another letter, this one with four dots. Combined, the eleven microdots contained over 150 questions—most containing several subparts—about every aspect of highly classified U.S. military production and war capability: production capacity for airplane and anti-aircraft weapons; armament of fighters; destination of war shipments; departure dates for aircraft carriers; casualties to aircraft and personnel to date; number of pilots in the army, navy, and civil aviation; methods of anti-craft and other defenses for shipping; and more.

Most importantly, a dot on the April 2 letter followed up on what Engels had mentioned in Rio—the Germans wanted details on the U.S. atomic bomb development, a program that was supposedly secret. It was a race, Berlin knew, and the German team was close. Dr. Otto Hahn, who would win the Nobel Prize in 1944 for the discovery of nuclear fission, was one of several scientists Hitler was pushing. From 1940 on, the Allies would sabotage and bomb again and again Hitler's Vemork heavy water production facility in Tinn, Norway.

What Dusko's questionnaire requested should have shocked the FBI: "Decay of Uran. . . . There is reason to believe that the scientific works for the utilization of the atomic-kernel energy are being driven forward . . . by the use of helium." The Germans wanted to know how the Americans were sending heavy uran, what other raw materials were being used, and where the tests were being conducted.

While Berlin was latching on to Dusko's possible doubling, Lisbon continued business as usual. Around this time von Karsthoff sent 250,000 escudos* to an account for Dusko at Manufacturers Trust Company. By May, however, Berlin had seen enough. They warned Ludovico that there were now "sound reasons for suspecting" that Popov was a British double agent.

On May 8 MI6 Major Felix Cowgill received the intercept from Station X and cabled the bad news: "We have heard from another source that Berlin definitely decided on May 5 (repeat May 5th) that both Tricycle and Balloon have been under control since the former arrived in America." Five days later Charles Cholmondeley, an Oxford-educated flight lieutenant who had joined MI5 from Air Ministry Intelligence, circulated a confirming memo: "Evidence is now available to us that the Germans do not trust this [TRICYCLE network] organisation and we are led to believe that they place the date when Tricycle came under control as being his arrival in America."

But again, British Intelligence couldn't reveal the information to Dusko, at least not directly. The dance continued. The FBI kept asking—in agent IVAN's name—for money from Lisbon. Von Karsthoff continued to stall. On May 20 Ludovico sent a message that he could send money by courier to a cover address. William Stott of BSC thought it was a trap, but Dusko, now running deeply into debt, was anxious to find out. They offered a rendezvous at the New Yorker Hotel and requested a date. Mysteriously, Lisbon never replied.

Three weeks later the FBI tried again and von Karsthoff said he could forward $3,000, a paltry and insufficient amount, Popov felt. Dusko had the FBI send a last request, but Lisbon once more fell silent.

»

Through early summer Dusko tried to lay low. With his FBI and Abwehr work stifled, he turned his attention to Simone. They became regulars at the Stork Club, El Morocco, and society parties. The nightlife was second nature to Dusko, but the entertainment was less appealing to his petite girlfriend. "I do crossword puzzles and play gin rummy," the Hollywood star later told an interviewer. "I drink one drink just to be polite but a second one puts me to sleep."

For Popov, sleep was impossible. Financially, he was at his wits' end. He had been spending lavishly—upward of $1,900 per month—on entertainment.

---

* About $10,250.

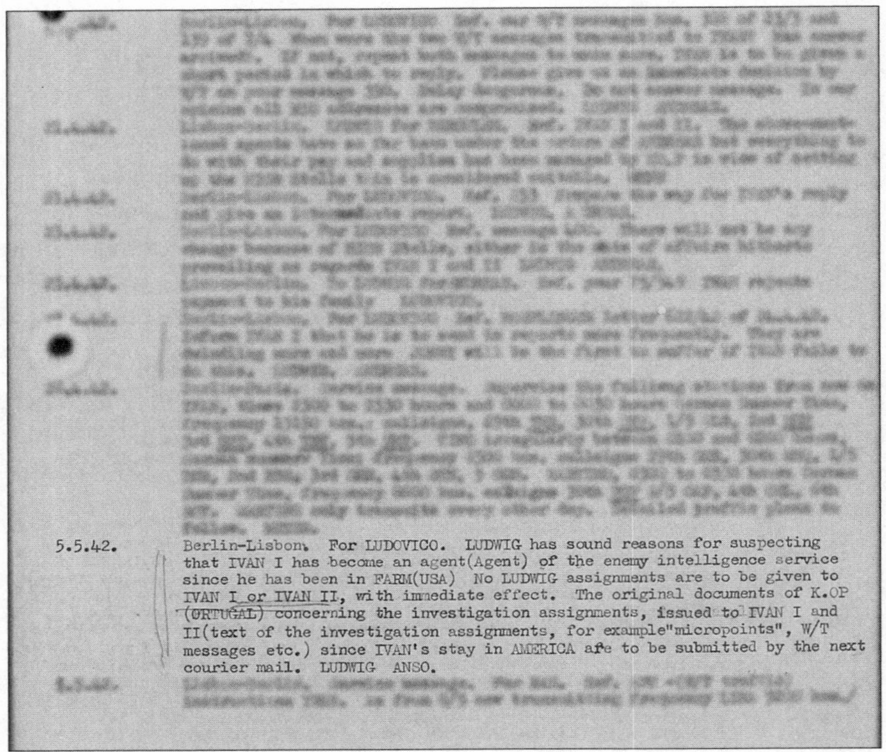

5.5.42. Berlin-Lisbon. For LUDOVICO. LUDWIG has sound reasons for suspecting that IVAN I has become an agent(Agent) of the enemy intelligence service since he has been in FARM(USA) No LUDWIG assignments are to be given to IVAN I or IVAN II, with immediate effect. The original documents of K.OP (ORTUGAL) concerning the investigation assignments, issued to IVAN I and II(text of the investigation assignments, for example"micropoints", W/T messages etc.) since IVAN's stay in AMERICA are to be submitted by the next courier mail. LUDWIG ANSO.

Station X intercept of Abwehr message May 5, 1942, warning von Karsthoff that Popov may be a British double agent. *The National Archives of the UK*

While extravagant, the expenditures were initially within his income. Upon his arrival in New York, the Abwehr paid him $3,000 a month, and then $4,000. But in May, with little production from agent IVAN, the Abwehr had cut him off. To make ends meet he spent $8,500 entrusted to him by his Yugoslav friends, the Bailonis, and borrowed $4,000: $3,000 from the FBI and $1,000 from BSC.

But the financial problem was merely humiliating; money could be repaid. Popov's real predicament was the Germans. After more than a year he had given them virtually nothing, and the Abwehr expected a full accounting upon his return. Broke, despairing over his family, and without a dragon to slay, Dusko again slipped into depression.

On July 4 he received a carefully disguised letter. Mailed from Zurich, the envelope was in Johnny's handwriting but the letter in Ivo's. Dusko could only weep as he read his brother's words:

Greetings Dear Dule:

I don't know where to start—first of all we are all well. We all are nice and thin thanks to the rationing of food and from a life full of excitement. Little Mischa alone knows nothing of war. For him we get milk and vegetables and he thrives like a wild plant (weed?). . . .

Our relations are all scattered: those who have paid with their lives so far are Joca, Dusko, Bata, Zagorka, Pejović, Milan from Sofia, Georgević from Bečej, and the brother of Jelić who worked in our shop. The last by the Germans, the others by the Ustashi and the Hungarians . . . and you can't swim in the Danube and the Sava for the corpses. . . . You have no idea how I long for you. We all think of you every day. When will the happy day come when we can go freely again to Dubrovnik and play in the waves . . . .

All the best from us all and I am dying to kiss you.

Yours,
Ivan

Two weeks later, Dusko received another blow from the unlikeliest of sources—a gossip columnist. No ordinary reporter, Walter Winchell was one of the most powerful—and feared—men in the country. In 1924 Winchell had invented tabloid journalism, filling articles with the latest celebrity marriages, affairs, and scandals. By the 1940s, his "On Broadway" column was carried by two thousand newspapers and his radio program was the country's top broadcast. Combined, they carried him into the homes of fifty million Americans (out of an adult population of seventy-five million). As one *New York Times* editor put it, "he possessed the extraordinary ability to make a Broadway show a hit, create overnight celebrities, enhance or destroy a political career." Winchell became such a household name that he was featured in popular songs, including Lorenz Hart's "The Lady Is a Tramp" and Cole Porter's "Let's Fly Away."

Like Dusko, Winchell was a regular at the city's most famous hot spot, the Stork Club. But like none other, Walter made his presence known. A *New York Times* reporter explained: "From Table 50 . . . Winchell held court like a prince, beckoning prizefighters, movie stars, debutantes, royalty and gangsters to his table." He was also well connected politically. With Winchell's support and FDR's victory in 1932, Roosevelt invited Walter to the White House, telling him to "call whenever he wanted." Equally important, Winchell was friends

Simone Simon. *Corbis Images*

with J. Edgar Hoover, who often supplied tidbits and favors in exchange for the columnist's public support.

One night Winchell apparently saw Dusko and Simone Simon at the club. While the actress was beautiful and famous, she and her date drew Winchell's attention for another reason: five years earlier Simon and Winchell had costarred in *Love and Hisses*, a musical comedy where Winchell had played himself. When Simon suddenly appeared at New York's top nightclub with a handsome man on her arm, Winchell couldn't resist. The third week of July 1942, virtually every newspaper in America carried Walter's latest:

"BROADWAY SMALL-TALK: . . . DUSKO POPOV (WHICH ISN'T DOUBLE-TALK AT ALL) OF THE YUGOSLAVIAN GOV'T AS SIMONE SIMON'S NEW TOY."

Such exposure was unthinkable for a spy; the Abwehr, MI5, MI6, and BSC would be outraged. On everyone's mind would be what Hoover's friend meant by linking Dusko's name with "double-talk." In addition, with Simon's celebrity, journalists might well investigate him to discover salacious details about Simone's "new toy."

The Germans saw the column.

»

Simone returned to Hollywood shortly thereafter, and Popov continued his downward spiral. On August 3 the FBI formally returned him to British control, wanting nothing more to do with him. It was no secret that Popov's lifestyle and Hoover's personality played a part, but the principal reason for the FBI's dismissal was overall strategy: Dusko had not been the German flytrap J. Edgar had hoped.

Yet Popov's issues with the FBI were far from over. Simone cabled him from Hollywood, asking why he had not been corresponding with her; it made no sense because he had sent several messages. Was Hoover intercepting his telegrams? Similarly, two cables he had recently sent—one to Gordana Bailoni, the daughter of his Yugoslav friends in Lisbon, and one to a German cover—mysteriously showed the sender's address as "Kosta 20 S. West St., Indianoplis, Ind." Dusko sent them from the Waldorf-Astoria; he had never been to Indiana.

Then the unthinkable. Little by little, evidence accumulated that Gordana was an Axis agent. On July 30 Ian Wilson received a report that she had been a sales agent for the Italian Caproni Aircraft Works, often calling at Rome and Berlin. In Lisbon, she was regularly seen at the Nina, a bar known to be patronized by Germans. Two weeks later MI5 received further proof that Gordana was indeed working for the Italians. Ian notified MI6 officer Frank Foley that the suspicions against Gordana also "rendered supect virtually the whole of the Yugoslav Legation at Lisbon. If TRICYCLE is to return . . . he should be warned to be extremely careful of this woman." Without question the entire Bailoni family knew of Popov's opposition to Nazism and love of France.

The news was crushing. They were more than family friends. The Bailonis, as owners of Savska Bank, had been Dusko's largest client, and representing the bank had been part of his cover. He was extremely close with both daughters and had conducted financial transactions with Gordana. He had spent considerable time at their home in Carnaxide.

And he still owed them $8,500.

If Dusko was not already blown—and it now seemed almost certain that he was—Gordana Bailoni or the Yugoslav Embassy would remove any doubt.

It was over.

»

Ian politely suggested that Popov retire from espionage. It was simple enough: The FBI had fired him, he was deeply in debt, and his cover was surely blown. He had served well, Ian said, and England was grateful.

Dusko would have none of it. Regardless of the danger, he wanted back in the game. He asked to be returned to Lisbon to re-engage.

Wilson was stunned. "You'd be a damned fool to play with them again."

Ian was right, of course, but Dusko knew that there were no other agents who had infiltrated the Abwehr and actually met with them. The radio traffic from GARBO* and BRUTUS† was helpful, but the Germans wanted in-person confirmation of wireless messages, which were often conflicting and obtuse. They wanted sources, names, places, dates. If Dusko didn't go, it would be a serious blow to British Intelligence and the Allied war effort.

But he also knew that if he returned to Lisbon, the SD and Abwehr III would be on him like buzzards on a dead carcass. If they caught him in one lie, one piece of inconsistent information, one flubbed FBI radio message, he was a dead man. Problem was, if he didn't go he was already dead. Dead to his cause. Dead to his conscience. Dead to his freedom.

He insisted on returning.

Tar Robertson, who had seen the German intercepts, gave Popov the blunt truth, pulling no punches. Ewen Montagu remembered the warning:

> He could end his double agent work with our gratitude or he could come back via Lisbon and try to explain away his failures in America and rehabilitate himself with his Abwehr masters. Tar Robertson warned him that his chances were nothing like even money. How was he to explain his complete failure in America in spite of having spent the large sum that they had given him? Even more difficult—how to explain his complete failure to do any of the things that he had been told to do? Worst of all, how to cover up his complete ignorance of anything that *he* had sent on the radio?

---

* Spaniard and double agent Juan Pujol, whom the Germans trusted and codenamed ARABEL.
† A Polish agent.

> The odds must be at least two to one that he was blown. And, if he was, it was pretty certain that he would be tortured to squeeze him dry of information about our system, and then there was equally probable death awaiting him at the end.

»

Hemingway once wrote that the bravery demanded of a bullfighter was the "ability not to give a damn for possible consequences; not only to ignore them but to *despise* them." Such disdain of consequences, Dusko believed, was critical to his success. "I think I survived because I didn't take anything too seriously. I learned—if this makes sense—to be lighthearted without being superficial."

But disregard of danger, of death itself, never eradicates fear. "Nearly all bullfighters are brave," Hemingway wrote, "and yet nearly all bullfighters are frightened at some moment *before* the fight begins." The same held true for Dusko. "There is always the feeling of danger," he would say after the war. "Fear can never be eliminated. You can throttle it, hold it down, but you can never get rid of it until the thing that causes it has disappeared."

Dusko would have much to fear in the days ahead. The game would soon play its final hand and, as with Pascal's Wager, he was betting his life.

INCOMPLETE CANVAS

If John Donne was right—that *every man's death diminishes me*—the thousands of bells tolling across Europe justified Dusko's decision to return to Lisbon. But his life, valuable as it was, was not MI5's only consideration in his re-engagement. If his cover was blown, or might be blown by an errant answer, other agents would be affected, as well as the overall deception game. Beyond that, they would be flying in the dark. MI5 had little idea what the FBI put over the radio to Berlin, and one contradictory message might compromise the entire TRICYCLE network. In an effort to discover what the FBI had sent, and also to assure that the Bureau was giving Popov adequate cover if he re-engaged, Wilson interceded. He asked the FBI for a log of what messages had been sent in Dusko's name, and for assurances that the Bureau was preparing the following: a story for how Popov acquired his wireless set and operator; the sources for the information and documents he acquired; and new material to take to Lisbon.

In a memo to the MI5 file, Wilson noted his disappointment in how the American agency responded: "I expected . . . that before I arrived in the U.S.A. the necessary stories would already have been prepared; or at least that the F.B.I. would have designated one of their officers to co-operate with me in preparing these stories. In fact, I found that the F.B.I. had taken no action on my note. . . . I was not supplied with any history of POPOV's stay in the U.S.A."

The Bureau's negligence—which endangered the life of his agent and the viability of the net—Ian found appalling: "I would be lacking in frankness if I did not record that I was deeply shocked by the failure of the F.B.I. to obtain for POPOV, to take with him to Lisbon, information deemed to have been acquired by him between June and October 1942. . . . Only two items were supplied—one a negative answer and one a re-hash of an item given by another agent. It was less than three days before his departure that I learnt that this was the extent of the information which the F.B.I. had obtained for him."

Dusko understood his options and risks. If he returned and could not convince the Germans of his loyalty, he'd be tortured for details and executed. On the other hand, he could retire with Britain's blessing and enjoy the fall and the holidays with Simone. She was back in California and her current film, *Cat People*, was being released on Christmas Day; the once-in-a-lifetime opportunity to escort a leading lady down the Fox Theater red carpet was hard to give up. On top of that, Simone had secretly introduced Dusko into the film: She played a Serbian girl named Irena Dubrovna Reed, a less than subtle nod to her Serbian boyfriend from Dubrovnik. It was the least he could do.

But it was more than the leisure of L.A. or the excitement of dating a Hollywood star—he had fallen in love. Grappling with the thought of not being able to see Simone for some time, he began calling more, openly expressing his affection. One evening he told her that he adored her and that his heart was breaking at the thought of leaving. Simone pointed out that they would be no farther apart than they were now, New York or London making little difference in the distance to Hollywood. He mentioned that he had seen Simone's mother yesterday and that she was a darling, suggesting that she wanted to take care of him while Simone and Dusko were apart. Before hanging up, he asked Simone to be a good girl and not fall in love while he was away; she told him not to worry, that there was no danger. He told her how badly he wanted to kiss her.

A night or so later they spoke again and she asked how he was doing. Very well from a physical point of view, he said, and very well from the mental point, but very bad from another perspective—where she was concerned. Simone asked if she could do anything for him.

"Yes, every morning after breakfast, say that you adore me."

Simone replied that she would be very bored if she did not have him to think about, and he said he wished he had a gramophone to hear her when she went to bed at night after speaking with him. Imagining that he could be back in the States for the holidays, Dusko planned their reunion. They would spend Christmas in Hollywood, he said, and then he'd take her skiing. Simone complained that she didn't ski well, but Dusko said she could do any sport well. She thanked him for his kindness.

"It is not kindness. It is that I am madly in love."

»

Over the next few days, Dusko wrestled with what to do. His heart ached to fly to Hollywood, and the choice should have been easy—likely torture and execution, or nights of blissful romance with the woman he loved. Yet the lives of Johnny, Ivo, and his parents still hung in the balance and, as long as Hitler remained in power, so did all of Europe.

He would return to Lisbon.

The British agreed to the redeployment, and in anticipation of his return, Wilson prepared a seventeen-point memorandum for what Dusko would have to overcome and answer. Why, for example, did he send his radio messages in English? How did he obtain a radio transmitter and wireless operator? What was his radio operator's name and address? What would he say if the Germans wanted to contact him? In addition, he would need intimate knowledge regarding the radio and other correspondence of his sub-agents, BALLOON/IVAN II and GELATINE/YVONNE. He would need a ready story of when and where he handed "Mr. Sand" the Midas money. Finally, he would need to provide a full accounting of his income and expenses, keeping straight fictional (Simon) and actual (Bailoni) loans.

On October 10, two days before his arrival in London and four days before his departure to Lisbon, Colonel Wren sent a telegram to Frank Foley at MI6:

> F.B.I. HAVE FAILED TO PRODUCE ANY WORTH WHILE INFORMATION FOR TRICYCLE TO TAKE WITH HIM.

Foley understood the emergency. Even if Dusko's cover had not not been blown, showing up in Lisbon empty-handed would seal his fate. Frank cabled Tar and asked if MI5 could come up with chicken feed at the eleventh hour. He noted that SIS had viable information on aircraft, and perhaps tidbits which notionally could have come from indiscretions of highly placed persons, but they needed more, much more. And fast.

"Can you at this late hour come to our rescue?" he asked.

Robertson put John Marriott on it, and the assistant worked around the clock. Victor Cavendish-Bentinck said the Foreign Office could supply a few items at six that evening if it was not shared with the Americans. General

Robert McClure, military attaché to the American Embassy in London, authorized the disclosure of certain U.S. troop activity in the U.K.:

1st Armored Division
1st Infantry Division (motorized)
8th Air Force
Parachute Battalion
Troops commanded by Major General John C. H. Lee

Commander Ewen Montagu offered naval updates: Three American shallow draft steamers, which were going to England in a trade convoy, were torpedoed and sunk at the end of September; two submarines—one of which was the *Severn*—had been refitted at Philadelphia; a third submarine, the HMS *Queen Elizabeth*, had been refitted in Norfolk.

In the meantime, Foley pieced together data on American production that had been made public, outlines of America's pressure on Brazil, and supposed details on the supply situation in North Africa and Britain's ability to contain Rommel. The information, however, had to be approved by Colonel John Bevan of the London Controlling Section, a secret department created to coordinate Allied strategic military deception. And even with Bevan's nod, risk remained.

After a year's worth of U.S. espionage, what Dusko would bring to Lisbon was meager. It would have to do.

On the eve of departure, Dusko called Simone one last time. Half-joking, he asked her if she'd get married while he was away. She promised not to, and he playfully said if she tried, he'd show up with a cannon. As the kidding waned, he harkened back to the danger he faced. He asked Simone to keep her fingers crossed for him as there were sometimes air attacks on the other side. She asked him to please not have her think of such things. Before saying good-bye, he said he'd seen an article—"The Girl You Like"—in *Esquire*, and that it had a questionnaire. With her in mind, he completed it.

The result, he said, was that Simone was "one in a million."

»

On Monday, October 12, Dusko returned to London, and two days later he left for Lisbon. That he did so in the face of probable arrest didn't go unnoticed by the Double-Cross Committee. "The greatest instance of cold-blooded courage that I have ever been in contact with," Ewen Montagu wrote after the war. Popov "had the steel within, the ruthlessness . . . that enabled him to go back to the German Secret Service Headquarters in Lisbon and Madrid time and again, when it was likely that he might be 'blown'; it was like putting his head into the lion's mouth. Bravely, in cold blood, he risked torture and death to reestablish German confidence in him so that he could continue to make his great contribution to the Allied victory."

Despite the peril, Dusko was exhilarated. "My reaction disturbed me in a way," he recalled after the war. "I was enjoying the game, the duel of wits, the aura of undefined danger. Yet that wasn't the reason I was there. I had a fierce hatred of Hitler and the Nazis to begin with, more so with my family and country under their oppression."

Around eight o'clock on Wednesday evening he arrived by Clipper in Lisbon. He checked into the Palácio and then headed to the casino with three officials from the U.S. State Department he'd met on the way. At midnight he slipped out to a public pay phone, called the embassy, and asked for von Karsthoff. The operator gave him another number, saying that Elisabeth wanted to speak with him. The "second's hesitation" in Elisabeth's voice, Dusko remembered, revealed her surprise that he'd returned. They agreed that she'd pick him up on the Rossio the following day.

Thursday morning the chauffeured sedan arrived at eleven. Elisabeth was in the front, but another man, not von Karsthoff, was in the back. He was Lieutenant Kammler*—six feet tall, clean-shaven, dark hair and eyes, and well dressed. He was around twenty-eight but appeared to have aged quickly—his eyebrows were speckled with white hair.

The car sped northwest up Avenida da Liberdade and then headed due north on Republica. They were not traveling toward von Karsthoff's villa in Estoril, Dusko realized, *but to where? And why was the other man with them?*

A few minutes later they arrived at Avenida Berne 8, a modest apartment building with interior parking. Von Karsthoff met him at the door and formally introduced Kammler, who he said was from Abwehr I and would be assisting with debriefing. Dusko apologized for the midnight call the prior evening, saying that he was in the company of three State Department officials who took him to the casino.

---

* Whose real name was Otto Kürer.

"I know," von Karsthoff said. Before Dusko could process that he had been followed, Ludovico cut to the chase: "Now, what happened?"

Dusko stiffened. It all came down to this. His demeanor and composure in the next two minutes, he knew, might determine whether he lived or died. J. C. Masterman explained the danger: "A lie when it is needed," the Double-Cross chief wrote in his postwar report, "will only be believed if it rests on a firm foundation of previous truth." Dusko's previous truth was that he had financial worries. But would that be enough to explain why he never left for Hawaii, or why he had provided almost nothing of significant value for over a year? And could he remain calm and steadfast with the thin story? "No mortal can keep a secret," Freud had taught. "If his lips are silent, he chatters with his finger-tips; betrayal oozes out of him at every pore."

Dusko would test the theorem. He rattled off the little information MI5 had collected and then went on the offensive. The trip to America "was a colossal error from beginning to end," he told the Germans. "In England, I had connections from before the war. Every door was open to me. But in the U.S.—you send me there with no help whatsoever, no contacts, a few miserable dollars . . . and you expect me to produce results in no time." He was in such financial straits, he said, that he had to stoop to borrowing from a girlfriend.

Ludovico mentioned her by name—Simone Simon—stating that Berlin thought he concentrated more on film stars than his job. Dusko countered that those were the people he knew, and that they provided his introduction in society circles. Besides, he said, it was part of his cover.

The major mulled the rebuttal and reiterated that Berlin was extremely unhappy with Popov's lack of work product. "Give Berlin a very rude message from me," Dusko shot back. He had contacts lined up, he said—men like Mr. Bacher from the Aeronautical Chamber of Commerce and journalist Boris Cassini—who could have provided valuable information if he'd had money to pay them. Dusko threw out the MI5 supplied military sources for good measure: Colonel Prime from Mitchel Field, Lieutenant Decker—husband of a girl known to Johnny—Commander Waldron from the U.S. Navy, and Captain Slaatten, a Norwegian Air Force officer in Canada.

Von Karsthoff backed off. Kammler said nothing.

"It is Berlin's fault and Johnny's fault," Ludovico finally said; they'd bungled the finances.

The interrogation continued, but Dusko had sufficiently maneuvered his interviewers that they avoided the sticky issues he was warned about by Wilson. They asked about the Allied invasion and morale in America, but never about Popov's movements, sources, or why he had not gone to Hawaii. Nothing about the Midas money. They never asked why, after his (fictitious) wireless operator refused to work, Dusko didn't continue writing in secret ink. They failed to ask about Dusko's letters before the wireless; he had mentioned in one that he had written the Germans fourteen times when in fact only seven of his letters had been sent by the FBI.

Instead, von Karsthoff asked about the radioman. Popov rattled off his planned answer, saying that the man was a Croat whom he had met in a bar frequented by Yugoslavs on West 45th Street. He was excellent on the radio, Popov said, but exaggerated his skills in other areas. He worked well as long as he was paid, but once Dusko couldn't pay him, he refused to be of further help.

Dusko offered that the wireless set was in a house in Long Island, but the Germans didn't ask for details or an address. He also said that the Croat was unable to build the radio, but that Dusko had acquired a set from an anti-British Indian he'd met in the British Library. Von Karsthoff asked nothing about the Indian, but returned to the operator.

"Are you very sure about that radioman?"

"What do you mean?"

He might have been caught, Ludovico explained, and been working under American control.

"But Ivan would not be here," chimed in Elisabeth.

The man didn't know the code, either, Dusko added, and didn't know what Popov was doing.

Seemingly mollified, Ludovico asked when Popov would be returning to the U.S.

Dusko blinked. He wouldn't. The FBI bridge had been burned and the good riddance was mutual. Yet, from the German perspective, he had no reason to decline the re-posting. He mumbled that he wasn't sure. Thinking fast, he argued that since the U.S. entry into the war effectively ended his usefulness with the Yugoslav Ministry of Information, he had planned on returning to London.

Von Karsthoff pressed. The Germans needed him in America because the radio was "of inestimable value." Too late, Dusko said; he had instructed the Croat to destroy it.

The discussion continued and shortly after three o'clock the major began wrapping up. He asked where Popov would like to work next.

Dusko breathed. He'd made it.

Ludovico said that if a return to the U.S. was impossible, he'd like for Popov to proceed to any English-speaking country under British or American control. Dusko nodded but suddenly had a sinking feeling in his stomach. *Too easy.* He had failed to go to Hawaii, had precious little information after a year's work, and the Abwehr had significant evidence he was a double. Yet, with a smattering of numbers and a few self-serving excuses, he was back in their good graces.

It was a trap.

18 »

THE ART OF THE SILENT KILL

Dusko remained coy. He said he wasn't sure what he was going to do, and that at the moment his only concern was his financial situation, which was dire. He couldn't do anything, he said, until he had repaid the Bailonis $8,500. They were influential bankers, and because they were in Lisbon, word of an embezzlement would travel fast. Their funds had to be returned before he would consider further work.

Kammler blanched. He begged Popov not to make difficulties over money because such trouble might result in Kammler's being sent to the Russian front. Dusko noted the weakness. His Abwehr supervisors had a vested interest in his success; if he failed, the lack of intelligence production from Lisbon would prompt Berlin to replace them.

Throughout the war, this self-serving relationship permeated every Abwehr station; case officers routinely overestimated the value of their agents. Von Karsthoff and Kammler had reason to see Dusko's results through rose-colored glasses, and did. In the end, it would cost Ludovico his life.

The meeting ended at quarter past three with Kammler saying he could take care of the Bailoni money. He told Dusko to meet him at four o'clock at Café Chave d'Ouro. On the hour, Dusko made it to the café and walked directly to the men's room. Setting his briefcase next to him, he began washing his hands. A moment later Kammler appeared at the sink next to him. Without a word, he slipped an envelope into the briefcase.

Cash in hand, Dusko headed to a meeting with the charge d'affaires at the Yugoslav Embassy and then to the Bailonis' farm—Quinta Los Grillos.

He was followed.

The next day, October 16, the Germans requested another meeting, and Elisabeth picked him up on the Rossio at half past twelve. Before he would

Café Chave d'Ouro, hotbed of spies.

Arquivo Municipal Lisboa

discuss future work, Dusko told von Karsthoff and Kammler, he wanted to settle the money. He had been forced to borrow $10,000 from Simone Simon, he said, a humiliating experience and money that had to be repaid. Von Karsthoff countered that Popov's predicament was self-inflicted since he had been "living like a prince."

He *had* been living like a prince, Dusko knew, and the German return on investment was paltry. Out of excuses, he pushed all in. Given the way he had been treated, he told the major, he was unwilling to continue as a German agent.

Ludovico called the bluff. Once anyone got involved in this type of work, he said, there was no leaving off. Dusko would continue his work, and it had to be better. Reaching for a telegram, he read aloud Berlin's assessment of agent IVAN's reports: very good in England, excellent in America up to the South America trip, medium for three months, and then terribly bad.

"Now you know what Berlin thinks of you."

Dusko replied simply: He needed money to work.

Again the pendulum swung—von Karsthoff concurred. Since Dusko's funds had been cut off in June, he said, it was perfectly normal for Popov to refuse further assignments. Kammler agreed: "Berlin are stupid fellows. They are sitting at desks making statistics and can't put themselves into your or my position and do not realize the difficulties of being without money. Therefore please work hard," he said, "or we shall all have trouble here."

Von Karsthoff acquiesced to Popov's financial demands and moved on to military information. "What about invasion?"

Dusko said he didn't think anyone really knew. His contacts had suggested that there wouldn't be one, which probably meant there would.

"Where will it be?"

Before Popov could answer, the major instructed that Dusko should press his contacts about the kind of training the army was receiving, if they were learning any languages, what exercises were being conducted, what fortifications were being simulated, and on what kind of beaches they were practicing. "You will see from the questionnaire," he went on, "you have some naval and military questions. Berlin wants information of direct use for military purposes."

At three o'clock they finished up and Dusko went to the British Embassy, where the air attaché gave him a letter with emergency numbers and additional chicken feed. Popov memorized the information and then destroyed the paper. That evening at six he met Kammler again at the Vivenda Pilar, an Estoril residential estate. With him was a Mr. Meyer, a middle-aged microdot and secret ink expert, and Kammler's secretary, an attractive twenty-four-year-old with dark shining eyes.

Popov's future instructions would come in the form of dots, Meyer said, but Dusko would continue to reply in letters. Meyer showed him five matches, explaining that Popov would communicate secretly with them. Each would write in invisible ink, he claimed, up to two hundred letters. Dusko was to convey his work on airmail paper; if that was unavailable, he would take ordinary stationery and rub it with wool cotton for several minutes until smooth. He would then affix one of the matches to a pencil and write very lightly in block letters.

At Dusko's next meeting, on October 19, Kammler's secretary sewed the matches into the shoulder of his coat. The following day he met again with Kammler in von Karsthoff's apartment to finalize instructions and money. After some debate over currencies—and amid Dusko's conviction that the lieutenant was skimming from what Berlin had sent—Kammler gave him $25,000 and 6,000 escudos for incidentals. He also produced an envelope containing microdots for Popov's future assignments.

Dusko held it to the light and shook his head. It was no good, he said; the points were clearly visible. He handed it back, and Kammler promised to send new ones to him in London.

»

Before leaving, Dusko met with Johnny, who had just arrived in Lisbon. They were returning from a meeting with von Karsthoff when Johnny suddenly pulled the car over. He had an idea, a scheme more or less, that he had conjured up with Ivo. It was dangerous, he said, but the windfall would be worth it. The critical point—that both sides would have to be in on it—was laughable. Brilliant as Jebsen was, the plan was outlandish. *A joint Allied-Axis espionage effort? Approved by the British and Germans, working together?*

Only Johnny could have envisioned such connivance.

And only one man had the gall to sell it.

»

On October 22 Dusko returned to England. The stakes were mounting with the Germans, and between the invasion deception and Johnny's dealings, he needed to be in top form. He wasn't, and he knew why—he missed Simone. At the end of the month he sent her a telegram at the Beverly Hills Hotel, where she occupied rooms 323 and 324: "Missing you darling much more than I thought. With love, Dusko Popov."

While he waited to hear back, he settled into London, signing a six-month lease for the Clock House, an upscale cottage in Rutland Gate, adjacent to Hyde Park. Tar Robertson notified the postmaster that if any mail came for Popov from neutral countries, such letters should be extracted so that MI5 could see them first. Days later a letter came for Dusko at the Yugoslav Legation. It was from Dusko's father. Inexplicably, Mr. Popov was in Zurich—alone—in a refugee camp. He wrote:

My dear Dusko,

Your nice letter from Estoril has given me the greatest pleasure. . . . Your news that it has finally been decided that you stay where you are has given me a special pleasure because I am very much frightened by all of the journeys you make in aeroplanes which can be dangerous both for one's life and one's health. . . . Unfortunately, I have not seen him [Ivo] for fifteen months, nor have I seen his wife, nor Iva, your mother, or Vlada. I am all right and living quietly. The food question is difficult here but we manage. . . .

Write to me often. . . . God grant the war will soon be over, which would be marvelous and that all our family meets together. . . .

With best wishes,
from Tata [Dad]

Hearing that his father had not heard from Ivo in fifteen months was distressing. Assuming that Ivo also would be double-crossing, Dusko had inquired with MI5 in late October about his activities and whereabouts. Ian Wilson confirmed that Ivo was working in the underground, but knew few details or his location. Worse, Dusko learned that his younger brother, Vladan, had also now disappeared.

Were his brothers dead?

»

Meanwhile, Dusko struggled with how to help his father. The money he had brought from Lisbon was in the safekeeping of his British handlers and would soon be allocated elsewhere. On November 29 Colonel Robertson did just that, forwarding $13,000 to MI6—$10,000 for repayment of SIS loans, $3,000 to cover FBI loans.

The following day Ian asked Dusko to sign a memorandum of agreement regarding finances. It noted that the Germans had forwarded—for reasons unknown to Dusko or Ian—$10,000 to a woman in Boston named Fanny Mason. Dusko was somehow supposed to collect it, and Ian assured him that MI5 would try to do so. Wilson added that they would also "take every step in our power" to prevent the FBI from confiscating the money. If the Bureau did, Ian assumed, they would bungle the pickup and endanger Dusko's cover.

The British would bear any of Popov's out-of-pocket expenses not borne by the Germans, the agreement stated, but MI5 would monitor and restrict his spending habits. Two-thirds of any sum received by the Germans would be deposited for Popov in a bank of MI5's choosing, but he could withdraw funds for actual living expenses or "capital investment purposes."

Popov must have smiled at the terms; "living expenses" went undefined and left plenty of room for his many devices.

He wasted no time in putting those devices to work. On December 5, 1942, he gave Ian a letter for transmission to Colonel Wren in New York. Addressed to "Mr. Thomas," the correspondence asked Wren if he would kindly forward Popov's belongings left in the storage closet of his New York penthouse. Since he had taken minimal luggage, he was now the "shabbiest and coldest man in London." That was not all; "You know that my heart is in very bad condition," stated the thirty-year-old agent. "My doctor who is my biggest fiend thinks that it is far too much alcohol, tobacco and sin." The only remedy, he wrote, was milk and chocolates, and would the good major also send along $100 worth of chocolate?

Continuing tongue-in-cheek, Dusko wrote: "There is something else I want you to do again to save my life. Xmas is getting very close. Everyone who arrives here from the States is looked upon by lady friends with an eye on stockings. So if I don't have them somebody will try a murder." To avert the heinous crime, Popov asked Wren to also send $100 worth of nylons, a scarce item during the war.

Two days later Wilson passed the message on to Tar, offering that he thought the request for chocolates and stockings was excessive. What Ian didn't realize was that the items were Popov's way of ingratiating himself with von Karsthoff's assistant, Elisabeth. Dusko was always thinking ahead, particularly when it involved women.

Tar sent Dusko's letter to MI6's Frank Foley for transmittal to Colonel Wren in New York, suggesting that a *reasonable* amount of chocolates and nylons would be appreciated. Robertson added: "TRICYCLE would like included in his luggage his camera, which I last saw in the possession of the New York office of the F.B.I." Why the FBI had Popov's camera, or how it was obtained, was not disclosed.

»

Around this time Popov's cover was again threatened. MI5 received a letter, dated December 8, 1942, sent to Dusko from the Keystone Collection Bureau in New York. The agency was writing to collect $215.85 for horticultural supplies delivered to Popov's retreat in Locust Valley, Long Island, just before he left for London. What shocked Dusko and everyone at MI5 was the address to which Keystone had sent the letter: "c/o British Ministry of War Information." If a New York collection agency found this information, how hard would it be for the Germans?

MI5 quietly paid the bill and hoped for the best.

»

For the next two months Dusko remained in England and worked on German questionnaires, carefully splicing in MI5 misinformation with his Abwehr matches and sending correspondence to one of four cover addresses. By late winter he was writing at least one letter every three days, each with two or three pages of secret text. While he was keeping an active social calendar, his new scrivener role was more than he could bear. With no travel or excitement or danger, he was going mad. He asked Wilson to find more stimulating work, and Ian advised Tar of Dusko's restlessness: "TRICYCLE stressed his desire to do something more active in the way of outwitting the Germans than merely writing letters at our direction. I told him that we were as anxious as he was to bring about some more agressive [*sic*] action."

Robertson had the perfect remedy.

»

In February and March 1943, MI5 records of Popov's activities are mysteriously silent for three- and four-week gaps. The dead weeks are odd since from November 1940 to the end of the war, Dusko's whereabouts and activities were recorded almost daily. Dusko's disappearance, however, coincides with the two stages of the highly secret SOE (Special Operations Executive) commando schools. It appears that Dusko attended the Stage 1 training the last three weeks in February, and the Stage 2 training from mid-March to mid-April. On February 24 a Captain D. Doran of S.I.M.E. (Security Intelligence, Middle East) sent a memo to MI5's Dick White, suggesting that Dusko be attached to SOE operations in Cairo. It was from this station that British operatives infiltrated the Balkans, Yugoslavia in particular. On March 17 Tar sent a letter to Masterman and White, explaining that he was working on finding a suitable cover for Popov's Middle East SOE station. Two days later Ian met Dusko—apparently after Stage 1 of his training—to discuss Popov's new assignment. Dusko's files are quiet again until April 16, when Wilson found him at home in bed with influenza.

His immune system was weakened for good reason.

»

In the spring of 1940 Britain's Directorate of Military Training had authorized the development of a small, fast-action guerilla force under the command of

Lieutenant Colonel Colin Gubbins. Fashioned for sabotage and raids behind enemy lines, the commando group was originally intended to be small—no more than five hundred. In July the Special Operations Executive was secretly established. The name was somewhat misleading, however, as the commandos created by SOE were hardly executives; the Germans would later call them *terrorists.*

Gubbins desired the best, toughest operatives and training was established in two stages. Stage 1, which was a three- or four-week course at one of several English country homes, focused on physical fitness and small arms training. Cross-country runs and other exercises were included, with practice in various pistols and submachine guns. The homes also included well-stocked bars, since SOE needed to know how recruits would behave after a few drinks.

If a candidate passed Stage 1, he would progress to Stage 2—an intense three-week course at a secret school in the forsaken town of Arisaig, near Lochailort, Scotland. One Dutch agent described the place as "a wretched, barren countryside, thinly populated; rain fell from a heavy sky that never cleared completely. . . . a most depressing place."

Here, Gubbins set up facilities for every aspect of guerilla warfare. In one area the agents would practice with every type of pistol and machine gun found on the battlefield; in another, they would learn map reading and demolitions. In yet another, they would learn how to kill—gun, knife, or with their hands.

Gubbins brought in as instructors perhaps the two best streetfighters in the world. Major William Ewart Fairbairn and Captain Eric Anthony Sykes, former Royal British Marines who had established long careers with the Shanghai Municipal Police, would teach all aspects of shooting, knife-fighting, and hand-to-hand combat. Fairbairn was particularly suited for the task.

After serving with the Royal Marines for six years, Fairbairn in 1907 had joined the International Police Force in Shanghai—a lawless city ruled by thugs, drug dealers, and criminals. The following year he was attacked by a gang, reputedly stabbed a dozen times, and left for dead. Fairbairn survived and, over the next eighteen years, turned himself into a lethal weapon. With extended stays at Tokyo's Kodokan, he studied under Kano Jigoro, founder of judo. By 1926 Fairbairn had earned black belts in judo and jiu-jitsu, and had supplemented those with training in boxing, savate, and kung fu. Combining these skills with lessons learned from the street, Fairbairn developed his own system and taught various police forces over the next fourteen years.

After a thirty-year career policing "red-light" and other tough districts, he was said to have been in some six hundred fights. His arms, legs, torso, and hands bore scars from knife attacks, and his nose appeared to be permanently broken. Thick-necked and broad-shouldered, he was lithe and explosive. When recruited to SOE in 1940, even at fifty-five, he remained one of the most dangerous men in the world. Students called him the "Shanghai Buster." In spite of his roughneck profession and back-alley history, Fairbairn neither drank nor swore. In civilized company he was an officer and a gentleman; in uncivilized, a killing machine.

Exactly what Gubbins had in mind.

Eric Sykes, the weapons expert, had met Fairbairn in Shanghai while working for the Remington rifle company. Together they invented the Fairbairn-Sykes commando fighting knife, a double-edged dagger used today by most elite forces. As Gubbins had dreamed, Fairbairn and Sykes would give the SOE commando agents every bit of training they needed, and more.

The small arms course included practice with every conceivable weapon, especially those stolen from the enemy. They shot German, Italian, American, and British pistols and rifles. Machine guns they fired included Germany's Schmeisser, MG 34, and MG 42; Britain's Vickers and Sten; America's Tommy Gun; the Anglo-Czech Bren; Italy's Fiat-Revelli; and the American-Greek Hotchkiss. They practiced firing at pop-up targets—including at the end of a rigorous obstacle course—and were expected to strip, reassemble, and load in total darkness every weapon they handled.

Fairbairn instructed his students to fire in a new, double-handed crouch position. In addition, he instituted the "double tap," used now by virtually every special ops squad in the world. Fairbairn also taught his commandos to be quick on the draw, so candidates practiced speed shooting from the hip, shoulder, and pocket.

Finally, Fairbairn taught his men how to fight. Dusko could not have had a better teacher. Even before he retired, Fairbain was widely regarded as the father of hand-to-hand combat. His tactics, by design, were "drastic and admittedly unpleasant." One commando remembered that Fairbairn's instructions typically ended with: ". . . and then kick him in the testicles."

The SOE training manual mirrored Fairbairn's serious, humorless approach: "Your object here is to learn how to kill but it is quite unnecessary to kill or damage your sparring partner, you will get no credit if you do."

Fairbairn's specialty—the "art of silent killing"—was an integral part of the course. Dutch operative Pieter Dourlein explained this as creeping up on an enemy and dealing with him "in a way that prevented him from uttering a sound." Dusko described it more bluntly: strangling and cutting throats.

In addition, students were taught how to slip tags, survive interrogation, board moving trains, and escape cafés and other meeting places by side and back doors. At night, staffers would listen to see if any candidates spoke in their sleep and if so, in what language. To prepare them for capture and ruthless cross-examination, Arisaig staffers would wake the commandos in the middle of the night, rush them before men dressed as Abwehr or SD officers, and interrogate them for hours. At the end of the program, up to a third of the students would be told that they had failed or were otherwise unqualified for service.

Years after the war Dusko spoke of surviving Arisaig, describing the training as merciless. It was "the hardest thing I ever had to go through in my whole life," he confessed to an interviewer. But the school fulfilled its purpose—those graduating were fearless and lethal, with or without a weapon. George Langelaan, an SOE operative who underwent plastic surgery so that he could reenter Vichy France, testified to the transformation:

> The "Shanghai Buster" gave us more and more self-confidence which gradually grew into a sense of physical power and superiority that few men ever acquire. By the time we finished our training, I would have willingly enough tackled any man, whatever his strength, size or ability. . . . It is understandable when a man knows for certain that he can hurt, maul, injure, or even kill with the greatest of ease. . . . [Fairbairn] made each of us a terribly dangerous man.

Langelaan wasn't exaggerating. The SOE training manual taught that blows with the side of the hand, properly executed to the the neck, were lethal. Popov's son, Marco, confirmed his father's training in this deadly game: "I remember very clearly Dusko mentioning he learned combat techniques whilst in Scotland. He once told us he learned how to kill a man with one blow of his opened hand on the neck."

The silent kill.

Fairbairn's reputation and training would soon cross the Atlantic. With the success of Arisaig, William Stephenson suggested to William Donovan that they open a similar, British-American commando school in Canada. Wild Bill's OSS men, after all, would benefit greatly from the rigorous course, and the BSC could send qualified Canadian trainees. Donovan agreed and Stephenson went to work. The course would be conducted on his farmhouse property in Oshawa, a village on the shores of Lake Ontario, near Toronto. The location, like Arisaig, was ideal—rural, isolated, and near water. Stephenson had several huts and other buildings constructed, and planned the course. He brought in Fairbairn and Sykes and gave them free rein.

Recalling the assistance he had received in drafting the OSS charter, Donovan invited Ian Fleming as an observer. Once there, Ian asked if he could participate in the exercises and everyone agreed. In addition to the normal instruction in firearms, hand-to-hand combat, and demolition, Stephenson added underwater operations. Using an old tanker moored on the lake, candidates would practice night swims to place limpet mines. A strong swimmer, Fleming was one of the few trainees who successfully placed the mine without detection.

Pleased with Ian's progress through the training, Stephenson chose him for a post-course assignment. A dangerous enemy agent had just checked into a cheap hotel in downtown Toronto, Fleming was told, and had to be eliminated. They went to the hotel, and Stephenson gave Ian the room number. Handing him a loaded police .38 revolver, he said the games were over.

"Open that door, draw fast, and shoot straight. It'll be his life or yours."

Fleming took the gun and headed up the stairwell.

In a small, dimly lit room with only table and chair, William Fairbairn was waiting.

19 »

"TURN AROUND SLOWLY"

Fairbairn had no weapon and wore no bulletproof vest. There would be no tricks. Fleming's gun was real and fully loaded. He had his instructions. The range would be close, fifteen feet or less. Ian merely had to pull the trigger, as Stephenson intended.

William Fairbairn would dodge the bullet.

It was a unique combat skill—diverting a shooter five yards away so that the shot would go wide—that Fairbairn had honed through the years. At fifty-five, however, his reaction time and movement would be considerably slower, the margin for error zero.

Fleming quietly crept up the stairs.

At the landing platform, he paused. *Could he shoot a man in cold blood?* For several moments he stood there, clutching the .38. Behind the wall in Fairbairn's room, Sykes watched through a peephole.

After another minute, Fleming turned back. He couldn't do it. "I just couldn't open that door," he told Stephenson. "I couldn't kill a man that way." The genteel Canadian understood. "Although Ian was an outstanding trainee," he told Fleming's biographer, "he just hadn't got the temperament for an agent or a genuine man of action."

Another SOE graduate would have gladly tested Fairbairn's reflexes.

»

As Ian Wilson spoke to an ill Popov, he didn't have the heart to tell Dusko that Cairo was off and that all of his rigorous training with SOE—for which he now likely suffered—was for naught. At the beginning of March, MI5 had again received warning signals about Popov's standing with the Germans. Days later Dick White sent a telegram to a Colonel Maunsell in Cairo, notifying the SOE officer that "our plans for sending TRICYCLE to you temporarily suspended owing [to] uncertainty as to enemy attitude towards him." Then, on April 13, the Political Warfare Executive, which would have run Popov in conjunction with the SOE and the Foreign Office, decided that running a covert operation with TRICYCLE would be unwise given the PWE's difficult situation in Cairo and its "delicate" relationship with the SOE.

Wilson advisedly refrained from telling Popov about the unsteady relationship with the Germans, or the SOE/PWE bureaucratic impasse. But MI5 had to find *something* their restless agent could do. By this time Dusko had sent twenty-four letters to four different cover addresses, and sick or not, he wanted action. Wilson worked to see what he could do.

On April 29 he, Robertson, and Masterman met with Dusko at the Clock House to discuss how they could better utilize him. Ian summarized the consensus: "That TRICYCLE should undertake some Intelligence work of a more active, ambitious and dangerous character." Further, "TRICYCLE stressed the fact that he was ready to take almost any risks to achieve anything that would be really useful."

Few agents, double or otherwise, invite risk. Fewer still actively seek danger. Dusko wanted both.

»

Tar Robertson, who had been promoted to lieutenant colonel in April, kept Dusko busy in May. Eugen Sostaric, a friend of Johnny's and Ivo's, had come through an escape route before one was formally established. An aide-de-camp to the King of Yugoslavia, Sostaric had failed to flee Belgrade during the German occupation. When he was imprisoned, Ivo assumed he would be tortured, and he tried to spare Eugen the ordeal by sending him poisoned cigarettes in a care package. Sostaric, who either didn't smoke or was exceedingly generous, gave them to fellow prisoners. By the time Eugen connected the deaths to the cigarettes, Johnny had devised a scheme to rescue him: a triple-cross.

Jebsen persuaded the Abwehr to bring Sostaric aboard as a double agent, and Eugen was transferred to Berlin for a month of training. The Germans sent him to Madrid, where Sostaric contacted the British Embassy. In April MI6 slipped him out to Gibraltar, and then to England. After three days of interrogation at the Royal Victoria Patriotic Building in Wandsworth, euphemistically called the "London Reception Center," he was cleared for potential work with British Intelligence.

Throughout his questioning, Sostaric claimed to be working with Johnny and Ivo, and contended that Ivo had instructed him to contact Dusko once he was in London. Initially, Eugen had notions of joining the RAF, but MI5 had in mind a higher calling. Robertson codenamed him METEOR, and tentatively included him in the TRICYCLE network. Tar asked Dusko to meet with Eugen, confirm his bona fides and his relationship with Ivo, and try to persuade him to become a triple. Popov did, and METEOR became Dusko's third sub-agent.

Around this time, Popov approached Robertson with an idea Johnny had suggested in Cascais. Dusko had envisioned an Allied escape route, he told Tar, to which Johnny added an ingenious twist. The Yugoslav government-in-exile was anxious to evacuate officers marooned in Switzerland, Dusko said. In addition, the Germans had been executing hundreds of Yugoslavs as punishment for resistance and a large number were being held in Belgrade as hostages. They all needed an escape route to England.

Johnny's idea, if they could pull it off, was to get the Abwehr involved. If MI5 approved, Dusko would pitch von Karsthoff on a crafty way of getting German spies into England—a Yugoslav escape route. By allowing a trickle of "harmless civilians" to escape—under the watchful control of Ivo and Dusko—the Abwehr could send in new spies disguised as escapees. Ivo would handle the initial flight from Yugoslavia and Switzerland, Johnny would coordinate transit through France, and Dusko would run the receiving end in Spain. From there the escapees would travel to Gibraltar and on to England. What the Germans wouldn't know, of course, was that Ivo and Dusko were double agents and the Yugoslavs and Germans coming in would be as well; Ivo would handpick the former and Johnny the latter. The Trojan Horse soldiers wheeled into England would all be friendlies.

On May 11 Popov met with Masterman to discuss the idea, and how Dusko could otherwise reengage the Germans in Portugal and Spain. J. C. stated that he was in favor of the route, but that it would have to be approved by the Yugoslav prime minister; Dusko would have to sit tight until then. About this time, Dusko received a telegram from a contact in Lisbon stating that von Karsthoff had deposited 187,500 escudos into Popov's Estoril bank account. The Germans, it seemed, had again placed their confidence in IVAN.

Throughout the month, MI5 and MI6 brainstormed to create a suitable cover for Dusko's return to Portugal. "C" had even weighed in, offering the ruse that Popov had tried to travel to America but was stranded in Lisbon for want of visa clearance. MI5 rejected the idea, but came up with a plan involving the Yugoslav government and Dusko's position as a reserve army officer.

Meanwhile, Ian Wilson was concerned that Popov might get tripped up if the Germans inquired about sources or information particulars. While Dusko was in London, MI5 had him send to von Karsthoff various numbers on shipbuilding and other items from unnamed naval sources; Ian expected questions to follow. In addition, Dusko would likely be quizzed on where he'd been. J. C. Masterman explained the risk: "A double agent should, as far as possible, actually live the life and go through all the motions of a genuine agent." In particular, Masterman wrote, there was an "imperative necessity of making the agent actually experience all that he professes to have done." The Oxford don's example of what typically happened during interrogation was especially relevant to Popov. "'And then you come to the little river,' says the interrogator, 'tell me about the ferry there, and what sort of man rowed you across?' The victim describes the ferry to the best of his inventive power," Masterman explained, when "he should have said, 'There is no ferry. I walked across the bridge.'"

Dusko's risk of this trap was high so Ian asked Ewen Montagu to supply Popov with verifiable sources, advising that Dusko should personally meet them. He also asked Major E. Goudie in the War Office for real names to connect to information supposedly coming from Canadian, American, and Welsh officers.

While Wilson sought sources, Dusko worked on the route. On June 3 he met with General Rakic, head of Yugoslavia's military cabinet and an aide-de-camp to the king. Dusko suggested that he go to Lisbon or Madrid to organize the escape of fifty Yugoslav officers marooned in Switzerland. The general approved, and later that day Dusko informed Ian that, for proper cover, he'd have to be mobilized in the Yugoslav Army. Two days later MI5 received approval from Yugoslavia's prime minister to conduct the operation in Spain, and the route was initiated on a dry-run basis before involving the Germans.

What MI5 didn't tell General Rakic or the prime minister, however, was that the British had another reason for sending Popov to Spain: Ewen Montagu's Operation Mincemeat. On April 30, a mile off the Spanish coast near Huelva, British submarine HMS *Seraph* had jettisoned a cadaver. The body, which had been kept in a cooler in anticipation of the operation, was dressed in a British uniform and made to appear as if the man had died from drowning. A briefcase attached to his wrist contained fictitious documents identifying him as "Major Martin." Also on his person were fabricated letters suggesting that the Allies would soon be invading Greece and Sardinia (rather than Sicily, the actual target).

British Intelligence knew that Adolf Clauss, an Abwehr agent in Huelva, was friendly with local officials. Montagu assumed that the Spanish would allow the German to copy the documents before returning the body to British authorities. As part of the operation, Popov would be sent to Spain to determine if the local officials had, in fact, showed the documents to the German and if so, what credibility the Abwehr attached to them.

Meanwhile, Ian was gathering a mountain of data for Dusko to deliver to von Karsthoff. In a six-page memorandum dated June 10, 1943—apparently for distribution to MI6 and Army and Navy Intelligence—Wilson set forth the information he wanted, and the details Dusko would have to keep straight. "TRICYCLE is supposed to have written 36 letters since he last arrived in this country," he wrote, seven of which were notionally intercepted by British censors. Popov's original German questionnaire, Ian stated, had requested information about the formation of new units, including: the number and location of county divisions; the number, purpose, and location of armored divisions; and how many and which army tank brigades were presently in England. Dusko should have this information when he returned.

In addition, he should or might also provide to von Karsthoff:

- » the names of high-ranking officers and commanders
- » bogus figures and tables regarding the output of copper
- » American divisional signs published by *Reader's Digest* and *Newsweek* magazine
- » documents detailing arrangements for special trains or food to liberated countries
- » information about an advance party to resume control of Yugoslav mines
- » an anti-aircraft regiment which had finished a course in Wales and was now stationed in Essex

Wilson also prepared a number of stories for Dusko to memorize, some verbatim, about information or rumors he had acquired from fictitious officers concerning British and American troop training and deployment, hospital accommodation for civilians, air-raid shelters, army lorries seen transporting barge sections, electrically propelled canoes manufactured, commercial shipping, construction of a "large plane" at Hartfordbridge Flats, Sherman tanks delivered, and the American development of blimps and helicopters for submarine warfare. Weaving in the finest details, Wilson also imagined that Dusko's tailor had mentioned a large number of senior officers having battle dress made or altered.

Finally, Ian connected Dusko's lifestyle to his duties: "It is proposed to take TRICYCLE to visit certain south coast towns. . . . He has already reported on his notional visit to Bournemouth and should therefore see the place, and, as a keen spy, he should I think have taken his girl friends to different south coast towns on various weekends." Popov would have no trouble with female names and von Karsthoff would have no trouble believing it.

That evening Wilson gave Dusko homework—independent of the data noted in his memorandum—"so that he should have the right general background": two volumes of press clippings and several books on the British Air Force, the Royal Armoured Corps, and other military matters. Although not recorded in MI5 files, it is likely that Popov cursed the day he had been given a lawyer as a case officer.

While Robertson, MI6, and half the British generals in England worked on producing Wilson's information, Ian took Dusko on a field trip: June 17 to Bournemouth, June 18 "on a tour of the coast between Brighton and Hastings."

Without girlfriends.

»

On June 20 Wilson heard from the Yugoslav Foreign Ministry that Popov's diplomatic passport had been prepared. The Portuguese visa would be forthcoming in a few days, they said, but since Yugoslavia had no diplomatic ties to Spain, Dusko was on his own for a Spanish visa. The British couldn't help either, Ian noted, since "the last thing we wish to intimate to the Spaniards is that we are interested in TRICYCLE's trip." Dusko would have to get to Spain by hook or by crook once he was in Lisbon.

Two days later Ian received instructions from MI6 on how Popov was to contact SIS agents in Madrid and Lisbon should he run into trouble. In

Madrid, he was to contact a "Senor Gallegos" at Orfila 7, or call him at 35059. Dusko was to identify himself as "Gregorio." In Lisbon, he was to contact Colonel Jarvis at Passport Control, calling 29105 from a pay phone. He was to speak in French and give his name as "Monsieur Jean." As before, the rendezvous would be at the Tennis Pavilion in Tapada da Ajuda, this time two hours early. At night he was to ring 29942 and ask for the duty officer, again giving his name as Monsieur Jean. Any meeting with MI6, the instruction stressed, was discouraged absent dire emergency.

»

The following week another scare arose. MI5's Anthony Blunt* received word that the Yugoslav Foreign Ministry had, with its issuance of Popov's diplomatic passport, recorded that "Doctor POPOVIC is going on a special mission to Spain for the British." Such a leak not only imperiled Popov's mission for Operation Mincemeat, it risked blowing his cover in general. Dusko had warned the British several times to be careful with his identity when dealing with Yugoslav emissaries, and it was discovered that the leak most likely emanated from Rakic or Vladimir Milanovic, assistant foreign minister.

Once again, Popov was on a tightrope.

It would get worse. Just before he was to leave, Popov wrote in his memoirs, Wilson and Robertson showed up at the Clock House with an urgent warning. "You may be walking into a trap in Lisbon," they said. One of the agents coming through the first escape route, the MI5 officers explained, was likely compromised. THE WORM, a twenty-seven-year-old Czech named Stefan Zeis, had disappeared during the trip and was now seen regularly at Hotel Lutetia, Abwehr Paris headquarters. The route had backfired, it seemed. Dusko couldn't believe it; Ivo had assured him that everyone coming through would be a double agent working in the underground. The danger was obvious. WORM had been working with Ivo for months, knew he was being sent to London as a double, and knew all secrets, Dusko's included.

"You're probably burned," Robertson said. "As a personal friend, I advise you not to go."

Dusko appreciated Tar's concern and the risk, but his mind was settled. He had asked for danger, for something important, and now he had it.

---

* Later exposed as a Soviet spy in the Cambridge Five ring.

"They won't kill me first thing."

Wilson winced. "You might wish they had."

»

On July 16 Popov boarded his flight at Whitchurch Airport with Wilson's words surely ringing in his ears. Watching the green squares of Bristol disappear beneath him, he assumed this would be his last trip. Von Karsthoff would unwind his maze of lies and the big cat would finally devour him.

Though he expected the Germans to kill him, Dusko was not afraid. He was *angry*. "I was angry that after all I would not see how it would work out, and that I would [not] know the end of Hitler," he later told an interviewer. The thought of not returning to Lisbon never crossed his mind. "I was completely engrossed in the struggle," he wrote, "and could no more think of abandoning it than, say, Rembrandt could allow himself his final gasp while in front of an incompleted canvas." Popov would finish the canvas.

He packed a Luger.

While he had no fear of dying, and largely expected it, he had no intention of being tortured. "I would shoot my way out of a tight situation, or be killed in the attempt."

»

On the flight over Dusko had much else to think about. His covers and assignments for the trip were precarious. In addition to his Portuguese visa, he was carrying an Egyptian visa, which Portugal had required in granting transit to Lisbon. He was also carrying a Yugoslav diplomatic bag containing a questionnaire and other documents—for the *British*. His official cover was as attaché to the Yugoslav Foreign Ministry, and he was supposedly traveling to Cairo and Lisbon as a diplomatic courier. But his duties were quite real: The Yugoslavs wanted him to continue running the escape route from Madrid; the British wanted him to visit Spain for Operation Mincemeat and Lisbon for pumping information from von Karsthoff; and the Germans wanted to interrogate him as a possible double. Over the next two weeks he would have to fool the Portuguese, Spanish, Yugoslavs, and Germans. He was, as it were, a Matryoshka doll—each identity hidden and layered inside another.

He aged.

»

Arriving safely in Portugal, he took up his usual suite at the Palácio. That evening, Dusko recalled in his memoirs, he headed to his pickup on the Estoril road. In pitch darkness he practiced what he had been taught at Arisaig: the quick draw from a shoulder harness. Again and again he drew his Luger, making sure the weapon slid freely and didn't catch on his coat.

The Abwehr car arrived, and as he jumped in the backseat, he noticed that the driver was new. At the villa she showed him to the drawing room and left to notify the major.

Dusko scanned the room. Two doors—one on the right, which led to the dining room, and double French doors on the left, which led to the garden. That would be his escape route. Slipping his hand inside his jacket, he pushed the Luger safety catch forward, unlocking it, and moved to the French doors.

Suddenly, steps behind him—

"*Turn around slowly*, Popov, and don't make any sudden moves."

Von Karsthoff's voice was hard. Ludovico had entered quietly through the hall entrance behind him. Dusko's heart pounded.

This was it.

He slipped his palm over the pistol.

TICKING

As he began to turn, intending to shoot in one motion, he caught von Karsthoff's reflection in the window. The major was alone, unarmed, and had a small monkey on his shoulder.

Dusko dropped his hand, his coat still concealing his weapon.

The animal was a gift from an agent in Africa, Ludovico said, and if frightened, might bite. Pulse still racing, Dusko chuckled as if mildly amused and asked the major to put the animal away.

»

Later that summer British Intelligence received evidence that Popov was wearing his mask well, observing what Lethbridge had told him—to act as if he were a genuine German spy. On August 1 MI6 Lisbon notified Frank Foley about a "Mrs. Jackson," whom Dusko had met the year before in New York. Celia Jackson, the report said, was astonished to see Popov at the Palácio, and complained to Passport Control. Given Dusko's "strong pro-Axis bias," she could not understand why he was allowed to travel from the UK to Lisbon. She also "thought it strange that he should be persona grata with the British authorities."

Thanking Mrs. Jackson for her patriotism, the British said they'd look into it.

Over the next week Popov met with von Karsthoff, Sahrbach, Jebsen, and Kammler. Ludovico didn't question Dusko's loyalty, and embraced the notion of a Yugoslav escape route wholeheartedly. He was excited about the possibility of sending German agents through, and suggested that Dusko could run it from Madrid or Berne.

The report Dusko turned in to MI6, however, raised a red flag. Kammler and Jebsen had told him privately, he wrote, that "they were sure he was

580

On His Majesty's Service

Original plan of members of the
Abwehr drawn by TRICICYCLE.

OHMS file cover.

The National Archives of the U.K.

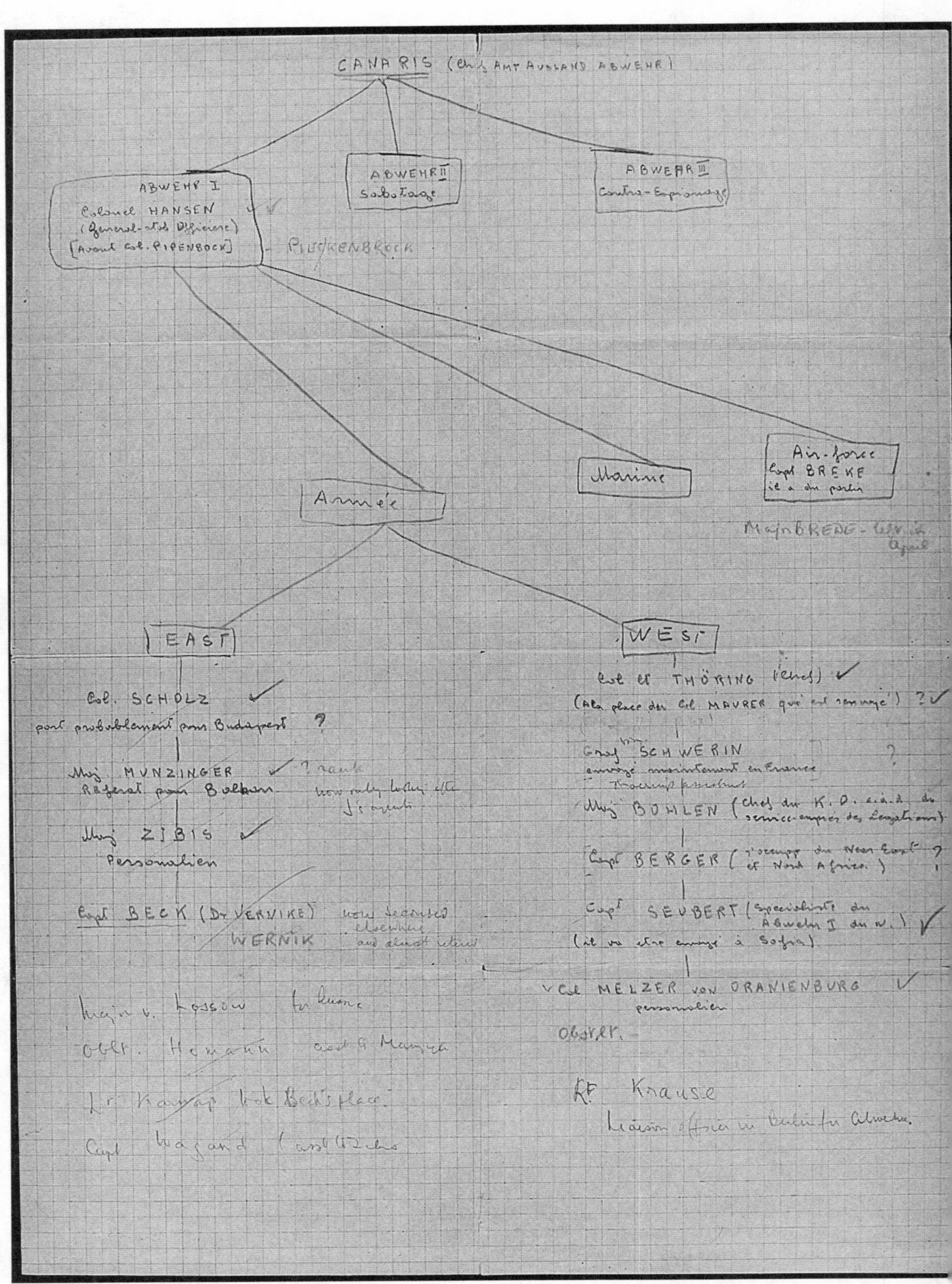

Popov's sketch of Abwehr structure given to MI6 Lisbon on August 10, 1943.

The National Archives of the UK

Le vrai nom de von Karsthoff est VON KREMER-AUENRODE
(CRAMER?)
" " " " Kammler " KURRER

Les noms employés dans les télégrammes:

LIZA = Lisbon
LUDOVICO = v Karsthoff
HERRIBERT = Kammler
GOLF-PLATZ = England
ANDREAS = ABWEHR I East
HIOB-ENRICO = " " WEST
RUDOLF = PARIS (pour le chef)
PARK-PLATZ = U.S.A (?) Paris
HOFLINGER = MUNZINGER
POLLUX = Chef Constantinople

Popov's notes regarding von Karsthoff and Kammler's real names and German code words.

The National Archives of the UK

working for the Allies—and that if he wasn't he was a fool!" Johnny, they expected, but Kammler? The man who had given Popov a bad mark for his work in America? The man whom Johnny had considered his worst enemy? Was the Abwehr supervisor playing Dusko and Johnny only to build a dossier to send to Berlin?

Dusko's report, which sketched out the Abwehr structure as he knew it, along with German code words, was highly regarded. Frank Foley sent both to Tar, together with Popov's other notes. Dusko's diagram, Ian Wilson noted the following day, was "remarkably accurate," the code names reported with "remarkable accuracy."

Meanwhile, the Germans made arrangements to create a forged Yugoslav diplomatic bag for Popov to carry to London. They had borrowed his official legation letter and sent it to Berlin for duplication. Weeks later the Abwehr returned the letter with a stamp and seal matching exactly the Yugoslav original. Dusko passed the information along, and Ian Wilson began working on a scheme whereby the British would take temporary possession of the real bag, and permanent possession of the forged bag. A triple-crossed diplomatic bag. The Germans, it turned out, wanted Dusko to sneak a wireless radio to London in the forged bag, while the British wanted him to carry secret materials.

Dusko made *two* forged Yugoslav bags.

»

Between 1942 and 1943, Popov's romance with Simone Simon had fizzled, but he wasted no time harvesting fresh fields. Days after his arrival in Lisbon, British censors intercepted a letter from London addressed to him at the Yugoslav Legation. The woman was new, but the tone familiar:

> *My darling,*
>
> *How have you been lately? . . . Darling, it seems ages and ages and ages since I last saw you and I can't tell you how much I miss you—I can't write it in a letter . . . and anyhow there is not enough paper around here for me to put it all down. . . .*
>
> *Darling, I haven't anymore* [sic] *news but I shall write again soon—All my love to you always sweetheart—Thinking of you all the time.*
>
> *Nani*

»

Weeks later, Nani would send a second letter to her darling Dusko, this one ending with all her love "and more—Nani xxx."

Dusko's darling in London, however, competed with another darling in Lisbon. In a memo to Tar on August 20, Ian Wilson noted that before Dusko left he had requested assistance in acquiring English visas for the Bailoni family, most particularly Ljiljana, who was now twenty-one.

"Evidence from various independent sources," Wilson wrote, "has recently reached us that TRICYCLE is paying considerable court to Ljiljana. TRICYCLE is doing an extremely good job of work under conditions of considerable risk at the present moment. He would undoubtedly be an easier agent to run if he became a little more settled in his domestic habits, which he probably would be if this girl were here, whether or not he entered into the marriage tie." Ever the thoughtful and thorough case officer, Ian asked Tar if MI5 could assist in bringing Ljiljana to London.

In the meantime, Dusko went to Spain to investigate Operation Mincemeat. "I checked in Madrid," he later said, "and found that they had swallowed the whole story." As Montagu had assumed, local police had photographed the papers Major Martin was carrying and had given copies to the Germans. Berlin perceived the documents as genuine and sent troops to Greece and Sardinia, submarines to Crete. The Allies would meet little resistance in Sicily.

»

By the time Dusko returned to Lisbon, the WORM had surfaced in London. On August 1 Wilson and Masterman interviewed him at the "Reception Center." WORM had not been turned, they happily discovered, and made an "extremely good impression." He was prepared to double, not only from national interest, but also to protect Ivo's position in Belgrade. WORM also carried particularly valuable information about Ivo and Johnny. In a meeting with Dr. Popov in Paris, Zeis said, Ivo informed him that Dusko was a German agent and that he was "90 percent certain, but not entirely sure" that he was doubling for the British. Ivo asked him, Zeis continued, to warn Dusko that the Germans might suspect that some of his information "had been faked," and to have a good explanation ready when he returned to Lisbon.

Zeis added that Dr. Popov had given him and two other escapees false passports which had been produced by the youngest Popov, Vladan. All Popov brothers, it appeared, had joined the Allied cause independently. Robertson placed WORM in the TRICYCLE network, and Dusko had his fourth sub-agent.

»

One day when Popov and Jebsen had an afternoon free from von Karsthoff and Kammler, they headed to Cascais.

"During an air-raid Hitler, Goering, Goebbels and Himmler took refuge in the same air-raid shelter," Johnny said with a grin. Their bunker "received a direct hit. Who was saved?"

Germany.

Johnny's joke about the Nazis confirmed their silent meeting of minds. While Dusko had not told Jebsen specifically that he was working for the British, he was certain Johnny knew. With their cards partially on the table,

Johnny told him to move from London due to the rockets the Germans were about to launch.

"What rockets?"

"Some new invention. From 120 to 150 are fired together, and each of them has the same effect as a two-thousand-kilo bomb."

"Don't be a fool, you are influenced by the German propaganda."

"It is true."

"Where should I go and live?"

"Scotland."

Jebsen was referring to the FZG-76—a rocket bomb later called the V-1 or doodlebug. Developed by Werner von Braun, it was launched from the ground and flew like a bird thousands of kilometers to hit a target.

Dusko noted the warning and asked Johnny what Berlin thought of agent IVAN's work.

"There are two types of people in the office in Berlin—Nazis, who are damned idiots, and reactionaries." The Nazis were too stupid, Johnny said, to question Dusko's genuineness. The others, who might suspect him, would remain silent since voicing their concern would be adverse to their own interests. Nevertheless, he warned, Dusko's work had to improve for the sake of Johnny's protection against the Gestapo.

The secret police had already tried to get rid of him, he said, and would try again. In one of Johnny's currency exchanges some Gestapo had given him forged notes; when he complained, rumors spread that "a group of Gestapo people were making money at the expense of the Third Reich."

Himmler had one of them shot.

Johnny couldn't return to Germany, he said, because the Gestapo would certainly execute him. Up till now the Abwehr had been protecting him, and the Lisbon station had specific orders to do so. Kammler had even said, "In case of emergency you had better go to England." But if he didn't return, his wife Lore would soon be receiving visitors. The Nazi protocol of *Sippenhaft*—exacting revenge on one's family—was swift and sure.

Complicating the matter for MI5 was Johnny's relationship with Dickie Metcalfe, Dusko's sub-agent BALLOON. On August 31 Ian Wilson prepared a memorandum for Robertson, Masterman, and Marriott. In it he gave an update on Metcalfe, and the delicate handling of him vis-à-vis Popov and Jebsen. "I cannot help feeling," he wrote, "that the Germans do no[t] place any real trust in information given by BALLOON." If that was the case, Wilson warned, Jebsen was caught in the middle. "I think we can assume that, as JEBSEN knows that TRICYCLE is controlled, he equally knows that BALLOON is controlled. He seems to have concealed from Berlin TRICYCLE's real position, but it is not clear that he is pretending to Berlin that BALLOON is also alright."

Wilson posed the dilemma: "It is, of course, illogical for Berlin to believe in TRICYCLE and at the same time regard BALLOON as controlled, but unless that is their attitude I cannot understand why TRICYCLE was not asked to bring a new ink, money and cover addresses to Lisbon." Ian countered—thinking as a German—that the British would not allow a controlled agent to travel to Lisbon. In either case, the situation was troublesome.

»

A day or so later Dusko visited the Bailonis. The farm offered quiet therapy and refuge, and for a few hours at least, he needed both. As he pulled in, Ljiljana rushed up.

"Dusko, let's go have a swim."

He shook his head. "I just got here. I want to collect myself."

As much as he admired the girl, he needed time to think. And rest. Undeterred, Ljiljana called for another visitor to accompany her. The young man, whom Dusko figured to be an American military attaché, waved his assent. Ljiljana smiled and asked if they could go in style in Dusko's Jaguar. He tossed her the keys, and moments later Ljiljana and her friend tore off for the beach.

They could not hear the ticking.

FIVE LIVES

Some four hours later, Dusko estimated, he noticed a car, not his Jaguar, racing down the drive. It was a cab, out of which Ljiljana jumped. "Your car, Dusko, it exploded," she cried as she ran toward him. "We were in swimming and it just exploded all by itself."

Dusko had wanted excitement, even danger, but not the endangerment of innocent girls. He contacted Cecil Gledhill, the British station chief who had replaced Colonel Jarvis.

"Who would want to get rid of me? It couldn't be the Germans. I'm graded number one with them, and anyway, they'd put me on the grill first if they suspected I was double-crossing them. And the same goes with you."

Gledhill agreed it couldn't be the Germans, and assured Dusko it wasn't the British. He surmised a surprising culprit.

The Americans.

"Some weeks ago an American service showed some curiosity about you," he said. "They asked if you were working for us. Naturally, we said no."

If Dusko was correct in assuming the officer with Ljiljana was American, it didn't make sense. Yet Sam Foxworth's words about putting an idea in Hoover's head echoed. Perhaps the American officer was not in counterintelligence and had no idea of a termination order. Ian Wilson took up the case and asked Arthur Thurston, FBI legal attaché at the U.S. Embassy in London, if he would determine the extent to which TRICYCLE was under suspicion by American authorities in Lisbon.

While Dusko waited to hear back, he returned to a favorite pastime—gambling. One night at Casino Estoril he was having quite a run at the baccarat tables, winning some six or seven thousand dollars, when a group of friends came by. With them was an attractive Belgian, Louise, who seemed enchanted with Popov's company. Dusko stuffed the chips in his pockets and suggested sharing a bottle of champagne in the lounge. An hour or so later they were at the Palácio getting better acquainted. Around four in the morning, Dusko remembered, he awoke to the "patter of little feet and the rustling of papers"; Louise was going through his desk drawers.

After several minutes she returned, slipping quietly back into bed. With a stretch and yawn, Dusko feigned waking up. "For whom are you working?" he suddenly asked.

"What?"

"For whom are you working?"

Louise acted ignorant and Popov slapped her, lightly. She began to weep and said she needed money to pay rent. "Well, this was a bloody lie," Dusko said later, recalling the incident, "because all she would have had to do was to reach in my coat pocket and lift a thousand dollars in chips and I never would have known the difference."

Louise was loyal to the part, never disclosing for whom she was spying, and Dusko let it ride. No sense in spoiling a nice evening, he figured, and besides, the employer might later send a replacement.

»

By fall 1943 Dusko's nerves were shot. He worried constantly about his parents, Ivo, and Johnny, not to mention another assassination attempt. Each day he lived five lives—German spy, British spy, Yugoslav diplomat, import/export businessman, and international playboy. He was drinking and smoking heavily, popping Benzedrine to stay in top form during the day, and sleeping pills to catch a few winks at night.

Internally, nine ulcers were eating their way through his stomach.

While he struggled to maintain work and cover, Jebsen's troubles with the Gestapo and SD were coming to a head. At summer's end MI6 had received a report that Johnny wanted to remain in Lisbon, and that "under no circumstances" would he return to Germany. On September 4 they heard that he had not been allowed to remain in Portugal, and would be traveling to Madrid and staying at the Ritz.

»

On the evening of September 13 Dusko left Lisbon and arrived at Whitchurch Airport at eight the next morning. Tar and Ian met him in London and drove to the Clock House, where they unloaded the Yugoslav diplomatic bags. In addition to a large number of silk stockings, the pouches included the fake Yugoslav seals, three cover addresses, an envelope with £2,500 (five hundred £5 notes), an envelope with $2,000 (twenty $100 notes), two German questionnaires, materials for making secret ink, a Leica camera with six rolls of film, a Penguin edition of John Galsworthy's *The Country House* (phrases from which Dusko was to use for coding messages), and a German wireless set contained in a sealed parcel. Inside the lid of the radio transmitter were instructions for setup, frequencies, times to contact, and call signs for the transmitter and control station.

Later that morning Wilson sent the British currency to the Bank of England for inspection. Of the five hundred £5 notes, 152 were forgeries. Dusko couldn't let von Karsthoff know, however; he'd have to wait two weeks and then report that a few notes he had used were found to be illegitimate, and that the police had asked how he received them. Naturally, he would ask the major to send replacements.

Back at the office Ian put the Galsworthy code book in the B1A safe and delivered the secret ink materials to a Professor Briscoe. In a follow-up letter, Wilson informed the professor that Popov's procedure was "to take the hollow part of a pen nib, put some of the crystals in it and then heat them by holding a match or cigarette lighter under it. When the crystals have melted he takes a match and dips the end into the molten mixture, turning the match stick round and round till the composition forms a match head on it." Popov was then to use the match for writing. Professor Briscoe, presumably with MI10, was asked to determine the crystal formula and duplicate the process.

Ian also placed in the file a note Popov had given him to clarify wireless messages while Dusko was in the U.S. Captioned "THE HAIRLESS DOCTOR," the note stated:

> Johnny explained to me that the equivalent of $10,000, which I was supposed to receive from Miss Mason of Boston was paid to Mrs. Ruza Simic in Belgrade by my brother, who is supposed to be "the hairless doctor." . . . I was supposed to understand that "the hairless doctor—Gonorrhoea specialist" is my brother because as a young doctor he worked on a new treatment for the cure of Gonorrhoea which required intensive concentration and to force himself not to go out he cut his hair very short.

»

Unknown to the Germans, agent PAULA—the "hairless Gonorrhoea doctor"—would soon become double agent DREADNOUGHT, Dusko's fifth subagent.

Meanwhile, Dusko received his answer—or at least strong evidence—as to who placed the bomb under his car. Days after he returned to London he met a U.S. military attaché at a social function. The man took an immediate and suspicious interest in him, Popov found, and asked to meet with Dusko later. About this time, Arthur Thurston got back to Wilson.

"During my recent visit to Lisbon," the FBI attaché wrote, "both the Counselor of the Legation and the Military Attaché inquired of me as to whether I had any information concerning Dusan Popov. These men advised that Popov had been in Lisbon several times during the past few years . . . and were concerned over the fact that he was possibly working for the enemy and were of the opinion that detailed inquiries should be initiated concerning his activities."

Thurston did not ask whether they had tried to kill Popov, but advised that Dusko was under British control and that they should refrain from making any inquiries, since "such action might endanger the agent's position."

Wilson did not share this information with Popov, but "C" later told Dusko that he suspected the assassination attempt was by Americans who had found out that he was a German agent, but had not discovered that he was a *double* agent.

»

On September 20 Wilson prepared for Tar and the Double-Cross Committee a seventeen-page report summarizing the significant information Dusko acquired on his trip. He began by stating that "TRICYCLE reports everything material to us with complete integrity and an exceptionally high degree of accuracy." As an example, Wilson stated that Dusko had accurately determined the real meanings of ten code words the Abwehr used in their telegrams. Ian also highlighted, however, a disturbing conversation between Jebsen, Kammler, and Popov:

> KARSTHOFF and KAMMLER asked TRICYCLE whether he had seen BALLOON much. TRICYCLE said he had seen him only occasionally and avoided talking to him. JEBSEN said that no man could have written all

> the letters BALLOON had written without being caught, and that KAMMLER had said to him—JEBSEN,—"No spy could write for three years on the same paper regularly without being caught."

Popov's relationship with Kammler was tenuous. Although not technically Dusko's boss, the Abwehr I man often acted as his case officer and sent reports to the Tirpitzufer about his work, which was universally regarded as bad. Kammler was working against Dusko, Johnny had said, and reported to Berlin that all of IVAN's material was "phoney or invented or cut out of newspapers." Fortunately, Wilson wrote, von Karsthoff hated Kammler and either didn't forward some of the reports or redacted them to mitigate IVAN's failures.

Ludovico then had Kammler recalled to Berlin, Popov told Ian, using the oldest trick in the book: "I learned from ELIZABETH," he wrote in his report, "that the First Secretary of the German Legation helped KARSTHOFF to get rid of KAMMLER because of a love affair between KAMMLER's fiancee, who was working in the legation, and the First Secretary." What von Karsthoff didn't realize was that Kammler could do more harm to Jebsen and Popov in Berlin than in Lisbon.

Dusko's relationship with Jebsen, on the other hand, couldn't have been stronger. "Johnny's attitude towards me is that of a great friend," he told Ian, "and I do not think there is anything, even very dangerous, that Johnny would not do for me."

Together, Dusko reported, they worked out a plan to get Johnny to England. On the German side, Johnny would pitch to his Abwehr superiors that he could better supervise IVAN and other agents working in Britain if he relocated to London. On the British side, Dusko would pitch MI5 on the benefits of having Johnny formally admitted as a double agent, and would work on getting him a visa. To assure effective communication, they established codes for telegrams. If Johnny wrote, "Because of illness cannot carry on with business," it meant that he was in acute physical danger. If Dusko sent a message to Johnny saying, "Operation successful Maria feeling better," it meant that Jebsen had received a visa to England.

Ian Wilson's September 20 memo also noted that Kammler was replaced by a Major Schreiber. Aloys Schreiber was Bavarian, fifty years old, dark, bald, and carried scars on the back of both hands. A doctor of chemistry, Schreiber had apparently been burned by acid.

Virtually everyone at MI5 and MI6, including "C," read Ian's report. In a memo to his colleagues the following day, Colonel Robertson noted: "Had it not been for the fact that we have ISOS [radio intercepts] against which to check the report I feel that we should not have believed the greater part of it and we should almost certainly have come to the conclusion that JEBSEN was double-crossing TRICYCLE."

The feedback from the intelligence officers was that everyone wanted Dusko to return to Lisbon and dig for details. Robertson agreed: "TRICYCLE is shortly going back to Lisbon at the request of the Germans and it seems to me that we are in a good position to play for very high stakes."

The stakes in Lisbon, however, would be upstaged by an unstable gambler in Madrid.

»

Around September 6 Jebsen had checked in to room 530 at the Madrid Ritz. Over the next several days he solicited the advice of two anti-Nazi Abwehr officers, Moldenhauer and Ruser. Unbeknownst to Johnny, Ruser had contacted British Intelligence about a year earlier and bore his own risks. While not actively engaging the German, MI6 had given Ruser the code name JUNIOR.

Jebsen, Moldenhauer, and Ruser shared similar fates. All knew that Kammler had been recalled to Berlin, and it seemed probable that he would betray at least Johnny and Ruser to the Gestapo. "You know of the charges you are up against, don't you?" Kammler had said to Ruser before departing. Moldenhauer, closely aligned with Ruser and Jebsen, would surely be suspect as well. But Johnny had the greatest risk; he was convinced that before leaving, Kammler had placed a microphone in his apartment and had secretly recorded a conversation between Johnny and Dusko when they discussed helping the British. Kammler, Johnny believed, would share this recording with the Abwehr, and probably the Gestapo, upon his arrival.

Johnny's currency troubles compounded the danger, and circumstantial evidence mounted. First, there was the summons from the Tirpitzufer to return to Berlin. Shortly thereafter a business associate in Frankfurt sent Johnny a telegram stating that he'd risk his life if he returned. Then Freddy von Kageneck, Johnny and Dusko's college buddy, sent word from Paris that Johnny should escape immediately to the home of Honorah Fitzgerald, their mutual friend in Dublin. Days later an Abwehr colleague in Berlin cabled that "the old Gestapo trouble" had resurfaced.

The pressure was too much.

On September 21 Johnny dictated a suicide letter to Moldenhauer. For Dusko, the note meant losing his best friend.

For IVAN, it was far worse.

SHOTS RANG OUT

Kenneth Benton, an MI6 agent in Madrid, recalled being summoned to the British Embassy one morning in late September 1943. In an upstairs room reserved for escaped POWs, a visitor would be waiting under guard. When Benton arrived he saw "a small man who was chain-smoking and looking rather sweaty and apprehensive." The man announced that he was an Abwehr officer and that he was there to ask the British for protection.

"You're in trouble?"

"The Gestapo are on my tail, because I made a report on their dealings in forged British bank notes."

"Have they followed you here?"

"No, I shook them off."

Benton asked for his name, and Johnny gave it, saying, "I suppose you are Mr. Benton." The SIS officer jumped. No one was supposed to know he was an agent, much less know his name.

Johnny explained that the Abwehr Madrid office had frequent discussions about the MI6 staff. Jebsen knew, for example, that Benton had been an assistant to a Vienna agent named Kendrick. Somewhat embarrassed, Benton asked what the Abwehr thought of the Madrid station. The general feeling, Johnny said, was that Benton and a man named Ivens were "sly foxes," but that Miss Gillott, a visa examiner, was who really ran the office. Pleased that Jebsen's information was at least incorrect there, Benton asked him to continue.

"I know one Abwehr agent," Johnny said, "a man I recruited myself, who has either been turned already or would go over to your side at the drop of a hat."

Benton asked for the name.

"Dusan Popov, a Yugoslav. He's a prolific agent, run from both Belgrade and Lisbon."

The discussion continued for a couple hours, Benton remembered, and Jebsen suggested he'd leave by the service entrance. Kenneth shook his head. Johnny would be staying in the embassy that night, Benton said, and the next day he'd move to a safe house. Jebsen gratefully consented.

That evening Benton sent an encoded summary of the meeting to London, and by ten the next morning a "Most Immediate" message had come back. "ARTIST is telling you the truth," London advised. "He is a *Forscher*, and well-known to us. Popov is one of our most successful double agents, pseudonym TRICYCLE. This contact has great potential value. Use utmost caution, but try to obtain names of other agents he has recruited, in case there is one we have missed."

The following morning Benton had the safe house watched and asked the French to check the British Embassy service entrance to make sure it was not under surveillance. With both clear, he escorted Johnny to the flat and continued debriefing. Jebsen gave him a copy of his suicide note, which was addressed to "Herr Oberstleutnant" (presumably a Colonel Toering) and "Herr Major" (presumably Munzinger), his Abwehr supervisors. Moldenhauer had the original, Jebsen said, but had not sent it.

Benton read the letter, not realizing that "Iwan" was Dusko and "Paula" was Ivo:

> *I cannot return to Germany because I would no longer be able to look you in the eyes.*
>
> *For the last fortnight I have been carrying a secret around with me. . . . I have therefore decided . . . to tell you the whole truth and take the consequences upon myself.*
>
> *When I met Iwan in Portugal, I had the gravest doubts, due to my discussions with Kammler in Berlin, that he was still genuine. . . . Shortly before his departure Iwan then confessed to me that he had not been genuine for a long time. . . . Torn as I was, either to fulfill my duty as a soldier or to break my word given to a friend, there was only one way out, and I have now decided to take it. . . .*
>
> *I know that a Court Martial would condemn me to death for what I have done. . . . By taking this step myself, I am hoping to save the "Amt" the shame and my wife the disgrace to bear a soiled name. . . . Do not be afraid that there will be a scandal. I shall cover up all traces carefully, I shall send*

my things to my Father Confessor for the poor. Then I shall take poison and swim far out into the sea. It may be days before my corpse will be washed up and it will then be no longer recognisable. . . .

You can only use Paula in future in Serbia as people sent to him by England are almost certain to come into contact with Iwan who then converts them.

Johnny mentioned that his plan was to have a witness—Moldenhauer—verify his state of despondency to give the note credibility. Feigning despair, he had dictated the letter and then made a copy. His intent, of which Moldenhauer was ignorant, was to send the letter and have the British immediately fly him to Gibraltar, and then to England. Would the British play along?

Benton forwarded the information to London.

At noon British Intelligence cabled back, asking for details about Jebsen's danger, stating that "at all costs" Johnny should be prevented from sending his letter. The telegram further instructed that Jebsen must keep his position with the Abwehr, and that MI6 would provide him sanctuary only when *they* felt it necessary. London suspected that Johnny exaggerated his danger to rush the British into an unnecessary evacuation.

The next day, September 24, Dusko cabled Johnny:

CALM DOWN. MY GENUINENESS TOWARDS THE GERMANS MUST AT ALL COSTS BE SAFE-GUARDED. ALL YOUR ACTIONS MUST PRIMARILY BE DIRECTED TO THAT OBJECT TO PROTECT BOTH OUR FAMILIES AND FRIENDS. IT WOULD MEAN DISASTER FOR THEM IF YOU CAME OVER HERE NOW. YOU MUST THEREFORE AT ALL COSTS KEEP YOUR POSITION IN THE ABWEHR AT LEAST UNTIL I GET BACK.

As Dusko and everyone in British Intelligence knew, if Johnny suddenly disappeared the Germans would suspect foul play not only with him, but with his principal agent, IVAN, and the entire Yugoslav network. Johnny would have to sit tight.

Four days later Ian Wilson coordinated the flurry of telegrams and evaluated the risk. As MI5 feared, Johnny's letter had already been leaked. "At once," Ian wrote, Moldenhauer had disclosed the matter to an SIS informant. The breach didn't sit well with Tar, and he sent a mitigating proposal to

Masterman, Marriott, and Wilson. "Should Johnny Jebsen decide to throw his lot unconditionally with us," Robertson wrote, he should contact Erich Schroeder, Lisbon SD chief, and present the following story:

> I have been approached by the British and have had several meetings with them . . . At these meetings the British proposed that (a) I should pass through as genuine intelligence British "Spiel" material. (b) I should disclose such German agents as I have cognisance of, and (c) I should continue in my capacity as an Abwehr recruiter and that I should recruit persons designated by the British I.S. who should then operate as double agents.

Boldly suggesting that Jebsen approach the Germans for a triple-cross, Robertson's quadruple-cross strategy was outlandish. But he was not done. Jebsen would say the British claimed that one in three Abwehr officers were in a similar position and were informing MI6 of all Abwehr matters. Johnny would then make an oblique (and false) reference to a Czech already double-crossing. The Germans would identify the agent as OSTRO,* and would assume that his case officer, Kammler, had also been turned. Robertson's scheme would continue with Jebsen arranging a second meeting with Schroeder, but on the following morning they would find that Johnny had been "kidnapped and spirited away."

Unknown to Tar, the Germans had already discussed kidnapping Ruser, and were making their own plans for Johnny.

»

The following day Masterman, Marriott, Foley, and Wilson met to discuss Robertson's idea and what to do. They could either secretly fly Jebsen to London and acquire his inside knowledge or, better yet, leave him in Madrid and operate him as a double. Foley informed them that MI6 was already referring to Johnny under the code name ARTIST, informally utilizing him as an informant. For now, the group decided, they would not implement Robertson's proposal, but would seek more information on the extent of Johnny's danger. His role as an Abwehr insider was extremely valuable, and one British Intelligence would not give up lightly.

---

* Paul Fidrmuc, who had recently survived poisoning.

A week or so later, Kenneth Benton remembered, London transferred Johnny to Lisbon. "I was very sorry to have to part with ARTIST," he wrote, "because he was an interesting and well-educated man and very good company." In Lisbon, Benton added, Johnny informed MI6— "with a visible shudder"—"that the Gestapo had a trained hijack team, skilled in entering foreign countries, seizing a wanted man and smuggling him back across the frontiers without arousing suspicion."

The Ablege Kommandos, Jebsen explained, were experts in kidnapping and elimination. They were said to have a tasteless and fast-acting poison which could be added to any food or drink. After twenty minutes the substance left no trace in the body and the victim would clear an autopsy. Where poison was not practicable, shooting was adopted. In Spain, Johnny said, the Germans had full cooperation of the police and Falange.*

While less formalized, the Abwehr had similar capabilities. That very year—1943—a snatch squad was ordered to kidnap a German driver who had been passing information to the British. A team of three was given the address of the man's mistress in downtown Madrid and told when he would be visiting. Their instructions were to overpower the man and take him to Abwehr headquarters without commotion—in broad daylight.

"We were all in civilian clothes," one of the kidnappers remembered. "Each carried a pistol and I also had a few tins containing cotton chloroform pads. . . . While W. waited in the car, ready to drive the captured deserter through the town quickly and quietly, I and the other man went into the house. . . . The door into the next room opened and there stood the man I was after. . . . A few shots rang out as I ran after him and tried to overpower him, but he crumpled up, killed by his own gun."

The snatch teams, however, were only the formal options.

»

Over the next few weeks Dusko worked on the escape route, where Britain, Germany, Yugoslavia, and Spain all spun in an unbalanced and invisible carousel. While Jebsen would have to work out the details on the German side, the broad picture was that Johnny would coordinate with Ivo in Belgrade and select up to a dozen people. Von Karsthoff, in turn, would work with

* A fascist political party and movement founded in 1933, and unified and absorbed by Franco in 1937.

Johnny and Ivo to select German agents to slip into the group. Johnny would coordinate with German authorities to arrange passage through France and into Spain. Dusko would meet the group in San Sebastian—twelve miles from the French border—where he would greet the German agents as old friends and pass them to the British Consul, who would arrange travel to England. Von Karsthoff would believe he was sending genuine German spies into the group, but Ivo, who would be handling final selection, assured Dusko and the British that all would be double agents.

The missing link in the escape chain was Dusko's visa to Spain. With the rise of a new Croatian state, relations between the Yugoslav government-in-exile and the Franco government were strained. British Intelligence had tried to get the Yugoslav charge d'affaires in Madrid to push Spain for Dusko's visa, but he refused, distrusting Popov and working independently on his own route. The Yugoslav Legation in Lisbon tried to help but was also unsuccessful.

Von Karsthoff told Dusko that the Abwehr had the power to deliver the visa, but the notion was dismissed since the British would realize Popov had received German help. If Dusko could contact some influential Yugoslavs in London, Ludovico suggested—friends of escapees—they could push the British into giving Popov a passport, with which he could acquire the Spanish visa. Dusko agreed.

The last piece was the escapees themselves. They would have to be notified—in a fashion approved by the British and Germans—to prepare for the journey. Each escapee, it was decided, would receive the following notice:

> *You will receive this letter through Dr. P. He is a friend of ours and he is in touch with us. He has an opportunity through some friends of his of helping you to escape from Yugoslavia and go to Spain. If you want to come over do exactly as Dr. P. tells you, even if it seems rather peculiar to you. In San Sebastian you will be met by a Yugoslav official who will send you on to England. In case you have not got the necessary funds for the tickets etc., Dr. P. will advance it to you. Keep all this very secret and burn this letter.*

»

During this time Johnny had second thoughts about his double-cross. The stigma of being branded a traitor weighed heavily on him, as well as the danger to his wife if he were exposed. He suggested to MI6 that he wanted to break off communication, but the Madrid station told him that he'd taken an irrevocable step. They would, however, allow Jebsen to be an "unconscious" source, discreetly delivering information to TRICYCLE and other agents.

Johnny agreed, with three conditions: (a) any German agents in the UK who were uncovered by information supplied by Johnny were to be treated as prisoners of war rather than spies (who would be executed); (b) the British would use "utmost caution" not to expose Johnny, even indirectly; and (c) Johnny would have liberty to travel after the war. MI6, meanwhile, prepared for an emergency. Frank Foley contacted an SOE agent in Madrid and told him to be on standby for an evacuation.

Johnny continued business as usual with von Karsthoff, and together they worked the German side of the route. On October 18 he submitted to the major a lengthy outline of how the operation would work. IVAN had received approval of the Yugoslav government-in-exile, he wrote, to slip through from Switzerland and Serbia to England specified Serbian officers. PAULA (Ivo) would purchase German alien passports to allow travel from Belgrade to France. The group would travel to Biarritz, where Johnny or an agent of his would receive them. The Yugoslav government would pay 4,000 French francs per escapee to bribe two Customs officials at the border. Johnny would escort the group to Madrid, where they would be handed over to the English. Von Karsthoff, Johnny, and PAULA would select German agents to include in the group, who would be treated no differently than the others. Neither the Yugoslav government nor the British suspected foul play, Johnny assured Ludovico.

The following day von Karsthoff notified Berlin of the plan, including Jebsen's full report. He explained that the Franco–Spanish border agent would be "Carlos," an Argentine employed by Jebsen's firm in Hamburg. Noting that the operation was "very delicate," the major added: "For safety's sake attention is drawn to the possibility of endangering also Ivan I* in case of suspicion or failure of the slipping-through operation."

While von Karsthoff was carefully protecting Popov's identity against the enemy, Robertson was incorporating Jebsen into the British fold. Informing him of Dusko's upcoming trip to Lisbon, Tar asked Johnny to list his local Abwehr supporters. Jebsen identified four: von Karsthoff, two secretaries, and Dr. Aloys Schreiber.

---

* Dusko was Ivan I, his sub-agent (Dickie Metcalfe/BALLOON) was Ivan II.

»

Dusko returned to Lisbon on November 10, this time checking into the Aviz. Given the significance and heightened danger of Popov's work, Ian Wilson arrived two days later to assist if necessary. To their mild surprise, Dusko was received exceedingly well. In a report back to London on the twenty-first, Wilson quoted Jebsen: "SCHREIBER has written to Berlin that in his opinion TRICYCLE is absolutely reliable and should be given biggest and most secret tasks for big money." Von Karsthoff appeared to concur. At one of their first meetings, the major gave Popov three new questionnaires and $15,000. Dusko deposited the money in the hotel safe.

Jebsen, in turn, began his new role, feeding MI6 an ongoing stream of information about Abwehr officers and their positions on various matters. For the first time, it seemed, Johnny and Dusko were working in tandem; the former gleaning information, the latter planting misinformation.

»

The smooth sailing lasted less than a month. On October 26 Johnny informed MI6 that the Abwehr had an informant—"with a name something like Martins"—who worked in the U.S. Embassy in Lisbon. Weeks later Martins stopped by the British Embassy and confessed that he had been supplying cover addresses for two German agents in Britain, BALLOON and GELATINE. Martins knew their real names, too. The Germans had been using his firm, the Portuguese said, to send payments to the agents.

The dilemma for Dusko was disconcerting: If Metcalfe and Gaertner stopped writing, the Germans would assume they had been arrested, and that Dusko's arrest would follow. But if they continued to write, Martins would suspect they were double agents and would inform the Abwehr. If the former, the Germans would cut Dusko off; if the latter, his cover was blown.

The British brainstormed. Wilson, Robertson, and Foley compared notes and came to a quick resolution. On November 28 London cabled Lisbon with a plan:

> MARTINS should be interviewed <u>in person</u> and told to carry on normally, but should be sworn to secrecy. He should be both complimented and frightened, but should be promised a reward if he carried out our

```
instructions. The Germans should be encouraged to
warn BALLOON and GELATINE to lay off the addresses.
```

The following day Wilson reported back. Martins had been interviewed, he said, but "cannot be trusted to keep his mouth shut indefinitely if he continues to receive correspondence, which after a time he must guess is controlled." Ian suggested shutting down Friedl's correspondence and waiting to see what happened.

»

About this time Dusko went to the Aviz front desk to retrieve his package from the safe. A few moments later, the employee returned empty-handed. The safe was empty.

The missing money had two possible explanations, Dusko knew: Either an employee had stolen the package, or the Abwehr was on to him. The former seemed unlikely, since an employee would not have known the package contained money. More importantly, how could he hope to have survived a hotel investigation? The only realistic explanation was the Germans. If Dusko's cover had been blown, as Wilson feared, the Abwehr would have wanted to retrieve their $15,000. But how would they have gotten into the safe, even if they assumed he had stashed the money there?

Unknown to Dusko, a man was working in the hotel who was not an employee; unknown to the hotel, he had a safe key.

TRUTH SERUM

Some days later von Karsthoff returned the money, explaining that an overzealous agent had assumed the package contained diplomatic papers. Ludovico didn't say how the man knew that Popov had placed something in the safe, and Dusko didn't ask. Later that month Johnny told MI6 that the hotel agent was highly valued by the Germans, and until this incident he had been known only by Jebsen, Schreiber, and one other Abwehr officer. The man was not actually an Aviz employee, Johnny explained; the Abwehr paid him 2,000 escudos per month and the hotel allowed him to work there—"for camouflage purposes." Johnny didn't know his name, but he knew his role: When English guests checked in, the agent would retrieve their passports so the Abwehr could make copies. Otherwise, he lingered about to "supervise" foreigners staying at the hotel.

Neither Popov nor MI6 desired supervision by this man—whom the British had code named VIPER—but for the time being they'd have to live with a snake in their midst.

»

In mid-November Popov was meeting regularly with Jebsen and von Karsthoff, both giving him plenty to pass to London. Jebsen's situation with the Gestapo and the SD had not improved, he told Dusko, and Major Munzinger had informed Johnny not to return to Berlin—even if Munzinger ordered it. Jebsen's protection still lay with the Abwehr, but that status was now determined by an unusual source: Ivo Popov.

Fully incorporated into the TRICYCLE net as double agent DREADNOUGHT, Ivo worked tirelessly in the underground, assisting in sabotage and counterintelligence. Dr. Popov's intellect, charm, and powers of persuasion were making significant inroads in Abwehr leadership, and like Dusko, he made the most of the opportunity. Ian Wilson summarized the British windfall: "ARTIST describes TRICYCLE's brother as having the most dominating personality of anyone he has met, and an exceptionally cool and keen brain in a crisis." In a very short time Ivo "[has] gained a tremendous influence with the Abwehr officials he has met, and is extremely highly regarded by them. In fact he is now in a position where he is able to use his influence to help ARTIST rather than vice-versa." So trusted was Dr. Popov that Munzinger stored 25,000 Swiss francs in Ivo's name for safekeeping when Germany collapsed.

Ivo's rising status was due in part to the fact that he was one of the Abwehr's chief sources of information on the activities of Draža Mihailovic, the Serbian general leading the Chetnik resistance guerillas. As agent DREADNOUGHT, however, he was feeding the Germans selected misinformation dreamt up by MI5.

Dr. Popov's influence was timely. When Colonel Hansen replaced Pieckenbrock as head of Abwehr I, Kammler had made a direct appeal to undermine Dusko and Johnny. Ivo met with the colonel shortly thereafter, however, and, in Johnny's words, "cooked him." Hansen now believed in the genuineness of his two Lisbon agents, and suspected that Kammler was working for the Gestapo.

Dusko, meanwhile, was using his considerable charm to keep von Karsthoff in tow. The major was enjoying happy days, driving a new Cadillac and entertaining at the Quinta de Condé, a sprawling farm near Cintra. At several meetings in late November, Ludovico expressed his pleasure in Popov's work. Even amid warning signs, von Karsthoff was impervious, blinded by Dusko's charisma and his ability to create answers and excuses on the fly. The major had even received a report which stated that IVAN was spending considerable time with Yugoslavs and the British and had "adopted a pro-British attitude."

Von Karsthoff congratulated him.

The British-friendly veneer was necessary, Ludovico acknowledged, for Popov to accomplish his mission. Along those lines the major asked him to investigate Beatrice Terry, a woman staying at the Aviz who had caught the attention of VIPER. She was a British spy, von Karsthoff said, and had come from Chile on a Czech passport. The major described her as a tall blonde, "ugly but with sex appeal." He also told Popov that when Dusko returned to

London, he should set up his radio outside of London. "It would be a silly thing," he said, "for you to be killed by German weapons."

»

During this time Ivo had recruited into the double-cross network an old friend of his and Dusko's, Marquis Frano de Bona. The de Bona family, like the Popovs, were well known Dubrovnik aristocrats, tracing their heritage in the city to the fifteenth century. Dusko knew Frano well, and Frano jumped at the opportunity to help defeat the Nazis. He went first to Belgrade for Abwehr debriefing and instruction by Munzinger, and then to Paris for wireless radio training. After several weeks he was given the code name GUTTMANN and cleared for duties as IVAN's radioman in London. Munzinger asked Major Helmut Wiegand, the hard-drinking Paris chief, to coordinate de Bona's transit to Madrid, but Wiegand sent a note to Johnny suggesting that the task would be difficult. Johnny was convinced, he told MI5, that Wiegand magnified the assignment's complexity simply to schedule a trip to Madrid or Lisbon.

On November 19 Johnny went to Madrid to coordinate with the Germans de Bona's arrival—a dry run through the escape route. A week later Dusko joined him to instruct British Passport Control. Around December 1 de Bona arrived and MI6 coordinated his transit to Gibraltar. Giving him the code name FREAK, SIS provided Frano with a false identity—Canadian Peter Banwedon—and travel documents for London. For the British, he was added to the TRICYCLE net to operate the radio for Popov, GELATINE, and METEOR. For the Germans, GUTTMANN was to make acquaintance with the highest lords of English society—particularly colleagues of Yugoslavia's King Peter, his friend exiled in London—and encourage them to seek terms with Germany.

Johnny and Dusko returned to Lisbon on December 3 and 4, respectively, only to find new squatters. Three new German intelligence officers had arrived, including two from the SD. The Abwehr had been steadily losing power and Schellenberg, the Nazi intelligence chief, had been gaining. Whereas Abwehr agents previously had been off-limits to the SD and the Gestapo, the Nazi intelligence arm now boldly ignored protocol.

Around December 6, Wolfgang Henss, the lanky SD chief in Porto, gave Jebsen a questionnaire to pass to Popov for his upcoming trip to London. The questionnaire was comprehensive, asking for information on everything from the English rationing system to the significance of changes in the English Cabinet. IVAN was asked to acquire copies of publications like the *Socialist Appeal* and the *British Weekly*, as well as documents pertaining to conferences in Moscow, Cairo, and Casablanca. Dusko submitted it to MI6 and a copy was sent to London. J. C. Masterman passed it along to Victor Cavendish-Bentinck, chair of the Joint Intelligence Committee, and Frank Foley forwarded a copy to the War Office.

On December 20 Major Wiegand arrived, and for the next several days he and Dusko went over details of the escape route. A condition precedent to Dusko's running of the operation, which Wiegand and the Abwehr accepted, was that Ivo would maintain sole authority over escapees selected. Explaining to Ian Wilson that his discussions with Wiegand were delaying his departure, Dusko wrote: "The man is very pedantic and I think it would be very unwise not to discuss the 'smuggling' with him in all detail."

Just before Popov left, Henss gave him a second questionnaire. When Dusko arrived in London on January 5, 1944, he carried a cache of espionage. John Marriott, who picked Popov up in Paddington, itemized the spyware:

1. Two envelopes containing $10,070 for Dusko's expenses
2. An envelope containing $1,380 for GELATINE
3. The principal SD questionnaire
4. The last-minute SD questionnaire
5. Microphotograph instructions and codes for the wireless transmitter
6. A list of seven new cover addresses
7. An envelope from Abwehr agent Hans Brandes to be given to a Mr. Rackwell
8. A code book, *Histoire des Etats-Unis*, by Andre Maurois
9. A report from Johnny on Germany
10. A package for GELATINE containing a five-page questionnaire and two styptic pencils
11. A paper containing the name and address of an Abwehr paymaster in Tangier

Marriott placed the dollars and documents in the MI5 safe and gave Dusko £250 for incidentals.

One of Popov's first stops was at the Public Control Department to obtain a visitor's driver's license. His card provided: "Dr. Dusan Popov, c/o Section

15c, Foreign Office, London, is hereby licensed to drive MOTOR CARS and REVERSIBLE TRICYCLES."

»

February 1944 was a tumultuous time for Britain and Germany. The Allies had launched Operation Fortitude South, the deception campaign preceding the invasion of France, and difficulties mounted. On February 18 Hitler sacked Admiral Canaris and ordered the Abwehr abolished, its functions to be assumed by Himmler's Reich Security Head Office (RSHA), governing body of the Gestapo and the SD. Abwehr station chiefs, including von Karsthoff, were summarily replaced as responsibility shifted to RSHA Amt (office) VI and foreign intelligence chief Walter Schellenberg.

British and American generals, including Eisenhower, realized that the war hinged on the invasion of France. The Atlantic front, however, was guarded by sixty infantry and nine Panzer divisions, all led by Germany's best, Field Marshal Erwin Rommel. The Allied landing spot—Normandy—would be exceedingly tough as it was; if Rommel placed the feared Fifteenth Army and one or more Panzer units there, the invasion would fail, perhaps costing the Allies the war. The goal was to convince the Germans that the Allies were attacking in the Pas de Calais area, some 150 miles northeast of Normandy, and that the best Allied commander, General George S. Patton, would be leading a massive notional army, the First United States Army Group (FUSAG). To assist the charade, the British would place dummy installations, landing craft, field hospitals, artillery, and trucks at Dover, the closest point across the channel.

The invasion deception success—at least in terms of direct misinformation—would fall largely on the shoulders of Dusko and a Spaniard named Juan Pujol (codenamed GARBO). "You and Garbo vie for the number-one spot on the German spy list for over a year," Colonel Robertson had told Dusko as the operation began. While not paired, the two agents provided a compelling team. What Popov found appalling—pushing a scrivener's pen—Pujol found appealing. Juan was regularly spending six to eight hours a day composing secret letters and radio transmissions. From his perch in London, he was sending hundreds of messages to Berlin from fourteen agents and eleven well-placed contacts—all fictional. In like fashion, Dusko found long hours of intense SD interrogation—often six or more—exhilarating. The duel of wits, the danger, the play for unlimited stakes, all suited Dusko's madcap desire for challenge and adventure.

But thrusting Popov into the bowels of German Intelligence was risky. Given the close calls with his cover and Johnny's tenuous situation with the Gestapo, MI5 and the Double-Cross Committee wondered whether the TRICYCLE net could be used at all. If Jebsen were tortured, they feared, he'd reveal the double dealing of Dusko, Ivo, METEOR, WORM, and others. But Dusko's influence on the highest levels of German Intelligence—perhaps at its zenith in late 1943—had to be utilized. In a memo to Colonel Robertson on December 20, Ian Wilson had urged his boss to risk it, and continue the net's activity: "There can be no doubt that at the moment TRICYCLE's stock in the eyes of the Abwehr is extremely high," Ian wrote. "He was treated like a hero by the Abwehr in Lisbon, and SCHREIBER, in addition to obtaining authority to pay him for three months in advance, took steps to obtain for him questions of the highest grade. Berlin gave a favourable evaluation of his material and I have myself seen a fulsome personal letter of congratulation from MUNTZINGER to ARTIST."

Wilson knew, too, that Aloys Schreiber's star also had risen and that Aloys was now one of the Abwehr's most influential senior officers. "The fact that SCHREIBER is a very strong supporter of TRICYCLE is of extreme importance," he noted, "because SCHREIBER is due at any minute . . . to become head of the western part of the Army Intelligence Section of the Abwehr. SCHREIBER will be responsible for passing on TRICYCLE's material . . . and it seems virtually certain that he will give that material the highest possible backing."

But it wasn't just the information; it was that Dusko Popov was a known entity. "Quite apart from the merits of the material, [Schreiber] is likely to pay more attention to the reports of an agent of whom he has personal knowledge than the reports which come to him from out-stations from agents of whose personal particulars he has no knowledge [i.e., GARBO and his stable of notional sub-agents]."

Returning to the risk involved, Wilson made his final point: "In the case of every double agent, however well run, there is always the chance that something will go wrong. . . . I do not believe that this risk at the present time is any greater in the case of the TRICYCLE group than with any other agent, and I think we are justified in thinking that TRICYCLE's material will be more strongly backed by Eins Heer [Army Espionage] than that of other agents."

Three days later the Double-Cross Committee discussed Wilson's memo, and the risk/reward gamble of continuing Dusko's operations and net. At the bottom of his original copy, Ian jotted a short note: "Discussed at XX Cttee 23/12/43. No ban."; the committee and W Board voted to continue running the TRICYCLE team. While various agents, including GELATINE, would contribute to the overall operation, the four principal operatives of strategic deception were TRICYCLE, GARBO, FREAK, and BRUTUS.

But the Allies had a problem: ARTIST's knowledge of GARBO. When Dusko returned to London in January, he had brought with him a report summarizing conversations with Jebsen. Included was a list Johnny prepared—as evidence of his loyalty to the Allies—of a number of the Abwehr's best agents in Lisbon. ARABEL, the German's code name for GARBO, topped the chart. Pujol's case officer, Tomás Harris, was petrified. If the British took no action against Pujol, Harris argued, Jebsen would realize that ARABEL was in fact a controlled British agent. If so, the army of notional sub-agents created by GARBO would be exposed, as well as the entire Operation Fortitude scheme. Harris was aware of Jebsen's relationship with Popov, but stressed that under duress or torture, Johnny could talk and bring down the house of cards.

Harris had a point and the committee discussed three options. They could evacuate Jebsen from Portugal, but if they did so the Germans would realize that Johnny had been captured or turned, and would assume that his contacts would be compromised. Alternatively, the British could do nothing and hope for the best, praying that the SD and the Gestapo had more pressing issues than the bona fides of ARTIST and GARBO. This had little appeal, too, since the SD and the Gestapo were already investigating Jebsen. The third option was proactive but messy.

Assassinate Johnny.

The committee discussed having MI6 do the job but decided that such action would trigger a massive German investigation that might expose Jebsen's relationship with the British in general, and Popov in particular. The committee opted to do nothing.

On the German side, intelligence gathering became at once chaotic and intense. Schellenberg's Amt VI and the General Staff's Amt Mil had to absorb some 13,000 Abwehr employees, while ferreting out incompetent and untrustworthy agents. The SD and the Gestapo had long disdained and distrusted the Abwehr, Canaris in particular, and Schellenberg inaugurated a spring cleaning. Popov's two principal supervisors, Major von Karsthoff and Major Munzinger, would soon be replaced. For the immediate future, Dusko would be managed by a team of SD and Abwehr officers.

With the invasion pieces in place, the game began. Popov returned to Portugal on February 26 and fired the first salvo of Operation Fortitude South—lies posed as questionnaire answers. The pressing issue for the Germans in early 1944 was the activity at Dover. It was the logical point from which to launch an invasion of France, and the place to which most radio traffic pointed. Were the British making preparations? Was an infrastructure being created from which to launch a massive campaign? What did IVAN see? Were troops already assembled?

Dusko's report to the Germans confirmed the Dover hoax:

> During this tour I satisfied myself that preparations were far from complete. I learnt from the claims officer, Major McKenzie, that little had been done since last summer to improve the permanent buildings, such as cook houses, wash houses, etc. used in conjuction with the tented camps which had been set up during the large exercises last summer, or R.A.F. advanced landing grounds in Kent. He said that an extensive programme for repairing and improving these buildings had been drawn up. . . . Chester Beatty* said that a lot of work still had to be done before full use could be made of Dover Harbour. He also said that a recent large-scale exercise in his neighborhood between the 43rd and 61st Divisions had been a shocking failure. . . . Feeding arrangements were hopeless and most of the troops got nothing for over 24 hours. There seemed to be no idea of making full use of cover for vehicles which bunched together in the open.

What Dusko didn't know was that the Germans had a bead on him. Two days before his scheduled departure, MI6 Lisbon sent London a startling cable: "WIEGAND states Berlin unhappy about authenticity [of] TRICYCLE's reports and that TRICYCLE's present tasks have been set so that answers could be checked." After almost two months of preparation by various British

---

* Mining engineer and Churchill's advisor on raw material supply.

military and intelligence sources, however, it was too late to modify answers to Popov's questionnaire. Discrepancies and inconsistencies would have to be overcome by Dusko's deftness. Compounding the problem was that he would no longer have a friendly ear—von Karsthoff had been reassigned to Vienna and the interrogation would not be conducted by Schreiber, but by new, aggressive SD and Gestapo officers.

Through what appeared to be an espionage sixth sense, Dusko stopped to see Jebsen before heading to his meeting with the Germans. He recalled Johnny's warning: "You will report to our SD friends, Schroeder and Nassenstein," he said. Jebsen's use of "friends" was sarcastic; Major Erich Schroeder was Lisbon's strident SD chief, and Major Adolf Nassenstein, whose real name was Nogenstein, was a fanatical Gestapo agent who would later stage a shoot-out reminiscent of the O.K. Corral.

With some trepidation Johnny added that a third officer was being sent specially from Berlin to interrogate Dusko after the first team finished. "The report you're making tonight has top classification," he advised, "important and urgent. They'll pick your brains down to the last curlicue, and they won't be gentlemen."

Suggesting that he and Jebsen meet afterward in case his story needed "patching up," Dusko gave Johnny a key to his hotel room and headed to the meeting. At 7:30 p.m. he met the Nazis in a barren villa. For seven hours the Germans took turns cross-examining him about the upcoming invasion. As always, Dusko provided the chicken feed supplied by British Intelligence. He sketched the insignia of Patton's mighty FUSAG troops and delivered commanding officer names—some actual, some notional. At three in the morning the Germans wrapped up. As they were walking out, Schroeder told Dusko that a superior officer from Berlin would be in town to interrogate him as well, confirming Johnny's warning.

When he returned to the hotel, Popov remembered, Jebsen was waiting. How did it go? he asked. The interrogators were party hacks, Dusko said, neither as smart nor as dangerous as von Karsthoff.

"Wait till the lord high executioner from Berlin gets hold of you," Johnny shot back. "I'm not sure you appreciate the extent to which the OKW is banking on what you've gleaned in London. They trust you but they'll want to be double sure you haven't been misled. I can't put it strongly enough, Dusko: be on your toes."

Popov shrugged. "I've been in the game for four years now and I'm a smarter fox than they are."

Johnny wasn't convinced. "Oh, you're a real fox. You can outwit them as long as your head stays clear, but what happens when they give you truth serum?"

Sodium thiopental—better known as sodium pentothal—had been developed in the thirties and the Germans had been experimenting with it in 1944. A patient under its influence was incapable of lying, Johnny said, and the Abwehr's Lisbon station had just received a delivery of it. Since IVAN was the only agent undergoing interrogation, Dusko was surely the intended recipient.

The Berlin specialist would likely ask Dusko's consent to accept an injection as a gesture of good faith, Johnny said. If Popov declined, they would inject it by force.

Dusko told Jebsen to finagle or steal a dose. Calling Cecil Gledhill to an emergency meeting, he asked the MI6 station chief to find a physician who "doesn't ask questions." Gledhill didn't ask why Popov needed a doctor, but told him one would show up at his room at six the following evening. On March 5, the day before the meeting with the "Berlin specialist," Johnny and a Portuguese doctor arrived.

Stating that twenty-five grams would be the appropriate amount to cause partial paralysis of the nervous system, the doctor plunged the syringe into Popov's vein. A few moments later Dusko felt dizzy and sleepy. "With it all," he wrote in his memoirs, "everything seemed gay and funny. I loved everyone." He called for Jebsen to bring on the Gestapo, and Johnny peppered him about why he had been arrested and expelled from Germany, what he thought of Hitler, and what he was doing in England. Throughout, Popov maintained composure and answered methodically.

Jebsen smiled. "Either this truth serum is for frightening children, or you have a will of iron."

Dusko asked for a larger dose and at 2:00 a.m.—sufficient time for the first dose to have worn off—the doctor returned and jacked him with fifty milligrams, double the prescribed dosage. Dusko remembered Johnny waking him twelve hours later, at five in the afternoon. He had responded brilliantly, Jebsen said, disclosing nothing. With a bite to eat and a cold shower, Dusko left for his meeting.

He would need the show of a lifetime.

Refreshed by his coma-like slumber, Popov felt terrific as he entered Club Sparta at eight. The "Berlin interrogator" appeared and introduced himself as Major Muller. The man was in fact Aloys Schreiber, who had just been promoted to Oberstleutnant and was now replacing von Karsthoff as head of the Lisbon station. Highly regarded, Schreiber for two years had interrogated prisoners of war and reported directly to Hitler. Kindly and patient, Dr. Schreiber probed about places Dusko had visited and sources he had cited, slowly and carefully dissecting every answer.

Aware that the soft, psychiatric approach was intended to lull the interrogatee into a false sense of security, Dusko remained alert. Every hour or so, Major Schroeder would take over and pick up the pace, apparently to throw Popov off. Question. Answer. Rephrased question. Answer. Cross-examination. Answer. And on it went.

For *nine hours.*

Around five in the morning, Aloys gathered his notes. Dusko was worried. He had visited the places where Schreiber probed, but the sources he claimed were all MI5 fabrications and Schreiber had put his finger on them several times.

"One more thing," Schreiber suddenly said, "we would like your consent . . ."

24 »

AUF

Dusko stirred. Truth serum.

He had to wonder if his ability to withstand Johnny's interrogation was due to his inability to see Jebsen any differently than as a friend playing a game. Even in his semiconscious, sleep-sticky state, he knew he could always make out Johnny's friendly voice. But could he maintain his deceit under legitimate, dunning, drug-enhanced interrogation?

The instructions at Arisaig—to start counting in your head so that when the drug took effect you'd only spout off numbers—was helpful but that pertained to interrogation with ether. They'd had no training or instructions about sodium pentothal.

Schreiber looked at him. ". . . your consent," he said, "to contact Guttmann and to ask him to gather some additional details." Popov sighed and nodded. GUTTMANN was the German code name for Dusko's radio operator.

Aloys told him to return the following evening, and the game continued.

While Dusko was uneasy about the first night, he was "definitely on top" the second, he told Ian Wilson. Feedback from the interrogation was stellar; not only were Popov's remarks well received, but Schreiber, Wiegand, and von Karsthoff waged fierce competition as to who would now run IVAN, and who would get to present his report in Berlin. Wiegand, it turned out, had been sent by Colonel Hansen to receive Popov's report because Hansen feared that Schreiber might have left Lisbon before Dusko arrived. Since Popov's information on the Allied invasion was the highest quality available, each German wanted credit for delivering it.

Von Karsthoff left immediately by train with the report. Wiegand, an ambitious lawyer in his early thirties, refused to be outmaneuvered and flew to Berlin to deliver an oral report before Ludovico arrived. In the end, Wiegand won the Popov sweepstakes, earning the right to control Germany's best agent; Schreiber retained directorship of the Lisbon station, while von Karsthoff, whose reputation for laziness saturated the SD, was reassigned to Austria.

So entrenched was Popov that he demanded $150,000 from the Abwehr or he would provide no further information on the Allied invasion plans. Further, since von Karsthoff had promised Dusko a postwar business benefit—ownership of some type of agency—he demanded that the Germans confirm allegiance to the offer. The requests were outlandish, and Johnny and Ivo had advised against them, but Dusko forged ahead without bothering to run it by MI5.

The demands had multiple objectives: The financial payment would reveal where Dusko really stood with the Germans, and would compensate him for what he was owed and what he would do in the future. If the Abwehr paid, he could assist Ivo and Johnny, who was having trouble exchanging currency in Lisbon. By pressing for von Karsthoff's promised postwar benefit, Dusko would feign assumption of German victory and exhibit steadfast loyalty to the cause.

Astonishingly, Wiegand and Schreiber took up Dusko's case, pointing out to Berlin that Popov was not German and therefore was not morally bound to constantly risk his life in England. IVAN's motives for being an Abwehr operative had been clear from the outset, Lisbon stressed, and von Karsthoff had indeed offered the postwar business to encourage Dusko to work hard. In short, the Lisbon station held, the Abwehr should retain "this valuable agent whatever the circumstances might be."

»

Throughout the spring, British Intelligence received varied reports about how the Germans viewed the TRICYCLE net. On March 10 an ULTRA intercept indicated that GELATINE's reports were viewed as "completely worthless." The damage to Popov, however, was negligible. A week and a half later, Johnny met with Ian and updated him on how TRICYCLE's information was being addressed in Berlin. Regarding Dusko's prior report, Jebsen said, the German General Staff was unwilling to make correcting military dispositions unless Colonel Hansen could guarantee—in writing—that the TRICYCLE report was genuine. Hansen wouldn't make the commitment and the staff postponed their decision until receipt of TRICYLE's next report. That questionnaire, Dusko's latest, "passed with flying colors," Johnny said. The decision was made, however, to wait for confirming reports from Spanish agents before making appropriate adjustments.

Hansen and the General Staff knew the stakes. The success or failure of the Allied invasion of France would be determined by information given to Hitler, and corresponding directions given to Field Marshal Gerd von Rundstedt and to Rommel. Everyone wanted a scapegoat in case they were wrong. If the General Staff ordered inadvisable military adjustments, they could point to Hansen as having given invalid intelligence. Hansen, in turn, could point to the Spain Abwehr station. But at this point, so far as Johnny could tell, both German Intelligence and the Wehrmacht generals believed Dusko's reports to be genuine and that they would indeed be influencing military decisions.

The General Staff circulated his reports to all Wermacht stations for consideration and possible modifications. Aloys Schreiber reported back to Johnny that Popov's information had been classified "as good as sure," an almost unparalleled evaluation. Colonel Hansen was so delighted that he boasted to Walter Schellenberg, his counterpart in the SD, that in IVAN the Abwehr had the one agent of real value in the UK.

Things were proceeding well for Dusko, and on March 23, Johnny presented him with a pleasant surprise—Ivo. Johnny had slipped Dr. Popov through the Yugoslav escape line and, in Paris, had given him a false German passport; from there Ivo flew to Madrid and on to Lisbon as "Hans Popper." It had been three years since the brothers had seen each other, and Ivo had changed. Dusko wrote in his memoirs that Ivo was still dapper and handsome, but at the time he told an MI6 agent that his brother "had grown thin and old since he had last seen him." The stress of living two lives, one laden with lies, was taking its toll.

Secret Intelligence prepared a small dinner, attended by Dusko and two MI6 agents, to welcome and honor agent DREADNOUGHT. "Ivo created the very best impression," one of the agents wrote. "He speaks with the authority and deep sincerity learnt from his long experience of fighting for the Serbs under the cloak of collaboration with the Germans and witnessing the destruction of his country. This experience has left him his great personal charm, but has given him a seriousness and depth of feeling which contrasts with TRICYCLE's expansive bonhomie."

After dinner the Popov brothers holed up in the Palácio, where Ivo updated Dusko on their family and Ivo's work in the Yugoslav resistance. Dr. Popov was practicing medicine by day, he told Dusko, and sabotaging Nazi trains by night. The Yugoslav economy had been destroyed, however—prices inflating twenty to eighty times—and Ivo couldn't make a living as a physician. With Johnny's help, he had purchased a shoe-polish company, and the supplemental income provided just enough to support the family.

When Jebsen wasn't checking up on Ivo and Vladan—whose school expenses in Bologna Johnny was covering—he worked his currency scheme. Gold and hard currency exchange rates for German occupation marks differed in each country, Ivo said, and Johnny profited by taking advantage of the spread from one country to the next. At the end of the trail, after an investment had doubled or tripled, Johnny would park the funds in Switzerland. Jebsen didn't need money, however, and took no part in the profits; his aim was to invest for Abwehr and SD officers and thereby bind them to him. Since the transactions were illegal, Jebsen assumed these men would protect him from the Gestapo in case rumors arose about Johnny's Allied assistance. For officers without means, Johnny even loaned the initial principal.

The scheme would prove to be a Faustian bargain.

The next afternoon Dusko took his brother to the Boca do Inferno ("Mouth of Hell") cliffs of Cascais. Here, watching breakers crash into rocks of hell, Dusko told his brother how the TRICYCLE net might do likewise. If the Gestapo followed Johnny's financial transactions, he said, the trail would eventually lead to them; in time the Germans would figure out that the entire TRICYCLE net was controlled. Ivo needed protection, Dusko said, or at least warning, if the Jebsen shoe fell. MI5's plan was that if Ivo was in imminent danger, a coded message would be included in the BBC's 8:00 p.m. Yugoslavian broadcast:

> *Mačka je dobila devet mačića.*
> The cat's got nine kittens.

If Ivo heard that phrase, he was to go to General Mihailovic's headquarters, report to the chief of the British Mission, and state that his name was "Sveta Popovic." The British, it was understood, would slip him out.

Dusko had another idea. The safest bet would be for Ivo to move to Madrid. With SIS contacts, he said, Ivo could disappear for the duration of the war. Dr. Popov slept on it but in the morning told Dusko that there were too many involved and that he couldn't desert the resistance; he had to return to Belgrade.

"But you won't be able to protect them," Dusko objected. "You'll be the first one arrested and put up against a wall."

"Then that will be their warning."

»

The night before heading back to England, Dusko also had a heart-to-heart with Johnny. The dribble of information over the last month had consistently brought distressing news regarding Jebsen's plight. On February 10 Johnny had received a call from Baroness von Gronau saying that, due to the recent defection of Dr. Erich Vermehren, the principal Abwehr agent in Istanbul, orders from Berlin were that Jebsen was to be "watched" because Johnny had spent time there and had at one point contacted Vermehren's wife, Petra. The Germans expected Vermehren to pass through Lisbon, possibly in disguise, and ordered Lieutenant Kramer from Abwehr III to investigate. Johnny met with Kramer around this time and told him that the only thing Kramer could do was to shoot Vermehren at the airport. It was a strange suggestion, particularly given Jebsen's predicament, but one that was largely impracticable. In any case, the baroness suggested that Johnny not return to Berlin.

About this time, Ivo also had discovered that the Gestapo was closing in on Johnny's deals. With the SD looking to make a name for itself in the Abwehr takeover, the exposure of Jebsen's illicit activity would be a high priority. Dusko recalled pressing Johnny about his precautions, hoping that by some miracle Johnny could escape to a small town in Spain.

"In theory," Johnny said, "the people I'm doing business with will protect me. They have to in order to protect their own interests and their own safety."

Dusko knew it wasn't that simple. "But they could try to silence you . . . forever."

"It's a horse race."

"But if you've backed the wrong horse?"

"I'm not backing. I'm the horse."

»

Ivo and Johnny were in the same boat—taking on water but without opportunity to bail. Dusko had his own worries, to be sure, and continuing to mislead the Germans at upcoming interrogations would be no mean feat, but the fates of his brother and his best friend were what churned his stomach.

He and Johnny needed a break. Mental. Physical. Emotional. Anything for distraction.

Casino Estoril.

Several hours at baccarat tables seemed a reliable antidote, but it wasn't; he and Johnny went through the motions, winning and losing with equanimity, their minds elsewhere. He walked Johnny home, Dusko wrote in his memoirs, and bid him good night. As he turned to leave, Johnny called out.

". . . Nothing . . . I just wanted to have a look at you," he said. "It's going to be a while. I feel we are . . . going in different directions. *Auf—*" Johnny's voice broke off. "Goodbye."

Dusko shuddered. Johnny's change of words thundered with an ominous permanence. He was about to say, *Auf Wiedersehen—* "Until I see you again."

»

On April 13, 1944, Dusko returned to London. In his possession were two Yugoslav diplomatic bags, one genuine, one forged. Per protocol, he opened the pouches in Ian Wilson's presence. In the forged bag were five reports from ARTIST, two Abwehr questionnaires about the invasion, a political questionnaire from the SD, $1,000 with instructions for GELATINE, $1,000 for FREAK, and $14,000 of Popov's own money. Dusko told Ian that the SD had also shown him a military questionnaire, from which he was to take notes and supply information.

The SD was sending an agent to Lisbon in April or May, Dusko told his case officer, to interrogate Jebsen. Until recently the Gestapo had orders to arrest Johnny at the German border, he said, but now—since the SD was pleased with Dusko's latest report—ARTIST was free from danger. Amazingly, Jebsen actually *wished* to return to Germany, Ian wrote in his debriefing report, saying that ARTIST wanted to "do something big for us." Wilson didn't like the idea and spoke to MI6's Foley and Lloyd the following day. They agreed. So long as the possibility of Jebsen being interrogated remained, British Intelligence wanted him to stay in Lisbon, where he would be safe. But was he?

One of Johnny's Lisbon sources, a colleague named Hans Brandes, was suspected by SIS of playing "his own game." An ULTRA intercept indicated that Brandes had reported to Berlin that Jebsen was "showing noticeable curiosity" about German agent OSTRO. MI6 was fearful that Brandes might be playing Johnny—luring him into a false confidence—to ascertain information about the activities of ARTIST and TRICYCLE. Was Brandes double-crossing Johnny?

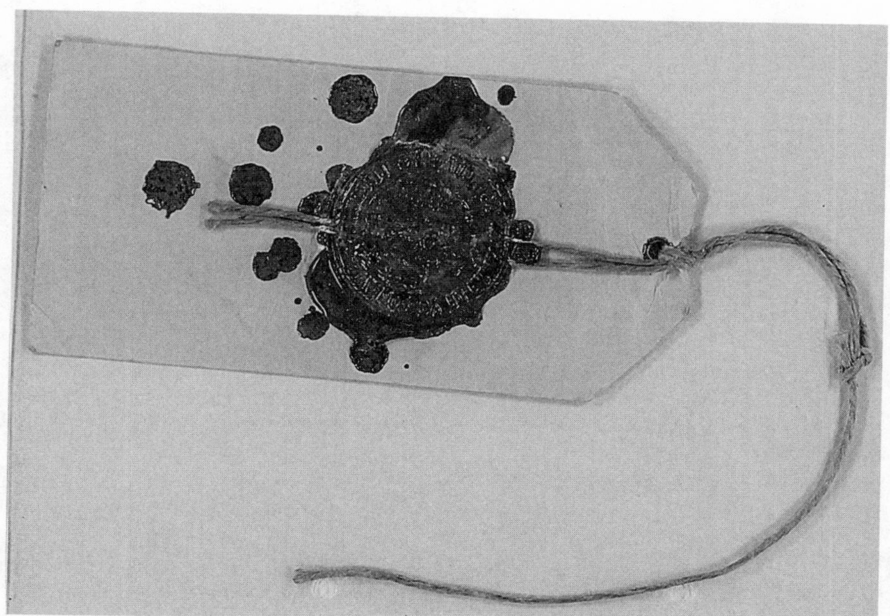

Popov's fake Yugoslav Legation seal. *The National Archives of the UK*

As April rolled on, Johnny received evidence that he was in the clear. Dr. Schreiber phoned and told Johnny that *Oberst* Kuebart in Berlin had requested that Jebsen meet with Schreiber and a Major Bohlen, administrative head of the war stations, in Biarritz on April 21. Johnny initially sensed it was a trap and demurred, suggesting that such a meeting would be unwise since it might blow his cover. He explained that the British knew that diplomats only operated in Lisbon and Madrid, and if he went to France it would reveal that he was more than a civilian.

It was a feeble excuse, but Schreiber seemed mollified and offered exciting news: IVAN's last report had made a tremendous impression on Berlin, he said, and Kuebart had agreed to pay Popov's financial demand. Aloys was authorized to give Johnny $75,000 now, the other half coming after IVAN produced the information in his questionnaire. Even better, Schreiber added, Jebsen was to be awarded a medal—the KVK* first class.

Schreiber said that he would see what Bohlen wanted to discuss, and in

* *Kriegsverdienstkreuz.*

T R I C Y C L E

Questionnaire
Given to TRICYCLE in Lisbon
At the Beginning of April, 1944.

Part I.

1) When will the landing (or part-landing) take place?

2) Where are the landing targets? Give centres of gravity and possible course of time.

3) Strength of the formations to be employed (Army, Air Force and Navy)?

4) Which ports are the starting bases?

5) Will unknown weapons (for instance gas) be used? If so, what weapons and by which formations?

6) Number of the infantry, airborne and armoured divisions in England, furthermore of the U.S. divisions in England, divisional number and locality.

7) Which British or American Armies are under the Army Group Montgomery or the 1st American Army Group?

8) Which English divisions are being re-formed into "air transported" (Lufttransportierten) divisions? Divisional numbers and localities.

9) Where are/

First questions of the "invasion questionnaire" given to Popov by the Germans (as translated by M15). The German original is three pages and has sixty questions, most with several subparts. First two questions: When and where? *The National Archives of the UK*

Part II

1.) Werden von Amerika Kampfstoffe nach England oder über England nach Russland geliefert?
Luft-Kampfstoffe und Gelände-Kampfstoffe.

2.) Fairey-Rückstosstriebwerk (Fairey Jet-Propulsion System)
a) entwickelt Fairey an diesem Triebwerk
b) wieweit ist die praktische Ausführung
c) wie urteilen Fackkreise über die Fairey Konstruktion.

3.) Flugzeug- und Flugmotorenfertigung in England 1943 (nach Viertel - jahren)

4.) Angaben über Umschlag in den wichtigsten Häfen, insbesondere London: Surrey Commercial Dock und Catherine Dock. Welche Häfen sind durch Luftwaffe zerstört, wie dst deren Wieder-Aufbau ?

5.) Genaue Angabe von Haupt-Vorratslagern für Getreide, sowie Groß-Kühl-Anlagen. Genaue Lage der Margarine-Fabrik Selby (25 km südl.York?) Leistungsfähigkeit.

6.) Auswirkung der Luftangriffe auf Coventry:
a) Feststellung, welche Werke wieder nach den großen An - griffen(April 41) arbeiten?
b) oder wohin verlegt? Industrie-Verlagerungen der jüngsten Zeit.

7.) Lage-Ermittlung folgender Werke:
Rolls Royce, Belper.
Bristol Aeroplane Ltd.Didcot
Hordern Richmond, Chesham
Jable Propellers Ltd. Manchester
Bendix Ltd., Birmingham
Brown Bros. (Aircraft Ltd. Warwick)
Redwing Aircraft Co.Ltd., Croydon
Lage innerhalb der Waddon Factory Estate.

8.) Evakuierung von Behörden aus London, sowie Verlegungen innerhalb Londons.

9.) Nach Möglichkeit Angaben über Lage, Kapazität, bzw. Ausbringungs-zahlen, von Kriegsmaterial (Waffen, Munition, auch Kugellager usw.) soweit in England hergestellt.

10.) wirtschaftliche und industrielle Schäden, verursacht durch die Luftangriffe im Jahre 1943.

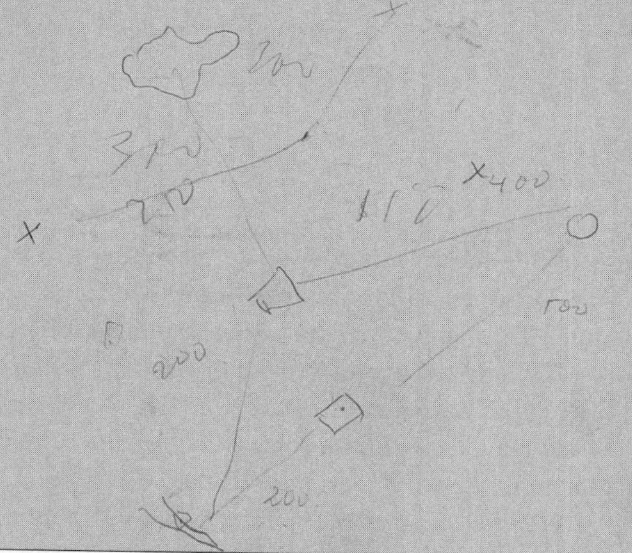

Page 3 of the questionnaire. Dusko appears to be marking Folkestone, Dover, and Ramsgate as British launch sites (London is the irregular shape), and the beaches of Boulogne, Calais, and Dunkirk as landing locations. The interior box may indicate St. Omer as a notional bombing target. *The National Archives of the UK*

the meantime he'd set up an award ceremony at the Lisbon Embassy; he could give Johnny IVAN's money then, and afterward they could go over whatever information Bohlen wanted.

About this time Johnny also received an unexpected windfall from the Gestapo. Wolfgang Henss, his SD friend in Porto, had just been promoted to head the Gestapo station in Lisbon. Informing Johnny of his promotion, Henss said: "If ever you get in trouble with my department and I have to organize a search for you, you had better hide in my house where no one will think of looking for you!"

It was the best protection he could hope for. Thrilled, Johnny met with an MI6 agent on April 21 to tell him that the investigation was over and that he and Dusko were out of danger. He also sent Popov a celebratory letter:

Dear Dusko,

. . . I congratulate you on being my Beloved Führer's best agent, who is genuine without any doubt. By "without any doubt" I mean with money because, after having hesitated for some time, the Abwehr decided that the money should be transferred to you as arranged here with Schreiber and Wiegand. I got 75,000 dollars, of which I send you 50,000 today. To Ivo I shall send the 20,000 Swiss francs tomorrow. . . .

Please give my best greetings to Ian, Frank and the Bentons. Be a good boy, and try to behave.

Yours always,
Johnny

While Jebsen and MI6 were celebrating in Lisbon, London followed suit. On April 26 Ian invited Dusko to a dinner party at the Hyde Park Hotel. The banquet hall had been festooned for a grand occasion, Dusko recalled, and the guests were all of London's senior officers from MI5 and MI6: Director-General Sir David Petrie, Colonel Tar Robertson, Major J. C. Masterman, Major Frank Foley, Major M. Lloyd, Captain Guy Liddell, John Marriott, Richard Butler, and Wilson.

As Popov observed the room, someone suddenly made a toast. Bewildered, Dusko was still trying to figure out the occasion when Wilson whispered to sit down. The toast and the banquet, he said, were for the guest of honor—

Dusko Popov. After a number of heartfelt remarks about Popov's exemplary feats, the evening was topped off when it was announced that he would be nominated for, and most likely receive, an order of chivalry. The Order of the British Empire, established by George V in 1917, was bestowed by the king in a ceremony at Buckingham Palace and was one of Britain's highest honors. "It would have been a splendid evening," Dusko remembered, "if I could have kept my thoughts on the festivities and not on Johnny."

»

Circumstances to follow would keep Jebsen on his mind. Throughout April Station X had intercepted several wireless messages regarding Dusko's demand for $150,000. On April 12 Berlin notified von Karsthoff that Major Wiegand, the Paris chief negotiating with Popov, was not up to the task:

> In spite of the most precise directions which he was given for negotiating with IVAN it is noted that Wiegand is not capable of persuading IVAN to accept these proposals or to continue his work on a similar basis. From the recent correspondence one has the impression that IVAN is not being directed but doing the directing himself. IVAN's present preliminary successes in no way justify a demand for such a large payment.

Nevertheless, the Abwehr was unwilling to lose their slippery spy over a few escudos. A week later Berlin authorized Lisbon to release the initial $75,000. The second installment, the message read, was to be "handed over after HARRY's oral report in Biarritz on 21/4." Lisbon replied:

> JONNY is maintaining his objections. HARRY will arrive in Biarritz alone on 21/4 towards the afternoon. The first installment of the sum in dollars was paid to JONNY on 20/4 in accordance with your HIOB I of 20/4.

On April 29 SIS London received through the diplomatic bag Johnny's April 21 letter and $50,000. MI5's monthly report to Winston Churchill—which included updates on significant espionage activities—contained information regarding but one British spy:

> The agent TRICYCLE has now returned from visiting his masters in Lisbon. He has once more succeeded in convincing them of his complete reliability and has extracted from them a large sum in dollars as an advance against future services. So far as the Germans knew, his reason for visiting Lisbon was that he is acting as the organiser of an escape route on behalf of the Yugoslav Government. This undertaking has now the cordial support of the German Secret Service, who hope to use it as a means of reinforcing their net-work in England. In practice, however, the effect will be the opposite, since the escapers are selected in London and sent from Yugoslavia by TRICYCLE's brother, DREADNOUGHT. . . . Apart from his work for German Military Intelligence, TRICYCLE has now also established a connection in Himmler's organisation [SD] to whom he has delivered a political questionnaire. . . . They appear to have the highest opinion of him and are taking steps to ensure that his work for them remains unknown to his other German masters.

It was almost too good to be true.

»

That afternoon in Lisbon, Aloys Schreiber called Jebsen and asked him to stop by Schreiber's office at six o'clock to go over details of the decoration. He asked Johnny to bring along his friend and houseguest, Moldenhauer, so that they could go over that agent's previous mission. Jebsen and Moldenhauer arrived at six and after a brief discussion, Aloys called Johnny into another room.

Earlier in the day, Dr. Schreiber had run two errands—to the pharmacy and to a variety store to purchase two large trunks.

D-DAY

On April 30, 1944, Station X intercepted and translated a German message from Berlin to Lisbon:

> Extreme caution in flip matters. In particular whatever the course of events, WALL (Abwehr) must be prevented from learning of the collaboration planned.

On May 4 they captured another. This one, "Most Secret," from Berlin to Biarritz:

> As special machine cannot be provided to pick up J and W, they are to be sent to Berlin immediately under the closest supervision and with all measures for security. Responsible officer in charge is instructed to report time of arrival promptly so that they can be met at station in Berlin.

The following day, May 5, Lisbon updated Berlin:

> FLIP taken by WALL to GEROLD (France) through BERN (Spain) on 29/4 as planned. . . . The fact that he has been taken has been kept absolutely secret. . . . The conversations we have had with FLIP served only the purpose of lulling him into a sense of security. QUETTING'S account of the agreement concerning FLIP reached between leiter STRAUCH . . . has naturally been kept secret. QUETTING requests you to arrange

that FLIP is placed at HOFMEISTER'S disposal as soon as possible.

Meanwhile, Ian Wilson met with Dusko on May 7 to give him a second letter from Johnny, and to tell him that MI6 Lisbon had just cabled: Jebsen missed his May 5 appointment and had not been at his house since April 29. Dusko could only wonder. It wasn't like Johnny to miss a meeting, and he'd not said anything about going to Madrid or Paris. Suicide was out of the question, but maybe Johnny was spooked and went to ground. Or maybe he had gone to Biarritz after all and had no time to notify MI6.

Dusko read the letter, touched by the close.

28th April, 1944

Dear Dusko,

Last time already I could tell you that your standing in the eyes of the Abwehr was really what you wanted. I don't remember if I pointed out that, in spite of the General Staff's and Abw. I's good opinion about your work, Department III still had some doubts about your genuineness.

In the meantime your friend Schreiber had a conference with the III people in Spain for the purpose of calming them down and convincing them that their doubts were absolutely without any foundation. . . . So the new judgment of Department III is . . . that the last reports certainly proved the genuineness of Dusko. . . .

A proof of the fact that Schreiber did not tell me stories is that I got another decoration and this time the K.V.K. First Class. First Class probably was given because you double-crossed them first-class! I feel a little bit ashamed of getting a decoration for the work you and Ian did. . . . I made up my mind to give it to Ian. . . . After all, he is an exceptional man and it is only in accordance with this that he, as a British intelligence officer, has the exceptional honour of getting a decoration with the swastika on it. . . .

I hope you will give my love to all you can give it to without spoiling your, my, or anyone else's cover. To you I can give my love anyhow, which I do. . . .

Yours, as always,
Johnny

With Johnny's disappearance and the assumption of foul play, J. C. Masterman circulated within B1A a memorandum entitled, "Effects of the Removal of ARTIST on Deception Plans." He notified those receiving the document—Robertson, Marriott, Wilson, and Tomás Harris—that it was unknown why Johnny had fallen under suspicion. The assumption was that Johnny's "unreliability" was due to his financial transactions, his "intrigues with the S.D.," or his inquisitiveness regarding Brandes and OSTRO. "There is no proof that treason on the part of ARTIST in connection with TRICYCLE is part of the charge," he wrote, but "under [torture] ARTIST may betray all."

Masterman suggested that the only way to find out if Dusko was compromised was to provoke a reaction through FREAK's radio messages. If MI5 sent something to Belgrade regarding Yugoslav affairs, he thought, with a comment about TRICYCLE's reliability, Berlin might bite.

In the meantime, J.C. recommended that TRICYCLE continue to operate at a high level but avoid all questions dealing with Operation Fortitude. "Any change in his procedure would surely blow the whole network and expose most of our operations," he warned. Masterman wondered aloud whether the other double-cross agents should continue deception efforts since if any were blown the Germans would read in reverse all radio traffic, collapsing the entire scheme.

What the British had in their favor, however, was time.

It would take considerable time, he figured, for the Germans "(a) to decide which of the agents were really controlled and which were not; (b) to decide which parts of their reports were true and which false; (c) to deduce therefrom what we wish [them to] believe."

Masterman's recommendation was that if the situation had merely deteriorated, the double agents could be used to "fill the German mind with confusion" rather than pitch a complete deception plan. On the other hand, if TRICYCLE and GARBO were blown, British Intelligence would have to shut down all agents shortly before D-Day. With the exception of Tommy Harris, GARBO's supervisor, everyone agreed that Masterman's observations and suggestions were on target. In a rebuttal to Robertson and Marriott that same day, Harris made his case.

MI5 had totally missed the radio traffic suggesting that ARTIST would be kidnapped, Harris wrote, and, like Jebsen, had felt that there was no danger from the Gestapo or the SD. In fact, he went on, the kidnapping "was put into operation the same night that our confidence in him was at its height."

Illustrating how badly British Intelligence had misinterpreted the situation, Tommy added: "MS.S. [Most Secret Sources] appeared to support ARTIST's belief that SCHREIBER was his ally and was fighting his battles against the suspicions of High Command, the Abwehr and the S.D. whereas SCHREIBER was in fact the man chosen to carry out his kidnapping."

In short, Harris didn't trust the Double-Cross Committee or B1A to determine whether GARBO had been blown, or would be blown. Tommy had his own idea. If MI5 decided to use GARBO "for the purpose of further implementing FORTITUDE, a task on which to date he has hardly embarked . . . I consider he could only be so used with any degree of safety" if radio traffic—which could be proved untrue—was sent through TRICYCLE, while counterbalancing traffic—which could be proved true—was sent by GARBO.

Without knowing whether Popov had in fact been blown, Harris was suggesting affirmative action to *prove* that agent IVAN was controlled in order to secure Pujol's position. But if Berlin had proof that Popov was a double, Harris surely knew, Dusko could expect an assassination or kidnapping attempt if he left Britain.

»

On May 9 Station X intercepted another German signal from Lisbon to Berlin:

```
DORA has arrived.
```

Connecting this message to earlier ones, the code breakers at Bletchley Park notified Wilson the next day to tell him of DORA and the "J" and "M"* message. Ian drafted two quick memoranda to Robertson, Masterman, and Marriott, pointing out that in Johnny's last meeting with MI6, on April 28, Jebsen had mentioned that Moldenhauer was staying with him. Moldenhauer was the "M" of the message, Wilson assumed, and presumably had been kidnapped as well. Because Moldenhauer knew about Johnny's true intentions, Ian warned, his abduction doubled the exposure of GARBO and the TRICYCLE net.

Since Popov couldn't know about "Most Secret Sources"—ULTRA—Ian was in the awkward position of keeping from Dusko knowledge that Johnny was in a Berlin prison. So far as Popov knew, Jebsen had simply missed his

* The intercept showed a "W," but Bletchley Park correctly identified it as an "M" to Wilson.

appointment. The dilemma that had to be decided by B1A and coordinated with Dusko, Wilson pointed out, was how agent IVAN should handle receipt of the $75,000. The Abwehr had not mentioned the money in their last radio messages and perhaps were waiting, too, to see if Jebsen had passed it along before the kidnapping. If they knew Johnny had sent it, they would expect Popov to reply with confirmation. But if Dusko signaled receipt and Jebsen had given the Abwehr no indication of handing it off, Popov's cover would be blown. It was a bit of a coin flip, but Ian figured that from the German viewpoint, Popov would not have known of Jebsen't receipt of the money. For the time being, MI5 would not mention the money in IVAN's radio traffic.

With D-Day looming, and the prospect of Dusko's cover hanging in the balance, Wilson and MI5 could only wait. The following day Ian received evidence that his assumption was correct. Frank Foley notified him that MI6 had no indication from Johnny that—from the *German* perspective—he was to have notified IVAN of receipt of the money. Dusko could make no reference to funds, then, unless the Abwehr mentioned it first.

That afternoon the Germans played their hand. MI6 Lisbon informed London that a Gaspar de Oliviera, a senior officer within the espionage section of the PVDE, had asked the British for information about Dusko Popov. Frank Foley assumed the inquiry was on behalf of the SD and asked Tar how he wished to respond. Robertson suggested playing it by the book: Popov visited Portugal from time to time as a Yugoslav diplomatic courier, and the Passport Control Office had been instructed to give him a visa to the UK upon application.

On May 12 an SIS agent repeated to Oliviera, through a local contact, the innocuous information. The Germans were waiting. No sooner than the contact had recited Popov's role as a Yugoslav diplomat, Oliviera handed him a report.

It indicated that Dusko was either a British or Russian agent.

»

As of mid-May, Dusko knew nothing about Johnny's imprisonment, or the "British or Russian agent" report. Unable to determine Johnny's fate or whereabouts, Dusko's thoughts turned to his brother. On May 17 he told Ian that if MI5 didn't have immediate use for him, he'd be prepared to parachute into Yugoslavia to try to contact Ivo, or at least find out if Ivo was still free in Belgrade. B1A declined. The TRICYCLE net was moving ever closer to the German furnace and Popov wouldn't be the bellows.

About this time, one of General Mihailovic's sources notified MI6 that FREAK had been charged with "accusations." Until British Intelligence could determine his status, Robertson felt, Dusko's radio would have to fall silent. Wilson allowed a few messages on May 18, but the next scheduled transmission, on the twenty-second, would not be sent. With D-Day two weeks away, the radio dialogue was delicate, and Ian decided that silence would trigger the least consequences.

Days later, on May 25, General Eisenhower's office called. A Colonel H. N. H. Wild from Supreme Headquarters Allied Expeditionary Force (SHEAF) sent a note to Colonel Robertson asking if Tar would let him know how TRICYCLE would be used after D-Day, "in the event of no further evidence coming to light." Tar put off responding to Colonel Wild, and it was fortuitous; further evidence did come to light. On May 28 Robertson received MI6's translation of the Lisbon secret police report. It contained numerous red flags about the bon vivant diplomat:

> Said to be a lawyer. . . . Is attaché in the Yugoslav Foreign Office with residence in London. Often travelled between Lisbon and Madrid, and his own Legation was doubtful as to his real nationality. Suspected of being Bulgarian or Russian (according to whether his name spelt with "ov" or "off"). Visa granted by authority of the Portuguese Embassy in London marked "in transit for Egypt" where he did not go. His interests are in Lisbon and Madrid, and it cannot be ascertained whether he is a British or Russian agent. . . .
>
> His category of attaché alone surely does not permit him to live in expensive apartments at the Hotel Aviz or at the Palacio Hotel Estoril. He gives us the impression of belonging to some secret organization with branches in Lisbon and Madrid. It is known that he has close connection in Lisbon with the BAILONI's [*sic*]. . . . They receive no official subsistence but live in great luxury giving expensive receptions and dinners attended by diplomats and military attachés. . . . One of the daughters left for Lisbon under the subject's influence. The mother and the remaining daughter installed themselves at the Quinta dos Grilos at Carnaxide.

»

Dusko's status as a bona fide German agent was hanging by a thread, and Tar, understandably, folded the intelligence tent. In a letter back to Eisenhower's office on the twenty-eighth, Robertson told Colonel Wild, "I am not in a position to prepare an appreciation on the employment of TRICYCLE after D. Day, nor indeed do I think any useful purpose would be served were the preparation of such an appreciation to be possible."

Days before D-Day, then, neither the British nor the Americans knew the status of TRICYCLE. Only one person knew Popov's true position—whether the Germans still believed in him—and whether the lies about the invasion pitched by him would hold.

Johnny.

Around this time, Popov remembered, Robertson and Wilson stopped by the Clock House. "Dusko, Artist has been arrested," Tar said. "Jebsen was kidnapped by the Gestapo. . . . They invited him to tea at the embassy and put knock-out drops in it. Then he was given an injection, placed in a large trunk, and driven that way to Madrid in a motorcar with diplomatic plates. From there he was taken to Biarritz and then flown to Berlin. He's in the Gestapo prison in Prinz-Albrechtstrasse."

Robertson's information was mostly correct, although there was no banquet and the knock-out occurred differently. When Dr. Schreiber called Jebsen into a separate room on April 30,* Aloys testified after the war, he told Johnny that he had orders to conduct him to Berlin—by force—since Jebsen had refused to attend the Biarritz meeting. Johnny bolted for the door, Schreiber said, and Aloys caught him and knocked him out. Meanwhile, another agent—Karl Meier—overpowered Moldenhauer in the adjoining room. When Johnny recovered, Schreiber told both men how he planned to sneak them across the border, and according to Aloys, both men submitted (perhaps at gunpoint) to an injection.

With Jebsen and Moldenhauer drugged and sleeping inside ventilated trunks, the kidnap party left Lisbon at 9:00 p.m. and crossed into Spain sometime after midnight. The following day they crossed the French border, also about midnight. A day or so later, Jebsen and Moldenhauer were flown from Biarritz to Berlin in Colonel Hansen's personal plane.

When Dusko heard Tar's report, he knew Jebsen's fate; Prinz-Albrecht-Strasse was notorious for torture and execution.

"He won't talk, not Johnny."

---

* MI5 files conflict as to whether the abduction occurred on April 29 or 30.

Wilson chimed in, saying that at the moment Lisbon believed the net was not compromised. The Gestapo had taken Jebsen in because of his financial dealings, but Johnny was under "reinforced interrogation." If Jebsen talked, Wilson warned, Dusko and every agent Jebsen had passed to him would be blown; the entire Operation Fortitude deception would go by the board.

Robertson could take no chances. Dusko and MI5 simply had to wait and see how the Germans responded.

Sitting idly, passively waiting for the stars to align, was almost a sin to Dusko. He met again with Tar and Ian on June 3 and pressed for action. Popov "urged with some vehemence," Wilson wrote, "that some active step ought to be taken to clear up the position of his case, such as trying to get in touch with DREADNOUGHT in Belgrade. . . . He suggested that if we did not have agents to whom we could safely entrust such instructions, he or The WORM might be sent out for the purpose." Dusko, however, had no idea of the scheduled invasion date—June 5—or that the Lisbon secret police had identified him as a British or Russian spy.

Reigning in their aggressive agent, the MI5 officers told Dusko that this was not the time for "hasty or violent action"; they would revisit the situation when the picture cleared.

»

The importance of TRICYCLE and GARBO in the grand scheme of Operation Fortitude cannot be understated. A victory on D-Day was critical to winning the war, and a successful invasion was critical to D-Day. The Germans knew this as well. As early as 1943 Hitler had warned that a successful Allied invasion of France would have decisive consequences for the war, and on May 5, 1944, General Jodl, OKW* operations chief, had said: "Today we are faced with the great landing by the western powers and with it battles decisive for the outcome of the war and for our future."

German commanders had two questions: Where and when? They had received countless signals and letters from agents and spies who suggested untold locations, from Norway to Normandy. The most frequent, however, and the one confirmed by their best two spies—IVAN and ARABEL—suggested that Calais was the principal spot. Radio traffic consistently sup-

---

**Oberkommando der Wehrmacht* (Supreme Command of the German Armed Forces).

ported that location, as did aerial photos of Dover, which showed a significant increase in boats, landing craft, aircraft, trucks, and tanks.

All made of rubber.

Hitler and his generals believed the invasion would occur principally in the Pas-de-Calais area, but that simultaneous attacks or feints would occur in other areas, perhaps the Somme, the Bay of Saint-Malo, the Gironde estuary, or even along the Mediterranean coast. Dr. Paul Leverkuehn, Abwehr station chief for Turkey and the Near East, remembered that as early as 1943 the Allies were flying coastal reconnaissance in distinct patterns. Calais, the Seine estuary, and the sector west of Bordeaux were most often reconnoitered. In April 1944 Hitler had specifically included Normandy in the list of probable landings, although, according to General Walter Warlimont, OKW deputy operations chief, the notice brought no change of defenses.

The second question—when?—was equally difficult. The German High Command had originally concluded that May 18 was the invasion date, and Rommel had readied his troops. The date came and went. As May turned to June, foul weather entered the picture and suggested that an invasion could only come in late June or July. Aside from reinforcements from the Eastern Front, the Germans were as ready as they could be.

»

In the spring of 1944 the German commander in chief of the western theater, Field Marshal von Rundstedt, had sixty divisions west of the Rhine, with estimates of soldiers under his command ranging from 950,000 to over 1.8 million. As commander in chief of Army Group B, Field Marshal Erwin Rommel was in charge of guarding the 2,500-mile Atlantic coastline.

According to General Hans Speidel, Rommel's chief of staff, Army Group B consisted of the Fifteenth Army—seventeen infantry or field divisions stationed around Calais—the Seventh Army—eleven divisions covering Normandy and the Channel Islands—and nine Panzer divisions scattered in various positions away from the coast and the reach of naval guns.

For the Allies, a successful invasion required that the Germans keep the massive Fifteenth Army in Calais, and the Panzer divisions where they were. Accordingly, in the weeks and months leading up to D-Day, British agents with wireless sets—GARBO, FREAK, and BRUTUS in particular—worked feverishly, sending hundreds of misleading radio messages and letters suggesting various invasion spots and times.

Yet that was not enough.

Understandably, the Germans wanted to corroborate wireless and written information with hard evidence—a warm body. Radio messages and letters cannot be cross-examined, and German Intelligence needed someone they could interrogate to provide what lawyers call "demeanor evidence" and poker players call "tells." If someone is lying or under stress, experts say, the body will provide reliable cues: certain postures, rapid blinking, throat clearing, crossed legs, jittery feet, lip biting, heavy breathing, swallowing, sweating, and so on. Very few people—even professional poker players—can consistently bluff without a tell. Only one in a million—Menzies's virtuoso—can lie again and again under extreme duress without a sign of insincerity or insecurity.

Dusko had been that virtuoso. He had sold the Germans, under countless hours of cross-examination by seasoned Abwehr and SD interrogators, on the bogus buildup at Dover, and on the massive but fictitious First U.S. Army Group to be led by Patton. He also had backed up the German view of timing—that an invasion couldn't commence yet—by posturing that the Dover preparations were far from ready.

»

On the morning of June 5, 1944, the weather at Normandy was abysmal. Sea swells were reaching four to five feet, it was drizzling, and heavy clouds were moving in. At Cherbourg the German naval commander for Normandy, Admiral Hennecke, was told by his meteorologist that the sea was rough, visibility poor, the wind was five to six knots, and that the rain would become heavier. The weatherman expected little change over the next few days. "Then that means," Hennecke concluded, "that the next day on which all the conditions of tide, moon and overall weather situation necessary for a landing . . . would not be until the second half of June."

Weather reports circulated among the army groups. From his headquarters in the Rochefoucauld castle at La Roche Guyon, Erwin Rommel wrote in his diary: "There is no indication that the invasion is imminent." Later that morning he left for Herringen to visit his wife Lucia, whose birthday was the sixth. From there he was planning to drive to the Berghof—Hitler's retreat in the Bavarian Alps—to personally plead with the Führer to let Normandy have two Panzer divisions and a rocket launcher.

It was a quiet day, Hans Speidel remembered. Reports from Abwehr agents, which suggested that an invasion was possible between June 5 and 15, had been distributed among the generals in France. Prior notices had all been false alarms, and the commanders received the updates with a grain of salt. The weather would prevent an invasion in any case. Reports of increased activity of the Free French resistance in the interior of France trickled in, and leaflets were distributed—particularly in Brittany—but Army Group B had been on full alert since the beginning of June. Speidel issued no further orders.

That evening at ten o'clock the Fifteenth Army stationed at Calais intercepted a coded message that the invasion was to begin. The report was relayed to Field Marshal von Rundstedt, as well as to troops on either side of the Fifteenth. Von Rundstedt decided not to notify the entire front, however. The seas were so rough that the navy patrols had been cancelled; surely this was another false alarm.

Not long after midnight General Speidel received word that enemy troops were parachuting into Caen and the Cotentin Peninsula. It was unclear whether the landings were isolated drops to assist the resistance, or part of an invasion force. Regardless, Speidel ordered all units to battle stations. Between 3:00 and 4:00 a.m., more landings were reported. Shortly thereafter, Allied planes began to bomb coastal defenses and the 21st Panzer Division was ordered to move into its battle position south of Caen. The 1st and reserve Panzer groups were told to be ready to move. Von Rundstedt and General Jodl at High Command headquarters in Zossen were notified.

At 5:30 a.m. it began.

»

Hundreds of Allied ships began raining down artillery on the Calvados coast, and Speidel ordered implementation of the German invasion defense, Operation Normandy. Just after six he called Rommel at home. Erwin approved Speidel's actions, ordered that all available resources be consolidated under one command, and suggested that the 21st Panzer Division would probably be needed for a counterattack. Rommel canceled his meeting with Hitler and left for La Roche Guyon. Hans passed word to General Marcks, commander of the 84th Army Corps.

No sooner than Speidel had hung up, he received word that Allied troops had stormed the beaches. He phoned Jodl and von Rundstedt again, but there was little they could do until a clear picture of the enemy's movement emerged. Hans knew Rommel would be furious. Throughout May the field marshal had repeatedly requested utilization of the 1st, 12th, and Panzer-Lehr divisions, intending to place them between Caen and Falaise. All requests had been denied, and this was part of what Erwin had planned to discuss with the Führer. As the battle on Normandy raged, Hitler denied Army Group B's requests for assistance from reserve armored divisions.

At ten o'clock the 21st Panzer Division, now pushing along the banks of the Orne, made contact with the besieged 716th Army Division. General Marcks, hearing that enemy troops had parachuted behind his line, abandoned the counterattack and moved his tanks to assist 716. At 3:00 p.m. the 1st Panzer Division was finally approved for release, but couldn't move during daylight hours due to Allied air superiority. At the same time, Allied ships were laying down a ring of fire inland to prevent the Germans from reinforcing.

Back at the Berghof, Hitler received the news. At his situation conference that morning, he mulled the probability of Normandy being a feint. In particular, he was concerned about the intelligence supplied by Germany's best spies. "How many of those fine agents are paid by the Allies, eh?" he asked his generals. "Then they deliberately plant confusing reports. I won't even pass this one on to Paris."

Hitler knew that the British had been flooding him with misinformation, but finding the right countermeasure was difficult. Albert Speer, Hitler's architect, armaments minister, and closest friend, explained: "The enemy intelligence service had deliberately played this information into his hands, Hitler maintained, in order to divert him from the true invasion site and lure him into committing his divisions too soon and in the wrong place. . . . During the previous several weeks, Hitler had received contradictory predictions on the time and place of the invasion from the rival intelligence organizations of the SS, the Wehrmacht, and the Foreign Office. . . . Now he scoffed at the various services, calling them all incompetent."

The Allies couldn't have asked for a better response. As Rommel begged for reinforcements, Hitler asserted that Normandy was only a distraction; the *real* invasion was yet to come. "During the following days and weeks," Speer wrote, "in characteristic but more and more absurd mistrust, Hitler remained convinced that the invasion was merely a feint whose purpose was to trick him into deploying his defensive forces wrongly. . . . For the time being he expected the decisive assault to take place in the vicinity of Calais. . . . This was the reason he did not commit the Fifteenth Army, stationed at Calais, to the battlefield on the coast of Normandy."

The exact opposite of what Rommel had requested—an immediate repelling defense by four Panzer divisions—was occurring. By the time Erwin arrived at his headquarters at 4:30 p.m., it was too late; the Allies had established several beachheads along the Normandy coast. Before sunset, Speidel was told, the U.S. First Army had landed two airborne divisions and at least three armored divisions; the British Second Army had pushed ashore four or five armored or infantry divisions, along with an airborne division; and bridgeheads would open between the Orne and the Ryles, and in the southeast corner of the Cotentin Peninsula. Reports indicated that the former was fifteen miles wide, six miles deep; the latter, nine miles wide, two deep. Before the day was out, Speidel heard that Allied air forces had pummeled the German positions with twenty-five thousand sorties.

Rommel's request that most of the eight infantry divisions in Calais be released to Normandy was denied. Available infantry and tank divisions were held back, released only piecemeal over the crucial invasion days: The 12th Panzer Division did not arrive until June 7; the Panzer-Lear and 346 Infantry divisions arrived on June 8 and 9; the 2nd Panzer, 3rd Parachute, and 77th Infantry divisions on June 13; the 1st Panzer Division on June 18. It was too little, too late.

General Speidel explained: "The reason for refusal was that Hitler and the High Command expected a second Allied landing on the Channel coast [Calais]. This question of a second landing was to play an important part in the first six weeks of the invasion. Marshal Rommel considered a second landing rather unlikely . . . but the bits of intelligence data that came in to us from above . . . reported between 30 and 50 divisions still in the British Isles. . . . From the middle of June on Army Group B thought it unlikely that Patton's Army would land north of the Seine. . . . The High Command again refused to let divisions of the Fifteenth Army be brought up . . . until the second half of July."

The Germans were waiting for Patton's massive army to launch from Dover and invade Calais. The "bits of intelligence"—agent IVAN's report of FUSAG troops, division insignia, preparations, officers, landing craft, and more—had been swallowed whole by the Abwehr and the High Command.

By all accounts D-Day was the turning point of the war, and Operation Fortitude was the turning point of the invasion. While Popov often didn't know if the Germans were buying his lies, Normandy was different: "Sometimes we never knew for sure," he later said. But regarding the invasion, "they must have—because after D-Day we captured maps which showed they had deployed their troops exactly as we had wanted them to."

The thousands of lives his Pearl Harbor information could have saved, his D-Day misinformation surely did.

»

While Allied soldiers battled and bled to secure ground in France, Popov secretly waged his own war. Soon after hearing of Johnny's arrest, Dusko had sent—without telling MI5 or MI6—a blackmail letter to the Abwehr station in Lisbon. If Johnny wasn't freed, he threatened, he'd terminate all efforts on their behalf. So long as he wasn't blown, Dusko figured, it might work. Since the war began, he had been Germany's top agent, and they wouldn't risk losing him needlessly.

In the meantime, he wanted work and he wanted to find out about Ivo. He suggested to Colonel Robertson that someone, namely himself, might go to Yugoslavia to meet with General Mihailovic. Since the country's politics underlying the war were in play—with the Partisan Communist Tito and Chetnik Royalist Mihailovic vying for power—British Intelligence surely needed a man on the ground. At the same time, Dusko could find Ivo and their parents and secure everyone's safety.

On June 19 Robertson and Wilson met with Popov and explained that such a trip would be too risky. If Dusko were to be captured—either by the Germans or the Communists—it would jeopardize the tremendous gains that had been achieved over the last four years. Dusko again would have to sit idle while MI5 monitored the situation. FREAK, meanwhile, had been asked by King Peter, Yugoslavia's monarch, to accompany him on an upcoming trip to Italy and Malta. Accordingly, the Germans were notified that he would be unable to transmit for a short while.

About this time, the king sent word that he also had a mission for Popov. If the British and Americans would allow it, Peter wanted Dusko to visit the U.S. to participate in a conference on international currency and postwar trade, and to garner support from Yugoslavs in the States for a pending compromise between the king and Tito. Ian Wilson supported the trip, since it would be a suitable reason why Popov could not continue to supply the Germans with reports, coinciding with FREAK's duties. "The present position is that the Germans are continuing to call FREAK," he wrote in a memo to

Robertson and Marriott. "The position is still too uncertain for us to resume normal traffic, and our principal concern must be to prevent the Germans from learning, if they do not already know it, that TRICYCLE and FREAK have been working under our control."

Ian suggested that FREAK, now back from his trip, could signal the Germans that Popov had been similarly called to duty by the king and was leaving for America. FREAK could report that Dusko "hoped that either on the way out or the return journey he would have an opportunity of reporting in person in Lisbon. (In fact we would make arrangements to ensure that he did not pass through Lisbon.)"

Robertson and Marriott agreed, and the Yugoslav Embassy immediately applied for Dusko's exit permit from England and visa to America. On June 30 FREAK radioed the Germans:

> Had to stop for reasons given in Ivan letter May twenty. Have since had to travel with my master. Am just back but may be sent away on further unavoidable mission for him at short notice. Thanks to him English doubts of me mostly overcome but still some exist. Ivan has been invited to go on official mission for our Government to Washington. He will try to pass through Lisbon as he has much material.

Around this time, Dusko remembered, Robertson showed up again at the Clock House. "News of Jebsen," he cried. "Your ruse seems to be working. We've had a report that the Abwehr is trying to obtain his release. The Gestapo is blocking it, but there's hope." Most importantly, Tar said, Johnny hadn't talked.

Dusko had his doubts about Johnny's release. Since the fall of Canaris, the Abwehr had little power. The only hope, it seemed, was his letter to Lisbon, which might—if Popov was lucky—end up on Schellenberg's desk. But feedback from the Germans about agent IVAN proved unsteady. On July 3 they responded to FREAK's messages:

> Yours thirtieth June, do not understand sudden unnotified interruption of work in present critical times. Letter Ivan twentieth not received in view of

```
postal restrictions. Please notify urgently date
departure Ivan for U.S. via Lisbon.
```

MI5, however, wasn't about to resume regular radio contact; FREAK and TRICYCLE needed to stay out of the loop until it was clear that Jebsen had not exposed them. Ian suggested that B1A toss in a countermeasure—a secret ink letter from Dusko to Lisbon complaining about the lack of activity on the escape route. If nothing else, he figured, it might provoke the Germans into revealing why they had abandoned the route, citing "technical difficulties."

As the TRICYCLE-FREAK pot simmered over Jebsen's heat, Dusko received more news.

Ivo had been arrested.

26

NAKED AND SHAVED

Ivo's arrest occurred not long after Johnny's kidnapping and was based, from what MI6 had heard, on Dr. Popov's participation in the currency deals. The Gestapo, Ivo later told Dusko, showed up one day at Dr. Popov's medical office and cashiered him to Glavnyaca prison without charges. During interrogation Ivo realized the Germans knew nothing of his underground activities, and questioned only about occupation marks he had purchased.

From time to time Ivo was allowed care packages from friends. One morning, Dusko explained in his memoirs, Ivo received a parcel from a patient who was working with him in the underground. Among the goods was a box of cigarettes. Ivo emptied it and found a small paper, which had separated the sections. On it was the floor plan of the Gestapo headquarters where he had been questioned. When the prisoners were next taken in for interrogation, Ivo bolted for the exit. Three weeks later he met up with General Mihailovic's resistance forces in the Serbian forests.

On August 2 SIS London received a "Most Immediate" telegram from an MI6 agent in Bari, Italy. The cable stated that a local SOE operative had received—perhaps intercepted—a radio signal from General Mihailovic. It requested that a message be forwarded to "I. Wilson" and stated that a Dr. Popov had escaped from the Gestapo and was with Mihailovic's resistance fighters. He was traveling as Dr. Predrag Ivanovic, it said, and desired evacuation from Foggia, Italy. The general noted that Dr. Popov could be transported by American aviators who were currently with his men. The SOE agent added that the evacuation could take place over the next few days and if London so desired, to send instructions. Frank Foley cabled back that the Bari agent was to evacuate Ivo at once to the U.K.

Dr. Ivo Popov, MI5 file. The scar above his left eye was courtesy of a German rifle butt. *The National Archives of the UK*

Ian rushed to the Clock House. While Dusko's heart was warmed by the news, he wrote, his nerves had been whittled raw by the stress of Johnny's and Ivo's imprisonments. Further, his planned trip to the U.S. for the king—after incessant questions and hurdles from the FBI and the SIS—had been scrapped. As a result, he had no present duties; he asked Ian for a break.

Someplace to get away. Away from prisons and spies and D-Day and doodlebugs. A place where he could just "read and walk and forget about the war" for a few days. Wilson agreed to work on it. In the meantime, Ian had another pressing issue. For several weeks the FBI had been pestering MI5 and BSC for reports on Dusko, asking for details of what he had been doing. Since all roads eventually led to Johnny, however, Ian and Tar were wary to provide too much. And why did the FBI care? Dusko had not been in their employ for two years.

That afternoon Wilson discovered the reason: The FBI had received a story—the source of which was allegedly the Poles—about various mysteries surrounding a playboy Yugoslav diplomat. The FBI, Ian found out, had received a recited summary of the PVDE report. Sensing no harm in the inquiry or the information, he prepared a full report of Popov's last year and forwarded it through the American Embassy. While at it, he also found time to locate Dusko's hideaway.

The first week of August Dusko was off to Scotland. Tucked in a forsaken corner of the northeast Highlands, near the coastal town of Tain, was a small lodge known as Fisherman Inn. Only sea and sheep for miles around, Ian had said. It was quiet all right.

On August 11 Dusko called John Marriott to tell him that he'd moved to Kinlochbervie, another small town but on the west coast. With a population of a couple hundred, Kinlochbervie's main attraction was the fish depot. Nonetheless, Dusko could rest, walk the craggy shore, and clear his mind. Marriott mentioned that Ivo had made it to Italy, and Dusko left his number—201—in case MI5 received word that Ivo had reached England. Four days later, Dusko recalled, he was awakened in the middle of the night by banging on his door. It was a policeman, who said that Popov was to report to the War Office.

Immediately.

At a military airport near Epsom, Dusko was met by his old chauffeur, Jock Horsfall, who raced to Waterloo Station. There, standing with Ian, was Ivo. Although haggard from months in the woods, Dr. Popov was in good spirits. They checked into the Savoy, and after hearing details of Ivo's escape, Dusko told him about Jebsen's arrest. Did Ivo know of anyone who might be able to help? he asked.

According to Popov's memoirs, Ivo mentioned Frederick Hahn as a potential lead. A senior official in the Reichsbank, Hahn had been in charge of controlling national banks in occupied countries, and had participated in Jebsen's currency deals. Hahn's fiancée, Jacqueline Blanc, was in Paris and had met Ivo while he was coming through the escape line with Johnny. If Hahn wasn't there, Ivo had said, Blanc might know of his whereabouts.

»

Dusko arrived in Paris at the end of August, days after the city's liberation. With any luck, he recalled thinking, he might find Hahn hiding out in Blanc's apartment as the Wehrmacht retreated.

Jacqueline Blanc was in her mid-twenties and beautiful, Popov remembered, but her eyes were filled with haunting terror. Dusko introduced himself and said he was looking for a friend, Johann Jebsen, and that Ivo had mentioned Mr. Hahn as a potential lead. Blanc invited him in but said that Frederick was away on business in Germany, and that she hadn't seen him for over a month. Dusko remembered offering her a cigarette, but she said she didn't smoke.

He glanced at the full ashtray.

"Mademoiselle Blanc, let me be very frank with you. I am determined to save Jebsen by any means necessary. If you refuse to help, I shall have to take disagreeable steps. You are quite vulnerable, Mademoiselle Blanc. Please don't force me to take action."

Jacqueline asked what he was talking about.

"Yesterday I was walking on the Champs-Elysées and saw a revolting sight. Some girls were being marched through the street naked with their heads shaven and swastikas painted all over them. They had been associating with the Germans."

"You *wouldn't—*"

"To save a friend's life, Mademoiselle Blanc, I'd go much further than that."

Suddenly, the bedroom door burst open and a tall German stormed into the room. He pointed a gun at Dusko.

ULLA

Popov told Hahn to put the pistol away. He simply wanted names of people involved in Jebsen's currency deals who might be able to help. After a bit of stalling, Hahn informed him that Johnny was being held in the Prinz-Albrecht-Strasse, and that several men had interrogated him, including an SS officer named Walter Salzer, Kaltenbrunner's* assistant.

Salzer was in his early forties, Dusko recalled Frederick saying, five-foot-ten or so, and would be easy to identify since he had a saber scar on his left cheek and his left hand had been so badly burned that he almost always wore gloves. As for who had the power to obtain Johnny's release, Hahn gave the name of Dr. Schmidtt, Schellenberg's aide-de-camp.

That night Dusko drafted a letter to Schmidtt, stating that unless Jebsen was released safely to Lisbon or Switzerland, he was shutting down his net. Adding that he knew numerous officers were involved in Johnny's deals, Dusko said he'd hate to see other heads fall. Schmidtt, who had likely participated, would get the point. Signing it as "Ivan," Dusko sent it the following day through a courier.

While Dusko chased the Hahn lead, Ian Wilson assisted from London. On September 10 he asked Frank Foley to have the Paris office interrogate two men who might have information on Johnny: Vladan Popov, Rue Maribeau, 19/v, Paris, and Mihail Glusevic, Rue Franqueville 15, Paris.

Vladan, Dusko's younger brother, was attending medical school in Paris,† Ian wrote, and Glusevic was a business agent of Johnny's and had participated

---

* Ernst Kaltenbrunner was director of the Reich Main Security Office, a combination of the Gestapo, Kripo, and SD.

† Dusko apparently was unaware that his brother was in Paris at this time.

in the financial scheme. In addition, Glusevic had been working with Jebsen and a group of financiers to fight the "German Economic State System." Apparently organized and secret, they were using the password "SENI." Ian also asked that the local agents let Vladan know they could carry back to Dusko and Ivo any personal letter.

An SIS agent apparently found Vladan, but the circumstances surrounding it were odd. On September 26 Dusko received a letter at the Yugoslav Legation. Strangely, the envelope contained two letters—one from Vladan and the other from Branko Milinovic, a Yugoslav friend. Dusko showed them to Ian the following day and noted that the writing was not of either man, but that Vladan's signature was in fact genuine. The letter read:

Dear brother Dule,

As Ivan told me to do, 15 days ago I sent you a message. But up to now I did not get a single answer from you; and I am very much worried.

Please help me to come to see you; otherwise I shall have to go to the Rhein. My financial situation is very very bad since two monthes [sic].

News = last news from our family I got before two monthes [sic]—Ivan has escaped from the Gestapo in the forests.—A bomb fell on our Belguzol's house. . . .

Hope to see you the sooner possible. Much love from your brother,

Vladan Popov

The unknown courier, Wilson figured, had required Vladan and Branko to record their correspondence in English as a precondition to carrying it, and may have been the scrivener. In any case, the letter made Dusko "keener than ever" to see his younger brother and Yugoslav friends. Wilson suggested to Tar that he (Ian) and Popov travel at once to Paris; Dusko could visit Vladan and at the same time they could pursue leads on Johnny.

Since the French border was strictly controlled, Robertson would have to appeal to Allied Supreme Headquarters for clearance. On the twenty-eighth, Tar made the request to a Lieutenant Colonel Speir, and two days later MI5 had their papers—formal approval by way of command and assignment from General Eisenhower himself.

»

The first week of October Dusko and Ian traveled to Paris and tried to make progress on Johnny. The endeavor was fruitless. None of Jebsen's Parisian contacts, including Johnny's mistress, had an inkling of what had happened to him. The good news was that since the Germans had made no attempt to arrest or interrogate any of Jebsen's associates (save Glusevic), it was apparent that Johnny had not disclosed that he, Dusko, or Ivo were British controlled. Glusevic, while taken in for interrogation in mid-August, had only been asked about Johnny's financial affairs; neither the Popovs nor any linking friends were mentioned. Surprisingly, the Germans asked nothing of the Yugoslav escape route, even though Glusevic had cashiered escapees through Paris.

By the end of the month Wilson had no further leads and no additional duties for Dusko. Given Johnny's situation, MI5 couldn't actively engage the Germans from the TRICYCLE net, and Popov was free, until further notice, to do as he pleased. On October 27 Ian gave Dusko the $10,000 that MI5 had been holding and told him to stay in touch.

With an authorized leave of absence, Dusko accelerated efforts to help Johnny. His correspondence to Dr. Schmidtt, he later found out, had made an impact. Shortly after receiving it, Schmidtt had Jebsen transferred from Prinz-Albrecht-Strasse to Oranienburg; no picnic itself, but the concentration camp was far better than the Prinz prison. After that, Dusko was told, Schmidtt sent Captain Kammler to the Gestapo to negotiate Jebsen's release. He also asked the captain to see Johnny and let him know what was happening.

The Johann the captain witnessed was jolting. "Dressed in prison clothes," Kammler said, Johnny "was starting to take on the look of the typical concentration-camp victim. His flesh and muscle had melted away, and his head looked enormous sitting on top of his wasted neck and shoulders. His hair had fallen out in patches." But Johnny's spirit was strong, Kammler reported, and his crystal eyes flashed when told that Popov was effecting his release.

"Tell Dusko I knew he wouldn't forget me," Johnny had said.

From Hjalmar Schacht, president of the Reichsbank, Dusko later learned of Johnny's unbreakable spirit. Schacht, who was imprisoned in the cell next to Jebsen's at Prinz, described what he witnessed when Johnny returned to his cell after an interrogation. "His shirt was drenched with blood," Schacht recalled, and as the guards were locking him in his cell, Johnny snapped with aristocratic authority, "I trust I shall be provided with a clean shirt."

»

On November 11 Popov met with Wilson to discuss another problem: Yugoslavia. At best, Dusko said, their friends and neighbors in Belgrade and Dubrovnik saw him and Ivo as cowards who had fled in time of need; at worst, their countrymen believed they were German agents. Partisan records in Cairo, Dusko had found out, listed him as a Fascist and Nazi collaborator. Yet Dusko and Ivo were not worried about reprisals against them personally—they were out of the country—but against family members. On October 20 Belgrade had been liberated, and scores were being settled with collaborators and their families. Neither he nor Ivo had heard from their parents, Dusko told Ian, or from Ivo's wife. Wilson agreed to speak to Foley, and said that London would ask local agents to look for them, and provide protection if possible.

Dusko also said that King Peter had asked him to visit Belgrade on a special mission. He didn't have details, but wanted to know if British Intelligence had any objection. Wilson said no. Popov's assumption was that the king sought his counsel about upcoming decisions Peter would have to make regarding Tito, Communism, and bridging the divide with the Partisans. While Popov was anti-Communist, he had not committed himself politically and favored compromise with Tito, a view which aligned with the king's.

Ten days later Dusko notified Ian of mission specifics. King Peter had told Dusko that he would fly him to Belgrade as special emissary, but that the need for certain approvals had caused delay. Dusko and Ian filled in the blanks: There was inherent danger in Popov arriving in Belgrade as a Royalist or Yugoslav officer. It was more than possible that a Russian or a Communist might "seek to do him harm." The "approvals," it appeared, was authorization to have Dusko arrive in Belgrade in a British uniform. The king had discussed this with Churchill, Peter told Popov, and the prime minister had had no objection if the king could arrange it with the Air Ministry.

Dusko also asked Ian to consider reengaging the Germans. Word could be sent to them that Popov was moving to Paris, and since the SD had numerous agents in Switzerland, Dusko could arrange a trip for personal contact. If the liaison between the king and the Communists was handled properly, he said, he could obtain necessary approvals from the new Yugoslav government. Wilson discussed the idea internally, but the conclusion was that reopening the dialogue might cause the Germans to reexamine the TRICYCLE net, exposing all.

The following day Ian met again with Dusko and told him that the notion of reconnecting with the Germans was off, but that the Paris trip could move forward. Due to the circumstances, however, Popov would have to do something out of character—lay low. Ian warned Dusko not to draw attention to himself in Paris—"by excessive expenditure or otherwise."

As Wilson had promised, he also worked on finding and protecting Dusko's parents and Ivo's family. Ian notified MI6 of Ivo's wife's name, Dragica, and the corresponding details. Their house had been destroyed by American bombs, he explained, the whereabouts of Ivo's wife and child unknown. Ian suggested that SIS might inquire with Dragica's father, George Vasic, who was a priest at St. Sava, a large church in Belgrade. The location and status of Dusko and Ivo's parents, he added, was also unknown.

The SIS work was dicey. If word got out that the British were trying to locate and protect certain Yugoslavs, rumors would spread that those protected were Allied agents. If the name of any Popov surfaced, the TRICYCLE net would be exposed and Johnny would be shot. And others. Heinrich Himmler had made clear in an order on September 10 that "every deserter . . . will find his just punishment. Furthermore, his ignominious behavior will entail the most severe consequences for his family. . . . They will be summarily shot."

»

At the end of November, Dusko wrote in his memoirs, he received a strange letter from Switzerland. Someone named "Ulla" had written him, as if a friend, saying that Johnny would be visiting her in Zurich a week or two before Christmas. Jebsen would be staying at the Hotel Baur au Lac, the letter stated, and would love to see him.

Popov could only wonder: *Who was Ulla?*

Unknown to him at the time, only one Ulla had surfaced in MI5, MI6, or BSC reports. On December 17, 1941, British censors in Bermuda had intercepted a secret German letter from Mexico to Sweden. Ostensibly from Agencia Commercial e Informadora International, the correspondence was addressed to an Ulla H. Moberg of 21 Styrmannsgaten, Stockholm. In invisible ink, the message to Ulla stated that since Germany had declared war on the U.S. and had broken diplomatic relations with Mexico, secret messages bound for Sweden, Portugal, and Chile would henceforth be sent via microdots.

Jumping at any lead, Dusko booked the trip. He flew to Paris and took up residence with his friend Branko. On December 14 he sent a letter to Wilson and provided the telephone number and address—95, Rue Taitbout—in case Ian needed to get in touch. He did not mention his planned trip to Switzerland, but told Ian that he'd let him know if any news arrived regarding the mission for the king. Closing with "Give my love to everybody in the office," he was off to Zurich.

He checked in at the Zum Storchen and went by the Hotel Baur au Lac to see if Jebsen had arrived. He had not, the clerk said, and for the next several days Dusko stopped by the Baur au Lac twice a day. No sign of Johnny.

Pacing the hotel daily, Dusko remembered, he was consumed with thoughts of his friend. As Christmas neared, hope of seeing Johnny waned, and on December 24 he gave up the vigil and returned to Paris.

»

Just before the New Year he met with Major Foley and agent Desmond Bristow. While MI5 had placed him on indefinite sabbatical, MI6 hadn't. They asked him to help build a new network in Paris. A considerable number of General Mihailovic's operatives, they said, had been imprisoned by the Germans but had escaped during the retreat. If Popov could supply names, MI6 would approach them to become "straight line-crossing agents." Others with suitable backgrounds might be sent to Switzerland as bait to become double agents. Dusko couldn't be visible in the operation, of course, since again one slip and his cover would be blown.

Meanwhile, Popov's mission for King Peter had fallen through. The Yugoslav Foreign Office—apparently from objection by the Russians—refused to authorize it "as a question of foreign policy." That was the good news. Dusko also received word that the Partisans had identified his brother as a Nazi collaborator. The situation was a frightening re-creation of the Ustaše nightmare in 1941: Since Ivo was in England, the sentence would fall on his wife and child.

Dragica and Misha were to be shot.

PARTISAN POLITICS

Near the end of February 1945 Dusko saw an old girlfriend in London. She was a Yugoslav and the former mistress of General Vlatko Velebit, a Serb who had joined the Partisans in 1941. She asked if Dusko was related to Dragica Popov, and he confirmed that she was his sister-in-law. Velebit had recently told her, she said, that the Partisans had robbed and arrested Dragica on the basis of Ivo's supposed collaboration with the Nazis. Ivo's wife and their small child were to be shot, she went on, but a Scottish brigadier—Fitzroy Maclean of the SAS—apparently had intervened. Maclean's credentials were above reproach: As Winston Churchill's personal representative, he had parachuted into Yugoslavia as commander of Britain's military mission to the Partisans, and worked directly with Tito.

Dusko passed this on to Wilson, and Ian to Major Bristow. In a letter to the MI6 agent on February 27, Wilson lamented the lack of information security in Yugoslavia. While Maclean was to be lauded for saving the Popovs, Ian wondered aloud whether the Scot could have achieved the result without compromising DREADNOUGHT and, by extension, the entire TRICYCLE net. Ian asked Desmond to find out exactly what had been told to which Yugoslavs, and by whom. Bristow might as well have been told to kick an anthill and record the activity of each insect.

On March 14 Belgrade SIS reported back. To secure Dragica's and Misha's release and safety, local agent L. H. Cohen wrote, Maclean had approached Tito directly. He told the Partisan general that Ivo was indeed working for MI5, and offered that the British would provide a flight for Dragica and her son to join Ivo in England. Tito assented and assigned General Velebit to assist.

Cohen added that "DREADNOUGHT's work for us is fully understood, but in the eyes of the general public Dragica must unfortunately suffer for what her husband agreed to do in Belgrade." As for the fallout of security, he went on: "Dragica, with some knowledge has unfortunately talked herself and it must therefore be assumed that many more people in Belgrade now believe her husband is in England and worked as a British, and not a German, agent." As a result, the Americans and Russians also now knew, and keeping it from the Germans would be difficult.

While accurate at the time, Cohen's report underestimated the danger to Dragica and Misha. In the end, they would flee Yugoslavia—Dragica dressed as a man in a British uniform, Misha (now four) drugged and sleeping in a duffel bag carried by Fitzroy Maclean—on a British bomber.

»

As spring brought warmth and new life, good news trickled in on all fronts. Dusko was living in Paris and had started a publishing business, which was flourishing. On April 6 he received word that his father had escaped to Switzerland, and that Dragica and Misha had arrived safely in Bari. Hoping that MI5 could pull strings to get him to Zurich, Dusko flew to London.

Milorad Popov had been outwardly working for the SD, Wilson and Bristow told Dusko, but, like his sons, had been double-crossing. Mr. Popov was now in a refugee camp, they said, and had little money. The intelligence officers didn't have information as to why Milorad fled to Switzerland, or why Mrs. Popov was not with him. Dusko's father would have trouble getting out of the camp, they added, as it required a sizeable payment to Swiss authorities. For the sake of Dusko's cover and possible repercussions to Johnny, however, British representatives could not contact Swiss authorities.

MI6 had already briefed an agent in Switzerland, Bristow said, who would try to contact Mr. Popov and give him money. In the meantime, they would find out what payment was required for the authorities, and Dusko could transfer funds from his Banco Espirito Santo account in Lisbon to his Schweizerische Bankverein account in Berne. If his visa came through normal channels and Dusko made it to Switzerland, Ian offered, he was free to find Johnny's friends and inquire about Jebsen's status.

Days later, promising news about Johnny arrived. Major Bristow reported that an American source in Lisbon had said that Jebsen was not only alive, but had left for England. Dusko couldn't celebrate, however, because SIS reported at the same time that his father was having a rough go in the Swiss camp. The situation was considered urgent, they said, and Dusko asked the Yugoslav Embassy to help with the visa. Unfortunately, that would take time.

On May 2 Dusko returned to Paris, still longing for a way to help his father. Meanwhile, the pillars of the Third Reich crumbled. General Patton had relieved Bastogne in late December 1944, concluding the Battle of the Bulge on January 16, 1945. On March 7 Allied troops had crossed the Rhine and encircled the Germans in the Ruhr. Two months later, at Rheims, France, on May 7, 1945, General Alfred Jodl signed on behalf of the German High Command Germany's unconditional surrender. VE* Day on May 8, 1945, was the largest outdoor party in the world, spanning from Los Angeles to Vladivostok.†

Dusko sent a congratulatory letter to Ian "and all my friends in the office, hoping that a terrific hang-over they might have will pretty soon disappear." Since Jebsen had not shown up in England, Dusko also mentioned that Johnny once had a hideout at a pub near Freiburg, and that the owner was a man named Schmidt. Perhaps MI6's Major Peter Hope, he suggested, might be able to pursue the lead. If not, Dusko was more than ready to go himself. He asked if Ian had any news about Johnny's wife, Lore, whom Dusko also believed to be in Freiburg. If Ian authorized him to go, he said, he could look for both. Wilson declined, deciding to let local MI6 agents handle it.

As summer approached, things seemed to unravel. Dusko still had not acquired the Swiss visa and had no further news of his father. Johnny's fate, which Dusko had clung to for a year now, seemed in doubt. On May 26 the Allies interrogated an Abwehr agent named Waetjen, who seemed to have intimate knowledge of Johnny and his activities. "In spite and because of good connections with the Gestapo and S.D.," he had said, Jebsen "helped many people who had difficulties with [the] Nazi organization. By his warnings many people were saved."

Waetjen believed Johnny had been killed.

Two weeks later the Allies interrogated a senior Abwehr officer, *Oberstleutnant*‡ Wilhelm Kuebart. As Major Wiegand's immediate superior, Kuebart had voiced numerous doubts about Popov, and was suspicious about Jebsen

---

* Victory in Europe.

† By the time Soviet General Zhukov ratified the surrender in a ceremony with German Field Marshal Wilhelm Keitel on May 8 in Berlin, it was May 9 Moscow time.

‡ Lieutenant Colonel.

as well. When Johnny refused to go to Biarritz, Kuebart stated, Colonel Hansen ordered his arrest. After Johnny arrived in Berlin, he went on, "Hansen had to turn him over to the S.D. on the direct instructions of Field Marshal Kietel, which produced a great deal of ill-feeling in the Abwehr." After that, Kuebart claimed, he heard nothing more about Jebsen.

On June 9 Ian finally received news about Dusko's father in Switzerland. The local SIS agents apologized for the delay, saying that they had heard Mr. Popov was in Ticino, but eventually traced him to the Bear Hotel in Baden. At the same time, Ian received through Major Hope correspondence from Dusko to Ivo, which Ian passed along. The letter stated that Dusko had finally received his Swiss visa, and hoped that the British could assist in transferring money to Switzerland and getting his father to France. Dusko was planning to leave the following day, so Ian passed word through MI6 to let him know that Mr. Popov was in Baden, that they would work on the money and entrance to France, and that Ian was still working on locating Jebsen or his wife. Johnny had not survived, Wilson thought, yet he had no particular evidence.

That evening Ian gave Dusko's letter to Ivo and asked if he knew Lore Jebsen's stage names during her acting career. Ivo didn't, only that she had worked at the State Theater in Hanover.

Two days later Ian updated Frank Foley, and reminded him of their promise to Jebsen: "You will remember when we were both in Lisbon, about the only assurance which we gave to JOHNNY was that if anything happened to him we would look after the welfare of his wife. He explained that he was not particularly worried about her financial future as he had taken other steps to provide for that, but that he would like to know that we were seeing that she did not meet any undue difficulties." Ian added that he felt Johnny's chances of survival were not very high, but that there was no evidence that Jebsen had disclosed any secrets about doubling or the TRICYCLE net. If Foley had the occasion, Wilson asked, Frank's assistance in finding Johnny would be appreciated.

On June 6 the SOE had forwarded an enciphered message that seemed to shed light on Johnny's plight. The message was dated February 1945 and was from Lieutenant Commander Cumberledge, an SOE operative who had been captured in Greece while trying to blow up the Corinth Canal. He was interned at Oranienburg, the note said, and was believed to have been shot prior to the camp's liberation by the Russians on April 30. Before he died, however, he passed a coded letter to another prisoner, Colonel Jack Churchill, who survived the war and made it back to England:

```
Johny Jebsen hun held high treason can D repeat D
Popoff Jslav Warminster help urgent F.O. know of
J. J. all charges against us are baseless.
```

Cumberledge also wrote a letter to his wife and enciphered the following sentence:

```
Johny Debsen hun held high treason can [MI5
concealed] of Selection Trust help?
```

Two weeks later Wilson received a note about "Mrs. ARTIST" from MI6. Through METEOR they learned that Lore's maiden name was Peterson, and that her father was a professor at a language school in Leipzig. Lore was about thirty-two, it said, five-foot-eight, with a good figure, very beautiful, and was fluent in German, French, and English. She was regularly employed, it also stated, as a leading lady at Frankfort-am-Oder theater.

On June 25 Popov sent a letter to Wilson, updating him on the trip to Switzerland. While helping his father, Dusko wrote, he had met another camp refugee, a Greek named Aframides, who had been imprisoned at Prinz-Albrecht-Strasse with Johnny. The principal Gestapo agent investigating Jebsen, the Greek said, was *Obergeheimrat* Quetting. Aframides went on to say that Quetting boasted of having sent men to Lisbon to bring Johnny to Berlin.

Knowing that British and American officers would be vetting war prisoners, Dusko thought Ian might pass word to keep a watch out for Quetting. "If you have luck and find the man," he wrote, "keep him alive until I come, I would love to have a few words with him." Nothing more was heard about Quetting.

Officially.

At the end of the month, Ian finally received encouraging news about Johnny. SHEAF sent a telegram which contained an extract from the interrogation of Walter Schellenberg the day before. "In Berlin handed to Mueller [Gestapo chief]," the message read, "was accused of working for Britain." Noting that the suspicion of Johnny stemmed from conflicting reports he sent to different departments, the telegram stated that Schellenberg "thinks that Jebsen has not been killed."

Clinging to any hope, Dusko met with Ian and William Luke to inquire if he could go to Freiburg to look for Johnny's wife. The MI5 officers said that they could not officially support it. Days later Luke checked with Trevor Wilson of MI6, who stated that SIS could probably "unofficially" assist Popov. Meanwhile, Dusko's father had made it to France and was planning to visit Ivo in London.

A month later Ian received another extract from the interrogation of *Oberstleutnant* Kuebart. Passing the testimony on to Masterman and Luke, Ian wrote that Kuebart did not seem "even now, to suspect that Tricycle's information was plant material nor that Tricycle was under our control." Equally important, it was evident that Johnny had not talked, as he was "clearly suspected of intending to desert but not of having already, for some time, acted as a British Agent."

About this time Ian sent a memo to Masterman, Luke, and Harris, summarizing MI5's deception with Operation Fortitude. Kuebart testified, Ian wrote, that Abwehr agents IVAN (Popov) and OSTRO* had sent information on English division numbers and locations, although the latter's were mostly unusable. "It is eminently satisfactory," Wilson stated, that "the man who held the position of head of the enemy military espionage services from July 1943 to July 1944 was relying for his information about England upon three controlled agents."

Things were looking up. The deception operation had been successful, Mr. Popov was now in France, and Kuebart's testimony indicated that Johnny had not talked and might still be alive. Ian sent letters to the army and the SOE to pursue Jebsen leads. The SOE, in particular, had contacts to a prisoner who had survived Oranienburg—Captain Payne Best from the Venlo kidnapping incident—and Wilson encouraged steadfast investigation.

By mid-August, however, the search had stalled. SOE found nothing from Oranienburg and Best's whereabouts were unknown. "I am still concerned at the lack of definite news about the fate of ARTIST," Ian wrote in a note to

---

* OSTRO was a Sudeten Czech named Paul Fidrmuc who operated from Lisbon and fed the Abwehr "intelligence" based on gossip, hunches, pre-war reference materials, and pure imagination. His network of sub-agents was entirely fictitious.

Major Luke. "TRICYCLE is himself going to try and seek information from friends of ARTIST's known to him."

Dusko went to Germany that month and located Lore Jebsen's friends, although he was unable to catch Lore. She was in the Russian zone, he found out, and was doing her best to cross into the American or English zone. Upon his return to Paris on August 27, he sent Ian a letter with Lore's address and telephone number, as well as the two cities where she was expected to appear. Dusko also told Ian that while on his trip, he had found out that a close relative in Belgrade had been attacked, robbed, and arrested.

His mother.

JOHNNY

On July 18 Partisans had attacked and robbed Dusko's mother of her money and jewelry. Ten days later she was arrested. "You can imagine how I feel about all that," Popov wrote to his case officer. With only slight exaggeration, Dusko suggested that he might use the same "nazi-gangster methods" and kidnap a Partisan general to assure his mother's safety.

Knowing that Ian would move heaven and earth to help, Dusko thanked him, saying that the entire Popov family should elect him as their "honorary father." Wilson went to work, as Dusko had expected, firing off letters and calls. The feedback from SIS Belgrade on September 6, unfortunately, was frightening: "I had heard subject [Mrs. Popov] was in prison and have been trying to discover reasons," wrote Major R. M. Hamer. Dusko's mother had been advised by family, he reported, to visit Dubrovnik for her health. The night before her departure, she was arrested.

Suspecting that the arrest was due to "foolish talking" by Mrs. Popov or her acquaintances, Hamer noted that "stories got put about" that she had sons in the U.K. and U.S. who had advised her to go to Dubrovnik, from where she might escape Yugoslavia. If this was the reason for her arrest, he warned, "it will not repeat not be easy for me to mediate and results for doing so might worsen matters." Hamer went on to say that the chances of springing Mrs. Popov were remote, and that the wiser plan would be to let the matter run its course. In all likelihood, he figured, Mrs. Popov would have to remain in prison to serve the "usual corrective period," or another three to six weeks.

Meanwhile, Ivo's wife dashed off letters to General Velebit and a Belgrade lawyer who she thought could help. Zora Popov never meddled in politics, Dragica told them, and "only lived for her children, and whose one ambition" was to see her children happy.

As the effort to free Mrs. Popov continued, MI5 received a lead on ARTIST. The Americans had arrested Baroness von Gronau, British Intelligence heard, and Johnny's old friend just might have information on his fate. In a letter to a Major Forrest on September 9, William Luke provided the Americans with Jebsen's background and asked that von Gronau be questioned about Johnny. "As we feel some sense of responsibility towards this Abwehr officer who ultimately came under our control," Luke wrote, "we should very much like to know his ultimate fate and, if, as now seems unlikely, he is alive, we would wish to secure his release."

While Popov awaited news about his mother and Johnny, King Peter called and Dusko again assumed duties as the king's emissary, this time to political and military officials in Austria and Italy. In particular, the king wanted Dusko to help raise an army to resist Tito. No sooner than that assignment started, however, reports came in about Johnny and Dusko's mother.

On October 17 Major Hamer notified MI5 that, according to Belgrade sources, Mrs. Popov had finally been released from prison. After an almost two-month incarceration, he said, Zora was going to the Vrnjačka Spa to recover. The leads on Johnny, unfortunately, proved to be dead ends. With no progress in sight, Dusko asked William Luke if British Intelligence would object to a trip to Hamburg so that he could at long last find out what happened to his friend. In a letter to MI6's Hamer, Luke passed on the request:

"As you know, we have been unable to find out from any Field Source anything about ARTIST. . . . I told TRICYCLE that I did not think he could obtain any information which would not also be available to us, or that his enquiries in Hamburg would get him any further, but he disagreed with me and felt that . . . he was mainly responsible for ARTIST's misfortunes and that if ARTIST was no longer in this world, which seems likely to be the case, he would wish to do something for the long suffering widow." Luke mentioned that MI5 would not sanction the trip, but would not object. Adding that the visit might help resolve the ARTIST mystery, Luke wrote that he would be glad if MI6 would stamp Popov's papers with "No Objection."

Major Hope and Major Bristow reported back that SIS did not object, and Popov left Paris for Hamburg on October 27. Hope had given Dusko a Mission Order to visit a Major Jo Stephenson in Germany, which Dusko would do on November 1. One of Johnny's friends, Dr. Max Bruecher, had previously offered help, so he would be Dusko's first call.

While Dusko scoured Germany for leads, a familiar name resurfaced in London: Quetting. The U.S. Forces European Theater Office, which had interrogated SS-*Standartenführer* Eugen Steimle, notified the London War Room on November 30 that Steimle might indirectly help with locating Jebsen. Steimle, USFET reported, had replaced Wilhelm Kuebart at Abwehr/SD Mil B after the failed July 20, 1944, putsch.* In the fall of 1944, the message went, Hermann Quetting, recently promoted to *Sturmbannführer* (major), had contacted Steimle to "discuss the Jebsen case." Quetting, it turned out, had been entrusted by the SD with Johnny's investigation and wanted to interrogate Jebsen's associate, Brandes. Steimle was certain, the report noted, that the Gestapo had made Brandes testify. Steimle had no further information, however, and Quetting's name quietly disappeared.

Dusko returned to Paris at the end of the year and on January 2, 1946, reported to London. He had not found Bruecher and otherwise had made no progress on Johnny.

Months passed.

The first week of April Tar sent a letter to a Lieutenant Colonel S. H. Noakes: "TRICYCLE is most anxious to have the JEBSEN case cleared up conclusively, and try to determine what actually happened to him at the end." Dusko had offered, Tar said, to go to Hamburg to interview Johnny's English secretary, Miss Harbottle, and Bruecher, who apparently was now living in Freiburg. Bruecher was a mutual friend of Jebsen's and Popov's, Tar wrote, and Dusko had entrusted Max to look after Lore Jebsen in Dusko's absence.

Robertson also requested that Colonel Noakes investigate the names of individuals exterminated at the concentration camp in Mauthausen. This camp, Tar wrote, was the typical place where prisoners were sent to be killed, and Johnny might have been transferred there from Oranienburg.

On April 10 Tar requested travel approval from the Military Permit Office, and on April 25, Dusko flew to Hamburg and stayed two nights. He made no progress on Jebsen, but did manage to meet with Johnny's wife, and apparently with Bruecher. While there, he also hunted for—and found—Jebsen assets unknown to Lore. At the Hendelsbank in Frankfurt, Johnny had stashed 400,000 Reichsmark. With a friend in Oberusel, he had hidden $20,000, thousands in Swiss Francs, and 2,700 gold pieces. With another friend, in Flens-

* The attempt by German senior officers to assassinate Hitler.

burg, he had cached silver, art, rugs, and other valuables. Dusko gave Tar and Dr. Bruecher the addresses and contact names for each location, and suggested that Max would be able to collect everything for Lore within a short time.

To assist Bruecher in the task, Tar sent a letter to Lieutenant Colonel B. Melland of the British Army of the Rhine, asking that Melland assist in providing Dr. Bruecher travel papers for all areas. Robertson's correspondence to Melland marks the first time that British Intelligence conceded that Johnny was dead, Tar referring to him as "late."

»

While the information does not appear in MI5 files, Popov would later state that Walter Salzer, the name given by Frederick Hahn, had killed Johnny. Dusko vowed to return the favor. "Getting Salzer became a personal vendetta," he told an interviewer. "Up until then the war, for me, had been a matter of fighting for ideals—and, of course, getting paid for it. But avenging Johnny's death had nothing to do with money or ideals. He was my friend and I was determined to kill the man who murdered him. In a sense *my* war didn't start until the war ended."

After scouring much of the country, Dusko wrote in his memoirs, he found Salzer in Minden, a small town west of Hanover. At gunpoint he forced Salzer into a jeep and then drove to a nearby wood "to put a bullet through his brain." When they reached a desolate area, Dusko asked who had ordered Johnny's execution. Salzer said, "My superiors."

Blood boiling, Dusko asked for names.

Salzer stuttered.

Dusko asked again.

No answer.

Popov raised the pistol.

Seconds hung as he stared into the bleak eyes of Johnny's killer.

He couldn't do it. He couldn't pull the trigger. Tossing the gun aside, he smashed Salzer's face with everything he had. The German crumpled. Fury inflamed and unrelenting, Popov pummeled the Nazi again and again, punching him mercilessly as Johnny had been beaten.

Exhausted, knuckles dripping blood, he stood.

Salzer was unconscious.

As Dusko turned to leave, he heaved and started vomiting. First the contents of his stomach, and then five years of stress and intrigue. "I vomited my sins and my shame and my pain," he wrote. The sleeping pills, the benzedrine, the seducers and shadows, truth serum and car bombs—all gone. The lies, the danger, the hatred—no more. The clutch of Nazi claws, pinning him as prey to be devoured, had finally been broken.

Dusko Popov had survived the lion's mouth.

EPILOGUE

"Spying is not a chivalrous business," Popov once said. To live as a double agent, a spy had to be an unflinching liar. Dusko was. It was a banner device that undoubtedly had saved his life time and again during the war.

And probably after.

One of the dangers in World War II espionage was gray areas. "Killing a German in Germany in August 1945 presented no difficulties," Dusko wrote. But it wasn't that simple. If you killed a Wehrmacht soldier on May 7 you were doing your job. If you killed him on May 8 you committed murder. But who would complain if a bloodthirsty Nazi was killed? The juridical answer was that war criminals would be tried at Nuremburg. But what if the Nazi in question committed war crimes yet did not have a high enough profile to catch Allied attention? Such was the case, Dusko believed, with Johnny's killer.

He would walk away scot-free.

Dusko found that reality unjust and maddening. For Johnny's sake, he longed to bring the killer to justice. And so he tracked down Salzer intending to shoot him, but in the end simply beat him and let him go.

Or did he?

In *Spy Counter-Spy*, Popov wrote that Tar Robertson told him of Johnny's death at the end of December 1944. MI5 files, however, reveal that Dusko went to Germany in October–November 1945 to find out what happened to Johnny. And while Tar had conceded Jebsen's death earlier, as late as August 1947 Allied Intelligence was still actively interviewing war prisoners to "provide a new lead to the elusive last chapter of the Jebsen story." Yet Popov's memoirs state that he hunted Walter Salzer two years prior, in August 1945. Strangely, in an interview promoting his book, Dusko claimed that Salzer survived the war, "was tried and served several years in prison." Popov even added that

"Walter Salzer is [presently] one of the heads of a chemical company in Germany."

The Nuremburg Trials show no record of a Walter Salzer. In addition, leading up to the trials the Allies interrogated principal SD and Abwehr officers still alive—including Kaltenbrunner, Schellenberg, Kuebart, Schroeder, Schreiber, and Kammler—and none of them mentioned a Walter Salzer. Schellenberg, who headed SD's foreign intelligence, did not mention the name in his memoirs. Nor did Wilhelm Höttl, who helped direct the SD's production and distribution of counterfeit currency, one of the alleged crimes for which Jebsen was investigated.

Salzer doesn't show up in Station X/Bletchley Park radio intercepts. He doesn't appear in the accounts of prisoners at Oranienburg. Most importantly, the last person to see Johnny alive—whom Popov mentions—was Mrs. Petra Vermehren. She testified in 1947 that a *Kriminalrat* Hofmeister was in charge of Jebsen and that a *Sturmbannführer* named Schmitz interrogated Johnny and took him away for the last time in February 1945. Vermehren did not mention a man named Salzer.

The reason is simple: Walter Salzer did not exist.

I posed the problem of dates and the unknown Salzer to Marco Popov, Dusko's son, and his answer resolved both discrepancies: "Although Dusko never actually admitted this to me or any other member of the family (he only winked for response)," Marco wrote, "I am convinced Dusko found the person who ordered JJ's execution and killed him. This in the aftermath of war would have been considered murder. I thus believe Walter Salzer is a borrowed name and Dusko's vendetta epilogue was a personal matter not to be found in MI5 files."

Marco's supposition is credible. If Walter Salzer was Johnny's killer and Dusko only beat him, why the need to change dates and names? Only if Dusko had actually killed the German would he need to craft an alternate story.

So who actually killed Johnny? And who, presumably, did Dusko kill? Three men are logical candidates: Hofmeister, Schmitz, and Quetting. Hofmeister and Quetting were the two officers implicated in the May 5, 1944, intercept revealing who was to be handling "FLIP" (Jebsen). According to Mrs. Vermehren, Hofmeister "was responsible for everything that happened to Jebsen," and it is possible that he ordered Schmitz to shoot Johnny. Quetting was the officer in charge of Johnny's investigation, and was the one who had bragged about having Jebsen abducted and brought to Berlin. Importantly, he was also the officer Popov suspected. "If you have luck and find the man," Dusko had written to Ian Wilson, "keep him alive until I come, I would love to have a few words with him."

The time that Popov would have hunted any of the three was on his October–November 1945 trip. Not that Popov would have informed Robertson of Johnny's killer, or that Dusko was going after him, but as late as April 1946 Tar was still inquiring as to what might have happened to Johnny, wondering if he had been sent to a termination facility at Mauthausen.

No one can prove that Hofmeister, Schmitz, or Quetting killed Jebsen, or that Popov killed any of them. The ultimate fate of Johnny and his killer will remain a mystery, as well as what Popov did or didn't do about it. If he did kill one of them, together with his acknowledged elimination of Bozidar, perhaps agent TRICYCLE would have earned Ian Fleming's double-0 designation:

003.

»

That Popov would terminate the man who murdered Johnny comes as no surprise. Dusko was not above what many would consider justifiable revenge, and would be the first to admit that he had many faults—incorrigible playboy, unrepentant spendthrift, impetuous, and a man for whom danger was a stimulant. He lived life on the edge, always peering over the precipice at the next treacherous challenge. But he was also courageous, loyal to a fault, and exceedingly kindhearted. Dusko looked after Johnny's widow after the war, clearing her debts, finding Johnny's assets, and making sure she was financially secure and safe. He even petitioned MI5 to pull strings, which they did, so that Lore could obtain ongoing work as an actress in Hamburg. He also gave money to fellow Yugoslavs in need, both during and after the war, some of whom he barely knew. To one individual, he gave his entire Yugoslav army salary.

But his great contribution to humanity was his success during the war. With no disrespect to Juan Pujol, it can safely be said that Dusko Popov was Britain's greatest WWII double agent, and perhaps history's best spy. He was involved in more operations (ten), had more actual sub-agents (eight), and faced greater danger than any other agent. While Pujol and Popov were both inducted into the Most Excellent Order of the British Empire, Pujol received an MBE (Member), while Dusko received the higher OBE (Officer). MI5's application for the decoration on Popov's behalf spoke volumes:

"Dusan POPOV is a Jugo-Slav national and originally offered his services to the British Embassy in Belgrade in 1940 at a time when his own country was neutral and the prospects for British victory did not look favorable. . . . The work of this agent was invaluable to the Allied cause and the channel of communication played an important part in deceiving the enemy prior to the Normandy invasion. At all times this agent has co-operated with the British authorities to the fullest extent at great danger both to himself personally and to his relatives in Jugo-Slavia."

As British Royal Navy Lieutenant-Commander Ewen Montagu wrote in the foreword to *Spy Counter-Spy*, Popov "put his head into the lion's mouth" by returning to Lisbon and Madrid time and again when his cover was surely blown. Spy novelist Graham Greene, who served with MI6 on the Iberian Peninsula and knew intimately the activities of agent TRICYCLE, would later say that Popov was "the most important and most successful double-agent working for the British during the war."

»

With the end of hostilities and the search for Johnny and his killer resolved, Dusko settled into his home at 3 Rue Dosne, Paris, and shocked his friends by getting married. On March 6, 1946, he wed a lovely French girl, Janine Ducasse, and they would have a son, Dean, two years later. He launched a publishing business with a tourist guide to France and continued the import-export business, maintaining his interest in Tarlair, Ltd., the company he had set up with Dickie Metcalfe as his London cover. Years later, the person still conducting the affairs of the office was Dusko's old MI6 secretary, Gisela Ashley. By the fall of 1947, Tarlair had offices in London, New York, Paris, and Rome, and Dusko had developed significant business for the company in Krefeld, Germany.

Yugoslavia had become Communist after the war, however, and Dusko was now stateless. He asked MI5 if he might become a British citizen, and the office felt it was the least Britain could do. Tar expedited the application, and on June 12, 1946, Dusko was naturalized. In a final letter to Colonel Robertson on June 17, Dusko wrote: "I just want to thank you very much for all you have done for me. . . . To express my thanks would not be enough," he said. Giving Tar his assurance of doing his best to be worthy of his new country, Dusko offered that he was at the disposal of MI5 whenever they thought he might be useful.

Dr. Ivo Popov—physician to King Peter and peasants alike—settled in

Italy, was decorated with the King's Medal of Courage in the Cause of Freedom (KMC) on April 18, 1947, and was naturalized as a British citizen on September 11, 1947. His application read: "Director of Medicine, 349 Corso Vitorio Emanuele, Rome." Two weeks later a "Hans Popper" from Germany was also naturalized, his occupation listed as "Serving Officer in His Majesty's Forces."

No address was given.

Misha—the baby twice condemned—would survive the war and go on to make his father proud, earning bachelor's and master's degrees at Oxford, a Ph.D. at Stanford, and serving as a consultant to the FBI, the U.S. Army, the U.S. Department of Defense, and the U.S. Attorney General.

Dusko's OBE, an award normally presented in a formal investiture at Buckingham Palace, was delayed because of the delicacy of decorating a double agent. MI5 chief General David Petrie was adamant that the award would have to be conferred in a private setting due to the restrictions of the Official Secrets Act. It was, on November 28, 1947, and at the place most suited for the Balkan playboy.

The Ritz bar.

»

In 1948 Dusko was nominated as secretary-general of the European Movement, a lobby organization promoting European unity, but he decided to focus on business. His import/export endeavors continued to thrive, and in 1951 he purchased Château Castellaras, a hilltop estate in southern France overlooking Nice. Built in the design of a sixteenth-century ruins castle, Castellaras would for the next ten years host lavish parties for Popov's business colleagues and government friends. His marriage, however, faltered, and he and Janine would divorce in 1960. The following year he sold the castle to Seligmann Bank and purchased La Grande Bastide, former summer palace of the Bishop of Grasse. Since the Bastide adjoined two hundred acres he had purchased seven years earlier, Dusko now had an estate worthy of an international mogul.

While on a business trip to Stockholm in 1961, Dusko met Jill Jonsson, a stunning blonde worthy in every respect to the girls of Bond. Even with their considerable age difference, Jill was smitten. "Dusko was such fun, so full of energy. . . . He was like a magnet, everyone was drawn to him. Every day he sent me flowers. . . . I didn't care what people thought. I knew that I could not live without him and he could not live without me."

They married on June 14, 1962. He was 50, she, 19.

Dusko and Jill Popov on the beach in the Bahamas.
Parade magazine

Over the next seven years they had three sons—Marco, Boris, and Omar—and embarked on a storybook marriage. Dusko's business, which continued to flourish, would take him to America, England, Germany, South Africa, and beyond.

In 1965 the Johannesburg *Sunday Times* interviewed Dusko regarding a $15 million business deal he was transacting with the government of South Africa. In an article about this "man of mystery," the *Times* journalist wrote that during the interview Popov's telephone was constantly ringing and that telex messages were buzzing in from New York, London, and Geneva. "He deals with governments, multi-million dollar corporations," the writer said. "He is a delightful person and for the half hour of our interview he charmingly told me practically nothing that I wanted to know. Then he showed me to the door and returned to his world of millions and mystery."

»

Dusko Popov *was* a man of mystery, to the world and to his family. Not until 1974, with the arrival of his memoirs, would Popov reveal to anyone, including his wife, that *he* was BICYCLE, of whom H. Montgomery Hyde had written in 1962's *Room 3603*; IVAN, of whom Ladislas Farago had written in 1971's *The Game of Foxes*; TALLYRAND, of whom Sefton Delmer had written in 1971's *The Counterfeit Spy*; and TRICYCLE, of whom J. C. Masterman had written in 1972's *The Double-Cross System*.

Yet there was one more British Intelligence officer who wrote about Popov, although indirectly, embellished, and in fiction: Ian Fleming. Dusko was also BOND in 1954's *Casino Royale*.

»

After publication of *Spy Counter-Spy*, Dusko was asked often about being the model for Fleming's famous playboy spy. While Popov admitted the connection as possible, he didn't like the comparison; the Fleming and Hollywood versions of a spy were too fanciful and unrealistic, he felt. A Bond in the flesh, he often said, would have been dead in forty-eight hours.

In a May 1974 interview with Jonathan Braun of *Parade* magazine, however, Dusko provided details and acknowledged his inspiring role: "In some ways, it's an insult to my intelligence to be known as the real-life James Bond," he said. "Nevertheless, I suppose I'm stuck with this Bond thing. I have been ever since Bond's creator, Ian Fleming, admitted using me as a model."

When Braun asked whether Popov had been called upon after the war to carry out tasks now and then for Her Majesty's Secret Service, Dusko smiled.

"That's a very foolish question, because either way my answer would have to be no."

SOURCES AND ACKNOWLEDGMENTS

During the early years of World War II, the Royal Air Force located Allied and enemy aircraft by triangulation of a plane's radio signal with three ground-based high-frequency direction finding ("Huff-Duff") receivers. By taking three readings, or measurements, the source of the transmission could be determined. Similarly, to establish an accurate portrayal of Dusko Popov's life as a double agent, one must process three perspectives: 1) Popov's account, recorded in his memoirs and interviews; 2) MI5's account, gathered in thousands of pages of officer letters, memoranda, diary entries, and documents maintained in the National Archives of the UK; and 3) the FBI's account, organized in thousands of pages of agent reports, memoranda, and exhibits housed at National Archives II in College Park, Maryland.

Espionage, like rugby, is a ruffian's game played by gentlemen. The World War II double-cross teams of MI5, MI6, and British Security Coordination (BSC) were led by giants of character and culture, including J. C. Masterman, Stewart Menzies, and William Stephenson. Yet the play was always muddy, often plagued by Pyrrhic dilemmas and invariably mired in intrigue. Circumstantial evidence, for example, suggests that BSC assassinated a German spy on U.S. soil, and that the Americans attempted to assassinate Popov on Portuguese soil. MI5 considered assassinating Johnny Jebsen, dismissing the option only for fear of a German investigation. Such activities, like all intelligence work, were meant to be closely guarded secrets.

Information, then and continuing until the early 1980s, was quarantined. The FBI rarely shared decisions affecting Popov with British Intelligence, and the Britons, in turn, often withheld details for fear the Americans might blow Dusko's cover. Internally, MI5 could not share with Popov wireless Enigma intercepts. Even writing almost thirty years after the war, Dusko had no access to MI5 or FBI files, their records protected by the Official Secrets Act and classification.

Like all biographies, though, the Dusko Popov story must begin with his memoirs, *Spy Counter-Spy*, and the interviews he offered in advance of the book. Neither is wholly trustworthy, however, and must be evaluated in light of MI5 and FBI reports written during the war. Dusko's account of Walter Salzer, in particular, must be considered pure fiction. Other events—as Popov biographer Russell Miller put it in *Codename TRICYCLE*—appear "embellished." Most difficult, I found, was tracing time through *Spy Counter-Spy*; in all but a few instances the material is dischronologized. Popov placed his banquet at Hyde Park Hotel, for example, as the battle was raging on the beaches of Normandy on June 6, 1944; MI5 records reveal, however, that the event occurred on April 26. Likewise, in numerous cases Dusko misremembered details, recounting that the Midas Plan resulted in his receiving $80,000 (rather than the actual $40,000), for instance, and that he met with Percy Foxworth on August 13, 1941, rather than with Sam's predecessor, Earl Connelley, on August 18. Dusko's account of the island rescue at Mljet is also incorrect; Misha Popov confirmed to me that he, his mother, and grandparents were found not by an Austrian sea captain hired by Johnny Jebsen, but by a German soldier hired by Ivo.

One might wonder whether Popov sometimes followed Kierkegaard's law of delicacy—an author's right to use what he has experienced, withholding verity for himself and only sharing with the reader a refraction of it. Since Dusko had no access to official files, most of his errors of dates, names, and details for events some thirty years prior are understandable. But Popov's recall of opponents during his marathon interrogations by Abwehr, SD, and Gestapo agents—von Karsthoff, Kammler, Warnecke, Schroeder, Schreiber, Wiegand, and Noggenstein—was amazingly accurate, all confirmed by MI5 reports. The risk of torture, it seems, had a wonderful way of searing the neurotransmitters.

Taken as a whole, the larger picture of agent TRICYCLE's operations—whether from Dusko's memoirs, MI5 or FBI files, or MI6 officer accounts—is remarkably consistent. Popov's cold-blooded courage, like his playboy and spendthrift "devices," can be seen everywhere. Most importantly, his two greatest activities—the Pearl Harbor warning and D-Day deception—have been established beyond question.

Of particular value in researching the German perspective, I found, were the memoirs of primary sources: General-Major Walter Schellenberg, General Hans Speidel, General Walter Warlimont, Dr. Paul Leverkuehn, and Albert Speer. Schellenberg's account of Nazi Intelligence, Speidel's account of D-Day, Leverkuehn's account of the Abwehr, and Speer's account of Hitler's mindset, proved especially helpful. Heinz Höhne's *The Order of the Death's Head: The Story of Hitler's SS* was a tremendous resource for understanding the founding and operation of the SS and SD. Likewise, the memoirs of British Intelligence officers—MI5's J. C. Masterman and Guy Liddell (diary), MI6's Kim Philby, Desmond Bristow, Graham Greene, and Malcolm Muggeridge, BSC's William Stephenson and H. Montgomery Hyde, and Naval Intelligence's Rear Admiral John Godfrey, Lieutenant-Commander Ewen Montagu, and Lieutenant-Commander Donald McLachlan—underscored the intricate involvement of multiple departments running World War II's greatest spy.

»

I owe a debt of gratitude to many who assisted in this work. Every writer, regardless of talent, needs skilled critics who are trusted enough to be candid. Hemingway loved being "balled out" by Gertrude Stein, he often said, and pulled no punches in his own critiques for F. Scott Fitzgerald. Additionally, writers need encouragers. An author's job is lonely and sometimes depressing. The story goes that James Joyce had worked all day and had collapsed, head in hands, frustrated. His friend asked him how many words he'd produced that day and Joyce said, eight. The friend saw the bright side, suggesting that James was eight words the richer, to which Joyce groaned: "But I don't know what *order* to put them in."

For the past three years I have been blessed to have a critic, editor, graphic artist, taskmaster, proofer, encourager, and friend in the same person—Susannah Hurt. Her steadfast support—a daily dialogue commencing June 2012—is simply incomprehensible. Gifted with an eye for noticing what looks slightly amiss, and an ear for assessing what sounds a bit awkward, Susannah has been a godsend. Without fail her comments were fair, insightful, and frank. On occasion she'd reward me with, "Not bad, Herr Loftis." More often she was Stein, calling me out when I'd forced a metaphor or missed an available nuance. In virtually every chapter she'd find a paragraph or ending and write, "This can be better." You and I (and my editor) are the beneficiaries of her demands for excellence. Through it all, Susannah's encouragement and enthusiasm has been relentless, shining beyond all expectations.

This book is for her.

For writers of nonfiction, research is critical and, where sources needed are in another country and language, the task becomes monumental. Popov's most exciting work was in Portugal and the sources—secret police files, hotel registrations, newspaper reports, land records—were not only difficult to find, but in Portuguese. Cristina Neves, of the Arquivo Municipal de Cascais, proved to be a guiding angel, spending countless hours assisting me. Books, photos, records, files, and documents I would never have found she passed along, all translated. Early on, I embarked on a mission (an obsession, truth be told) to find Major von Karsthoff's villa, identified in MI5 files as the Toki-Ona. Since "von Karsthoff" was an alias and the Abwehr officer put his name on nothing locally recorded, the goal was difficult. Compounding the problem was the change of street names and the sub-division of lots. Through Cristina's persistence, however, we identified the house, which stands today. While in disrepair, its grandeur remains, the pillars and Moorish arches echoing whispers of secrets past. A photo of the house and a copy of the original blueprints can be seen on my website.

To Cristina, my deepest gratitude.

Many thanks to the Popov family—Marco Popov, Misha Popov, and Nicolas Popov—for their patience in answering countless questions, and filling in so many details about Dusko and Ivo. Even today, I am amazed to have corresponded with Misha—the baby twice condemned—who is as kind and humble as his father.

Thanks also to John Boberg for brainstorming an early version of the book, and for providing a splendid tour of Quebec's Château Frontenac, where Popov was to meet the "bald-headed doctor"; and to my translators, Theresa Beer (Portuguese), John and Abigail Boberg (French), and David Hutchison (German).

I am indebted also to Dr. John Fox, FBI historian, who provided details of Percy Foxworth's personnel history, as well as photos of Foxworth, Lanman, and Connelley; to Russell Miller for his fine Popov biography and his helpful comments; to Stephen Sharp for his personal details about Dusko and Mr. Sturrock; to Rollins College, which provided access to important journal articles and the Nuremburg Trials transcripts; to Mark Murphy of the National Archives and Records Administration, who graciously assisted me time and again, even though my requests were beyond the scope of his FOIA department; to Mary Leong and Paul Johnson of the British National Archives; to Carol Hernandez and Mike Coleman of Ewell Castle, and Alexander Zahoransky of the University of Freiburg, for accessing Popov's student records; to Michael Johnson for the location and background of Jack Dempsey's Club and Bar; to Mrs. Eric Glass, spouse of the theatrical agent who played a chilling role in Plan Midas; to Patricia Domingues of the Palácio Estoril Hotel; to Alison Peters of the Brandman Agency; to Josephine McMullin and Erin Allsop of the Waldorf Astoria; to Shannon Besoyan of the Sun Valley Resort; to Gabriela Gurgel of the Belmond Copacabana Palace; to

Jacqueline Ferreira of the Câmera Municipal de Lisboa; to Ana Barata of the Calouste Gulbenkian Foundation; to Sharon Tune and Vanessa Varin of the American Historical Association; to Craig Murray of the Imperial War Museums; to Larry Jewell of the HyperWar Foundation; to Emily Morris, Louise Watling, and Sophie Bridges of the Churchill Archives Centre; to William Baehr and Kirsten Carter of the Franklin D. Roosevelt Presidential Library; to Steve Hersch of the University of Miami Libraries, Special Collections; to Jonathan Braun of *Parade* magazine; and to Emma Kapotes of *Reader's Digest*.

I am especially grateful to fellow lawyer and best-selling author, Steve Berry, for his outstanding counsel on writing in general, and to those who encouraged along the way, including Stuart Menzies III, Ron Bond, Chris Hurt, Dave Hutchison, Scott and Angela Crews, Christen Rogers, Jayson Rawlins, Danielle Gober, Dave and Sherry Seligson, Kerry and Cindy Lucas, Don and Denise Carr, the Ragsdale family, Benjamin Seyler, and so many others.

And to my peerless and gracious editor, Tom Colgan, and everyone at Penguin Random House; to Lauren Paverman at Trident Media Group; and to the late Dale King, who provided encouraging feedback on my early work, and who greatly enriched my love of words.

APPENDIX 1

The correspondence from FBI Assistant Director E. J. Connelley to Director J. Edgar Hoover was twelve pages, and Exhibit C (Pearl Harbor Questionnaire) was two pages. Following are the pertinent pages of the Connelley letter (1–3, 12), and the exhibit.

SECRET

Director August 19, 1941

In a separate communication I am covering certain situations which arose as to the arrival of Mr. Popov in the country and which may cause some difficulty in his operation here.

Very truly yours,

E. J. CONNELLEY,
Assistant Director

Encls. 24

SPECIAL DELIVERY

-12-

SECRET

Federal Bureau of Investigation
United States Department of Justice

EJC:NB

New York, N.Y.

Class. & Ext. By SP
Reason - FCIM II, 1-2.4.2
Date of Review 5/16/92

SECRET

August 19, 1941

ALL INFORMATION CONTAINED
HEREIN IS UNCLASSIFIED
EXCEPT WHERE SHOWN
OTHERWISE

PERSONAL AND CONFIDENTIAL

Classified by
Declassify on: OADR

Director
Federal Bureau of Investigation
Washington, D. C.

RE: DUSAN M. POPOV,
Confidential Informant
ESPIONAGE - G

Dear Sir:

Pursuant to my conversation with Mr. M. C. Spear and Mr. Carson of the Bureau and Mr. E. A. Tamm, arrangements were made through Mr. ELLIS to contact the Informant, DUSAN M. POPOV. As a result of these arrangements, a confidential meeting was had with Popov, lasting about three hours, participated in by myself, Special Agent Charles F. Lanman, who will handle this Informant in the future, and Mr. Ellis, at the Commodore Hotel on August 18, 1941. (S)

Mr. Ellis, whose identity is known to the Bureau, furnished me with a brief resume of the activities of Popov, wherein he has acted as an agent for the British Government while also acting as an agent for the German Government, and a copy of this resume is being attached hereto as Exhibit A. (S)

Also in this same connection, Mr. Ellis furnished me with a brief resume of the past history of Popov which gives his complete history up to and including his activity as an agent on October 10, 1940. A copy of this resume is attached hereto as Exhibit B. Mr. Ellis has agreed to furnish me with an additional memorandum bringing this summary concerning Popov up to date, and he will have this available for me probably within the next forty-eight hours. (S)

INDEXED

65-36994-4

In the three-hour interview I had with Popov in the presence of Mr. Ellis, many of the things covered in Exhibits A and B were briefly covered by me. However, it is planned to cover all of these situations in greater detail

-1-

SECRET

Director SECRET August 19, 1941

as we have further opportunity to interview Mr. Popov and during such time as we work out the plan of operation which will be hereinafter indicated. (S)

Supplementing the information contained in Exhibits A and B attached hereto, Mr. Popov advised me that after leaving England on the last occasion, he contacted the German chief agent at Lisbon and advised such agent that he, Popov, had been solicited by the British Ministry of Information to act as a propaganda agent in the interest of Jugoslavia. He of course indicated to the German representative that he had accepted this assignment to facilitate his work being carried on with the Germans. He indicated that the British had approached him, by reason of his connections in Jugoslavia and his family background, to possibly come to the United States and maintain close contact thereafter with the British Library of Information and other agencies of Great Britain who are concerned with propaganda in the interests of the Allied cause. The Germans readily agreed that this was a very desirable act upon his part and they indicated to him that he should maintain close contact with the British and the Jugoslavian representatives in England and the United States, and that in this connection he should assume an attitude hostile to the German Government in order that he would not disclose to anyone the fact that he was acting in the interests of the German Government. The pretext assumed in this connection was arrived at as a result of a discussion between Popov and the British representatives prior to his contact with the German representatives. (S)

To further facilitate his pretext being pursued, (S) he contacted the Prime Minister of Jugoslavia located in London, England, General DUSAN SIMOVITCH, who gave him a letter of introduction to the Jugoslavian Minister to the United States, Mr. K. FOTITCH, located in Washington, D. C. He exhibited this card to me, and due to the fact that he indicates he expects the Jugoslavian Minister in the United States to be in New York either today or very shortly thereafter, he retained this as his introduction to the Jugoslavian Minister. This message indicates that he, Popov, is engaged on a confidential mission and that Fotitch should facilitate his activities here in any way possible. He indicated that the Prime (S)

-2-

SECRET

Director SECRET August 19, 1941

Minister at London and also the Minister located in the United States are familiar with his family background and readily understand he might be engaged in some secret mission. However, he advises that neither Simovitch nor Fotitch know of the fact that he is acting as a British agent and also a German agent under the plan as has been carried out at the present time. (S)

Popov indicated that he understood upon his arrival in the United States, he would work with officers of the U. S. Government as related to him by the British authorities, that thereafter, shortly before the time he took the clipper to come to the United States, he contacted the head of the German Secret Service at Lisbon, in the presence of the latter's secretary, ELIZABETH SAHRBACH, and received his instructions as to how he was to operate in the United States. (S)

Mr. Popov was furnished with a letter of instructions in German, which letter was turned over to the British authorities here, and Mr. Ellis furnished me with an English translation of these instructions, a copy of which is attached hereto as Exhibit C. Reference to these instructions indicates considerable information as to what the German authorities already have as to some of these, and of course definitely indicates the detailed information which they expect him to obtain while in the United States. I will obtain the original German document later from Mr. Ellis. (S)

There were also furnished to Mr. Popov at this time the instructions for operating a radio station. These instructions are in English. The original of this was furnished to us. A photostatic copy of the instructions for the operation of the radio station is attached hereto as Exhibit D. (S)

There was also furnished to Mr. Popov at this time a list of eight addresses, the original document of which was furnished to me, and a photostatic copy of which is attached hereto as Exhibit E. (S)

The names and addresses listed from 1 to 7 inclusive are mail addresses to which he, Popov, will direct

-3-

SECRET

ATTACHMENT NO. 4345

Naval Information:

Information regarding loadings and shipping of war material and food, name of ship and speed.

Concentration of troops at points for shipment overseas in Canada and United States. Strength, number of ships.

Information regarding ship construction, both warships and others, docks, wharves, new ships laid down, condition of ships already under construction, time of construction.

Information regarding U.S. military and naval depots and bases, particularly in Florida, organization of bases for motor torpedo boats and other ships, coastal defense and organization.

HAWAII.

Munition dumps and mine depots.

Naval units, munition and mine depots on the Island of Kusha. (Pearl Harbour) Where possible drawings or sketches. Naval and munition deptos in Lualueai. Exact position. Railway connections. The exact munition munition reserve of the army believed to be in the crater Aliamanu. Information regarding exact position required. Ascertain if the crater Punchbowl at Honolulu is being used as a munition depot. If not, what other military depots are there2

AIR BASES.

Lukefield Airdrome. Details if possible with sketches, showing the position of the hangars, workshops, bomb depots and tank fields. Are there any underground tank depots? Exact position of naval air station.

Naval air support base at Kaneohe. Exact details of position, number of hangars, depots and workshops. Equipment.

Army air base at Wichamr Field and Wheeler Field. Exact position. Number of hangars, depots and workshops. Are there underground depots?

Bodger Airport. Will this depot be taken over by the Army or the Navy in wartime? What preparations are being made? Number of hangars; are there Possibilities for landing of seaplanes here?

Pan American Base. Exact position, sketches. Is the airport identical with Rodgers Airport, or is it a part of it? (A radio station belonging to P.A. is on the Monapuu Peninsula)

Naval Base at Pearl Harbour.

Exact details and sketches of the position of the shipyards, piers, workshops, oil tanks, drydocks and the new drydocks believed to be under construction. Details of submarine depots and exact position.

Where is the minesweeper depot? How far has work developed in the east and southeast lock ? depth of water; number of MOORINGS: Is there a floating dock at Pearl Harbour or is it intended to have one there?

Details regarding new British and American torpedo net defenses. To what extent are these in use? British and American anti-torpedo defense apparatus on warships and other ships. How used at sea? Details of construction.

Exact details regarding the tank units in America required. Tanks, particularly the type which are being sent by U.S. to the Near East. All possble details regarding tanks and the formation of tank units are of greatest interest. Organization tables (TO) of U.S. infantry divisions and of their units (infantry regiments, artillery, etc. etc.) as well as of American armoured divisions and their units. These tables of organization are of confidential nature and are produced by the War Department.

What is the new type of armoured vehicle? What new types are being brought into use? Weight, armament, armour.

Details regarding British credits and assets in the U.S. in June, 1940. What new obligations have been accepted by the British in connection with the Lend-Lease law? What payments has Eng. made to the U.S. since the outbreak of war for (1) goods (2) construction of plants or manufacture of war material and (3) for the development and extension of existing plants?

The exact details regarding expenditure and proposed expansion in the ~~half~~ years 1939-40, 40-41, 41-42, 42-43, particularly for the Army and for armament.

Financing of the munition program through taxation, loans and bonds. The part played by the metal Reserve Corp., Rubber Reserve Corp., Defense Plant Corp., Defense Supplies Corp and Defense Housing Corp in the financing of re-armament.

Growth of national debt and possibilities of liquidating the same.

All possible details regarding American air re-armament. The following points are of the greatest importance and urgent.

1. What is the total monthly production of aircraft?

2. Monthly production of fighters?

3. " " chasers?

4. Training machines?

5. Civil aircraft?

Quantities and types of planes delivered to the British Empire, in particular to Great Britain, Canada, Africa, the Near East, the Far East and Australia.

How many U.S. pilots finish their training monthly? How many U.S. pilots join the R.A.F.?

All possble details regarding the Canadian Air Force. Information regarding the number of front line planes, their numbers, position and headquarters. All possible details regarding air training scheme in Canada, particularly regarding the type, position and capacity of individual schools. Indicate clearly whether schools are for beginners, advanced or for observers.

APPENDIX 2

POPOV OPERATIONS

DATE(S)	SIDE	OPERATION	PURPOSE	ROLE
Spring 1941	British	Machiavelli	Deceive Germany about fictional mines around Britain.	Deliver and pitch dubious mine charts to Abwehr.
Spring 1941	British	Midas	Trick Germany into funding MI5 budget.	Creation and implementation.
Spring 1941–1944	British	Yugoslav Escape Route	Allied escape line; trick Germans into sending double agents.	Creation and implementation.
Summer 1941–1942	German	Unnamed	Establish U.S. spy network.	Create spy network in U.S. by recruiting sub-agents.
Summer 1941–1942	German	Pearl Harbor Questionnaire	Investigate defenses at Pearl Harbor naval base.	Investigate and provide written report to Abwehr.
Fall 1941	German	Unnamed	Atom bomb research.	Investigate U.S. uranium purchases and activity.
1943	British	Mincemeat*	Deceive Germany about the invasion of Sicily.	Investigate in Spain whether Germans bought the charade.
1943	British	Cicero*	Elyesa Bazna, as valet of British ambassador in Ankara, stole British military secrets and sold them to the Germans.	Discovered that Cicero was a German agent and notified MI6, which took no action.

DATE(S)	SIDE	OPERATION	PURPOSE	ROLE
Spring/ Summer 1944	British	Fortitude	Deceive Germany about date and location of Normandy invasion.	Hand-deliver false military material; give false information during interrogation.
May 1944	British	Copperhead (Monty Double)*	Convince Germany that General Montgomery was in Gibraltar instead of planning an Allied invasion of France.	Parade Monty double Lieutenant Clifton James before Abwehr agent, suggesting that it was General Montgomery.

* Books/movies made:

Mincemeat—*The Man Who Never Was* (book and movie)

Cicero—*I Was Cicero* (book); *5 Fingers* (movie)

Monty Double—*I Was Monty's Double* (UK book and movie), *The Counterfeit General Montgomery* (U.S. book title).

APPENDIX 3

IAN FLEMING'S BOND AND POTENTIAL MODELS

The framework of Ian Fleming's *Casino Royale*, his first Bond novel, was a thinly veiled re-creation of what he saw in Estoril, Portugal, in 1941. Casino Royale was Casino Estoril, the Brittany cliffs were the Cascais cliffs, and the Hermitage and Splendide hotels were the Palácio and the Parque. Even today, the Palácio Hotel remembers its role as a watering hole for World War II spies. In the opening pages of its bar menu the hotel highlights secret agents who operated in Estoril. The Palácio also seems to recognize the relative importance of their espionage visitors. In their list of spies Dusko Popov is mentioned first and, of the three hotel registrations reproduced, two are Popov's, one is Fleming's.

In 2014 the Palácio hosted *Le Bal de la Riviera*, a gala honoring Ian Fleming on the fiftieth anniversary of his death. The Fleming family, as special guests, presented a Tribute Award recognizing Fleming's literary legacy. The official invitation for the event, which was sponsored under the patronage of Their Royal Highnesses Prince and Princess Michael of Kent and His Royal Highness Prince Charles-Philippe d'Orléans, Duc d'Anjou, included a page describing the role of the Palácio and Casino Estoril in Fleming's *Casino Royale*. The summary identified *one* man "rumoured to have inspired the character of James Bond":

Dusan Popov.

Many individuals, like Ian's friend Ivar Bryce, surely contributed to Fleming's characterization of James Bond over thirteen novels and two short stories. There can be little doubt, however, that the inspiration for the 007 we see in *Casino Royale*, Fleming's first Bond novel, was Dusko Popov. Set forth below are the individuals most often claimed to be models (not necessarily the *inspiration*) for James Bond. In the far left column are the traits of Bond as revealed in *Casino Royale*.

	James Bond	Dusko Popov	Ian Fleming	Wm. Stephenson	Peter Fleming	Patrick Dalzel-Job	Fitzroy Maclean	Wilfred Dunderdale
Age (During WWII)	34 (in *CR*)	29–34	32–37	45–50	33–38	30–35	30–35	40–45
Nationality	1/2 Scot, 1/2 Swiss	Serbian	English	Canadian	English	English	Scot	?
MI6 Field Agent	Yes	Yes	No	No	No	No	SAS	Station Chief, Paris
Female sub-agent	Yes[1]	Yes[2]	No	No	No	No	No	No
Affair with sub-agent	Yes	Yes	No	No	No	No	No	No
Carried gun	Yes[3]	Yes[4]	No	No	?	Yes	Yes	No
Crack shot	Yes	Yes[5]	No	No	?	Yes	?	No
Killed enemy	Yes	Yes[6]	No	No	No	?	?	No
Assassination attempt	Yes[7]	Yes[8]	No	No	No	No	Yes	No
Wealthy background	Yes	Yes	Yes	?	Yes	No	Yes	Yes
Playboy reputation	Yes	Yes	No	No	No	No	No	No
Highly intelligent	Yes	Yes[9]	No[10]	Yes[11]	Yes[12]	No	Yes	?
Heavy drinker	Yes	Yes[13]	Yes	?	?	No	?	?
Heavy smoker	Yes	Yes[14]	Yes[15]	?	?	?	?	?
Met with enemy	Yes	Yes	No	No	?	Yes	Yes	No
High stakes baccarat	Yes	Yes	No	No	No	No	No	No
Bond connection	N/A	Admitted[16]	Denied[17]	Denied[18]	?	Denied[19]	No	No
Languages	3	5	?	?	?	2	?	3?
Eyes	Grey-blue	Grey-blue	Blue	?	?	Blue	Blue	?
Hair	Black, combed back, receding hairline	Brown, combed back, receding hairline	Black	Black/Gray	Black	?	Black	Black

[1]Vesper Lynd.
[2]Friedl Gaertner.
[3]Beretta .25.
[4]Luger 9mm.
[5]University of Freiburg two-time moving target champion.
[6]Planned and paid for the killing of Bozidar, a German spy informant.
[7]Avoided bomb in Splendid hotel walkway area.
[8]Avoided car bomb, which exploded his Jaguar.
[9]Law degree, Belgrade University; Doctorate in Law, University of Freiburg.
[10]No college degree; failed foreign office exam.
[11]Oxford, Cranwell Aeronautical College.
[12]First honors at Christ Church, Oxford.
[13]Not initially but developed during the war.
[14]Balkan cigarettes, Chesterfields.
[15]Half Balkan, half Turkish mix; Morelands.
"Three gold bands" matches Bond.
[16]*Parade* magazine, May 19, 1974.
[17]Interview with Canadian Broadcasting Company aired on August 17, 1964, five days after Fleming's death.
[18]*See* Stevenson, *A Man Called Intrepid*, p. 171. Some have mistakenly concluded that Fleming's reference of super-spy and hero qualities suggested that Fleming was saying that Stephenson was Bond. *See* Fleming Foreword.
[19]"I have never read a Bond book or seen a Bond movie. They are not my style... And I only ever loved one woman." *See* Ben Macintyre, "Was Ian Fleming the real 007?" *The Times*, April 5, 2008. Macintyre stated that Fleming told Dalzel-Job he was an inspiration for Bond, *See* Macintyre, *For Your Eyes Only*, p. 71.

SOURCES CITING DUSKO POPOV AS INSPIRATION FOR IAN FLEMING'S JAMES BOND

SOURCE	DATE	QUOTE
Alan Road, "Double-Agent Popov and the James Bond Affair," *Observer*, May 13, 1973	1973	"Dusko Popov was a real-life James Bond in World War Two." p. 22.
To Tell the Truth, TV program hosted by Garry Moore, April 23, 1974	1974	"There is a spy, in real life, who was the prototype for James Bond. We have that superspy with us."
Dusko Popov, *Spy Counter-Spy* (Grossett & Dunlap, 1974)	1974	"I'm told that Ian Fleming said he based his character James Bond to some degree on me and my experiences." p. 150
Jonathan Braun, "Superspy Dusko Popov: The Real-Life James Bond," *Parade*, May 19, 1974	1974	Popov: "I suppose I'm stuck with this Bond thing. I have been ever since Bond's creator, Ian Fleming, admitted using me as a model." p. 24
Penelope McMillan, "A James Bond Affair," *New York Daily News*, May 19, 1974	1974	"Dusko Popov, a WWII agent who may have been the model for Bond . . . It was bound to happen some day—the real James Bond, as it were, would stand up." p. 14.
Photo excerpt from "A Spy's Spy Tells It All," *People*, June 17, 1974	1974	"A reputed model for James Bond, Popov's aplomb in bed is still up to standard." p. 21
Publishers Weekly (*Spy Counter-Spy* jacket cover)	1974	"Popov was . . . reputedly the model for Fleming's James Bond."
Frederick Bear, "Dusko [007] Popov: Exclusive Interview," *Genesis*, November 1974	1974	"Dusko Popov was probably the inspiration for James Bond. . . . To reinforce the assumption it might be noted that in the first Bond book, *Casino Royale*, one of the female characters describes Bond as looking like Hoagy Carmichael. . . . And Dusko does look somewhat like Hoagy." pp. 34–35

SOURCE	DATE	QUOTE
Stephan Saunders, Executive Editor/Co-Publisher, *Genesis*, November 1974	1974	"Dusko Popov was one of the master spies of the Second World War. Known as *Tricycle* . . . he became the model for Ian Fleming's James Bond." p. 9
"James Bond existe: il s'appelle Popov." Le Figaro, December 19, 1974	1974	"James Bond exists: he is called Popov."
Richard Farrington, "Super Spy Dusko Popov: He Lived the James Bond Legend," *True Action*, June 1975	1975	"Ian Fleming is said to have called him the model for his fictional super agent James Bond." p. 78
Günter Peis, *The Mirror of Deception: How Britain Turned the Nazi Spy Machine Against Itself* (Pocket, 1977)	1977	"It has been said that Ian Fleming modeled his James Bond on Dusko Popov." p. 160 "Dusko Popov, said to have been the inspiration for Ian Fleming's spy, James Bond." p. 14 of photo section
"Dusko Popov, Ex-Spy, Dies: Aided British in World War II." *New York Times*, August 24, 1981	1981	"Dusko Popov, a double agent for Britain in World War II who was thought to have been the model for James Bond . . . has died at the age of 69. . . . In one incident, he gambled $50,000 in a night at a Portuguese casino as Mr. Fleming, who was then a British naval intelligence officer, looked on. Mr. Popov won, and the incident became part of the Fleming thriller *Casino Royale*. p. D15
Curt Gentry, *J. Edgar Hoover: The Man and the Secrets* (Norton & Co., 1991)	1991	"British agent Dusko Popov, the man said to be the model for Ian Fleming's James Bond . . ." p. 269
Stevan Petrovic, *Dzems Bond Se Zvao Dusko Popov* (DJuro salaj Bgd., 2001)	2001	"James Bond Named Dusko Popov."
Mark Riebling, *Wedge: From Pearl Harbor to 9/11: How the Secret War Between the FBI and CIA Has Endangered National Security* (Touchstone, 2002)	2002	"By the 1950s, when Ian Fleming wove into his books both Dusko Popov's daring and the theme of FBI-CIA competition . . ." p. 81

SOURCE	DATE	QUOTE
Claire Hills, "The Name's Tricycle, Agent Tricycle," *BBC News Online*, May 9, 2002	2002	"But although Agent Tricycle may have come across as an early James Bond type, he was vital to Britain's intelligence gathering and, some say, the country's most important agent." http://news.bbc.co.uk/2/hi/uk_news/1973962.stm
Russell Miller, *Codename TRICYCLE: The True Story of the Second World War's Most Extraordinary Double Agent.* (London: Secker & Warburg, 2004)	2004	"Popov was told that Ian Fleming . . . used it [Dusko's stunt in Casino Estoril] as the inspiration for James Bond's epic baccarat battle in his first book, *Casino Royale*." p. 89
Mario de Queiroz, "Will the Real James Bond Stand Up?" *Inter Press Service English News Wire*, December 1, 2005	2005	"The wealthy Yugoslav lawyer and spy whose life was the basis for Ian Fleming's James Bond character was considered to be one of the most important British agents operating in the nest of spies in Portugal during World War II. Dusan 'Dusko' Popov, who . . ."
Augustino von Hassell and Sigrid MacRae, *Alliance of Enemies* (New York: Thomas Dunne, 2006)	2006	"The character of James Bond was said to be modeled on Popov." p. 106 "As Tricycle had been a model for Ian Fleming . . ." p. 207
Simon Adams, *DK Eyewitness Books: World War II* (DK Children, 2007)	2007	"Author Ian Fleming was so impressed by the Yugoslavian-born spy Dusko Popov (1912–1981) that he based his character 007 on him." p. 65
True Bond. Released June 22, 2007	2007	Video produced by Jane Armstrong and distributed by Starz Entertainment and CineNova Productions, Inc.
Andrej Zivanic, *Britic: The British Serb Magazine*, two-part series: "The Name Is Popov, Dusko Popov," December 13, 2009; "The Man with the Golden Gusle! Dusko Popov," May 13, 2010	2009–2010	"The real life inspiration for the fictional superspy James Bond, his name was Popov, Duško Popov!"
Joshua Levine, *Operation Fortitude: The Story of the Spy Operation That Saved D-Day* (London: HarperCollins, 2011)	2011	"Dusko Popov, lawyer, playboy and *perhaps* 007 prototype . . ."

SOURCE	DATE	QUOTE
The Real Life James Bond: Dusan-Dusko Popov, video	2011	Uploaded February 10, 2011.
Julia Gorin, PoliticalMavins .com, "The Name Is Bond. James Dusan Popov Bond," March 28, 2011	2011	"As Bond creator Ian Fleming himself told newspapers in the early 60s, James Bond is actually Dusan Popov." http://politicalmavens.com/index.php/2011/03/28/the-name-is-bond-james-dusan-popov-bond/
Dwight Jon Zimmerman, "Dusko Popov, Real Life James Bond, Ran Afoul of the FBI," *Defense Media Network*, September 1, 2011	2011	"Popov was credited with being one of the inspirations for Fleming's spy, James Bond, and the casino scene in its various permutations would become the most famous scene in the Bond novels and movies." http://www.defensemedianetwork.com/stories/when-%E2%80%9Cjames-bond%E2%80%9D-ran-afoul-of-the-fbi/
Secret War: Double Agent TRICYCLE. History Channel documentary, May 30, 2012, Executive Producer—Matthew Barrett	2012	History Channel documentary on Dusko Popov as the real James Bond, narrated by Alisdair Simpson and with archives from the BBC Motion Gallery, Getty Images, the Imperial War Museum, the British National Archives Kew, and the U.S. National Archive. http://www.youtube.com/watch?v=Vtupvfr1m4I
Edward Stephens, "Just Like Bond, It's Suave and Sophisticated," *Birmingham Post*, June 7, 2012	2012	"I've got a shock for James Bond fans everywhere. Believe it or not, the archetypical British spy wasn't born in the UK at all, but in Portugal. In Estoril to be precise, at the Hotel Palacio. . . . And it was in that environment of intrigue, adventure and mistrust that Fleming created 007, based in part, I'm told, on a roguish character of the time called Popov, who always had a girl on his arm and more often than not was in the company of two or three."
Double Agent Dusko Popov—Inspiration for James Bond, produced by Stephane Krausz and Barbara Necek	undated	http://www.youtube.com/watch?v=fvZyy-_gXvE

APPENDIX 4

LIVING *CASABLANCA* AND *DR. NO*

As one author put it, 1941 Lisbon resembled Casablanca more than the movie's film set. Indeed, when Rick Blaine finished his farewell in the fog, it was to Portugal's capital that Ilsa Lund and Victor Laszlo fled. And as *Casablanca* mirrored Lisbon, so Rick Blaine's life was strangely similar to Dusko Popov's. In the movie Blaine had met and fallen in love with Lund (played by Swedish actress Ingrid Bergman) in Paris in 1940. In 1939 Dusko met and fell in love with French actress Simone Simon. *In Paris.* As Blaine rekindled his love affair during the war, so did Popov. Simone moved to Hollywood in 1940 to work for RKO Studios; when Dusko arrived in New York the following year, their relationship began anew and Simone flew to see him around the time she was filming *Cat People.*

Almost prophetically, as Humphrey Bogart was filming *Casablanca* and scheming against the Nazis on the Warner Bros. Morocco stage, Dusko was doing it in real life in New York's El Morocco. While Bogart was feigning romance with Bergman in Rick's Café Americain, Popov was romancing Simon in the Stork Club.

Like Rick Blaine, Popov lost his love, Simon moving on the following year. But while he lost his Ilsa, Dusko would later marry his Ingrid—Swedish beauty Jill Jonsson. Thirty-one years Dusko's junior, the stunning blonde brought comparisons to a woman seven years her senior—Swiss actress and the first "Bond girl," Ursula Andress. The year Ian Fleming's first James Bond movie was released—*Dr. No* in 1962—Dusko and Jill were married. As Sean Connery was feigning romance with Andress on the beaches of Jamaica, the real James Bond was romancing his "Bond girl" bride on the beaches of the Bahamas.

Humphrey Bogart and Sean Connery, it seems, acted the part that Dusko Popov lived.

NOTES

"He had the steel within" Ewen Montagu, Foreword to Dusko Popov's *Spy Counter-Spy*, vi.
"My own life" Dusko Popov letter to Tar Robertson (undated but approximately August 9, 1941), KV 2/849 (p. 196b).

DRAMATIS PERSONAE

For German Intelligence and Abwehr structure, see Paul Leverkuehn, *German Military Intelligence*, 28–32, and Lauran Paine, *German Military Intelligence in World War II*, 8–14. For SS, Gestapo, SD, and RSHA organization and structure, see Heinz Höhne, *The Order of the Death's Head*, x–xi, 218, 226–27 and Walter Schellenberg, *The Memoirs of Hitler's Spymaster*, X–XII, 10–12.

PREFACE

1 *"You might wish they had"* Dusko Popov, *Spy Counter-Spy*, 255.
1 *Luger* While Popov recalled carrying the German sidearm, it is more likely he carried a Wembley revolver, the British standard issue service pistol. MI5 files indicate that Dusko requested a "revolver" from his first case officer, William Luke, to carry back to Lisbon. "TRICYCLE" memo, March 5, 1941, KV 2/846 (p. 47J); Luke memo, February 24, 1941, KV 2/845 (p. 41A).
1 *"Turn around slowly"* Popov, *Spy Counter-Spy*, 256; Russell Miller, *Codename TRICYCLE*, 194–95.

CHAPTER 1 FORGING THE ANVIL

3 *"must be prepared to be a villain"* Donald McLachlan, *Room 39*, 355.
3 For Popov background and family, see Ian Wilson MI5 memo of March 26, 194, KV 2/852 (p. 456B); author correspondence with Marco Popov, Milorad ("Misha") Popov, Nicolas Popov. See also Miller, 13–14.
3 *water polo and tennis, and riding horses* Dusko Popov, interview with Alan Road, "Double-Agent Popov and the James Bond Affair," *Observer*, May 13, 1973, 24.
4 *whom Dusko idolized—was six-foot-two* Author correspondence on February 12, 2015, with Nicolas Popov (son of Ivo Popov).
4 For the education of Vladan and Ivo: Vladan's universities are mentioned in the MI5 files at Kew, while Ivo's universities and degrees are noted in the author biography of his book *Stay Young*, inside cover back flap.
4 *enrolled him at Ewell Castle* Dusko enrolled August 22, 1928. Popov personnel file of February 27, 1941, Aliens Office, KV 2/845 (p. 45). See also Ewell Castle student records.

4 For Ewell Castle history, see Ewell Castle website: http://www.ewellcastle.co.uk/about-us/history-of-the-school.html.

4 *Dusko snatched the cane* Author correspondence with Ewell Castle archivist and development manager Mike Coleman, June 21, 2013. Dusko was expelled by the headmaster at the time, Mr. Budgell.

4 *"Germany sits at the heart"* James Rickards, *The Death of Money: The Coming Collapse of the International Monetary System*, 136.

5 *Heidegger* Julian Young, *Heidegger, Philosophy, Nazism*, 11–12; Emmanuel Faye, *Heidegger: The Introduction of Nazism into Philosophy*, 8.

5 For Hitler, Heydrich, Himmler, and chronology of events, see Heinz Höhne, *The Order of the Death's Head: The Story of Hitler's SS*, x–xi. See also Reinhard Rürup, *Topography of Terror: Gestapo, SS and Reichssicherheitshauptamt on the "Prinz-Albrecht-Terrain": A Documentation*, 11, 44.

5 *"Ordinance for the Protection"* Höhne, x.

5 *in some cases murdering* Erik Larson, *In the Garden of Beasts: Love, Terror, and an American Family in Hitler's Berlin*, 16.

5 *"preventive arrest" and* Schutzhaft Höhne, 197, 199–200; Rürup, 99.

6 *SD formed "Working Associations"* Höhne, 216.

6 *three thousand full-time employees* Ibid., 218.

6 *Walter Schellenberg* Walter Schellenberg, *The Memoirs of Hitler's Spymaster*, 22.

6 *Joseph Schachno* Larson, *In the Garden of Beasts*, 3–4, citing "Conversation with Goering," unpublished memoir, 5–6, and July 11, 1933, and July 18, 1933, letters of George Messersmith to Cordell Hull.

6 For boycotts of Jewish businesses, see Rürup, 44.

6 *Mrs. Birlinger* Ian Wilson memorandum of December 8, 1942, to Guy Liddell, KV 2/851 (p. 368a); Popov, *Spy Counter-Spy*, 6.

7 For Karl Laub and the saber duel, see Popov, *Spy Counter-Spy*, 8–9; Richard Farrington, "Super Spy Dusko Popov: He Lived the James Bond Legend," *True Action*, June 1974, 74; Russell Miller, *Codename TRICYCLE*, 16.

7 *"a code of honor and duelling"* Schellenberg, 20.

7 *Mark Twain described a bout* Mark Twain, *A Tramp Abroad*, 12–13. Twain described several bouts in Heidelberg in 1878.

8 *Otto von Bismarck* "Dueling in Berlin," *Galveston Daily News*, November 9, 1886.

8 *duty bound by his Yugoslav cavalry* Popov, *Spy Counter-Spy*, 9; Farrington, 74; Miller, 16. The excuse was wholly fabricated, but Dusko and Johnny knew the referee and student court had no way of checking.

8 *"The Vivovdan and the September Constitution of Yugoslavia"* University of Freiburg records, Faculty of Law and Political Science, 1937.

8 *pro-democracy speech, foreign-student club* "The Story of SKOOT," December 23, 1940, KV 2/845 (p. 6x); Ian Wilson "Tricycle" memo, March 26, 1943, KV 2/852 (p. 456B).

CHAPTER 2 EXITING FEET FIRST

9 *team of Gestapo guards, arrest* "The Story of SKOOT," December 23, 1940, KV 2/845 (p. 6x); Ian Wilson "Tricycle" memo, March 26, 1943, KV 2/852 (p. 456B); Popov, *Spy Counter-Spy*, 11; Russell Miller, *Codename TRICYCLE*, 17.

9 Politika A Yugoslav paper. "The Story of SKOOT," December 23, 1940, KV 2/845 (p. 6x).

9 *speeches at the foreign-student club* "The Story of SKOOT," December 23, 1940, KV 2/845 (p. 6x); Ian Wilson "Tricycle" memo, March 26, 1943, KV 2/852 (p. 456B).

9 Kadavergehorsam Augustino von Hassell and Sigrid MacRae, *Alliance of Enemies: The Untold Story of the Secret American and German Collaboration to End World War II*, xix.

9 Reichsführer-SS Reinhard Rürup, *Topography of Terror*, 11, 36.

9 Konzentrationslagers Erik Larson, *In the Garden of Beasts: Love, Terror, and an American Family in Hitler's Berlin*, 54.

9 *"that attacked the political"* Raphael Lemkin was one of the drafters of Poland's legal code after World War I. Quoted from Krystyna Wituska, *Inside a Gestapo Prison: The Letters of Krystyna Wituska, 1942–1944*, xiii, xiv.

9 *Gestapo agents interrogated* Popov, *Spy Counter-Spy*, 11–13; Farrington, 74; Miller, 17–18.

10 *von Kageneck* In his memoirs, Dusko refers to him as "Freddy von Kaghaneck." This appears to be Alfred Alexander Heinrich Maria Faustinus, Graf von Kageneck (or "Count of Kageneck"), son of Heinrich Karl Alfred Joseph Kaspar, Count of Kageneck, and Baroness Alice Böcklin von Böcklinsau. Born in Freiburg on February 15, 1915, Freddy would have been twenty-one when Dusko met him in 1936. MI5 files refer to him as Count Alfred Kageneck. See, e.g., KV 2/845, (pp. 15B, 17b).

10 For the von Kagenecks: The noble line of the von Kageneck family can be traced back to at least the twelfth century. It appears that Freddy had a cousin, also in Freiburg and about Freddy's age, who was named after Erbo Graf von Kageneck (1185–1258). See http://www.genealogieonline.nl/de/stamboom-helmantel/I16909.php. Freddy's cousin, Erbo Graf von Kageneck (1918–1942), was a German fighter pilot and ace who recorded sixty-seven aerial victories before being mortally wounded in North Africa. MI5 files refer to "Count von Kageneck" as a "member of a wealthy Catholic landed family." See June 16, 1942, memorandum to Guy Liddell, KV 2/850 (file 3).

10 For the Jebsens: The Jebsens were Danish, and Johnny on at least one occasion mentioned his split nationality (Danish heritage but born in Germany). Johnny's grandfather, Michael Jebsen, Jr. (1835–1899, Denmark) had five children: Jacob (1870–1941), Johanne (1879–1907), Heinrich (1880–1944), Friedrich (1881–?), and Michael III (1883–?). Mr. Jebsen (grandfather) died in Berlin in 1899. The eldest son, Jacob, appears to have been Johnny's uncle. Jacob studied in Berlin and apprenticed in Hamburg. In 1895, Jacob cofounded Jebsen & Co. in Hong Kong (as shipping agent for father Michael) with partner Heinrich Jessen. In 1899, Johanne married Heinrich Jessen, Jacob's partner, and in 1909 the family expanded operations, setting up Jebsen & Jessen Hamburg. By the time Johnny enrolled at Freiburg, both of his parents were dead. Jebsen & Co. seems to have progressed through Jacob (Johnny's uncle), and then by his sons, Michael and Hans Jacob. Hans Jacob's son, Hans Michael Jebsen (b. 1956), currently lives in Hong Kong and is the CEO and chairman of Jebsen & Co. In 2009, *Forbes* estimated his net worth at $680 million.

10 Johnny as shipping heir: MI5 files describe Johnny as "the son of [a] rich Hamburg shipping family"; Dusko Popov, undated "Dramatis Personae," KV 2/849 (p. 177b); Ian Wilson memo, March 26, 1943, KV 2/852 (p. 456B). MI5 files also refer to him as "the son of the owner of Jebsen and Jebsen, export and import company, dealing with China, with headquarters in Hamburg," extract from FBI report of November 11, 1943, KV 2/855 (sub-file 1).

10 *of it . . . "sports cars and sporting girls"* Popov, *Spy Counter-Spy*, 19, 5; Ben Macintyre, *Double Cross*, 7, Miller, 16.

10 *"encyclopedic," his recall infallible* Popov, *Spy Counter-Spy*, 7.

10 *intelligent, cultured, clever, English* See, e.g., December 20, 1940, memo, KV 2/845 (p. 2); "The Story of SKOOT," December 23, 1940, KV 2/845 (p. 6x); Ian Wilson's "Tricycle" memo, March 26, 1943, KV 2/852 (p. 456B); Dusko Popov, undated "Dramatis Personae," KV 2/849 (p. 177b).

10 *under Johnny's spell* Popov, *Spy Counter-Spy*, 7; Macintyre, 8.

10 *"He is courageous"* "Tricycle" memo, March 26, 1943, KV 2/852 (p. 456B).
11 For Jebsen description Dusko Popov, undated "Dramatis Personae," KV 2/849 (p. 177b).
11 *black, tobacco-stained teeth* December 20, 1940, memo, KV 2/845 (p. 2).
11 *water polo, horsemanship, tennis* Dusko Popov, interview with Alan Road, "Double-Agent Popov and the James Bond Affair," *Observer*, 24; Dusko Popov, interview with Jonathan Braun, "Superspy Dusko Popov: The Real-Life James Bond," *Parade*, 24.
11 *thin and frail* While Dusko graciously described Johnny as "handsome, strong, wiry" (Popov, *Spy Counter-Spy*, 7), extant photos of Jebsen suggest otherwise. In addition, British agent Kenneth Benton, who met Jebsen in Madrid in 1943, described Johnny as "a small man who was chain smoking and looking rather sweaty and apprehensive." Kenneth Benton, "The ISOS Years: Madrid 1941–3," *Journal of Contemporary History* 30, no. 3 (July 1995), 395.
11 *Orwell's poor Winston* George Orwell, *1984*, 1.
11 *Johnny suffered from varicose veins* Ian Wilson memo, KV 2/852 (p. 456B).
11 *willing to pay $600* Dusko Popov, "Report by Tricycle," May 1, 1941, KV 2/847 (sub-file 2, part 3) (p. 86b).
11 *prison* "The Story of SKOOT," December 23, 1940, KV 2/845 (pp. 2a, 6x).
12 *"The blankets"* Dietrich Bonhoeffer, *Letters & Papers from Prison*, 248–49. See also Irene Tomaszewski, *I Am First a Human Being: The Prison Letters of Krystyna Wituska.*
12 *"In a very few weeks"* George Langelaan, *Knights of the Floating Silk*, 136–37.
12 Schutzhaft Rürup, 99.
12 *Courts* §7 of the law of February 10, 1936, concerning Secret State Police provided: "Orders and concerns of the Secret State Police are not subject to the scrutiny of the courts of administration." Rürup, 58.
13 *"feet first"* Popov, *Spy Counter-Spy*, 15; Russell Miller, *Codename TRICYCLE*, 18.
13 *By 1937 such camps* United States Holocaust Memorial Museum, Holocaust Encyclopedia, "Concentration Camps, 1933–1939." http://www.ushmm.org/wlc/en/article.php?ModuleId=10005263.
13 Sonderbehandlung Rürup, 99.
13 *scheduled for transfer to a camp and eventual extermination* Richard Farrington, "Super Spy Dusko Popov: He Lived the James Bond Legend," *True Action*, 74.

CHAPTER 3 SPYING FOR HITLER, KILLING FOR CHURCHILL

14 *February 4, 1940* "The Story of SKOOT," December 23, 1940, KV 2/845 (p. 6x); Popov, *Spy Counter-Spy*, 2.
14 *von Stein* Dusko Popov, "Dramatis Personae" memo, KV 2/849 (p. 177b); "The Story of SKOOT," KV 2/845 (p. 6x).
14 *more and better work* "The Story of SKOOT," KV 2/845 (p. 6x); "Tricycle" memo, KV 2/852 (p. 456B).
14 *"You are well acquainted"* "The Story of SKOOT," KV 2/845 (p. 6x).
14 *Dr. Jaksitch* "The Story of SKOOT," KV 2/845 (p. 6x); "Summary of Tricycle Case," July 15, 1941, KV 2/849 (177b); Ian Wilson "Tricycle" memo, March 26, 1943, KV 2/852 (p. 456B).
14 *"Lapad, Dubrovnik"* John Marriott "SKOOT" memo, January 8, 1941, KV 2/845 (p. 13a); author correspondence with Marco Popov (Dusko's son), October 27, 2014.
15 *vacationed annually a month or more in Paris* William Luke "SKOOT" memo, February 23, 1941, KV 2/845 (p. 38a).
15 *owned a yacht,* Nina Ibid.; Ewen Montagu memo, January 2, 1941, KV 2/845 (p. 10a).

15 *"born in the sun"* Dusko Popov, interview with Alan Road, "Double-Agent Popov and the James Bond Affair," *Observer*, 24.

15 *cable from Berlin* Russell Miller, *Codename TRICYCLE*, 20; Macintyre, *Double Cross*, 9.

15 *Johnny looked like hell* Popov, *Spy Counter-Spy*, 17; Miller, 20; Kenneth Benton, "The ISOS Years: Madrid 1941–3," *Journal of Contemporary History* 30, no. 3 (July 1995), 395.

15 *100 to 150 cigarettes a day* KV 2/856 (sub-file 3).

15 *ships in the Norddeutche Lloyd fleet* "The Story of SKOOT," KV 2/845 (p. 6x); Ewen Montagu memo, January 2, 1941, KV 2/845 (p. 10a); "Tricycle" memo, KV 2/852 (p. 456B). For Jebsen as director of the company, see Felix Cowgill correspondence to Tar Robertson, April 19, 1941, KV 2/846 (p. 82c).

16 *"a bloody tyrant"* Popov, *Spy Counter-Spy*, 19.

16 *"The King of Prussia"* Augustino von Hassell and Sigrid MacRae, *Alliance of Enemies: The Untold Story of the Secret American and German Collaboration to End World War II*, xviii.

16 *"the home of thought"* Hans Schoeps quoting Madame de Staël, who described Prussia as *la patrie de la pensée*—"the home of thought." Von Hassell and MacRae, xix (citing Madame de Staël, *De l'Allemagne*, 1813).

16 *Mr. How* It appears that either Ian Wilson was confused at times about the man's identity, or Mr. How used aliases. In various memos this man is referred to as "Mr. Dow" ("The Story of SKOOT," December 23, 1940, KV 2/845, p. 6x); "a British representative" ("Summary of Tricycle Case," July 28, 1941, KV 2/849, p. 183A); "Mr. How" ("Tricycle" memo, March 26, 1943, KV 2/852, p. 456B); and "Mr. Dew" (August 18, 1944, memo at KV 2/859, p. 972B).

16 *willingness to work for the Germans* "The Story of SKOOT," December 23, 1940, KV 2/845 (p. 6x); "Summary of Tricycle Case," July 28, 1941, KV 2/849 (p. 183A); "Tricycle" memo, March 26, 1943, KV 2/852 (p. 456B).

16 *H. N. Sturrock* Popov identifies this man as "Mr. Sturrack" in his memoirs (*Spy Counter-Spy*, 20), misspelling the name. Sturrock's formal title was "Commercial Secretary to His Majesty's Legation in Belgrade." Author correspondence with Sturrock's grandson, Stephen Sharp, December 13–31, 2014. Sturrock and Sharp were good friends of the Popovs, and Sharp later lived with Dusko's family for a short while after the war.

17 Forscher Kenneth Benton, "The ISOS Years: Madrid 1941–3," *Journal of Contemporary History* 30, no. 3 (July 1995), 395.

17 *"greater world"* Von Hassell, 5.

17 *Lethbridge* In his memoirs Popov states that the man gave his name as "Spiradis," a name Dusko later understood was a cover. Popov, *Spy Counter-Spy*, 35. Ian Wilson in his memo of March 26, 1943, refers to the man as "Mr. Fickis" of Passport Control; this also appears to have been an alias. KV 2/852 (p. 456B). In a memo on May 5, 1943, Wilson noted that the man was an MI6 representative. The six places where the man's name appeared in the memo have been censored, as well as his cover name. "Meteor" memo, KV 2/852 (p. 489a). The secrecy surrounding his name appears to have been necessary due to later work: The May 5 memo suggests, and a May 18, 1943, memo confirms, that this officer of the Belgrade PCO (Passport Control Office) in 1940 became an operative with SOE. Ian Wilson "Tricycle" memo, KV 2/854 (p. 504a). In all likelihood the man was St. George Lethbridge, SIS station head in Belgrade. See Nigel West, *MI6: British Secret Intelligence Service Operations*, 208.

17 *Ivanovitch* "The Story of SKOOT," December 23, 1940, KV 2/845 (p. 6x); "Interview with SKOOT," February 5, 1941, KV 2/845 (p. 19b); Ian Wilson "Tricycle" memo, KV 2/852 (p. 456B).

17 *Jebsen delivered three questionnaires* Ian Wilson, "Tricycle" memo, KV 2/852 (p. 456B).

18 *"now both in the same service"* "The Story of SKOOT," KV 2/845 (p. 6x); "Summary of Tricycle Case," KV 2/849 (p. 177b); "Tricycle" memo, KV 2/852 (p. 456B).

18 *wanted an easier living* Ibid.

18 For Ollschlager, Munzinger, Hoeflinger, Anzueto, see Dusko Popov report of May 1, 1941, KV 2/847 (p. 87a); "Summary of Tricycle Case," KV 2/849 (p. 177b); Tar Robertson letter to Frank Foley, March 23, 1943, KV 2/852 (p. 453a); Ian Wilson "Tricycle" memo, March 26, 1943, KV 2/852 (p. 456B).

18 *head of the Abwehr's I. H. Ost.* Robertson letter to Foley, March 23, 1943, KV 2/852 (p. 453a).

18 For Munzinger description, see "Summary of Tricycle Case," KV 2/849 (p. 177); Robertson letter to Foley, KV 2/852 (p. 453a).

18 *At a restaurant outside Belgrade* "The Story of SKOOT," December 23, 1940, KV 2/845 (p. 6x).

19 *spies were excluded* Convention relative to the Treatment of Prisoners of War, Geneva, July 27, 1929, and Laws and Customs of War on Land (Hague IV), October 18, 1907, Annex to the Convention, Articles 1 and 29.

19 *"You're being sold out"* Popov, *Spy Counter-Spy*, 40–42; Dusko Popov, interview with Frederick Bear, "Dusko [007] Popov: Exclusive Interview," *Genesis*, November 1974, 48; Russell Miller, *Codename TRICYCLE*, 25.

20 *"Bozidar is a cancer"* Popov, *Spy Counter-Spy*, 42–43; Miller, 26.

CHAPTER 4 MAGIC

21 *"A world at war"* Dusko Popov, interview with Frederick Bear, "Dusko [007] Popov: Exclusive Interview," *Genesis*, November 1974, 36.

21 *"Have I been running"* Popov, *Spy Counter-Spy*, 45.

21 *Bozidar had been shot* Ibid.; Miller, *Codename TRICYCLE*, 26; Popov, *Genesis*, 48.

21 *"could have caused death"* Popov, *Genesis*, 48.

21 *"Would you kill"* Popov, *Spy Counter-Spy*, 46.

22 *"Act as if"* Ibid., 48–49; Miller, 27.

22 *Arthur Owens (codenamed SNOW)* See, generally, Nigel West and Madoc Roberts, *Snow: The Double Life of a World War II Spy*; J. C. Masterman, *The Double-Cross System*, 36–45. See also, Guy Liddell Diaries, KV 4/187 (particularly pages 815, 851–54). After a meeting with J. C. Masterman, Tar Robertson, Dick White, and John Marriott on April 10, 1941, Liddell recorded in his diary that "the future control of Snow and Celery was not finally decided on. There was general agreement that they would have to be kept under close supervision and that it might be necessary to shut Snow up or alternatively to remove him from the country." KV 4/187 (p. 853).

Toward the end of the war, Owens was released from prison, continued nominal MI5 duties, and eventually moved to Canada. After the war, MI5 never resolved whether Owens was loyal to Germany or Britain. At the very least, he was an opportunist looking for adventure, money, and/or business advantages.

23 *Popov's talents* Dusko Popov, interview with Jonathan Braun, "Superspy Dusko Popov: The Real-Life James Bond," *Parade*, 24.

23 *SKOOT* See, e.g., "The Story of SKOOT," KV 2/845 (p. 6x), KV 2/845 (p. 1); Guy Liddell Diaries, KV 4/187. Perhaps due to his still learning English in 1940, Popov misremembered his initial code name as "SCOUT." Popov, *Spy Counter-Spy*, 57. In a few instances, MI5 reports show the name as "Scoot." See, e.g., KV 2/845 (p. 2).

23 *"Rubicon"* "A. D. SKOOT" Minute Sheet, undated, KV 2/845 (p. 1); "Summary of Tricycle Case," KV 2/849 (p. 177); Ian Wilson "Tricycle" memo, KV 2/852 (p. 456B).

24 *On November 17, 1940* Ibid. "The Story of SKOOT" memo records the dates as November 16 and 18. KV 2/845 (pp. 2x, 6x).

24 *Ala Littoria . . . Ambasciadore . . . Rome 44168* "The Story of SKOOT," KV 2/845 (pp. 2x, 6x); "Summary of Tricycle Case," KV 2/849 (p. 177).

24 *"Dear Dusko"* "The Story of SKOOT," KV 2/845 (p. 6x).

24 *"receiving attention"* Ibid. (p. 2x). See also Dusko Popov's "Dramatis Personae," KV 2/849 (p. 177b); Wilson's "Tricycle" memo, KV 2/852 (p. 456B).

24 *Ardanghi description* Popov, "Dramatis Personae," KV 2/849 (p. 177b).

24 *Dusko met Johnny for drinks* "The Story of SKOOT," KV 2/845 (p. 2x); "Summary of Tricycle Case," KV 2/849 (p. 177); "Tricycle" memo, KV 2/852 (p. 456B).

24 *the ENIGMA machine* I. C. B. Dear and M. R. D. Foot, *The Oxford Companion to World War II*, 1165.

24 *Bletchley Park* Officially known as the Government Code and Cypher School, Bletchly Park was the location—and unofficially the name—of the British code breaking organization.

24 *By the end of July* F. W. Winterbotham, *The Ultra Secret*, 70.

25 *Major Ludovico von Karsthoff* Popov, "Dramatis Personae," KV 2/849 (p. 177b); Popov, *Spy Counter-Spy*, 56.

25 *"Albert von Karsthof"* PVDE records contain the official German embassy list of diplomats and staff, and "Albert von Karstof" (one "f") appears second from the bottom on page 2 and is listed as an "Adjunto" (deputy). *Polícia de Vigilância e Defesa Estado, Serviços de Informação, Biblioteca Nacional, Lisboa.* MI5 files sometimes spell his name as "Karsthof" (see, e.g., KV 2/845, p. 6x) but most often as "Karsthoff."

25 *Ludovico, Anzuweto* Popov, "Dramatis Personae," KV 2/849 (p. 177b).

25 *Anzuweto* Dusko Popov MI5 report, May 1, 1941, KV 2/847.

25 *"He was a terribly likeable person"* Popov, *Genesis*, 48.

25 *rendezvous instructions* Popov, *Spy Counter-Spy*, 56–57; see also Miller, 51.

26 *Venlo* For an analysis of the Venlo incident from the British perspective, see Anthony Cave Brown, *C: The Secret Life of Sir Stewart Graham Menzies, Spymaster to Winston Churchill*, 208–23; from the German point of view, see Walter Schellenberg, *The Memoirs of Hitler's Spymaster*, 82–98.

26 *"full lists"* Schellenberg, 133.

26 *intercepting so many radio signals* Joshua Levine, *Operation Fortitude: The Story of the Spy Operation That Saved D-Day*, 57.

26 *Radio Security Service was intercepting* Nigel West, *MI6: British Secret Intelligence Service Operations*, 107.

26 *German agents operating in England* Masterman, 3.

26 *"C" had a secret passageway* Anthony Cave Brown, *C: The Secret Life of Sir Stewart Graham Menzies, Spymaster to Winston Churchill*, 225.

26 *"a small fortress"* Schellenberg, 241–42.

26 *his belongings would be searched* Popov, *Genesis*, 68.

27 *Major Conti* "The Story of SKOOT," KV 2/845 (p. 2x); "Dramatis Personae," KV 2/849 (p. 177b); "Tricycle" memo, KV 2/852 (p. 456B).

27 *gave instructions on a better formula* "The Story of SKOOT," KV 2/845 (p. 2a).

27 *Don Augustin Mutiozobal . . . "Still . . . waggons deliverable,"* Ian Wilson "Tricycle" memo, KV 2/852 (p. 456B).

CHAPTER 5 THE BEE HIVE

28 *"The most fascinating place"* Ronald Weber, *The Lisbon Route*, 1, citing *Irish Times*, October 23, 1941, 4.

28 *Duke and Duchess of Windsor* Neill Lochery, *Lisbon: War in the Shadows of the City of Light, 1939–45*, 71 *et seq.*; Weber, 146–48.

28 *Duke of Alba, King of Romania* William D. Bayles, "Lisbon: Europe's Bottleneck," *Life*, April 28, 1941, 77–78; Harvey Klemmer, "Lisbon—Gateway to Warring Europe," *National Geographic*, August 1941, 274.

28 *Prince of Sweden, the Prince of Poland, and the Princess of Greece and Denmark* See Cristina Pacheco, editor, *Hotel Palácio: Estoril-Portugal: Boletins de Alojamento de Estrangeiros/Boletins Individuais, 1939–1945*, 160, 208.

28 *Guggenheims* Countless Guggenheims fled to Lisbon upon the German occupation of Paris on June 14, 1940. On December 11, 1940, Reine, Charles, Caroline, Jacques, Madeleine, Michel Ernest, Micheline, and Suzanne Guggenheim all checked into Estoril's Palácio Hotel. See Pacheco, *Hotel Palácio, Estoril-Portugal: Foreigners' Accommodation Registration Forms/Individual Registration Forms, 1939–1945*. Peggy Guggenheim, daughter of millionaire Benjamin Guggenheim (who died a heroic death aboard the RMS *Titanic*), initially stayed in downtown Lisbon's Hotel Francfort before moving to the Monte Estoril Hotel. Lochery, ix, 99 (with Monte Estoril photo and registration on page 17 of the photo section).

28 *City of Light* Lochery, 2.

28 *City of Refuge* William Bayles, "Lisbon: the City of Refuge," *Picture Post*, June 28, 1941, vol. 11, no. 13, 9.

28 *"last of the gay capitals"* Klemmer, 270.

28 *"port of good hope"* Weber, 5, citing Lilian Mowrer, "Fiesta in Lisbon," *New Yorker*, July 20, 1940, 36.

28 *"veritable bee hive"* Weber, 5, citing Alva E. Gaymon, *New York Times*, July 28, 1940, 4.

28 *languages heard* See, e.g., Bayles, *Life*, 77, 86 (English, French, German, Japanese, Polish); Klemmer, 260, 274 (Italian, Spanish, Romanian); Bayles, *Picture Post*, 9 (Japanese); Lochery, 39 (Russian).

28 *no rationing* Demaree Bess, "American Strategy Pains Portugal," *Saturday Evening Post*, August 30, 1941, 36.

28 *McVitie's petits beurres* Weber, 74, citing Andy Marino, *A Quiet American: The Secret War of Varian Fry*, 313.

28 *aircraft rested side by side* Klemmer, 260; Weber, 2.

29 *signed in 1373* Klemmer, 274.

29 *Salazar* Lochery, 14, *et seq.*

29 *Portugal's colonial empire* Bess, 36.

29 *May 27, 1940, President Roosevelt announced* Bess, 18.

30 *The joke* Weber, 4.

30 *"Youth Movement"* Klemmer, 265; Weber, 3.

30 *fascist salute* Klemmer, 265.

30 *"Felix" . . . "Isabella"* William Shirer, *The Rise and Fall of the Third Reich*, 817.

31 wolfram Donald G. Stevens, "World War II Economic Warfare: The United States, Britain, and Portuguese Wolfram," *Historian* 61, no. 3 (1999), 539–55.

31 *demanded payment in gold* Lochery, 201.

31 *Germany, by comparison, held 133 tons* George Dorgan "Gold Tells the History of the 20th Century," SNBCHF.com, http://snbchf.com/gold-history/gold-tells-20th-century-history/.

31 *Casino Estoril pulsed all night* Klemmer, 274.

31 *generals slept in attics* Weber, 14, citing W. E. Lucas, *Times*, December 3, 1940.

31 *more than eighty thousand* Weber, 13, citing *New Horizons*, May 1942, 18. The figure was later confirmed by the PVDE. In 1940, it reported, 43,540 *European* refugees entered Portugal, most of whom swarmed the streets of Lisbon. Lochery, 43.

31 *forty thousand refugees* Klemmer, 261; Bayles, *Picture Post*, 9.

32 *"bottleneck of freedom"* Bayles, *Life*, 77; *Picture Post*, 9.

32 *one ship a week* Bayles, *Picture Post*, 9.

32 *disguised as refugees* Weber, 19, citing Samuel Lubell, "War by Refugee," *Saturday Evening Post*, March 1941.

32 *Operation Willi* The secret police's scheme to kidnap the Duke of Windsor while he stayed in Lisbon was planned for months. Fortunately, the operation was never initiated.

32 *croupiers greeted him in German* Bayles, *Life*, 78.

32 *inside a refrigerated meat locker* Richard Farrington, "Super Spy Dusko Popov: He Lived the James Bond Legend," *True Action*, June 1975, 76.

33 *"Don't worry about them"* Klemmer, 275.

33 *PVDE* Lochery, 3.

33 *"over-zealous Germanophiles"* Desmond Bristow, *A Game of Moles: The Deceptions of an MI6 Officer*, 150.

33 *"devils"* Ibid., 151.

33 *"Senhor . . . please show me"* Ibid., 154.

33 *up to five PVDE agents* Bristow refers to the secret police agents who shadowed him in 1944 as being from the Polícia Internacional e de Defesa do Estado (PIDE). Ibid., 150. The PIDE, however, did not originate until 1945, when it replaced the PVDE.

33 *"Better we see them"* Ibid., 156.

34 *November 22, 1940, he flew to Barcelona* "The Story of SKOOT," KV 2/845 (p. 2a); Ian Wilson "Tricycle" memo, KV 2/852.

34 *Calouste Gulbenkian, the world's richest man* Muggeridge, *The Infernal Grove*, 137. Muggeridge, apparently relying on memory, mistakenly refers to the Avis Hotel as the "Avish." For background on Gulbenkian, see Neill Lochery, *Lisbon: War in the Shadows of the City of Light, 1939–1945*, 11.

35 *The Germans controlled it* Popov, *Spy Counter-Spy*, 59.

35 *According to Popov's memoirs* Dusko's account of his first few days in Lisbon are slightly different from what Ian Wilson recorded in his March 23, 1943, "Tricycle" memorandum, KV 2/852 (p. 456B). Wilson has Popov moving to the Palácio on November 28, before meeting von Karsthoff, and meeting the major at the German Embassy rather than at the Estoril villa.

35 *"Schmidt" code* Popov, *Spy Counter-Spy*, 57; Miller, *Codename TRICYCLE*, 29.

35 *Portuguese physician* Cristina Pacheco, *Hotel Palácio: Estoril-Portugal: Boletins de Alojamento de Estrangeiros/Boletins Individuais, 1939–1945*, 44, 46.

35 For Axis and Allied hotel preferences, see Pacheco, 49 (Palácio and Atlântico); Miller, 50 (Palácio and Hotel de Parque). While Germans visited the Palácio and Allies the Aviz, the numbers were significantly in one direction. In 1941, for example, 111 Axis nationals visited the Palácio (78 German, 27 Italian, 6 Japanese), while over 1,350 Allied nationals stayed there (779 American, 381 English, 84 French, 34 Norwegian, 23 Dutch, 20 Canadian, 12 Irish, 11 Belgian, 10 Czech). Pacheco, 133. Dusko also mentioned that the Palácio's manager, George Black, was English. Popov, *Spy Counter-Spy*, 63.

35 *Von Karsthoff was an imposing figure* KV 2/845 (p. 6x) (describing him as forty, tall, and thin) and KV 2/849 (p. 177b) (describing him as forty-five, five-foot-ten, and thin). Both reports record his other characteristics.

36 *"being in the company of a domesticated panther"* Popov, *Spy Counter-Spy*, 62.

36 *Elisabeth Sahrbach* KV 2/845 (p. 6x) and 2/849 (p. 177b). She was listed on the German legation file as a "secretary." Official embassy staff list, *Polícia de Vigilância e Defesa Estado, Serviços de Informação, Biblioteca National, Lisboa.*

36 *the major's mistress* KV 2/849 (p. 177b).

36 *Von Karsthoff's villa* In his memoirs, Popov describes von Karsthoff's residence as: (1) being close to Estoril Casino (p. 57, and again later when he *walked* from the Palácio to the major's residence, p. 107); (2) having Moorish architecture (p. 57); (3) including a garage (p. 57); (4) including a salon (p. 57); (5) including interior stairs from the garage; (6) being bordered by a "high stone wall" in the rear; and (7) including a garden and "old pine tree" (p. 146).

37 *"Villa Toki-Ona" and the "Villa Toki-Ana"* Popov incorrectly refered to the property as the "Villa Toki-Ana" in one report (KV 2/849, p. 177b), but in his May 2, 1941, debriefing, he correctly identified it as the "Villa Toki-Ona." (KV 2/847, p. 86b). FBI files also incorrectly refer to the property as the "Villa Toki-Ana."

37 *"Chalet Toki-Ona"* See, e.g., permits filed with the Câmara Municipal de Cascais for improvements at "chalet Toki-Ona, Estrada de Bicesse em Estoril" filed by Dr. Pedro Monjardino on April 5, 1944, and August 19, 1946. On the contruction plans for an adjacent property, the Toki-Ona is cited as the "Vivenda" (Villa) Toki-Ona.

37 *Luís Teixeira Beltrão* Plans filed with the Câmara Municipal de Cascais on June 23, 1923. Notice of completion filed May 23, 1928.

37 *an ad appeared O Estoril*, November 15, 1936, 3. See also Maria Cristina de Carvalho dos Anjos, *O Turismo no Eixo Costeiro Estoril-Cascais (1929–1939): Equipamentos, Eventos e Promoção do Destino*, Anexos, Figura 6.

37 *Bom Refúgio, and the Toki-Ona Villa were all one and the same* The Cascais municipal public records for building permits, plans, and improvements reveal only one property that matches all of Popov's requirements—the Bom Refúgio (later, Toki-Ona) on Estrada Bicesse (the street name was changed in 1944 to Avenue Dom Nuno Alvares Pereira). The Bom Refúgio ad indicates several items of Popov's description: (1) two hundred yards from the Casino; (2) garage; and (3) gardens. A high stone wall (as Dusko describes climbing) and pine trees can be seen today in a Google Earth view of the backyard area. The original blueprints reveal the Moorish architecture and interior stairwell. Sadly, over the last seventy years the property has fallen into disrepair.

37 *Margot Seco de Topete* In May 1937, Ms. Topete filed a permit to repair plumbing drains at "Estrada de Bicesse, Guest House Bom Refúgio."

37 *Venezuelan, Palácio registrations reveal*, ed. *Hotel Palácio: Estoril-Portugal: Boletins de Alojamento de Estrangeiros/ Boletins Individuais, 1939–1945*, 76–77, 116–117.

37 *Associated Press release The Independent*, St. Petersburg, Florida, April 18, 1939, 19.

CHAPTER 6 TOO MANY DEVICES

39 *Ilena Fodor* Popov, *Spy Counter-Spy*, 59–61; Miller, *Codename TRICYCLE*, 31.

39 *"stop trying to find"* Ibid.

39 *Graham Greene* Norman Sherry, *The Life of Graham Greene: Volume II, 1939–1955*, 174.

39 *two thousand names* Ibid., Weber, *The Lisbon Route*, 272.

40 *November 28, 1940, he transferred to Estoril's Allied-friendly Palácio* "The Story of SKOOT," KV 2/845 (pp. 2x, 6x).

40 *"Still 5—15 waggons"* Ibid.

40 *The major also delivered a questionnaire* Ibid. (p. 2a). On December 13, 1940, von Karsthoff cabled Berlin, stating that "Popov is also in need of money." Five days later Berlin responded, stating that the major was to "refund him his travel expenses." "Top Secret 'U'" wireless intercepts catalogue, KV 2/860, sub-file 2 (unpaginated).

40 *new secret ink formula* "Report on INTERVIEW with SKOOT," February 7, 1941, KV 2/845 (pp. 21b, 21c).

41 *"When our troops are there"* Ibid.

41 *Maria Helena Barreto de S. Anna* "The Story of SKOOT," KV 2/845 (p. 2x).

41 *December 20, Popov finally acquired a KLM ticket* Night Duty Officers Report, KV 2/845 (p. 1x).

41 *on business for the Savska Bank* Extract from Report of S.C.O. Avonmouth, December 21, 1940, KV 2/845 (p. 5a); Tar Robertson memo, February 21, 1941, KV 2/845 (p. 36a).

41 *Jock Horsfall, Mr. Andrew* Night Duty Officers Report, December 20, 1940, KV 2/845 (p. 1x). (Horsfall telephoned from the Savoy upon arrival for further instructions.); extract from Report of S.C.O. Avonmouth, December 21, 1940, KV 2/845 (p. 5a); Popov, *Spy Counter-Spy*, 65.

41 *exceedingly fast* Popov, *Spy Counter-Spy*, 65.

41 *St. John Horsfall* See www.historicracing.com. Horsfall, who was Britain's best at Le Mans that year, also placed second at the 1938 RAC Tourist Trophy at Donnington. During the war, Horsfall played a key role in Operation Mincemeat by driving the van ferrying the now-famous cadaver to Greenock, Scotland. On April 18, 1943, Horsfall and Commander Ewen Montagu delivered "Major William Martin" to the British submarine depot at Holy Loch for placement aboard the Royal Navy submarine HMS *Seraph*. Ewen Montagu, *The Man Who Never Was*, 97–101. After the war, in 1948, Horsfall won the Spa 24-Hour Race, again driving an Aston Martin. The following year he was fatally injured while driving in the BRDC International Trophy Race. Each year the Aston Martin Owner's Club holds the St. John Horsfall Memorial Trophy Race in England.

41 *ten o'clock . . . room 430 . . . Tar Robertson* Night Duty Officers Report, December 20, 1940, KV 2/845 (1x); Popov, *Spy Counter-Spy*, 66.

41 *Royal Military Academy Sandhurst . . . Seaforth Highlanders* Nigel West, *MI5: The True Story of the Most Secret Counterespionage Organization in the World*, 43; Christopher Andrew, *Defend the Realm: The Authorized History of MI5*, 249.

41 *sporting his tartan trews* Andrew, *Defend the Realm*, 14 of photo section.

41 *Winsome* Christopher Harmer, at Robertson's memorial service on October 13, 1995, called him "immensely personable." Cited in Ben Macintyre, *Double-Cross: The True Story of the D-Day Spies*, 37, 364.

41 *twinkling eyes* Peter Darling, at Robertson's memorial service on October 13, 1995, said that Tar had an "unmistakable twinkle." Ibid, 37, 364. See also Miranda Carter, *Anthony Blunt: His Lives*, 284 (describing Robertson with "friendly eyes").

41 *"A born leader"* J. C. Masterman, *On the Chariot Wheel: An Autobiography*, 218–19.

42 *joined MI5 in 1933* West, *MI5*, 43.

42 *Wireless Board* Ewen Montagu, *Beyond Top Secret Ultra*, 40. See also, West, *MI5*, 169; Andrew, *Defend the Realm*, 255.

42 *Twenty Committee* Montagu, *Beyond Top Secret Ultra*, 48. Commander Montagu was a member of the XX Committee and "survived through" to the 226th and last meeting of the Committee on May 10, 1945. See also West, *MI5*, 170.

42 *"We had in him"* J. C. Masterman, *The Double-Cross System in the War of 1939 to 1945*, 56.

42 *interviewed and vetted* "The Story of SKOOT," KV 2/845 (p. 13b), item 6.

42 *New Year's Eve party* Popov, *Spy Counter-Spy*, 71–72; Miller, 7.

43 *The ideogram had been inherited* See, e.g., H. Montgomery Hyde, *Room 3603: The Story of the British Intelligence Center in New York During World War II*, 18, 21; F. W. Winterbotham, *The Ultra Secret*, 39; Malcolm Muggeridge, *Chronicles of Wasted Time: Vol. 2, The Infernal Grove*, 122; Ewen Montagu, *Beyond Top Secret Ultra*, 32; H. Montgomery Hyde, *Secret Intelligence Agent: British Espionage in America and the Creation of the OSS*, 3; Anthony

Cave Brown, *C: The Secret Life of Sir Stewart Graham Menzies, Spymaster to Winston Churchill*, 1, 224–25; Keith Jeffery, *The Secret History of MI6, 1909–1949*, 328.

43 *internal phone directory* Malcolm Muggeridge, *Chronicles of Wasted Time: Vol. 2, The Infernal Grove*, 122.

43 *Menzies reputedly could draw checks* On one occasion, Menzies drafted a check for £500 on an account at Drummond's, a subsidiary of the Royal Bank of Scotland, signed it simply with "C," and the check was honored. Cave Brown, 227.

43 *Reinhard Heydrich, chief of the SD, began to use "C"* Heinz Höhne, *The Order of the Death's Head: The Story of Hitler's SS*, 215, citing the untranslated dissertation of Heinrich biographer Schlomo Aronson: "*Heydrich und die Anfänge des SD und der Gestapo 1931–1935*," Inaugural Dissertation of Faculty of Philosophy in the Free University of Berlin, 1966, 96–97.

43 *no less than fifteen hundred times* Cave Brown, 2.

43 *the power behind the throne* Ibid., 14.

44 *James Bond's "M"* Cave Brown, 10. On January 29, 1964, Menzies said to Anthony Cave Brown: "Ian Fleming tells me that I am James Bond's 'M.'" The official Ian Fleming/James Bond website states that Fleming's boss at Naval Intelligence, Admiral John Godfrey, was Ian's model for "M." Fleming's biographer, John Pearson (who worked with Fleming at the *Sunday Times*), however, stated that this was not the case. Unlike the Bond/M relationship, Pearson noted, Commander Fleming and Admiral Godfrey were close friends. Strangely, Pearson believed that Fleming's *mother* was more likely Ian's model for M. John Pearson, *The Life of Ian Fleming*, 175–76.

44 Stewart Graham Menzies's background Ibid., 16.

44 *Edward Impey* Ibid., 31, 33.

44 *would demonstrate leadership in every citcle* Nigel West, *MI6*, 77 (German, cricket, steeplechase, Beagles, "Pop"); Cave Brown, 39–41 (French, captain of house, "Pop").

44 *"power to amuse"* Cave Brown, 39, quoting Martin Green, *Children of the Sun* (New York: Basic Books, 1976), 116.

44 *transferred to the exclusive Life Guards* Cave Brown, 41, 43; West, *MI6*, 77. When Stewart's father died, his mother remarried Lieutenant Colonel Sir George Holford and Stewart shortly thereafter transferred into his father-in-law's regiment of the Life Guards. Cave Brown, 42–43.

44 *the Battle of Ypres* West, *MI6*, 77.

44 *Military Cross* Ibid., 78.

44 *"One man out of a thousand"* Popov, *Spy Counter-Spy*, 74–75.

45 *"You have too many devices"* Dusko Popov, interview with Alan Road, "Double-Agent Popov and the James Bond Affair," *Observer*, May 13, 1973, 31; Miller, 8.

45 *"You have the makings of a very good spy"* Dusko Popov, interview with Jonathan Braun, "Superspy Dusko Popov: The Real-Life James Bond," *Parade*, May 19, 1974, 27; Miller, 8.

CHAPTER 7 PASSION AND ADDICTION

46 *"an absolute crook"* Ian Wilson memo, August 18, 1944, KV2/859 (p. 972B).

46 *Montagu . . . second thoughts* John Marriott memo, KV2/845 (p. 31d).

46 *"I cannot help"* William Luke memo, February 13, 1941, KV 2/845 (p. 31b).

47 *killing a rogue double agent* On January 16, 1941, MI5 Section B chief Guy Liddell recorded in his diary that agent SUMMER "must be eliminated." Guy Liddell diaries, KV 4/187.

47 *asked him to meet with Popov again* Major Tar Robertson "SKOOT" memo, January 1, 1941, KV 2/845 (p. 9a).

47 *"I found him a most charming person"* Lieutenant-Commander Ewen Montagu memo, January 2, 1941, KV 2/845 (p. 10a).

47 *Foster Brown* Ibid.

48 *"Over the question of money"* Tar Robertson memo, January 2, 1941, KV 2/845 (p. 11a).

48 *January 3* Popov left England for Lisbon on January 3, 1941 (KV 2/845, p. 13b), but did not check into the Palácio until January 7 per Palácio registration records. It appears that Dusko stayed four nights at the Aviz before moving to Estoril.

48 *he rang von Karsthoff* The MI5 "Report on INTERVIEW with SKOOT" has a slightly different account of Popov's arrival, stating that Dusko called von Karsthoff the following day, and arranged for a rendezvous "at 4 or 5 p.m. in the German Legation." Popov, *Spy Counter-Spy*, 90–91; "Report on INTERVIEW with SKOOT," February 7, 1941, KV 2/845 (p. 21b); Miller, *Codename TRICYCLE*, 51.

48 *"a friend of the major's cousin"* Ibid.

49 *the major left for Paris* "Report on INTERVIEW with SKOOT," KV 2/845 (p. 21b).

49 *every foreign guest* Cristina Pacheco, ed., *Hotel Palácio: Estoril-Portugal: Boletins de Alojamento de Estrangeiros/Boletins Individuais, 1939–1945*, 34–35, 39–40.

49 *lawyer* Dusko Popov January 7, 1941, Palácio registration, Arquivo Municipal de Cascais.

49 *information was considered too general* Tar Robertson "Memorandum to S.I.S. re TRICYCLE," March 16, 1941, KV 2/846 (p. 69a).

49 *"I'm sorry I behaved"* Popov, *Spy-Counter-Spy*, 91; Miller, 51.

49 *"entertain SKOOT"* Tar Robertson memo, February 9, 1941, KV 2/845 (p. 23a).

50 *the more pleased he would be* William Luke "SKOOT" memo, Febrary 12, 1941, KV2/845 (p. 27a).

50 *He requested navicerts* February 5, 1941, telegram from Guy Deyris and corresponding memo from Tar Robertson on February 10, 1941, KV 2/845 (p. 25a).

50 *Where are planes of the Botha type* German questionnaire (translated February 6, 1941), KV 2/845 (unpaginated).

50 *"slightly wrong positions"* Ewen Montagu, *Beyond Top Secret Ultra*, 58; Tar Robertson "SKOOT" memo, January 10, 1941, KV 2/845 (p. 14c); J. C. Masterman, *The Double-Cross System*, 83, 96.

51 *"I thought you had realized"* Montagu, *Beyond Top Secret Ultra*, 59.

51 *Writing as "John Danvers"* Original envelope and letter (with translations and developed ink) at KV 2/845 (group entry at p. 34a). See also Popov's three cover addresses at KV 2/846 (p. 69a).

51 *he and Luke left for Scotland* "TRICYCLE's Itinerary," KV 2/846 (p. 58A).

51 *"I have come to the conclusion"* William Luke "SKOOT" memo, February 23, 1941, KV2/845 (p. 38a).

52 *Popov's physical attributes* John Marriott "Description of TRICYCLE" memo, March 11, 1941 (p. 61); Tar Robertson "Description of TRICYCLE" memo, March 12, 1941 (p. 61A).

52 *Dusko's lifestyle* "TRICYCLE's Itinerary," KV 2/846 (p. 58A).

52 *Major Isham* William Luke memo, February 27, 1941, KV 2/845 (p. 44d).

52 *Friedl Gaertner* First meeting (William Luke memo, February 28, 1941, KV 2/846, p. 45a); age and background (William Luke "TRICYCLE" memo, March 7, 1941, KV 2/846, p. 50a); "TRICYCLE, BALLOON, GELATINE" memo (undated, unpaginated), KV 2/862 (sub-file 2); plan and pitch to the Germans ("GELATINE" memo, KV 2/849, p. 214h); dates with

Popov ("TRICYCLE's Itinerary," KV 2/846 (p. 58A). In his memoirs, Popov misremembered meeting Friedl (whom he referred to as "Gerda Sullivan"), thinking they had met at the New Year's Eve party, *Spy Counter-Spy*, 72–73.

53 *Friedl Gaertner's note of March 1, 1941* KV 2/863 (file 1).

53 *Menzies's brother's sister-in-law* Nigel West, *MI6: British Secret Intelligence Service Operations, 1909–45*, xv, 208; Anthony Cave Brown, *C: The Secret Life of Sir Stewart Menzies, Spymaster to Winston Churchill*, 306.

53 *passion that had become addiction* Popov, *Spy Counter-Spy*, 83.

CHAPTER 8 DEATH IN THE AFTERNOON

54 *full understanding of the escape plan* William Luke "TRICYCLE" memo, March 5, 1941, KV 2/846 (p. 47J).

54 *A revolver* Ibid.; William Luke memo, February 24, 1941, KV 2/845 (p. 41A).

54 *"jolly little thing"* Nigel West, *Seven Spies Who Changed the World*, 13.

54 *TRICYCLE* Two authors have parroted a tabloid version of why Dusko's code name was changed—that he fancied "three-in-a-bed" sex. See, e.g., Ben Macintyre, *Double-Cross: The True Story of the D-Day Spies*, 68 ("He was rechristened 'Tricycle.' This may have been, in part, a reference to Popov's insatiable appetites and his reputed but probably apocryphal taste for three-in-a-bed sex."); Ben Macintyre, *Agent Zigzag: A True Story of Nazi Espionage, Love and Betrayal*, 116 ("It was said that Dusko Popov, a rather louche Yugoslavian agent, had been named 'Tricycle' because of his taste for three-in-a-bed sex."); Christopher Andrew, *Defend the Realm: The Authorized History of MI5*, 253 ("Codenamed TRICYCLE because of his fondness for three-in-a-bed sex, Popov became . . .").

Since neither Macintyre nor Andrew provides a citation or source for the prurient allegation, their assertion is puzzling, particularly given contradictory evidence. MI5 records confirm that Popov's code name was changed from SKOOT to TRICYCLE in February 1941 when MI5 planned and authorized two sub-agents, BALLOON and GELATINE ("TRICYCLE, BALLOON, AND GELATINE" memo, KV 2/862, p. 1156a). The first use of "TRICYCLE" in MI5 records is February 26, 1941 (correspondence from Felix Cowgill to Tar Robertson, KV 2/845, p. 44b), followed by Tar Robertson's "TRICYCLE" memo on February 27, 1941, to William Luke (KV 2/845, p. 43a), a memo regarding sub-agent Friedl Gaertner, on which is a handwritten note: "Copy in GELATINE."

In 2004, Popov biographer Russell Miller attempted to lay the matter to rest: "With an embryonic 'network' in place, MI5 decided to change Popov's code name to 'Tricycle,' reflecting the fact that he was about to run an operation with two sub-agents. Years after the war scurrilous rumors circulated, without the slightest evidence, that his new codename more accurately reflected his proclivity for what British tabloid newspapers were usually pleased to describe as 'three-in-a-bed sex romps.'" Russell Miller, *Codename TRICYCLE: The True Story of the Second World War's Most Extraordinary Double Agent*, 65.

See also Nigel West, *MI5: The True Story of the Most Secret Counterespionage Organization in the World*, 198 ("He was authorized to recruit two MI5 nominees . . . Dickie Metcalf and . . . Friedle Gaertner. Popov's value had tripled overnight and his code name was changed from SCOUT to TRICYCLE."); Nigel West, *A Thread of Deceit: Espionage Myths of World War II*, 72 ("The code name was chosen for him by his case officer, Ian Wilson, because he was to head a ring of three double agents."); Nigel West, *Seven Spies Who Changed the World*, 13 ("As Dusko acquired his two sub-agents so MI5 gave him a new, more appropriate cryptonym: TRICYCLE."); Joshua Levine, *Operation Fortitude: The Story of the Spy*

Operation That Saved D-Day, 103 ("It has often been said—wrongly, unfortunately—that the name *Tricycle* derived from Popov's fondness for sexual threesomes.").

55 *"TRICYCLE . . . had some"* J. C. Masterman memo, March 5, 1941, KV 2/846 (p. 47k).

55 *Saturday, March 15* "TRICYCLE's Itinerary," KV 2/846 (p. 58A). Popov appears to have stayed that night at another hotel (perhaps the Aviz), as Palácio records show that Dusko checked in the following day, March 16, 1941. See Cristina Pacheco, *Hotel Palácio: Estoril-Portugal: Boletins de Alojamento de Estrangeiros/Boletins Individuais, 1939–1945*, 154–55.

55 *At what London station* Miller, 67.

55 *sound them out* Popov, *Spy Counter-Spy*, 95.

56 *March 16 and 18 meetings, "some gentlemen from Berlin"* Dusko Popov, "Tricycle's Report," May 1, 1941, KV 2/847 (p. 86B).

56 *Canaris had been very close* Paul Leverkeuhn, *German Military Intelligence*, 130.

56 *Hitler and Franco met at Hendaye* Stanley G. Payne, *Franco and Hitler: Spain, Germany, and World War II*, 87–95. A protocol was prepared on October 23, 1940, (and presented on November 4 after changes requested by Italy) between Germany, Italy, and Spain, whereby Spain would join the Axis Tripartite Pact (Germany, Italy, Japan) and enter the war against England at a future date after Spain had received sufficient war materials. The agreement was signed by Spanish foreign minister Serrano Suñer about November 8, and both sides considered the protocol a success: Hitler had procured Franco's enlistment in the war and Franco had attached such conditions so that his commitment could be delayed indefinitely.

56 *Hitler sent Canaris* Ibid., 103.

56 *Spanish Air Force would regularly train in Germany* KV 2/849 (p. 177b).

56 *Von Karsthoff warned* Popov, "Tricycle's Report," KV 2/847 (p. 86B); Popov, *Spy Counter-Spy*, 97.

56 *every German organization competed* See, generally, Walter Schellenberg, *The Memoirs of Hitler's Spymaster*; Albert Speer, *Inside the Third Reich (Memoirs)*; Heinz Höhne, *The Order of the Death's Head: The Story of Hitler's SS*.

57 *Operation Punishment* William Shirer, *The Rise and Fall of the Third Reich*, 826.

57 *"specialists" . . . "very diplomatic"* Popov, "Tricycle's Report," KV 2/847 (p. 86B).

57 *$10,000* Popov, *Spy Counter-Spy*, 100; Richard Farrington, "Super Spy Dusko Popov: He Lived the James Bond Legend," *True Action*, 77. Dusko did not mention this payment in his May 1 report. See "Tricycle's Report," KV 2/847 (p. 86B).

57 *Colonel Pieckenbrock* Piecki, as he was nicknamed, was director of Abwehr I, which handled foreign espionage. See Richard Bassett, *Hitler's Spy Chief: The Story of Wilhelm Canaris*, 111, 114.

57 *"I am not cruel enough"* Popov, "Tricycle's Report," KV 2/847 (p. 86B).

57 *"You're my closest friend"* Popov, *Spy Counter-Spy*, 101.

58 *active espionage and counterespionage* Walter Schellenberg, *The Memoirs of Hitler's Spymaster*, 133.

58 *Samuel Hoare* Lochery, *Lisbon*, 62, citing Samuel Hoare, *Ambassador on a Special Mission*, 22.

58 *April 9, the "specialist" from Berlin* Popov, "Tricycle's Report," KV 2/847 (p. 87a). Warnecke's name is variously spelled "Wernecke" in MI5 files, sometimes occurring both ways in the same report. See, e.g., Ian Wilson's "TRICYCLE'S FIFTH VISIT TO LISBON," KV 2/851 (p. 383A).

58 For Warnecke description, see Popov, "Tricycle's Report," KV 2/847 (p. 86b); KV 2/849 (p. 177b); Wilson, KV 2/851 (p. 383A).

58 *Osten, Lido, "Joe," Ludwig, "Konrad"* H. Montgomery Hyde, *Secret Intelligence Agent: British Espionage in America and the Creaton of the OSS*, 124–27; William Stevenson, *A Man Called Intrepid*, 175–76.
59 *"Phil's things"* Ibid., 125.
59 *"Rather reluctantly, BSC indicated"* Stevenson, 176.
60 *All were tried, found guilty* The last member of the spy ring, a German-born Argentinian named Teodore Erdman Erich Lau, was not captured until 1946.
60 *as Hemingway said of Villalta* Ernest Hemingway, *Death in the Afternoon*, 308–309.
60 *"He's collapsing like Yugoslavia"* Popov, *Spy Counter-Spy*, 129.

CHAPTER 9 "HE'S NOT DEAD"

61 *On April 23* Popov, "Tricycle's Report," May 1, 1941, KV 2/847 (p. 87a).
61 *"Popov, are you a Serb"* Popov, *Spy Counter-Spy*, 129–30; Russell Miller, *Codename TRICYCLE*, 69.
62 *$14 million . . . "is still on our side"* Correspondence of Felix Cowgill to Major Tar Robertson, April 19, 1941, KV 2/846 (p. 82c).
62 *record serial numbers of bills* Popov, *Spy Counter-Spy*, 119.
63 *"high-class procuress"* KV2/847 (91a).
63 *"French popsie" . . .* Daily Mail Dusko Popov, interview with Alan Road, "Double-Agent Popov and the James Bond Affair," *Observer*, May 13, 1973, 29. In *Spy Counter-Spy*, Dusko refers to his date as "Margo Broche" and mentions that the Palácio manager told him to take Ms. Broche "back to her room" (p. 111), indicating that the woman was a guest at the hotel. There is no entry in the Palácio registration records for a "Margo Broche" at this time, but Dusko mentioned in his Foreword that he changed a few names, either by request of the individual, or to prevent embarrassment. Broche appears to have been one of them. Russell Miller, in *Codename TRICYCLE*, suggests that Broche was "Pinta de la Rocque" (p. 54). Miller appears to be referring to Edna La Rocque; however, she did not check into the Palácio until May 19, well after Dusko's return to London on April 30. See Cristina Pacheco, ed., *Hotel Palácio: Estoril-Portugal: Boletins de Alojamento de Estrangeiros/Boletins Individuais, 1939–1945*, 156. As a result, the woman's true identity remains a mystery.
63 *"I had to" . . . kicked the man in the face* Dusko Popov, interview with Alan Road, "Double-Agent Popov and the James Bond Affair," *Observer*, May 13, 1973, 29.
64 *football* Dusko Popov, interview with Frederick Bear, "Dusko [007] Popov: Exclusive Interview," *Genesis*, November 1974, 36.
64 *"He's not dead"* Popov, *Spy Counter-Spy*, 111.
64 *matched the manager's* Popov, *Observer*, 29.
64 *sixty-five tons of turpentine* Popov, "Tricycle's Report," KV 2/847 (p. 87a); J. H. Marriott memo and attached Extract from PF. 55032, March 21, 1942, KV 2/849 (p. 236a).
65 *"man from the Phoenix"* Guy Liddell diaries, KV 4/187 (pp. 860, 869, 897).
65 *"He is to take a bus"* Ibid., p. 912.
65 *counterfeiting currency* Under Operation Bernhard, the Germans began counterfeiting millions of British pounds. Schellenberg reported that he had two paper mills in full operation solely for the counterfeiting. Walter Schellenberg, *The Memoirs of Hitler's Spymaster*, 419. When the German spy CICERO was leaking documents from the British Embassy in Ankara, the German Secret Service paid him an outlandish sum of money—all in counterfeited British currency. See Wilhelm Höttl, *Hitler's Paper Weapon: How the Nazis Forged Millions of British Banknotes*.

66 *Plan Midas* Masterman, *The Double-Cross System in the War of 1939 to 1945,* 85–86, 94, 96; KV 2/848 (p. 138b).

66 *"the party is over"* See multiple MI6 memoranda, including "POPOV" note at KV 2/848 sub-file 2 (unpaginated and undated) and correspondence to William Luke on June 16, 1941 at KV 2/848 (p. 148B).

66 *June 28, 1941* Correspondence from William Luke to Felix Cowgill, June 28, 1941, KV 2/848 (p. 169a); BOAC Civil Air Transport Warrant, June 28, 1941, KV 2/848 (p. 169b).

67 *"Don't do anything"* Popov, *Spy Counter-Spy,* 122.

67 *It was a lovely day* MI6 Lisbon reported to Major Tar Robertson on July 6 that "TRICYCLE is of the opinion that he is not compromised in any way." KV 2/849 (p. 175a).

CHAPTER 10 TARANTO AND THE TARGET

68 *Ivo had been condemned to death* Milorad ("Misha") Popov (Ivo's son), unpublished memoirs.

68 *Dr. Ante Pavelić* Wilhelm Höttl, *The Secret Front: Nazi Political Espionage, 1938–1945,* 110–13.

68 *campaign of genocide* See, e.g., Marko Attila Hoare, *Genocide and Resistance in Hitler's Bosnia: The Partisans and the Chetniks, 1941–1943*; Misha Glenny, *The Balkans: Nationalism, War, and the Great Powers, 1804–1999,* 498–502.

68 *official doctor* Milorad ("Misha") Popov, unpublished memoirs.

68 *treated countless patients free of charge* Ibid; correspondence of Nicolas Popov with the author, February 12, 2015.

68 *Disguised as a monk* Milorad ("Misha") Popov, correspondence with the author, February 13, 2015. The escape ruse was unconfirmed, Misha Popov believed, but this was what he later heard.

69 *"Pavelić's accession to power"* Fitzroy Maclean, *Eastern Approaches,* 334–35.

69 *von Gronau . . . Matsuoka* Popov, *Spy Counter-Spy,* 142–44.

69 *British raid at Taranto* See, generally, A. J. Smithers, *Taranto 1940: Prelude to Pearl Harbor*; Major-General I.S.O. Playfair, *The Mediterranean and Middle East, Volume 1, The Early Successes Against Italy (to May 1941), History of the Second World War, United Kingdom Military Series.*

70 *first aerial assault against a defended port* Ibid., 84.

70 *Fairey Swordfish* Ibid., 48.

70 For ships involved, and damage, see Ibid., 78–79, 118–22.

70 *twenty-seven barrage balloons* Ibid., 84.

71 *Taranto map* Major-General I.S.O. Playfair, *The Mediterranean and Middle East, Volume 1, The Early Successes Against Italy (to May 1941), History of the Second World War, United Kingdom Military Series,* Chapter XII, map 14, p. 235 (reprint at ibiblio.org/hyperwar/UN/UK/UK-Med-I/U).

71 mikropunkt Popov, *Spy Counter-Spy,* 146; Russell Miller, *Codename TRICYCLE,* 86; Dusko Popov, "Pearl Harbor: Did J. Edgar Hoover Blunder?" *True,* October 1973, 47.

71 *Englishman John Dancer* William White, *The Microdot: History and Application,* 4, 8.

71 *Frenchman René Dagron* Ibid., 10–12.

71 *Dr. Emanual Goldberg* Ibid., 25–27. Ironically, the invention of the microdots has widely been credited to the inventor of the MINOX 9.5 mm subminiature camera, Walter Zapp. FBI Director J. Edgar Hoover, in his fictional account of how the FBI captured Popov and discovered the secret German technology of microdots, stated that "the Balkan playboy" studied under "the famous Professor Zapp, inventor of the micro-dot process, at the Tech-

nical High School in Dresden." J. Edgar Hoover, "The Enemy's Masterpiece of Espionage," *Reader's Digest*, vol. 48, April 1946, 3. Popov may have informed Hoover that Zapp was the inventor. Popov, too, cites Zapp as the inventor, in *Spy Counter-Spy*, p. 103, but the FBI denies that the two ever met. Further, Popov studied law at Freiburg rather than technology in Dresden, and Zapp was never a professor. Countless authors and historians have furthered Hoover's statement that Zapp was the inventor. See, e.g., Leslie B. Rout, Jr., and John F. Bratzel, *The Shadow War: German Espionage and United States Counterespionage in Latin America During World War II*, 8 (identifying him as "Dr. Rudolf Zapp").

Dr. William White addresses and refutes the "Zapp Myth," including as an Appendix a letter from Zapp to Frederic Luther on August 10, 1981, detailing his entire career. Zapp, White contends, had no involvement with microdot technology, and White's chronology of dot development, particularly with Dr. Goldberg and Dr. Ammann-Brass, seems compelling. William White, *The Microdot: History and Application*, 65–67, 128–147.

72 *Dr. Hans Ammann-Brass* Ibid., 39, 44–45.

72 *microdot-producing apparatus in the fall of 1940* See Stanley E. Hilton, *Hitler's Secret War in South America, 1939–1945: German Military Espionage and Allied Counterespionage in Brazil*, 34–35. See also Rout and Bratzel.

72 *Dusko's 1941 questionnaire* German original and British translation at KV 2/849 (p. 207, group entry). The German original as contained on the four microdots Popov carried into the United States can be found in the FBI archives at Record Group No. 65, Box 6, Entry ID: 146913 (A1 38-B), 65-HQ-36994-7, NARA. The FBI English translation can be found in FBI Special Agent C. F. Lanman's report regarding Informant ND-63 [Dusko Popov] dated September 17, 1941, and located in the archives at Record Group No. 65, Box 6, Entry ID: 146913 (A1 38-B), 65-HQ-36994, Section 1, Serial 34x, pp. 6–9, NARA.

72 *would not see this questionnaire until 1972* J. C. Masterman, *The Double-Cross System in the War of 1939 to 1945*, 196–98.

76 *the next section—Hawaii* Popov, *Spy Counter-Spy* , 148; Popov, *True*, 47 *et seq*; Dusko Popov, "A Spy's Spy Tells It All," *People*, June 17, 1974, 19.

76 *transferred the death sentence* Milorad ("Misha") Popov, unpublished memoirs.

CHAPTER 11 CASINO ESTORIL

77 *"The Twenty Committee"* Guy Liddell diaries, KV 4/188. Liddell's confusion about the plan would continue, as on August 3, after TATE had arrived for the pickup, Liddell recorded that MI5 would receive a £20,000 credit to a bank in New York.

77 *"In Lisbon Tricycle represented"* J. C. Masterman, *The Double-Cross System in the War of 1939 to 1945*, 85.

78 *Berlin had approved the exchange* According to MI5 files, the exchange rate was £2/$, or $40,000. Felix Cowgill accounting memo to Tar Robertson, September 6, 1941, KV 2/849 (p. 210a).

78 *Erik Sand* While Popov remembered in his memoirs that he had given von Karsthoff the name of "*Charles* Sand," MI5 files reveal that the name given was "Erik." See below, Eric Glass.

78 *10 percent commission* June 7, 1941, correspondence of Felix Cowgill to Tar Robertson, KV 2/848 (p. 136b).

78 *Eric Glass* Guy Liddell noted in his August 3 entry that Dusko's telegram was addressed to "Erik Sand," resulting in complications that were eventually resolved. Liddell diaries, August 3, 1941, entry, KV 4/188 (p. 4). Interestingly, Mr. Glass's theatrical agency, Eric Glass, Ltd., continues in business to this day, run by his family. Correspondence of Janet Glass, Eric Glass's widow, with the author on December 9, 2014.

78 *On July 31, 1941, Dusko sent the telegram* Original telegram at KV 2/849 (p. 192a).

78 *the arranged code* "PLAN MIDAS" memorandum, KV 2/849 (p. 186b); Felix Cowgill memo to Tar Robertson on September 6, 1941, KV 2/849 (p. 210a).

79 *"HARRY should confirm"* MI6 correspondence to John Marriott, August 1, 1941, KV 2/849 (p. 186c).

79 *increments of £5* August 5, 1941, memo to file of J. C. Masterman at KV 2/849 (p. 191a).

79 *£85,000* Masterman, *The Double-Cross System*, 15.

79 *another $30,000* Popov's remembrance of the dollars received was foggy. In *Spy Counter-Spy*, he mentions collecting $80,000 in the exchange (p. 150), then states that he carried $60,000 to the U.S., $40,000 from von Karsthoff "the day before," $12,000 of his own money, and $8,000 belonging to the Bailonis (p. 153). In interviews promoting his memoirs, he consistenty claimed that he received $80,000 in the exchange, and had $80,000 on him the night of the casino scene with Bloch. See Dusko Popov, interview with Frederick Bear, "Dusko [007] Popov: Exclusive Interview," *Genesis*, November, 1974, 48; Dusko Popov, interview with Alan Road, "Double-Agent Popov and the James Bond Affair," *Observer*, May 13, 1973, 22; Dusko Popov, interview with Jonathan Braun, "Superspy Dusko Popov: The Real-Life James Bond," *Parade*, May 19, 1974, 27.

MI5 files reveal, however, that Popov received $40,000 in the Midas exchange (see Felix Cowgill accounting memo to Tar Robertson on September 6, 1941 at KV 2/846, p. 210a), insufficient to fund his $50,000 bet at Casino Estoril.

FBI files show that Popov brought $70,000 into the United States on August 12, 1941, and that he told the FBI that most of the funds were from the Germans. FBI report of Special Agent C. F. Lanman, September 17, 1941, Record Group 65, Entry ID 146913 (A1 38-B), Box 6, 65-HQ-36994, Section 1, Serial 34x, NARA.

Popov's statement of carrying $60,000 to the U.S. matches neither his reference to having $80,000 at the casino, nor the $70,000 the FBI recorded upon his arrival. It appears that Dusko jumbled several numbers. If one adds the $10,000 given to him by Johnny in Madrid, his total would equal the $70,000 that the FBI recorded. It appears that, writing some thirty-two years after the event, Dusko confused the original Midas exchange *goal* of $80,000 (an exchange rate of £4/$ being originally discussed), or perhaps rounded up to $80,000 the $70,000 he carried into the States. In either case, the amount he carried into Casino Estoril was sufficient for his $50,000 bet.

79 *"I had in my possession"* Popov, *Genesis*, 48.

80 *Fleming and Godfrey were returning from a visit to the U.S.* Admiral Godfrey recorded in his memoirs that the trip was to "co-ordinate the arrangement for exchange with the United States of all forms of intelligence." John H. Godfrey, *The Naval Memoirs of Admiral J. H. Godfrey*, Vol. V, 1939–1942, Naval Intelligence Division, Part I, 128. See also Ian Fleming, Foreword to H. Montgomery Hyde, *Room 3603: The Story of the British Intelligence Center in New York During World War II*, xi; William Stevenson, *A Man Called Intrepid: The Secret War*, 270–71; Patrick Beesly, *Very Special Admiral: The Life of Admiral J. H. Godfrey C. B.*, 181; David Eccles, *By Safe Hand: The Letters of Sybil and David Eccles, 1939–1942*, 283; Keith Jeffery, *The Secret History of MI6, 1909–1949*, 448.

80 *"In 1941 . . ."* Ian Fleming, Foreword to H. Montgomery Hyde, *Room 3603*, xi.

80 *"expressed himself firmly"* Stevenson, 163.

80 *checking in on May 20* Fleming biographer John Pearson cited the first leg of the Godfrey/Fleming visit to Lisbon as occurring "at the beginning of June" (*The Life of Ian Fleming*, 95), but Fleming's hotel registration reveals that he checked into the Palácio on May 20, 1941. Pearson also assumed that Godfrey stayed at the Palácio with Fleming ("their Estoril

hotel," page 96). There are no records, however, of Godfrey lodging at the Palácio or any Estoril hotel during the war. (Arquivo Municipal de Cascais, Divisão de Arquivos Municipais, Departamento de Inovação e Comunicação.) Admiral Godfrey's biographer, Patrick Beesly, a Room 39 (Naval Intelligence) staffer, wrote that Godfrey and Fleming left London on May 15 and reached New York a week later. Beesly, *Very Special Admiral*, 181. This schedule coincides with Fleming's Palácio registration, although Fleming's accommodation on May 15–19 is unknown.

81 *Traveling under a diplomatic passport* Pearson, *The Life of Ian Fleming*, 95. Palácio registrations are courtesy of Arquivo Municipal de Cascais, Portugal. A record of all guests (including Fleming and Popov) staying at the Palácio in 1941 can be found in Cristina Pacheco, ed., *Hotel Palácio: Estoril-Portugal: Boletins de Alojamento de Estrangeiros/Boletins Individuais, 1939–1945.*

81 *second night in Lisbon* Pearson, 96. Godfrey biographer and Room 39 staffer Patrick Beesly recorded that the Admiral and his assistant arrived in New York around May 23. If so, Ian would have had to depart Lisbon on May 21 and Pearson's "second night in Lisbon" could only refer to the return trip.

81 *Canadian Broadcasting Company interview* "Ian Fleming: the Brain Behind Bond." Interview at Goldeneye, Jamaica, before Fleming's death on August 12, 1964, the broadcast aired August 17, 1964.

81 *"Fleming himself has described"* Pearson, 96.

82 *Around May 23* Room 39 staffer Patrick Beesly wrote that Godfrey and Fleming departed London on May 15 and arrived in New York "a week later." Beesly, 181. If that is accurate, Fleming would have stayed one night at the Palácio and taken the Clipper the following day, May 21.

82 *one intelligence security boss—Colonel William Donovan* John Godfrey, *The Naval Memoirs of Admiral J. H. Godfrey*, Vol. V, 1939–1942, Naval Intelligence Division, Part I, 132, 137.

82 *June 10 he met with FDR* Calendar entry for President Franklin D. Roosevelt on June 10, 1941, 7:30–11:05 p.m., Franklin D. Roosevelt Library; Godfrey, 135–36.

82 *on June 18 Donovan became the coordinator of information* Hyde, *Room 3603*, 153.

82 letters from Ian Fleming to Colonel Rex Applegate and Cornelius Ryan Pearson, 101. Fleming's letter to Ryan on May 8, 1962, stated: "I wonder if during your research [on Ryan's *The Longest Day*] you came across my memorandum to Bill on how to create an American Secret Service? this was in fact the cornerstone of the future OSS."

82 *"General Donovan was a close personal friend"* Ibid. Fleming's letter to Applegate was written in March 1957.

82 *"For Special Services"* Ibid., 100.

82 *"I enclose a memorandum"* David Eccles, *By Safe Hand: The Letters of Sybil and David Eccles, 1939–1942*, 283.

83 *David Eccles* Eccles was shown as "Economics Counsellor" on the official British Embassy staff list filed with Lisbon's PDVE. *Arquivo Salazar, Biblioteca Nacional, Lisboa*, 232.

83 *"My darling love—Ian Fleming is here"* Eccles, 303. Fleming's stay with Eccles is corroborated by Ian's reference to Eccles in his July 30, 1941, memo to Admiral Godfrey (from Lisbon), and his September 27, 1941, letter to Eccles (from London). ADM223/490 C666650, National Archives of the UK.

83 *Fleming left Lisbon for London on August 12* Fleming memo to Admiral Godfrey, August 10, 1941. ADM223/490 C666650, National Archives of the UK.

83 *the memos of Fleming* Fleming's memos from Lisbon (July 18, 30, August 1, 10, 11) are part of a special Ian Fleming collection and can be seen at group entry ADM223/490 C666650, National Archives of the UK.

83 *Fleming followed him* Popov, *Spy Counter-Spy*, 151. In his memoirs, Popov states: "I'm told that Ian Fleming said he based his character James Bond to some degree on me and my experiences. Could be. . . . Fleming and I did rub shoulders in Lisbon, and a few days before I took the clipper for the States he did follow me about. . . . Probably Ian Fleming got wind of the deal. I came down from my apartment to the lobby of the Palácio Hotel, the packets of bills in the breast pocket of my jacket. . . . I noticed Fleming in the lobby but thought nothing more about it. Then I went to a café for a drink before dinner and there was Fleming skulking about outside. At dinner, he appeared in the same restaurant. . . . He followed me thereafter as I walked in deliberately leisurely fashion through the gardens leading to the Casino." After the war, Dusko couldn't decide whether Fleming was operating on his own (memoir account), was instructed to follow him (Bear interview account, *Genesis*, 48), or followed perhaps for another reason (Braun interview account, 27; Road interview account, *Observer*, 22).

83 *"The scent and smoke"* Ian Fleming, *Casino Royale*, 1.

83 *He was remembering Casino Estoril* But see Pearson, 171.

83 *"grand, with red velvet curtains"* Desmond Bristow, *A Game of Moles: The Deceptions of an MI6 Office*, 151.

83 *Lithuanian named Bloch* Popov, *Genesis*, 48; Popov, *Spy Counter-Spy*, 151; Popov, *Observer*, 22; Popov, *Parade*, 27.

83 *Dr. Lippmann Bloch or Dr. Albert Bloch* Raul Hilberg, *The Destruction of the European Jews, Vol. 2*, 607.

84 *they had lodged at the Palácio* The Bloch brothers left Holland in 1940, Hilberg reports. (Ibid.) On August 5, 1940, the brothers checked into the Palácio for two weeks. See *Boletim individual de alojamento de Lippmann Bloch no Hotel Palácio* and *Boletim individual de alojamento de Albert Bloch no Hotel Palácio*, Arquivo Histórico Municipal de Cascais. Where the brothers lodged after this is unknown.

84 *"must look upon the gaming table"* Fyodor Dostoyevsky, *The Gambler*, 468–69.

84 *"I don't know what prompted me"* Popov, *Genesis*, 48; Popov, *Observer*, 22; Popov, *Parade*, 27.

85 *"I hope the management"* Popov, *Genesis*, 48.

85 *"It is a disgrace"* Popov, *Spy Counter-Spy*, 152; Russell Miller, *Codename TRICYCLE*, 89.

85 *a smile creased his lips* Popov, *Parade*, 27; Popov, *Genesis*, 48.

85 *the Splendide and the Hermitage* Ian Fleming, *Casino Royale*, 29.

85 *amount of the bets* In 1941, Popov bet $50,000. In 1953's *Casino Royale*, there are two large bets: 16 million French francs (pp. 73–74), and 32 million francs (pp. 76–78). To determine the value of these bets, one must adjust for inflation and currency exchange rates (value of French francs in 1952 in U.S. dollars), an inexact science. The value of Popov's bet in 1941, in 2012 U.S. dollars, would have been approximately $783,064. To estimate the value of the Bond bets (using 1952 as the guide, when Fleming was writing), I have used the following formula (based on extensive research) for exchange rates and inflation: 1 U.S. cent in 1952 = .2856 francs; $1 = 28.56 francs; 16 million francs bet = $560,000; 32 million francs bet = $1.23 million. Thus, Popov's bet would have been just above Bond's first bet, and just below his second. Regardless of exactitude in inflation and exchange rate adjustments, the amount of the Popov and Bond bets would have been outlandish—exactly what Dusko Popov and Ian Fleming intended.

85 *Ian's authorized sketch* The *Daily Express* comic strip artist, John McLusky, desired a more rugged Bond, and his version would appear in the series, commencing in 1958. See "JAMES BOND, by Ian Fleming, Drawing by John McLusky," *Daily Express*, September 29, 1958. The writer of the *Casino Royale* comic series was Anthony Hern.

86 *"the son he never had"* Beesly, *Very Special Admiral*, 112.

87 *co-agent flings* See, e.g., William Luke's "TRICYCLE" memo at KV 2/847 (p. 91a); Guy Liddell's diary entry March 15, 1941, Liddell Diaries, KV 4/187 (referring to Gaertner as Popov's "girl friend").

87 *"World War II offers us"* John H. Godfrey, *The Naval Memoirs of Admiral J. H. Godfrey*, Vol. V, 1939–1942, Naval Intelligence Division, Part I, 98.

CHAPTER 12 PEARL HARBOR WARNING

88 *"From every fruition of success"* Winston Churchill, *The Second World War: Volume Two, Their Finest Hour*, 613.

88 *"After discussions between 'C'"* Ewen Montagu, *Beyond Top Secret Ultra*, 73.

88 *"When the offer of Tricycle's services"* Ibid., 75.

89 *Stephenson and the Double-Cross Committee had strong reservations* H. Montgomery Hyde, *Secret Intelligence Agent: British Espionage in America and the Creaton of the OSS*, 206.

89 *"Stephenson's activity in the United States"* Kim Philby, *My Silent War: The Autobiography of a Spy*, 73.

89 *"which would have greatly restricted"* Curt Gentry, *J. Edgar Hoover: The Man and the Secrets*, 268.

89 *"No one has given us"* Ibid.

90 *"Hoover's negative response"* John Pearson, *The Life of Ian Fleming*, 97.

90 *When the death sentence fell* Milorad ("Misha") Popov, unpublished memoirs.

90 *their friends contacted Mirko Ucovic, . . . Gustav Richter* Ibid. Dusko's account in *Spy Counter-Spy* of the Mljet ordeal (which he places in the fall of 1942), with Johnny hiring an Austrian sea captain to rescue them, is incorrect, Misha Popov confirmed to the author.

91 *"The news from Yugoslavia"* Dusko Popov's letter (undated and in French) to Tar Robertson, and William Luke's correspondence to Robertson on August 14, 1941, indicating arrival of the Popov letter, with Luke's attached translation, at KV 2/849 (pp. 197–99).

91 *August 10, 1941* Winston Churchill, *The Second World War: Volume Three: The Grand Alliance*, 431. Popov's August 10 departure is confirmed by MI5 records (see August 9, 1941, correspondence from Tar Robertson to Felix Cowgill at KV 2/849, p. 193a) and Palácio Hotel records (see Chapter 11).

91 *treasure trove worthy of an international spy* FBI Special Agent C. F. Lanman report regarding Informant ND-63 [Dusko Popov], September 17, 1941, Record Group No. 65, Box 6, 65-HQ-36994, Section 1, NARA ("Lanman Report"). See also FBI Laboratory Report, September 3, 1941, Record Group No. 65, Box 6, 65-HQ-36994, Section 1, NARA. The two copies of the Pearl Harbor questionnaire, in German and English, are referenced in E. J. Connelley's memo to J. Edgar Hoover on August 19, 1941, p. 3. BSC retained the German copy, Connelley wrote, and Dick Ellis gave him the English translation. Connelley included this English translation of the questionnaire as Exhibit C to his memo to the director. Record Group No. 65, Box 6, 65-HQ-36994, Section 1, NARA ("Connelley Report"). On the torn business card, letter from unknown girl, see "Tricycle" memo (undated) at KV 2/850 (p. 354A).

92 *$70,000* Correspondence of Lieutenant Colonel Frederick D. Sharp (MID) to A.C. of S., G-2, Governors Island, with copy to FBI Special Agent in Charge, E. A. Soucy, August 15, 1941, Record Group 65, Box 6, Section 1, 65-HQ-36994, NARA ("Sharp letter"). See also Lanman Report; Correspondence from Assistant Director E. J. Connelley to Director J. Edgar Hoover, August 19, 1941, Record Group No. 65, Box 6, Section 1, 65-HQ-36994-19, NARA, page 7.

92 *Hamish Mitchell . . . August 12, 1941* Sharp letter, ibid. Popov's arrival in New York on August 12 is also confirmed by FBI agent in charge Percy Foxworth in his "Memorandum

for the Director Re: Duchan Popov," dated August 14, 1941, Record Group No. 65, Box 6, Section 1, 65-HQ-36994-19, NARA ("Foxworth Memo"). See also "Activities of Tricycle in the United States," October 5, 1943, KV 2/855 (p. 662B). For Hamish Mitchell, MI6 agent stationed in Bermuda, see May 9, 1942, correspondence of R. D. Gibbs to John Marriott, KV 2/849 (p. 253c).

92 In his memoirs, Popov stated that the man joining his flight in Bermuda, and to whom he gave his entire briefcase, was John Pepper from BSC. *Spy Counter-Spy*, 154. It appears, however, that Popov confused Pepper with Mitchell. FBI files make no reference to Pepper, and Sharp indicates that Popov had his briefcase—stuffed with $70,000—at Immigration.

92 *shared a taxi to town* Sharp letter, ibid. In his memoirs, Popov stated that an FBI agent met him after Customs, ushered him to a second agent, who ushered him to a chauffeured sedan where Special Agent Charles Lanman was waiting. Together, Dusko wrote, they drove to the hotel. *Spy Counter-Spy*, 154–55. In his report of September 17, 1941, however, Lanman stated that he did not meet Popov until the August 18 meeting at the Commodore Hotel. Lanman Report, 2. See also "Activities of Tricycle," KV 2/855 (p. 662B). The initial meeting on the eighteenth is consistent with multiple FBI memos and letters from Connelley, Foxworth, Lanman, M. C. Spear, and C. H. Carson, and with Colonel Sharp's correspondence of August 15. FBI Assistant Director E. A. Tamm's memo to J. Edgar Hoover on September 16, 1941, also confirms the taxi story, as Tamm identifies the MID and ONI officers shadowing the taxi. Record Group No. 65, Box 6, Section 1, 65-HQ-36994-19, NARA ("Tamm memo").

92 *They were followed* Captain Stuart Murray, under authority of Colonel Sharp at MID, and Lieutenant Chambers, under authority of W. B. Phillips of ONI, followed Popov's taxi from the airport to the Waldorf-Astoria, and witnessed the document transfer. Tamm memo, 1. Since Popov took a taxi from the airport with Mitchell, and the FBI files show no contact until August 18 (when Lanman, Connelley, and Ellis met with him), it appears that Foxworth intended surveillance in his August 11, 1941, letter to Assistant Director Tamm, rather than greeting, although the FBI files contain no reference to a Bureau shadow.

92 *silently slipped Mitchell a document* See Sharp letter; Tamm memo, 1. The document Murray and Chambers witnessed Dusko passing to Mitchell remains a mystery. In the FBI's summary of Popov's work in the U.S. ("Activities of Tricycle in the United States," October 5, 1943, KV 2/855 [p. 662B]), the Bureau states that Popov's questionnaire was "turned over to British authorities upon his arrival in the United States, who in turn handed it over to our representatives." The "letter" given to Mitchell in the taxi could have been the two copies of the questionnaire, which Hamish would have passed along to Dick Ellis. On the other hand, it seems unlikely that Popov would have made a public transfer of a critical espionage document.

92 *Buick . . . belongings had been searched* On car purchase, see Lanman Report, 15. On belongings searched, see Popov, *Spy Counter-Spy*, 156.

93 *"The British say" . . . "Without the knowledge of Popov"* Foxworth memo.

93 *"should not be contacted"* C. H. Carson memo to P. E. Foxworth, August 14, 1941, 8:50 p.m., Record Group No. 65, Box 6, Section 1, 65-HQ-36994-19, NARA.

93 *$70,000 "for special purposes"* Sharp letter, 1.

93 *Sharp . . . Soucy* Ibid.

93 *"lay strictly off"* C. H. Carson memo to P. E. Foxworth, August 16, 1941.

93 *not been able to reach Ellis* Popov twice tried to call Ellis (at Ci 5-5176) during the visit by Murray and Chambers, but could not reach him. Sharp letter, p. 1.

93 *He called Agent Soucy* C. H. Carson memo to Mr. Foxworth, August 16, 1941, Record Group No. 65, Box 6, Section 1, 65-HQ-36994-19, NARA.

93 *Three days later, on Monday, August 18* In his memoirs, Popov states that he met Lanman upon arrival in New York (August 12, 1941), and the next day (August 13) met with Lanman and Percy Foxworth in Foxworth's office at Rockefeller Center. It was here, Dusko wrote, that he provided the FBI with his questionnaire, microdots, and warning. *Spy Counter-Spy*, 156–60. In his report of September 17, 1941, however, FBI agent Lanman wrote that he did not meet Popov until the August 18 meeting at the Commodore Hotel. Lanman Report, 2. See also "Activities of Tricycle," KV 2/855 (p. 662B). The initial meeting on the eighteenth is consistent with the FBI memos and letters from Connelley, Foxworth, Lanman, M. C. Spear, and C. H. Carson, and with Colonel Sharp's correspondence of August 15, all cited herein.

94 *confusing Earl Connelley with Foxworth* While Foxworth eventually became Popov's supervisor, Connelley ran the FBI New York office in August 1941. Until October 1941, Foxworth was the assistant director, Security Division (Counterintelligence) and based in Washington. In October, he was promoted to assistant director in charge of the New York Division and head of the Special Intelligence Service. Personnel file for Percy Foxworth, supplied to author via correspondence with official FBI historian Dr. John Fox, on December 30, 2014.

94 *"Mr. Popov was furnished with"* Correspondence from Assistant Director E. J. Connelley to Director J. Edgar Hoover, August 19, 1941, Record Group No. 65, Box 6, Section 1, 65-HQ-36994-19, NARA. Pages 1–3, 12, and Exhibit C of the Connelley letter are included herein as Appendix 1.

94 *Lanman met again with Popov* Correspondence from Assistant Director E. J. Connelley to Director J. Edgar Hoover, August 21, 1941, Record Group No. 65, Box 6, Section 1, 65-HQ-36994-19, NARA; Lanman Report, 2.

95 *"It will be remembered"* . . . *"The whole"* J. C. Masterman, *The Double-Cross System in the War of 1939 to 1945*, 79–80.

95 *August 25 Lanman personally delivered* Correspondence from Assistant Director E. J. Connelley to Director J. Edgar Hoover, August 25, 1941, Record Group No. 65, Box 6, Section 1, 65-HQ-36994-19, NARA; Lanman Report, 4.

95 *September 3, the lab released an eight-page report* FBI Laboratory Report, September 3, 1941, Record Group No. 65, Box 6, Section 1, 65-HQ-36994-19, NARA.

95 *Hoover sent Assistant Director Connelley* Correspondence from Director J. Edgar Hoover to Assistant Director E. J. Connelley, September 4, 1941, Record Group No. 65, Box 6, Section 1, 65-HQ-36994-19, NARA.

95 *"The American Embassy in London"* Correspondence from Director J. Edgar Hoover to Assistant Director E. J. Connelley, August 21, 1941, Record Group No. 65, Box 6, Section 1, 65-HQ-36994-19, NARA.

96 *"Confidential Informant ND-63"* Correspondence from Assistant Director E. J. Connelley to Director J. Edgar Hoover, August 21, 1941, Record Group No. 65, Box 6, Section 1, 65-HQ-36994-19, NARA.

96 *"Views on Preparations for War"* Edwin T. Layton, *And I Was There: Pearl Harbor and Midway—Breaking the Secrets*, 72–73.

97 *"This will be of interest"* Hyde, *Secret Intelligence Agent: British Espionage in America and the Creation of the OSS*, 124.

97 *the FBI's second warning* Ibid, 125–31. See also, William Stevenson, *A Man Called Intrepid*, 175–76.

98 *penthouse two blocks from Central Park* Correspondence from E. J. Connelley to J. Edgar Hoover, September 5, 1941, Record Group No. 65, Box 6, Section 1, 65-HQ-36994, NARA, p. 1.

98 *couldn't provide the landlord with references* Correspondence from E. J. Connelley to J. Edgar Hoover, August 19, 1941, Record Group No. 65, Box 6, Section 1, 65-HQ-36994-19, NARA, p. 6.

98 *received a letter from home* Correspondence from E. J. Connelley to J. Edgar Hoover, September 5, 1941, Record Group No. 65, Box 6, Section 1, 65-HQ-36994, NARA, p. 1.

98 *Bata—a world champion water polo player—was crucified* Milorad ("Misha") Popov, unpublished memoirs; author correspondence with Misha Popov, February 14–15, 2015.

CHAPTER 13 COVER-UP

99 *fired off a letter to Major General Edwin Watson* Official File 10 "Justice Department," Box 14, Franklin D. Roosevelt Library.

104 *the President had a forty-five-minute meeting* Franklin D. Roosevelt calendar for September 3, 1941, Franklin D. Roosevelt Library.

104 *"I thought you might be interested"* Official File 10 "Justice Department," Box 14, Franklin D. Roosevelt Library.

104 *Hoover had a meeting with the President* Franklin D. Roosevelt schedule for September 4, 1941, Franklin D. Roosevelt Library.

104 *Chen-Yen* Correspondence of FBI agent R. G. Fletcher to P. E. Foxworth, September 12, 1941, Record Group No. 65, Box 6, Section 1, 65-HQ-36994-19, NARA.

104 *flying lessons at Mitchel Field* Ian Wilson memo, November 13, 1942, KV 2/850 (sub-file 1).

105 *Terry Richardson* Popov refers to her as "Terry Brown" in his memoirs (*Spy Counter-Spy*, 164) and as "Laura" in his *True* magazine (October 1973, p. 107) account, likely because he offered to kill her.

105 *Dusko would have to take it up with Hoover* Dusko Popov, "Pearl Harbor: Did J. Edgar Hoover Blunder?" *True*, October 1973, 107.

105 *"Sam: see Connelley in N.Y."* Correspondence of P. E. Foxworth to J. Edgar Hoover, September 8, 1941, Record Group No. 65, Box 6, Section 1, 65-HQ-36994-19, NARA.

105 *Hoover with his partner Clyde* Anthony Summers, *Official and Confidential: The Secret Life of J. Edgar Hoover*, 125.

105 *stay at any hotel the FBI wished* Correspondence of Assistant Director E. J. Connelley to J. Edgar Hoover, September 9, 1941, Record Group No. 65, Box 6, Section 1, 65-HQ-36994-19, NARA.

105 *checked into separate rooms* Correspondence of FBI agent R. G. Fletcher to P. E. Foxworth, September 18, 1941, Record Group No. 65, Box 6, Section 1, 65-HQ-36994-19, NARA.

105 *Dempsey Vanderbilt Hotel* Author interview with Michael Johnson, Setai Project executive, on September 6, 2014. See also, "Jack Dempsey's Restaurant in Miami Beach," *Miami Heritage*, August 9, 2008. http://miamiheritage.org/2008/08/09/jack-dempseys-restaurant-in-miami-beach/.

105 *"was drawn to a man"* Dusko Popov, *True*, 107.

105 *White-Slave Traffic Act* 18 U.S.C. §2421-2424.

106 *Bureau records state* Correspondence of E. J. Connelley to J. Edgar Hoover, September 9 and September 27, 1941, Record Group No. 65, Box 6, Section 1, 65-HQ-36994-19, NARA. Popov's account of being accosted by FBI agents on the beach seems illogical since the FBI

didn't object to his leaving and sent agent Lanman to Miami to supervise. However, it also seems illogical that Terry Richardson, who had limited funds, would suddenly abandon an all-expenses-paid vacation to Miami Beach and fly alone to New York after a few days, and on a Saturday night (FBI records indicate that she was looking for a house, found nothing, and decided to return). In addition, Connelley's September 9 letter includes a handwritten note that agent Thurston "will leave Monday, 9/15," indicating that two FBI agents would be on the Miami scene, as Popov wrote.

106 *Hoover had blocked the Hawaii trip* Anthony Cave Brown, *Wild Bill Donovan: The Last Hero*, 196.

107 *Behind Sam's desk* Foxworth became assistant director in charge of the New York Division in October and likely would have moved to Manhattan just days prior to this meeting.

107 *"looking like a sledgehammer"* Dusko Popov, *True*, 110; Dusko Popov, "A Spy's Spy Tells it All," *People*, June 17, 1974, 20–21.

107 *"Hoover had no use for me"* Dusko Popov, interview with Jonathan Braun, "Superspy Dusko Popov: The Real-Life James Bond," *Parade*, 27.

107 *some challenge the veracity of Popov's story* Troy Thomas, a former CIA officer, claimed that the two never met, and that Popov warned no one about Pearl Harbor. Troy Thomas, "The British Assault on J. Edgar Hoover: The Tricycle Case," *Intelligence and Counter-intelligence* 3, no. 3, 1989. But see Summers, 127. Popov and Hoover certainly had occasion to meet, Summers noted, as FBI records confirm that during this time Popov was in Washington four days in late August 1941 and Hoover was in New York.

107 *Popov and Hoover never met* FBI Director Clarence M. Kelley correspondence to *True* magazine publisher, William Dunn, of Fawcett Publications, on October 1, 1973. Kelley stated: "Mr. Popov never personally met Mr. Hoover." Record Group 65, Box 13, Part 19, 65-36994, NARA. Kelley admits, however, that Popov went to FBI headquarters on October 24, 1946, and appeared in Hoover's reception room, but he contends that Dusko spoke only to two aides, not to the director himself.

107 *Hoover's "Do Not File" system* See Athan Theoharis, *From the Secret Files of J. Edgar Hoover*, 127, 339.

107 *"Edgar made an art form"* Summers, 128.

108 *"He [Stephenson] said Popov had indeed met Hoover"* Ibid., 128, 468.

108 *"He [Popov] was debriefed"* Ibid., 128.

108 *"had no doubt"* Ibid, 441, fn. 9. Two other principal sources confirmed in 1990 Summers's statement that Popov and Hoover had met. Chloe MacMillan, who worked for MI6 in Portugal, stated that she met with Dusko upon his return to Lisbon in 1942. "He did see Hoover, I'm sure," she told Summers, "and he did give them his warning about Pearl Harbor before it happened. When I saw him months later, he was still so depressed about what happened." Yugoslav author Branko Bokun, a friend of Popov's who recalled their discussion in 1946, remembered a similar encounter: "He [Popov] told me then, and many times afterwards, there are some things in life that shock us so much that they never leave you. It marked him the rest of his life." Ibid., 128.

108 *"As a matter of fact"* J. Edgar Hoover letter to Major General Edwin M. Watson, October 1, 1941, Franklin D. Roosevelt Library.

108 *"Tricycle was furnished with"* FBI memo to MI5, "Activities of Tricycle in the United States," October 5, 1943, KV 2/855 (p. 662B).

109 *eight investigations* Edwin T. Layton, *And I Was There: Pearl Harbor and Midway—Breaking the Secrets*, 511–17.

109 None *of them mention* Curt Gentry, *J. Edgar Hoover: The Man and the Secrets*, 296.

109 *"There have been official inquiries"* Popov, *True*, 113.

109 *none of the "Magic" intercepts* Husband E. Kimmel, *Admiral Kimmel's Story*, 83–86. Kimmel explained: "On September 24, 1941, the Japanese government instructed its consul general in Honolulu as to the type of report it desired from him concerning vessels in Pearl Harbor. . . . The dispatch stated:

With regard to warships and aircraft carriers, we would like to have you report on those at anchor . . . tied up at wharves, buoys, and in docks. (Designate types and classes briefly. If possible we would like to have you make mention of the fact when there are two or more vessels alongside the same wharf.)

The dispatch was decoded and translated on October 9, 1941. This information was withheld from me. . . . On September 29, 1941, Kita, the Japanese consul general in Honolulu, replied to his government's dispatch of September 24. . . . This dispatch of the consul general was decoded and translated on October 10, 1941. This information was never supplied to me. . . . On November 15, 1941, Togo sent the following dispatch:

As relations between Japan and the United States are most critical, make your "ships in the harbor report" irregular but at the rate of twice a week. Although you are no doubt aware, please take extra care to maintain secrecy.

This dispatch was decoded and translated by the Navy in Washington on December 3, 1941. This information was never supplied to me. . . . On November 18, 1941, Togo sent the following dispatch to Honolulu:

Please report on the following areas as to vessels anchored therein: Area N, Pearl Harbor, Mamala Bay (Honolulu), and the Areas Adjacent thereto. (Make your investigation with great secrecy.)

This dispatch was decoded and translated on December 5, 1951. This information was never supplied to me. . . . On November 18, 1941, the Japanese consul general in Honolulu reported to Tokyo . . . that in Area A there was a battleship of the 'Oklahoma' class; that in Area O there were three heavy cruisers at anchor, as well as the carrier 'Enterprise' or some other vessel; that two heavy cruisers of the 'Chicago' class were tied up at docks KS. . . . This dispatch was decoded and translated in Washington on December 6, 1941. This information was never supplied to me."

109 *"As far as the FBI's role"* Gentry, 296.

110 *revealed by countless sources* J. C. Masterman, *The Double-Cross System in the War of 1939 to 1945*, 79–81, 196–98; Ewen Montague, *Beyond Top Secret Ultra*, 75–77; William Stevenson, *A Man Called Intrepid: The Secret War*, 257–60; H. Montgomery Hyde, *Secret Intelligence Agent: British Espionage in America and the Creation of the OSS*, 204–210; Curt Gentry, *J. Edgar Hoover: The Man and the Secrets*, 269–73, 296–97; Anthony Summers, *Official and Confidential: The Secret Life of J. Edgar Hoover*, 122–30; Anthony Cave Brown, *Wild Bill Donovan: The Last Hero*, 195–96; Anthony Cave Brown, *C: The Secret Life of Sir Stewart Graham Menzies, Spymaster to Winston Churchill*, 371–73; John F. Bratzel and Leslie B. Rout, Jr. "Pearl Harbor, Microdots, and J. Edgar Hoover," *American Historical Review* 87, no. 5 (December 1982), 1342–51; Roger S. Young, John F. Bratzel, Leslie B. Rout, Jr., Otto Pflanze, and John Toland. "Once More: Pearl Harbor, Microdots, and J. Edgar Hoover: Letters and Replies," *American Historical Review* 88, no. 4 (October 1983), 953–60.

110 *"The Enemy's Masterpiece of Espionage"* J. Edgar Hoover, "The Enemy's Masterpiece of Espionage," *Reader's Digest*, April 1946.

111 *"Arrangements have been made"* Liddell diaries, March 15, 1941, KV 4/187.

111 *"It would be of value"* Correspondence of J. Edgar Hoover to Adolf A. Berle, Jr., June 5, 1941, Record Group No. 65, Box 6, Section 1, 65-HQ-36994-19, NARA.

111 *"honesty, his reliability, and his loyalty"* Correspondence of J. Edgar Hoover to E. J. Connelley, August 21, 1941, Record Group No. 65, Box 6, Section 1, 65-HQ-36994-19, NARA.

112 *"Since the names of all German instructors"* William White, *The Microdot: History and Application*, 65.

112 *Walter Zapp, White points out* Ibid., 65–75, 128–47 (Zapp letter).

112 *"innocent telephone messages"* Hoover, "The Enemy's Masterpiece"; FBI image indicating two microdots: Record Group 65, Box 6, 65-HQ-36994, NARA.

113 *Sousa did see it* Popov, *True*, 113.

113 *he called Hoover's office* Ibid., 114.

114 *"Truth to tell"* Ibid.

114 *September 6, 1946, Popov sent a letter to J. Edgar Hoover* Record Group No. 65, Box 13, Part 19, 65-HQ-36994, NARA.

114 *Director Clarence Kelley in 1973* In a letter to *True* magazine publisher William Dunn of Fawcett Publications on October 1, 1973, Kelley stated: "Mr. Popov never personally met Mr. Hoover." Acknowledging Popov's September 6 letter, Kelley went on: "On October 24, 1946, Mr. Popov appeared at FBI Headquarters and went to Mr. Hoover's reception room. He did not see Mr. Hoover personally but did speak briefly to two of Mr. Hoover's aides. That meeting is recorded." Record Group 65, Box 13, Part 19, 65-36994, NARA.

114 *"that he, Popov"* Memorandum of FBI agent C. H. Carson to D. M. Ladd, October 24, 1946. Record Group 65, Box 13, Part 19, 65-36994, NARA.

114 *"Popov was affable"* Ibid.

114 *"Just who is this?"* Hoover's handwritten note appearing on Popov's letter of September 6, 1946. Record Group 65, Box 13, Part 19, 65-36994, NARA.

CHAPTER 14 I'LL KILL HER

115 *Stefan Otto Feldmann* "Dusan M. Popov, Confidential Informant" memo of FBI agent R. G. Fletcher to D. M. Ladd, October 13, 1941, Box 6, Section 1, 65-HQ-36994, NARA ("Fletcher memo"). Popov told Charles Lanman the man's full name was Stefan Otto Feldmann von Bortham, but the FBI found no records of a Bortham. See also "Activities of Tricycle in the United States," October 5, 1943, KV 2/855 (p. 662B).

115 *microphone in his study* Correspondence from E. J. Connelley to J. Edgar Hoover, September 5, 1941, Record Group 65, Box 6, Section 1, 65-HQ-36994, NARA; Dusko Popov, interview with Frederick Bear, "Dusko [007] Popov: Exclusive Interview," *Genesis*, 68.

115 *"The informant has frequently"* Connelley, September 5, 1941 letter.

116 *The switch was a dummy* Popov, *Genesis*, 68.

116 *"Hoover is very jealous"* Popov, *Spy Counter-Spy*, 175.

116 *October 13 Popov met again with Lanman* Fletcher memo.

116 *Feldmann appeared to have been "planted"* "Activities of Tricycle in the United States," KV 2/855 (p. 662B).

116 *he'd kill her* Fletcher memo.

117 *When he next met with Foxworth* Popov, *Spy Counter-Spy*, 176–80.

117 *messages to Buenos Aires, Mexico City, Quito* FBI confidential report, "Totalitarian Activities—Brazil Today," December 1942, NA, RG 59, 800.20232/44, cited in Stanley E. Hilton, *Hitler's Secret War in South America, 1939–1945*, 28.

117 For Engels's background, see Hilton, 28–31, 33, 50.

118 *tables of organization* Record Group 65, 65-HQ-36994, Box 6, NARA.

118 *"It would be impossible"* "Activities of Tricycle in the United States," KV 2/855 (p. 662B).

119 *"Elizabeth departed for Rio"* Ibid.; cables sent and received by TRICYCLE, KV 2/863 (sub-file 3).

119 *numbers supplied by the War Department and the navy* For the tables of organization and production numbers supplied to Popov, see Record Group 65, 65-HQ-36994, Box 6, NARA.

119 *"Elizabeth will visit"* December 24, 1941, report of FBI agent C. F. Lanman (p. 4) summarizing Popov's Rio trip, Record Group 65, 65-HQ-36994, Box 6, NARA ("Lanman Report"); "Activities of Tricycle in the United States," KV 2/855 (p. 662B); FBI memo given to Ian Wilson in New York on November 16, 1942, KV 2/850 (p. 356 ma) ("FBI/Wilson memo"); cables sent and received by TRICYCLE, KV 2/863 (sub-file 3).

119 *"Having to leave"* . . . *"Everything possible"* Ibid.

119 *naval and military attaché* Lanman Report, p. 4.

119 *austere man with heavy, puffy eyes* Hermann Bohny photograph, courtesy of *Arquivo Nacional*, Hilton, photographs, image 2; Lanman Report, 10.

120 *"Elizabeth"* . . . *$10,000* Ibid., p. 5; "Activities of Tricycle," KV 2/855 (p. 62B). The "Elizabeth" password and authorized payment of $10,000 were confirmed by Germany to Rio in wireless intercepts on November 17, 1941; delivery of the $10,000 to Popov was confirmed by Rio to Germany in wireless intercepts on November 25, 1941. "Top Secret 'U'" catalogue at KV 2/860, sub-file 2 (unpaginated).

120 *room where a number of Germans were secretly working* Lanman Report, 1–3; Ian Wilson "TRICYCLE" memo for Tar Robertson (undated), point 34, KV 2/850 (p. 354A).

120 *he stopped by the apartment on Atlanticia* "Activities of Tricycle in the United States," KV 2/855 (p. 662B); FBI/Wilson memo, KV 2/850 (p. 356 ma); Lanman Report, 5–6.

120 *blond hair, blue eyes, fair complexion* Lanman Report, 5, 11.

120 *"Mrs. Dubois"* "Activities of Tricycle in the United States," KV 2/855 (p. 662B); FBI/Wilson memo, KV 2/850 (p. 356 ma); Lanman Report, 6.

120 *Albrecht appeared to be an accomplished athlete* Albrecht Engels photograph, courtesy of *Arquivo Nacional*, at Hilton, photographs, image 1; Lanman Report, 10–11.

120 For Popov's discussion with Engels, see "Activities of Tricycle in the United States," KV 2/855 (p. 662B); FBI/Wilson memo, KV 2/850 (p. 356 ma); correspondence from W. H. Blyth to Tar Robertson, December 31, 1941, KV 2/849, p. 229A.

121 *Portuguese captain* Dusko told the FBI nothing about the attempted acquisition of a microdot apparatus, only telling them that a sea captain would be a source for sending secure mail and microdots. Following MI6's instructions, Popov was careful to protect the captain's identity, telling the FBI that the captain ran from Rio to New York, rather than Quebec. See also, "Activities of Tricycle in the United States"; FBI/Wilson memo, KV 2/850 (p. 356 ma).

121 *bald-headed doctor, Château Frontenac* Popov, *Spy Counter-Spy*, 184–85.

121 *On December 1 Dusko met again* "Activities of Tricycle in the United States," KV 2/855 (p. 662B); FBI/Wilson memo; Lanman Report, 9 (Charles Lanman describes the hotel slip as a "scrap of paper").

121 *$8,500* German intercepts confirm that Engels paid Popov a total of $18,500. On March 9, 1942, Lisbon cabled Berlin: "Please inform me in detail of what sum IVAN received in Rio." Three days later Berlin cabled back: "For LUDOVICO. . . IVAN received . . . W/T operator Dec. to Feb. 1500; traveling expenses 1500; Total 18500." KV 2/860 (p. 1040b). See also Hilton, 176.

122 *S.S.* Uruguay Moore-McCormack was the only cruise ship company providing luxury cruise service between Rio de Janeiro and New York, running three, 33,000-ton liners: the *Uruguay*, the *Brazil*, and the *Argentina*. The *Uruguay* is recorded as Popov's ship in Special Agent

Charles Lanman's December 24, 1941, report. Record Group 65, Box 6, 65-HQ-36994, NARA.

122 *a small pilot boat approached* Popov, *Spy Counter-Spy*, 187; Miller, 113.

CHAPTER 15 BUTTERFLIES AND CARNAGE

123 *Several crew members disappeared* Report of FBI Special Agent Charles Lanman, December 24, 1941, Record Group 65, Box 6, 65-HQ-36994, NARA ("Lanman Report") (p. 13). While it is possible that MI6 removed the crew members because Popov tipped them off about the butterfly trays, it seems unlikely; in his memoirs Dusko does not mention telling Major Wren of the trays, and neither MI5 files nor FBI files mention Popov informing Wren, or noticing the trays before the Trinidad stop.

123 *captain called everyone to the first-class lounge* Dusko Popov, "Pearl Harbor: Did J. Edgar Hoover Blunder?" *True*, October 1973, 110, 113.

123 *"I was very, very proud"* Ibid.

124 *how they were coming* Ibid.

124 *killed 2,388 persons* USS *Arizona* Memorial, National Park Service; Edwin T. Layton, *And I Was There: Pearl Harbor and Midway—Breaking the Secrets*, 320.

125 *John Toland wrote to the FBI in 1978* Roger S. Young, John F. Bratzel, Leslie B. Rout, Jr., Otto Pflanze, and John Toland, "Once More: Pearl Harbor, Microdots, and J. Edgar Hoover: Letters and Replies," *American Historical Review* 88, no. 4 (October 1983), 958–60. Note that Toland believed that FDR had prior knowledge of Japan's intent to attack Pearl Harbor. See John Toland, *Infamy: Pearl Harbor and Its Aftermath*.

125 1982 article for American Historical Review John F. Bratzel and Leslie B. Rout, Jr., "Pearl Harbor, Microdots, and J. Edgar Hoover," *American Historical Review* 87, no. 5 (December 1982), 1342–51.

126 *Roger S. Young, FBI assistant director in charge* Ibid., 1347, fn. 14 and accompanying text.

126 *"neither the Naval Historical Center nor"* Ibid., 1347.

126 *"The FBI had sent"* Roger S. Young, John F. Bratzel, Leslie B. Rout, Jr., Otto Pflanze, and John Toland, "Once More: Pearl Harbor, Microdots, and J. Edgar Hoover: Letters and Replies," *American Historical Review* 88, no. 4 (October 1983), 954.

126 *The professors countered* Ibid, 953–57.

126 *"questionnaire . . . had been paraphrased"* Ibid., 956.

127 *"that J. Edgar Hoover"* Ibid.

127 *"It should also be pointed out"* Ibid., 954.

128 *"Hoover was to drop the ball"* Edwin T. Layton, *And I Was There: Pearl Harbor and Midway—Breaking the Secrets*, 105.

128 *"Hoover had shown his total incompetence"* William Casey, *The Secret War Against Hitler*, 10.

129 *On December 15, 1941* Lanman Report (p. 2).

130 confiscation of butterfly trays Ibid.

130 *"Mr. Popov told Mr. Foxworth"* J. Edgar Hoover memo of December 15, 1941, to Mr. Tolson, Mr. Tamm, and Mr. Ladd. Record Group 65, Box 6, 65-HQ-36994, NARA.

130 *Atelier Elizabeth* Lanman Report (p. 3). In his report, Lanman misspelled Industria as "Industra." See also Ian Wilson "TRICYCLE" memo for Tar Robertson (undated), point 34, KV 2/850 (354A).

132 *"lapse of memory" . . . "truth beyond your reach"* Popov, *Spy Counter-Spy*, 195–96; Miller, *Codename TRICYCLE*, 115.

CHAPTER 16 BLOWN

133 *Sonja Henie* Popov, *Spy Counter-Spy*, 205; Miller, *Codename TRICYCLE*, 117.

133 For Sun Valley history, see Sun Valley Resort website: https://www.sunvalley.com/about-sun-valley.

133 *Hemingway, who worked on* For Whom the Bell Tolls Jeffrey Meyers, *Hemingway: A Biography*, 326, 343.

133 *"My family was in occupied territory"* Popov, 205; Miller, 118.

134 *"Wishing you and all our friends"* KV 2/849 (p. 228A).

134 *"You know what that means"* Popov, 207.

134 *tapping his phone and keeping open files on his girlfriends* The FBI tapped Dusko's phone, maintained mail surveillance on Terry Richardson, tapped Simone Simon's phone, and maintained tight surveillance on Simon, reporting back to Hoover whom she was dating, whom she spent time with, and where she went.

134 *an apartment close to Dusko's* Popov recorded that Simone had taken a unit on the seventh floor of his building (*Spy Counter-Spy*, 208). FBI files, however, indicate that her apartment was in another building but on the same block of Park Avenue. Popov may have confused girlfriends, as Terry Richardson did move into his building. See "Dusan M. Popov, Confidential Informant" memo of FBI agent R. G. Fletcher to D. M. Ladd, October 13, 1941, Box 6, Section 1, 65-HQ-36994, NARA .

134 *sipping coffee on the terrace of Café de la Paix* Jacques Lory, "Tender Little Savage: France's Favorite Descends upon the Hollywood Scene," Screen & Radio Weekly, *Oakland Tribune*, December 29, 1935, 3.

134 *favorite haunt of Oscar Wilde's* Café de la Paix website: http://www.cafedelapaix.fr/uk/index.php#une-institution-parisienne.php.

135 *"Please remember to send"* Russell Miller, 123-24.

135 *"Keep main attention, Difficult to obtain"* Ibid., 124.

136 *"Blindfold me"* Popov, 209.

136 *"very proper"* Anthony Summers, *Official and Confidential: The Secret Life of J. Edgar Hoover*, 125.

136 *"Her mother is a sensationally beautiful woman"* Earl Wilson, "It Happened Last Night," *Tucson Daily Citizen*, August 1, 1944, 5.

136 *"enthusiastic about everything"* Popov, 211.

136 *air conference in Ottawa . . . removed him from the plane* Ian Wilson "TRICYCLE" memo for Tar Robertson (undated), point 25, KV 2/850 (p. 354A). Popov recalled in his memoirs (*Spy Counter-Spy*, 212–13) that he had driven to the border and was turned back for want of an income tax declaration, but Wilson recorded at the time that Dusko was removed from his flight for want of a proper exit permit, which the FBI had prepared. Since when leaving for London Popov incurred difficulties with the U.S. Revenue authorities, which the New York FBI office was to have cleared (resulting in MI6 paying $480 on Popov's nominal salary from the Yugoslav Ministry of Information), Dusko may have confused the two trips or may have encountered the hurdle on both trips. See also Wilson memo, point 23, KV 2/850 (p. 354A); Ian Wilson "TRICYCLE and Money Affairs" memo, November 12, 1942, KV 2/850 (p. 353a).

137 *"As there is a suspicion"* March 20, 1942, wireless intercept at KV 2/860 (p. 1040b).

137 *"IVAN may be playing"* March 21, 1942, wireless intercept at KV 2/860 (p. 1040b).

138 *"Before he left England"* Miller, 124–25.

138 *On March 26 he received two letters . . . "Decay of Uran"* "Activities of Tricycle in the United States," KV 2/855 (p. 662B).

139 *"sound reasons for suspecting"* May 5, 1942, wireless intercept, KV 2/860 (p. 1040b).

139 *"We have heard"* Felix Cowgill cable, May 8, 1942, KV 2/849 (p. 250).

139 *"Evidence is now available"* "Tribage Organisation" memorandum of Charles C. Cholmondeley, May 10, 1942, KV 2/849 (p. 254B).

139 *The Stork Club, El Morocco* Dusko Popov, interview with Frederick Bear, "Dusko [007] Popov: Exclusive Interview," *Genesis*, 68.

139 *"I do crossword puzzles"* Earl Wilson, "It Happened One Night," 5.

140 *$1,900 per month* Ian Wilson July 4, 1942, memo, KV 2/849 (p. 275b). The Germans eventually paid Popov and he was able to repay all loans. Some authors have written that Dusko borrowed $10,000 from Simone Simon, but this is untrue; he had borrowed $10,000 from MI6 but couldn't show such accounting to the Germans. Accordingly, the fiction was created—*to show the Abwehr*—that he had borrowed $10,000 from Simon. Ian Wilson explained the accounting in his memorandum of March 29, 1943: "The notional receipts are the same as his actual receipts except that TRICYCLE did not of course receive any salary from the Ministry of Information and the $10,000 loan was not from his girlfriend Simone SIMON but from S.I.S." KV 2/853 (p. 457a).

140 *a carefully disguised letter* KV 2/850 (p. 297); Ian Wilson memo, December 22, 1942, KV 2/851 (p. 383A).

141 *"Greetings Dear Dule"* KV 2/850, sub-file 2 (unpaginated, following 299).

141 *Walter Winchell was one of the most powerful* See Neil Gabler, *Winchell: Gossip, Power, and the Culture of Celebrity*; Bernard Weinraub, "He Turned Gossip into Tawdry Power; Walter Winchell, Who Climbed High and Fell Far, Still Scintillates," *New York Times*, November 18, 1998, www.nytimes.com/1998/11/18; Ralph D. Gardner, "The Age of Winchell," http://www.evesmag.com/winchell.htm (2001).

141 *invented tabloid journalism* Gabler, xii; Weinraub.

141 *carried by two thousand newspapers* Gabler, xi; Weinraub, Gardner.

141 *"he possessed the extraordinary ability"* Gardner.

141 *featured in popular songs* The full lyrics (as sung by Ella Fitzgerald) of Lorenz Hart's "The Lady Is a Tramp" mention him in refrain 2 (removed in Sinatra's version):

I go to Coney, the beach is divine/I go to ballgames, the bleachers are fine/I find a Winchell, and read every line/That's why the lady is a tramp

In Cole Porter's "Let's Fly Away":

Let's fly away And find a land that's so provincial, We'll never hear what Walter Winchell Might be forced to say!

141 *"From Table 50"* Weinraub.

141 *"call whenever he wanted"* Ibid. Calendar entries for President Roosevelt show that Winchell met with FDR on May 4, 1936; May 10, 1938; January 27, 1939; October 8, 1940; October 20, 1942; May 11, 1943 (just before FDR had dinner with Prime Minister Winston Churchill); March 24, 1944; and October 13, 1944. President Roosevelt calendar, Franklin D. Roosevelt Library.

141 *friends with J. Edgar Hoover* Gardner. According to President Roosevelt's calendar, Winchell had cocktails with Hoover and President Roosevelt at the White House on May 4, 1936. Franklin D. Roosevelt Library. See also photo of Winchell and Hoover in Summers, photo #18.

142 *"Broadway Small-Talk: . . . Dusko Popov"* Walter Winchell, "On Broadway," syndicated column from New York *Daily Mirror*. See, e.g., reprints in: *High Point Enterprise*, July 16, 1942, A-4; *Panama City News-Herald*, July 19, 1942, 6; *Port Arthur News*, July 22, 1942, 4; *Wisconsin State Journal*, July 22, 1942, 6.

143 *Germans saw the column* Ian Wilson telegram to Colonel Wren, November 17, 1942, KV 2/850 (p. 356Q).

143 *returned him to British control* August 3, 1942, telegram from Colonel Wren to Major Frank Foley, included in Foley's cable to Tar Robertson, KV 2/850 (p. 285a).

143 *Hoover intercepting his telegrams?* Ian Wilson "TRICYCLE" memo, November 11, 1942, KV 2/850 (p. 349a); correspondence from Tar Robertson to Frank Foley, November 13, 1942, KV 2/850 (p. 351).

143 *"Kosta 20 S. West St."* KV 2/850 (p. 352k).

143 *Ian Wilson received a report* Ian Wilson memo, July 30, 1942, KV 2/849 (p. 281a).

143 *"rendered suspect virtually the whole"* Ian Wilson memo to Major Frank Foley, August 10, 1942, KV 2/850 (p.288). See also Wilson memo, July 27, 1942, KV 2/849 (p. 279a).

144 *"You'd be a damned fool"* Popov, *Spy Counter-Spy*, 217.

144 *"He could end his double agent work"* Montagu, *Beyond Top Secret Ultra*, 80-81.

144 *"ability not to give a damn"* Ernest Hemingway, *Death in the Afternoon*, 58 (emphasis added).

145 *"I think I survived"* Dusko Popov, interview with Jonathan Braun, "Superspy Dusko Popov: The Real-Life James Bond," *Parade*, 27.

145 *"Nearly all bullfighters"* Hemingway, *Death in the Afternoon*, 58.

145 *"There is always the feeling"* Dusko Popov interview with Frederick Bear, "Dusko [007] Popov: Exclusive Interview," *Genesis*, 36.

145 *Pascal's Wager* Blaise Pascal, *The Mind on Fire,* 131–32.

CHAPTER 17 INCOMPLETE CANVAS

146 every man's death diminishes me John Donne, Meditation 17, *Devotions upon Emergent Occasions and Death's Duel*, 63.

146 *"I expected"* Ian Wilson, "POPOV" memo, March 26, 1943, KV 2/852 (p. 457k).

146 *"I would be lacking"* Ibid.

147 Cat People Two weeks after Winchell's public disclosure of Simone and Dusko's relationship, Simon began filming *Cat People*. Released on Christmas Day, the movie was a smashing success, and overnight Simone Simon became an international sensation. Released almost the same time as *Casablanca*, *Cat People* easily bested Bogart at the box office. On a budget of only $134,000, *Cat People* grossed a whopping $8 million, earning $4 million domestically and another $4 million abroad. *Casablanca*, released only a month after *Cat People*, made $3.7 million domestically on a budget of $878,000. *Casablanca*, *Cat People* budgets and box office receipts from Thomas Schatz, *Boom and Bust: American Cinema in the 1940s* (University of California Press, 1999), 218; Nash Information Services, LLC, http://www.the-numbers.com/movie/Cat-People#tab=summary.

Astonishingly, since the advent of feature sound film in 1927, on a cost to gross box office basis, *Cat People* remains today—after more than seventy years—the second most profitable major studio (non-animated) motion picture. With a cost of $134,000 and worldwide gross receipts of $8 million, *Cat People* earned almost 60 times its budget. By comparison, 1939's *Gone with the Wind* (cost: $3.9 million, gross: $198 million) earned 50 times its budget; 1953's *Peter Pan* (cost: $4 million, gross: $142 million) earned 35 times its budget; 1965's *The Sound of Music* (cost: $8.2 million, gross: $163 million) earned 20 times its budget; 1975's *Jaws* (cost: $12 million, gross: $220 million) earned 19 times its budget; 1978's *Grease* (cost: $6 million, gross: $190 million) earned 32 times its budget; 1997's *Titanic* (cost: $200 million, gross: $2.2 billion) earned 11 times its budget; 2009's *Avatar* (cost: $425 million, gross: $2.8 billion) earned less than 7 times its budget.

Where costs are available for calculation, only one non-animated major studio movie has bested *Cat People*: Sylvester Stallone's *Rocky*, in 1976 (cost: $1 million, gross: $117 million), earning an astounding 117 times its budget. Two animated motion pictures have also exceeded *Cat People*: 1937's *Snow White and the Seven Dwarfs* (cost: $1.49 million, gross: $185 million), earning 124 times its budget, and 1942's *Bambi* (for which cost is not available, but gross receipts exceeded $102 million). Nash Information Services, LLC, http://www.the-numbers.com/movie/budgets/.

147 *"Yes, every morning"* All conversation between Popov and Simon cited from FBI wiretaps. FBI Agent H. Frank Angel, "Simone Simon" report, December 29, 1942, Record Group 65, Box 6, 65-HQ-36994, NARA.

147 *"It is not kindness"* Ibid.

148 *seventeen-point memorandum* Ian Wilson memo, August 24,1942, KV 2/850 (p. 292a).

148 *"F.B.I. HAVE FAILED"* Foley telegram to Tar Robertson, October 10, 1942, KV 2/850 (p. 305y).

148 *"Can you at this late hour"* Ibid.

148 *Robertson put John Marriott on it* See John Marriott, "TRICYCLE" memo to Major Robertson, October 11, 1942, KV 2/850 (p. 305a) and accompanying notes.

149 *Ewen Montagu offered naval updates* John Marriott memo to Major Robertson, October 12, 1942, KV 2/850 (p. 307B).

149 *"The Girl You Like"* Conversation between Popov and Simon cited from FBI wiretaps. FBI Agent H. Frank Angel, "Simone Simon" report, December 29, 1942, Record Group 65, Box 6, 65-HQ-36994, NARA.

149 *October 12, Dusko returned to London* Colonel Wren "POPOV" memo (undated), KV 2/850 (p. 355b).

149 *"The greatest instance of cold-blooded courage"* Ewen Montagu, *Beyond Top Secret Ultra*, 81.

150 *"the steel within . . . putting his head into the lion's mouth"* Ewen Montagu, foreword to Popov, *Spy Counter-Spy*, vi.

150 *"My reaction disturbed me in a way"* Popov, *Spy Counter-Spy*, 220; Popov, *Parade*, 27.

150 *He checked into the Palácio* Dusko Popov, MI5 report of October 23, 1942, KV 2/850 (p. 313A) ("Popov October report"); Ian Wilson memo, "TRICYCLE'S FIFTH VISIT TO LISBON: 14th–21st Oct: 1942," December 22, 1942, KV 2/851 (p. 383A) ("Wilson memo").

150 *The "second's hesitation"* Ibid.; Popov, *Spy Counter-Spy*, 220–21.

150 *Thursday morning* Popov October report; Wilson memo. In his memoirs, Dusko misremembered the details of the rendezvous, thinking that he had been picked up on "the road outside Estoril" by von Karsthoff and Elisabeth the evening of his arrival and driven to Ludovico's country house. Popov, *Spy Counter-Spy*, 220–21.

151 *"I know"* Popov October report; Wilson memo. From the major's comment Popov knew that he had been followed when he arrived in Lisbon.

151 *"Now, what happened?"* Popov, *Spy Counter-Spy*, 221.

151 *"A lie when it is needed"* J. C. Masterman, *The Double-Cross System*, 20.

151 *"No mortal can keep a secret"* Sigmund Freud, *Dora: An Analysis of a Case of Hysteria*, 69.

151 *went on the offensive* Wilson memo.

151 *"was a colossal error"* Popov, *Spy Counter-Spy*, 222.

151 *borrowing from a girlfriend* Wilson memo.

151 *Simone Simon* Ibid.

151 *"Give Berlin a very rude message"* Popov October report.

151 *Mr. Bacher . . . Boris Cassini* Wilson memo. Bacher also recorded as "Becher." See, e.g., correspondence from J. C. Masterman to Frank Foley, October 28, 1942, KV 2/850 (p. 322a), telegram at KV 2/850 (p. 319B).

151 *"It is Berlin's fault"* Popov October report.
152 *never asked about Popov's movements* Wilson memo.
152 *radioman* Ibid.; Popov October report.
152 *"Are you very sure"* Popov October report.
152 *when Popov would be returning to the U.S.* Popov October report; Wilson memo.
153 *after three o'clock* Ibid.
153 *any English-speaking country under British or American control* Ibid.
153 *trap* "The ease with which I was being reintegrated in the Àbwehr," Dusko said in his memoirs, "made me slightly suspicious. I had come prepared for a thorough interrogation and at least a good dressing down." Popov, *Spy Counter-Spy*, 223.

CHAPTER 18 THE ART OF THE SILENT KILL

154 *Bailonis $8,500 . . . sent to Russian front* Dusko Popov, MI5 report of October 23, 1942, KV 2/850 (p. 313A) ("Popov October report"). Ian Wilson memo, "TRICYCLE'S FIFTH VISIT TO LISBON: 14th–21st Oct: 1942," December 22, 1942, KV 2/851 (p. 383A) ("Wilson memo").
154 *Café Chave d'Ouro* Ibid.
154 *charge d'affaires . . . Quinta Los Grillos* Ibid.
154 *He was followed* Ibid.
155 *$10,000 from Simone Simon* Wilson memo. The loan from Simon was a ruse; he never borrowed from her.
155 *"living like a prince"* Popov October report, KV 2/850 (p. 313A); Wilson memo.
155 *unwilling to continue as a German agent . . . no leaving off* Wilson memo.
155 *"Now you know what Berlin thinks"* Ibid.; Popov October report.
155 *cut off in June* According to Popov's report to MI5, the Germans cut off funding in April. See Wilson memo. The German contention was that his April payment was to have included part of May and that funding ceased when Popov provided no information from May to June.
155 *"Berlin are stupid fellows"* Popov October report; Wilson memo, KV.
156 *"What about invasion?"* Popov October report.
156 *air attaché* Wilson memo; Popov October report.
156 *That evening at six* Ibid.
156 *Kammler's secretary sewed the matches into the shoulders of his coat* Popov October report.
156 *$25,000 and 6,000 escudos* Popov October report; J. C. Masterman, "TRICYCLE" memo, October 24, 1942, KV 2/850 (pp. 312a, b); Wilson memo.
157 *held it to the light* Popov October report.
157 *conjured up with Ivo* Popov, *Spy Counter-Spy*, 232.
157 *Beverly Hills Hotel* H. Frank Angell, "Simone Simon" memo, December 29, 1942, Record Group 65, 65-HQ-36994, Box 6, NARA (p. 1).
157 *"Missing you darling"* The telegram, which was intercepted by American Censorship and forwarded to the FBI, was roughly worded and incorrectly spelled in transmission: "IS SAD TO BE IN THE ENTRANCE EUROPE WITHOUT GO INSIDE. MISSING YOU DEARLING MUCH MOOR THAN I THOUGHT WILL LOVE DUSKO POPOV." J. Edgar Hoover memo to Special Agent in Charge, New York City, November 14, 1942, Record Group 65, 65-HQ-36994, Box 6, NARA.
157 *Clock House* Clock House lease agreement at KV 2/851 (p. 359Bk).
157 *Robertson notified the postmaster* KV 2/851 (p. 359e and f, respectively).
157 *"My dear Dusko"* Letter from Dusko's father dated November 17, 1942, KV 2/850 (p. 356).

158 For the disappearance of his brothers, see Ivo: J. C. Masterman memo, October 24, 1942, KV 2/850 (p. 312a); Vladan: Ian Wilson "TRICYCLE" memo, November 11, 1942, KV 2/850 (p. 349a).

158 *"take every step"* Ian Wilson memo, December 2, 1942, KV 2/851 (p. 361B).

158 *"capital investment purposes"* Ian Wilson memo, November 30, 1942, KV 2/851 (p. 360a).

159 *"shabbiest and coldest man"* Dusko Popov letter to "Mr. Thomas" (Colonel Wren), December 5, 1942, KV 2/851 (p. 368).

159 *"TRICYCLE would like included"* Ian Wilson memo, December 7, 1942, KV 2/851 (p. 368).

159 *"c/o British Ministry of War Information"* KV 2/851 (p. 390).

160 *"TRICYCLE stressed his desire"* Ian Wilson "TRICYCLE" memo, February 8, 1943, KV 2/851 (p. 417a).

160 *SOE (Special Operations Executive) commando schools* The exact date of Popov's commando training is uncertain, but given the weeks required and Dusko's known schedules in Lisbon and London, this window appears to be the only time he could have participated. Dusko discusses attending the training in his interview with Frederick Bear ("Dusko [007] Popov: Exclusive Interview," *Genesis*, 36) and also in his interview with Jonathan Braun ("Superspy Dusko Popov: The Real-Life James Bond," *Parade*, 27). On the MI5 side, in addition to the Doran letter and Tar memos, Ian Wilson stated that on May 28, 1943, Popov informed him that a Yugoslav intelligence officer was being sent to Scotland for parachute training, which was part of the SOE program (KV 2/853, 511a).

160 *On February 24, a Captain D. Doran* KV 2/852 (p. 431B).

160 *On March 17, Tar sent a letter* KV 2/852 (p. 440a).

160 *Two days later* Ian Wilson "TRICYCLE" memo, March 20, 1943, KV 2/852 (p. 450a).

161 *Lieutenant Colonel Colin Gubbins,* See, generally, M. R. D. Foot, *S.O.E.: The Special Operations Executive, 1940–46.*

161 terrorists Ibid., 69.

161 *Stage 1* See Pieter Dourlein, *Inside North Pole: A Secret Agent's Story*, 79–80. Dourlein's Stage 1 training occurred in Reading, England. Dusko makes no reference to attending Stage 1 of the SOE training, although his seven-week disappearance would have given him time for both stages.

161 *well-stocked bars* Foot, 80.

161 *Stage 2* Denis Rigden, introduction, *How to Be a Spy: The World War II SOE Training Manual*, 5. Stage 2 was later lengthened to five weeks. See also, Foot, 79–85.

161 *"a wretched, barren countryside"* Dourlein, 81.

161 *William Ewart Fairbairn* See Tank Todd and James Webb, *Military Combat Masters of the 20th Century*, 58; George Langelaan, *Knights of the Floating Silk*, 65.

162 *"Shanghai Buster"* Langelaan, 65.

162 *"drastic and admittedly unpleasant"* W. E. Fairbairn, *Defendu: Scientific Self-Defense—The Official Text Book for the Shanghai Municipal Police, Hong Kong Police and Singapore Police*, p. 1 of foreword.

162 *"and then kick him in the testicles"* David Stafford, *Secret Agent: The True Story of the Covert War Against Hitler*, 28.

162 *"Your object here"* Denis Rigden, *How to Be a Spy: The World War II SOE Training Manual*, 362.

163 *"art of silent killing"* Foot, 84; Dourlein, 81; Rigden, 361.

163 *"in a way that prevented"* Dourlein, 81.

163 *strangling and cutting throats* Dusko Popov, interview by Frederick Bear, "Dusko [007] Popov: Exclusive Interview," *Genesis*, November, 1974, 36.

163 *slip tags, survive interrogation* Rigden, 68–70, 82–85.
163 *trains, and escape cafés . . . cross-examination* Foot, 86, 237.
163 *up to a third of the students* Ibid., 84–85.
163 *"the hardest thing"* Popov, *Genesis*, 36.
163 *"The 'Shanghai Buster' gave us"* Langelaan, 68.
163 *"made each of us a terribly dangerous man"* Ibid., 74.
163 *SOE training manual* Rigden, 363.
163 *"I remember very clearly"* Correspondence of Marco Popov with the author, October 4, 2014.
164 *British-American commando school* John Pearson, *The Life of Ian Fleming*, 102.
164 *brought in Fairbairn and Sykes* Since the information was yet to be declassified, Pearson referred to Fairbairn and Sykes as "Colonel Wallace" and "Murphy," respectively. Ibid., 103.
164 *"Open that door"* Ibid., 105.

CHAPTER 19 "TURN AROUND SLOWLY"

165 *"I just couldn't open"* John Pearson, *The Life of Ian Fleming*, 105.
165 *"Although Ian was an outstanding"* Ibid., 104.
165 *Cairo off* Ian Wilson memo, April 16, 1943, KV 2/852 (p. 474B).
165 *"our plans for sending TRICYCLE"* Ibid.
166 *"delicate"* April 13, 1943, letter from the Political Intelligence Department of the Foreign Office to Brigadier General Harker, KV 2/852 (p. 472a).
166 *twenty-four letters* Ian Wilson "TRICYCLE in England" memo, April 3, 1943, KV 2/852 (p. 464a); Ian Wilson memo, March 20, 1943, KV 2/852 (p. 450a).
166 *"That TRICYCLE should undertake"* Ian Wilson "TRICYCLE" memo, May 2, 1943, KV 2/852 (487a).
166 *promoted to lieutenant colonel* See April 16, 1943, Robertson letter to Major Frank Foley, KV 2/852 (p. 474c).
166 *Eugen Sostaric* Sostaric became one of Dusko's best friends, later serving as Popov's best man at his wedding with Jill. Dusko would later give his German car business to Eugen. Correspondence from Marco Popov to the author, December 5, 2014. See also Nigel West, *MI5*, 200–201, 204, 242.
167 *METEOR* Ian Wilson, April 22 and April 28, 1943, memo, KV 2/852 (pp. 480a, 484a).
167 *On May 11 Popov met with Masterman* J. C. Masterman memo, May 12, 1943, KV 2/852 (p. 499A).
167 *187,500 escudos* Telegram of Guy Deyris and Ian Wilson memo of May 13, 1943, KV 2/852 (pp. 500b, 501a).
168 *"A double agent should"* J. C. Masterman, *The Double-Cross System*, 19–20.
168 *Ian asked Ewen Montagu* Ian Wilson letter to Commander Montagu, June 3, 1943, KV 2/853 (p. 515a).
168 Wilson letter to Major E. Goudie June 3, 1943, KV 2/853 (p. 516a).
168 *General Rakic* P.T.O. letter to Frank Foley on May 29, 1943 (p. 512a); Ian Wilson "TRICYCLE" memo, June 3 (p. 519a); Haldane Porter letter to Wilson on June 5 (p. 520KA); and Wilson memo to the file on June 6 (p. 524a). All at KV 2/853.
168 *approval from Yugoslavia's prime minister* Haldane Porter letter, KV 2/853 (p. 520KA).
168 *Operation Mincemeat* Dusko Popov, interview with Alan Road, "Double-Agent Popov and the James Bond Affair," *Observer*, May 13, 1973, 24–26. See, generally, Ewen Montagu, *The Man Who Never Was.*
169 *"TRICYCLE is supposed" . . . "It is proposed"* Ian Wilson memo, June 10, 1943, KV 2/853 (p. 525b).

170 *"so that he should have"* Ian Wilson "TRICYCLE" memo, June 11, 1943, KV 2/853 (p. 526a).

170 *Ian took Dusko on a field trip* Ian Wilson "TRICYCLE" memo, June 20, 1941, KV 2/853 (p. 533a).

170 *"the last thing we wish"* Ibid.

171 *"Senor Gallegos"* June 22, 1943, correspondence from Captain M. Lloyd (for Frank Foley) to Ian Wilson, KV 2/853 (p. 536B).

171 *"Doctor POPOVIC is going on a special mission"* Anthony Blunt notice, June 27, 1943, KV 2/853 (p. 546a); see also Guy Liddell's diary entry of even date at KV 4/191.

171 prime minister leak Ian Wilson memo, June 29, 1943, KV 2/853 (p. 551a).

171 *"You may be walking into a trap"* Popov, *Spy Counter-Spy*, 254.

171 *THE WORM* Ian Wilson August 4, 1943, memo, KV 2/853 (p. 572xa). See also West, *MI5*, 206–207, 204, 243.

172 *"They won't kill me"* Popov, *Spy and Counter-Spy*, 255.

172 *On July 16 Popov boarded* Ian Wilson "TRICYCLE" memo, July 16, 1943, KV 2/853 (p. 566a).

172 *"I was angry"* Popov, interview with Alan Road, "Double-Agent Popov and the James Bond Affair," *Observer*, 29.

172 *"I was completely engrossed" . . . "I would shoot my way out"* Popov, *Spy Counter-Spy*, 255. See also endnotes for Preface regarding the pistol Dusko carried (a Wembley).

173 "Turn around slowly" Ibid., 256; Russell Miller, *Codename TRICYCLE*, 195.

CHAPTER 20 TICKING

174 *monkey* Von Karsthoff's pet monkey is confirmed in MI5 files. See, e.g., Dusko Popov "Dramatis Personae" entry for von Karsthoff at KV 2/849 (177b).

174 *"Mrs. Jackson"* Frank Foley, August 1, 1943, memo to Ian Wilson, KV 2/853 (p. 570a); see also Ian Wilson memo, September 17, 1943, KV 2/854 (p. 609a).

174 *"they were sure he was working for the Allies"* Major Frank Foley (MI6) memo to Tar Robertson (MI5), August 20, 1943, KV 2/853 (p. 578B).

177 *"remarkably accurate"* Ian Wilson letter to Gilbert Ryle, August 21, 1943, KV 2/853 (p. 580a).

177 For the chart and Popov's notes on code words, see KV 2/853 (p. 580a).

177 *forged Yugoslav diplomatic bag* Ian Wilson "TRICYCLE" memo, August 21, 1943, KV 2/853 (p. 581a); Ian Wilson "TRICYCLE" memo, September 20, 1943, KV 2/854 (p. 619k).

178 *"My darling"* The return address gives "RIESE" as the sender. KV 2/853 (p. 584a).

178 *"Evidence from various independent sources"* Ian Wilson memo, August 20, 1943, KV 2/853 (p. 577B).

179 *Dusko went to Spain* The exact dates of Popov's visit are unknown, but his trip seems to coincide with this time frame. MI5 files indicate that at one point Popov could not get a visa to Spain, yet Dusko states going there for Operation Mincemeat. Popov, *Observer*, 24–26.

179 *"I checked in Madrid"* Popov, *Observer*, 26.

179 *"extremely good impression"* Ian Wilson "The WORM" memo, August 4, 1943, KV 2/853 (p. 572xa).

179 *"90 percent certain"* August 30, 1943, memo of PP-J at KV 2/853 (p. 573W).

179 *"During an air-raid Hitler"* Ian Wilson "TRICYCLE" memo, September 20, 1943, KV 2/854 (p. 619k).

179 *While Dusko had not told Jebsen* In his defriefing with Ian Wilson soon after landing in London on September 14, 1943, Popov told his case officer: "In spite of not having told Johnny that I am working with the British, I am absolutely sure that he knows it." Ian Wilson "TRICYCLE" memo, September 20, 1943, KV 2/854 (p. 619k).

180 *"What rockets?"* Ibid.; Tar Robertson memo ("TRICYCLE'S INFORMATION ABOUT THE ROCKET GUN") to the Twenty Committee, September 18, 1943, KV 2/854 (p. 617c).

180 *"There are two types of people"* Ian Wilson "TRICYCLE" memo, September 20, 1943, KV 2/854 (p. 619k).

180 *"a group of Gestapo people"* Ibid.

180 *"In case of emergency"* Ibid.

180 Sippenhaft Sefton Delmer, *The Counterfeit Spy: The Untold Story of a Phantom Army that Deceived Hitler*, 51.

180 *"I cannot help feeling"* Ian Wilson memo, August 31, 1943, KV 2/854 (p. 592a).

181 *"Dusko, let's go have a swim"* Dusko Popov, interview with Frederick Bear, "Dusko [007] Popov: Exclusive Interview," *Genesis*, 80.

181 *admired the girl* Ian Wilson memo, August 20, 1943, KV 2/853 (p. 577B); Popov, *Genesis*, 80.

CHAPTER 21 FIVE LIVES

182 *four hours later* Dusko Popov, interview with Frederick Bear, "Dusko [007] Popov: Exclusive Interview," *Genesis*, 80.

182 *"Your car, Dusko, it exploded"* Popov, *Spy Counter-Spy*, 285; Popov, *Genesis*, 80.

182 *"Who would want"* In his memoirs Popov misspells Cecil's name as "Gladhill." Popov, 285. See also Nigel West, *MI6*, 83, 186; Nigel West, *Historical Dictionary of World War II Intelligence*, 118.

182 *six or seven thousand dollars* Popov, *Genesis*, 68.

182 *Louise* Popov, *Spy Counter-Spy*, 286.

183 *"For whom are you working?"* Popov, *Genesis*, 68.

183 *"Well, this was a bloody lie"* Ibid., 80.

183 *Benzedrine . . . sleeping pills* Popov, *Spy Counter-Spy*, 265; Richard Farrington, "Super Spy Dusko Popov: He Lived the James Bond Legend," *True Action*, June 1974, 78.

183 *nine ulcers* Popov, *Genesis*, 36.

183 *"under no circumstances"* Correspondence from M. Lloyd (for Major Frank Foley) to Tar Robinson, August 26, 1943, KV 2/854 (p. 588).

183 *staying at the Ritz* Correspondence from M. Lloyd to Ian Wilson, September 8, 1943, KV 2/854 (p. 594a).

183 *the evening of September 13* Night Duty Officer Reports, KV 2/854 (p. 604).

184 *large number of silk stockings* Ian Wilson "TRICYCLE" memo, September 20, 1943, KV 2/854 (p. 619k).

184 *Inside the lid of the radio transmitter* The B1A internal memorandum states: "Original document received with the Radio appartus. These papers were inside the lid of the Transmitter." See also Ian Wilson's memo of September 14, 1943, regarding details and equipment of the radio. Memoranda and instructions at KV 2/854 (602a).

184 *152 were forgeries* Bank of England September 15, 1943, notice of finding 152 forgeries and memorandum of Sir Edward Reid of B1B to Ian Wilson of even date at KV 2/854 (p. 604B).

184 *Galsworthy code book in the B1A safe* September 17, 1943, "TRICYCLE" memo, KV 2/854 (p. 611a).

184 *"to take the hollow part of a pen nib"* Ian Wilson letter of September 17, 1943, to Professor Briscoe, KV 2/854 (p. 612a).

184 *"THE HAIRLESS DOCTOR"* Ian Wilson memo, September 17, 1943, KV 2/854 (p. 617k).

185 *met a U.S. military attaché* Ian Wilson note on Thurston letter at KV 2/854 (p. 616a).

185 *"During my recent visit"* Arthur Thurston letter of September 17, 1943, at KV 2/854 (p. 616a).

185 *"C" later told Dusko* Popov, *Genesis*, 80.

185 *"TRICYCLE reports everything material"* Ian Wilson September 20, 1943, memo, KV 2/854 (p. 619k).

185 *"KARSTHOFF and KAMMLER"* Ibid.

186 *"I learned from ELIZABETH"* Ibid.

186 *"Johnny's attitude towards me"* Ibid.

186 *"Because of illness"* Ibid.

187 *"Had it not been for"* Lieutenant Colonel Tar Robertson memo, September 21, 1943, KV 2/854 (p. 619k).

187 *"TRICYCLE is shortly going back"* Ibid.

187 *room 530 at the Madrid Ritz* September 16, 1943, "JOHANN JEBSEN" memo from MI6 Madrid station, KV 2/854 (p. 607b).

187 *"You know of the charges"* Ibid.

188 *On September 21, Johnny dictated a suicide letter* See Ian Wilson memo, September 28, 1943, KV 2/854 (p. 632B); telegrams from Madrid on September 17, 22, and 23, 1943, KV 2/854 (pp. 1, 2, 9); and Jebsen's suicide letter, German original and translated copy, KV2/854 (group entry at p. 646c).

CHAPTER 22 SHOTS RANG OUT

189 *"a small man who was chain-smoking"* Kenneth Benton, "The ISOS Years: Madrid 1941–3," *Journal of Contemporary History* 30, no. 3 (July 1995), 395. Benton thought the meeting had occurred in February 1943, but MI5 files show that Frank Foley notified Tar Robertson on September 24 that Johnny had visited the Madrid MI6 office on the twenty-second. KV 2/854 (p. 8). See also, generally, January 13, 1944, correspondence from Frank Foley to Colonel Robertson regarding ARTIST, TRICYCLE, and Benton at KV 2/856 (p. 759B).

189 *"sly foxes"* Benton, 396.

190 *"ARTIST is telling you the truth"* Ibid., 397.

190 *"Herr Oberstleutnant"* MI5 has the original note, which does not identify names in the address, but there is some confusion as to the intended recipient(s). Ian Wilson's memorandum of September 28, 1943, at KV 2/854 (p. 632B) suggests that the letter was addressed to a Rohrscheidt, Abwehr III's Madrid station head. Frank Foley of MI6, however, noted on September 25 that the suicide note was addressed to Munzinger and Toering (KV 2/854, p. 12).

190 *"I cannot return to Germany"* The suicide letter, German original and translation, is collected as a group entry at KV 2/854 (p. 646c).

191 *"at all costs"* Cable to Madrid, September 23, 1943, KV 2/854 (p. 6).

191 *"Calm down"* The cable was sent to MI6 Madrid September 24, 1943, for forwarding to Jebsen. KV 2/854 (p. 10).

191 *"At once"* Ian Wilson memorandum, September 28, 1943, KV 2/854 (p. 632B).

192 *"Should Johnny Jebsen decide"* . . . *"I have been approached"* Colonel Robertson memorandum, September 28, 1943, KV 2/854 (p. 632).

192 *OSTRO* See interview of ARTIST on October 26, 1943, at KV 2/855 (p. 699c).

192 *discussed kidnapping Ruser* Ibid.

192 *Masterman, Marriott, Foley, and Wilson met* Ian Wilson memo, September 29, 1943, KV 2/854 (p. 635a).

193 *"I was very sorry"* . . . *"hijack team"* Benton, 398.

193 *Ablege Kommandos* October 23, 1943, memorandum of M. Lloyd to Colonel Robertson at KV 2/855 (p. 673B).

193 *"We were all in civilian clothes"* Günter Peis, *The Mirror of Deception,* 229.

194 *"You will receive this letter"* Ian Wilson October 4, 1943, memorandum at KV 2/854 (p. 646a). Wilson does not disclose who drafted the letter, but Ian and/or Ivo Popov would have been the probable authors.

195 *"unconscious" source . . . three conditions* See "ARTIST" memorandum of September 30, 1943, at KV 2/854 (p. 648B). Johnny's request for "liberty to travel after the war" is perplexing: If he expected to be imprisoned for being a German spy, he'd certainly not be allowed to travel; if he were not imprisoned, the request would have been unnecessary.

195 *Frank Foley contacted an SOE agent* Foley correspondence of October 6, 1943, to Colonel Robertson, KV 2/854 (p. 647k).

195 *submitted to the major a lengthy outline* Jebsen's "Serbian Slipping-through operation" memo, October 18, 1943, KV 2/855 (p. 709B), as translated.

195 *"Carlos" . . . "very delicate" . . . "For safety's sake"* Correspondence of Ludovico von Karsthoff, October 19, 1943, KV 2/855 (p. 709B), as translated.

195 *list his local Abwehr supporters* See October 26, 1943, debriefing of ARTIST at KV 2/855 (p. 699c).

196 *"SCHREIBER has written"* Memorandum of M. Lloyd to Colonel Robertson on November 21, 1943, KV 2/855 (p. 702A).

196 *"with a name something like Martins"* October 26, 1943, debriefing of ARTIST at KV 2/855 (p. 699c).

196 *"MARTINS should be interviewed"* Letter of M. Lloyd to Colonel Robertson on November 28, 1943, KV 2/855 (p. 705a).

197 *"cannot be trusted"* Letter of M. Lloyd to Colonel Robertson on November 29, 1943, KV 2/855 (708a).

197 *Unknown to Dusko* See MI6 "ARTIST" memorandum dated January 7, 1944, KV 2/856 (p. 743a).

CHAPTER 23 TRUTH SERUM

198 *"for camouflage purposes" . . . VIPER* See ARTIST memorandum dated January 7, 1944; Frank Foley correspondence to Colonel Robertson of even date; and Robertson letter to Foley on January 11, 1944; all at KV 2/856 (pp. 743, 746).

198 *even if Munzinger ordered it* Ian Wilson "TRICYCLE, ARTIST and connected agents" memo, November 26, 1943, KV 2/856 (p. 716B).

199 *"ARTIST describes" . . . "cooked him"* Ibid.

199 *"adopted a pro-British attitude"* Wilson memo, November 26, 1943, KV 2/856 (p. 716B).

199 *"ugly but with sex appeal"* "Source: TRICYCLE" memo, November 27, 1943, KV 2/856 (unpaginated, sub-file 4).

200 *"It would be a silly thing"* Ibid.

200 *Marquis Frano de Bona* Ian Wilson "TRICYCLE, ARTIST, and connected agents" memo, November 26, 1943, KV 2/856 (p. 716B); Frank Foley memo, November 20, 1943, KV 2/855 (p. 709B); M. Lloyd memo, November 30, 1943, KV 2/855 (p. 712B); Ian Wilson "TRICYCLE and ARTIST" memo, December 16, 1943, KV 2/856 (p. 727y). See also, Russell Miller, *Codename Tricycle*, 195–96; Nigel West, *MI5*, 202–203.

200 *Johnny went to Madrid* Ian Wilson "TRICYCLE and ARTIST" memo, December 16, 1943, KV 2/856 (p. 727y).

200 *Canadian Peter Banwedon* H. W. Astor memo (B1A) to (D4) Captain Kennedy, December 4, 1943, KV 2/855 (p. 715a).

200 *Henss . . . Wiegand* Ian Wilson debriefing report, January 11, 1944, KV 2/856 (p. 747). Wiegand's real name was Wrede. Ian Wilson, "TRICYCLE's Lisbon Visit: 26.2.44–13.4.44," KV 2/857 (p. 871a).

200 *questionnaire* KV 2/856 (p. 716B).

201 *J. C. Masterman passed it along to Victor Cavendish-Bentinck* Masterman letter, December 12, 1943, KV 2/856 (p. 722a). See also Colonel Robertson letter of January 12 (misdated 1943) to Cavendish-Bentinck at KV 2/856 (p. 754a). For Cavendish-Bentinck, see generally Stephen Dorril, *MI6: Inside the Covert World of Her Majesty's Secret Intelligence Service.*

201 *Foley forwarded a copy to the War Office* Frank Foley letter to Colonel Robertson, December 22, 1943, KV 2/856 (p. 734).

201 *condition precedent* See English translation of German questionnaire at KV 2/856 (p. 752a).

201 *"The man is very pedantic"* December 21, 1943, letter from Dusko Popov to Ian Wilson, KV 2/856 (p. 733c).

201 *Henss gave him a second questionnaire* January 6, 1944, letter from Frank Foley to Colonel Robertson, KV 2/856 (p. 740).

201 *itemized the spyware* See January 7, 1944, letter from J. H. Marriott to Colonel Robertson and Ian Wilson at KV 2/856 (p. 741a).

202 *"REVERSIBLE TRICYCLES"* Dusko Popov driver's license, No. 17993, issued February 23, 1944, KV 2/862 (unpaginated, sub-file 2).

202 *The Allies had launched Operation Fortitude South* Joshua Levine, *Operation Fortitude: The Story of the Spy Operation that Saved D-Day, 225 et seq.*

202 *Hitler sacked Admiral Canaris* See William Shirer, *The Rise and Fall of the Third Reich*, 1026; Walter Schellenberg, *The Memoirs of Hitler's Spymaster*, XII; Walter Warlimont, *Inside Hitler's Headquarters*, 409; J. C. Masterman, *The Double-Cross System in the War of 1939 to 1945*, 151–52.

202 *Walter Schellenberg* Schellenberg, XII.

202 *The Atlantic front* Hans Spiedel, *Invasion 1944*, 40–43.

202 *FUSAG* Masterman, 156; Popov, *Spy Counter-Spy*, 225; Miller, 207; Levine, 225; Farrington, *Super Spy Dusko Popov*, 78.

202 *"You and Garbo vie for"* Popov, *Spy Counter-Spy*, 273–74. See also, J. C. Masterman, *The Double-Cross System in the War of 1939 to 1945*, 148.

202 *Juan was regularly spending six to eight hours a day* Masterman, *The Double-Cross System*, 142.

202 *fourteen agents and eleven well-placed contacts* Masterman, *The Double-Cross System*, 143. See also, Juan Pujol with Nigel West, *Operation GARBO*, 8–9.

203 *"There can be no doubt"* Ian Wilson memo ("The use of the TRICYCLE Group for deceptive purposes") to Tar Robertson, December 20, 1943, KV 2/856 (p. 731B).

204 *"Discussed at XX Cttee 23/12/43. No ban."* Ibid. See also Masterman, *The Double-Cross System*, 148.

204 *four principal operatives of strategic deception* Masterman, *The Double-Cross System*, 149.

204 *ARTIST's knowledge of GARBO* Pujol, 148–49; Masterman, *The Double-Cross System*, 154; Popov, *Spy Counter-Spy*, 225–26.

204 *the Committee discussed three options* Pujol, 149.

204 *13,000 Abwehr employees* Schellenberg, XIII.

205 *"During this tour"* Ian Wilson February 24, 1944, correspondence to Hesketh at KV 2/857 (p. 832a).

205 *"WIEGAND states Berlin unhappy"* Telegram from Lisbon to Frank Foley, February 24, 1944, KV 2/857 (p. 833a).

206 *"You will report"* Popov, *Spy Counter-Spy*, 289.

206 *Schroeder and Nassenstein* The German officers who conducted Popov's interrogations, and the number of interrogations, during this trip to Lisbon is somewhat unclear. Dusko states in his memoirs that Schroeder and Nassenstein conducted a first meeting, while Schroeder and a man using an alias of Major Muller conducted a second meeting. MI5 files show that Dr. Aloys Schreiber conducted an intensive two-day interrogation. See MI6 Lisbon telegram to London on March 3, 1944 (KV 2/857, p. 838b), correspondence from Frank Foley to Colonel Robertson on March 4 (KV2/857, p. 838c), and memorandum of Ian Wilson on April 19 (KV 2/857, p. 871a). It appears that Schroeder and Nassenstein conducted a first interrogation, with Schreiber conducting an intensive second interrogation. Given Schreiber's expertise with prisoner interrogations, and the fact that he was not on the Lisbon Legation staff, it appears that he may have been the "specialist from Berlin" whom Dusko referred to as Major Muller, which Popov believed was an alias. The account is somewhat clouded in that Dr. Schreiber testified after the war that he had met Popov only twice, in September 1943 and January 1944, although his testimony as a potential war criminal would be suspect. See January 6, 1947, report of Capt. John Heinig, U.S. Army Military Intelligence Service Center Headquarters, "Reinterrogation Report No 7, Prisoner: Obst/Lt SCHREIBER, Aloys,"p. 5 KV 2/3568 ("Heinig Report").

206 *Nassenstein, whose real name was Nogenstein* Listed on the official German Legation staff as Adolf Nassenstein (see Legação da Alemanha in the Arquivo Salazar, Biblioteca Nacional) but his real name was Nogenstein. KV 2/1326.

206 *shoot-out reminiscent of the O.K. Corral* At the end of the war Nogenstein was captured but escaped by shooting his way out. He hid in Portugal until 1947, when he and two other Germans were discovered by Interpol. During the arrest attempt another shoot-out occurred, resulting in the death of two of the Germans (one being shot, the other taking poison to avoid capture). Nogenstein was arrested and during imprisonment made several attempts to commit suicide. The attempts failed and he was repatriated to Germany. See KV 2/1326.

206 *"Wait till the lord high executioner"* Popov, *Spy Counter-Spy*, 290–91.

207 *physician who "doesn't ask questions"* Ibid., 292–93.

208 *Dr. Aloys Schreiber* See May 20, 1946, and January 6, 1947, Heinig Report.

208 *Kindly and patient, Dr. Schreiber posed* See MI6 Lisbon telegram of March 3, 1944 (KV 2/857, p. 838b), correspondence from Frank Foley to Colonel Robertson of March 4 (KV2/857, p. 838c), and memorandum of Ian Wilson of April 19 (KV 2/857, p. 871a). See also list of ARTIST sub-sources at KV 2/856 (p. 753a) and Heinig Report.

208 *"we would like your consent"* Popov, *Spy Counter-Spy*, 296.

CHAPTER 24 AUF

209 *"your consent . . . to contact Guttmann"* Popov, *Spy Counter-Spy*, 296.

209 *"definitely on top"* Ian Wilson memo, April 19, 1944, KV 2/857 (p. 871a).

209 *Wiegand won the Popoff sweepstakes* Ibid. See also Wilson memo, April 20, 1944, KV 2/857 (p. 872a).

210 *$150,000* Jebsen letter, April 22, 1944, KV 2/858 (p. 892b); Ian Wilson memo, April 20, 1944, KV 2/857 (p. 872a).

210 *"this valuable agent"* Wilson memo, April 20, 1944.

210 *"completely worthless"* Ian Wilson memo, March 14, 1944, KV 2/857 (p. 840c).

210 *"passed with flying colors"* Ian Wilson "ARTIST report," March 21, 1944, KV 2/857 (p. 848b).

211 *"as good as sure"* April 19, 1944, memo, KV 2/857 (p. 871).

211 *"Hans Popper"* Unsigned MI6 Lisbon memo, March 29, 1944, KV 2/857 (p. 861b). NB: Popov's memoirs are dischronologized in several places during this period. Popov's account of the Ivo reunion, for example, occurs before his chapter 24, which begins February 1944, but MI5 records show that Ivo visited him in March 1944.

211 *still dapper and handsome* Popov, *Spy Counter-Spy*, 279.

211 *"had grown thin and old"* March 29, 1944, memo, KV 2/857 (p. 861b).

211 *two MI6 agents* Neither the March 29 memo nor Popov's account identifies the agents. One agent was most likely Cecil Gledhill, Lisbon station chief; Popov mentions that Ivo met Cecil during Ivo's stay to give Gledhill an update on the situation in Yugoslavia. See Popov, *Spy Counter-Spy*, 282. The other agent, who prepared the March 29 memorandum anonymously, is unknown.

211 *"Ivo created"* March 29 memo, KV 2/857 (p. 861b).

211 *sabotaging Nazi trains* Popov, *Spy Counter-Spy*, 279.

212 *prices inflating twenty to eighty times* Ivo Popov letter to Dusko, December 23, 1942, KV 2/851 (p. 386a).

212 *purchased a shoe-polish company* Ibid.

212 *school expenses in Bologna Johnny was covering* Ibid.

212 *he worked his currency scheme . . . Ivo needed protection* Popov, *Spy Counter-Spy*, 281–82.

212 *"The cat's got nine kittens"* Ian Wilson February 26, 1944, memo to John Marriott, KV 2/857 (p. 833c); MI6 Lisbon March 29, 1944, memo to file, KV 2/857 (p. 861b).

213 *"But you won't be able"* Popov, *Spy Counter-Spy*, 284. See also correspondence of Captain M. Lloyd to Colonel Robertson, April 10, 1944, KV 2/857 (p. 863a).

213 *a call from Baroness von Gronau* Ian Wilson February 16, 1944, memo regarding meeting with ARTIST on February 14, KV 2/857 (p. 835); Ian Wilson memo to Colonel Robertson, February 25, 1944, KV 2/857 (p. 833a). See also Jock Haswell, *D-Day*, 49.

213 *"In theory" . . . "Nothing . . . Auf"* Popov, *Spy Counter-Spy*, 297–98.

214 *In the forged bag were* Ian Wilson memo to file, April 16, 1944, KV 2/857 (p. 867a).

214 *"do something big"* Ian Wilson "TRICYCLE" memo, April 16, 1944, KV 2/857 (p. 868a).

214 *"his own game"* Ian Wilson April 17, 1944, memo to J. C. Masterman and John Marriott, KV2/857 (p. 870a).

215 *KVK first class.* Jebsen letter to Popov, April 28, 1944, KV 2/858 (p. 892b).

218 *"If ever you get in trouble"* Wilson memo, April 19, 1944, KV 2/857 (p. 871).

218 *MI6 agent, Johnny and Dusko in the clear* See April 21, 1944, memo from MI6 Lisbon to London at KV 2/858 (p. 883a). The MI6 agent may have been Kenneth Benton, whom Johnny mentions in his April 21 letter. In a follow-up letter to Colonel Robertson on April 23, Frank Foley withheld the name of the MI6 agent (KV 2/858, p. 883b).

218 *"Dear Dusko"* KV 2/857 (p. 880c).

218 *dinner party at the Hyde Park Hotel* Ian Wilson "TRICYCLE" memo, April 28, 1944, KV 2/858 (p. 890a). Dusko erroneously remembered the dinner occurring on D-Day (Popov, *Spy Counter-Spy*, 302).

219 *"It would have been"* Popov, *Spy Counter-Spy*, 303.

219 *"In spite of"* Wireless intercept of April 12, 1944, at KV 2/860 (file 3).

219 *"handed over after" . . . "JONNY is maintaining"* Wireless intercepts of April 20, 1944, KV 2/860 (file 3).

219 *$50,000* April 29, 1944, memo to Ian Wilson, KV 2/858 (p. 893a).

220 *"The agent TRICYCLE"* "Report on the Activities of the Security Service During April, 1944," May 5, 1944, KV 4/83 (659408).

220 *houseguest, Moldenhauer* MI6 Lisbon May 1, 1944, memo, KV 2/858 (p. 898d).

220 *Dr. Schreiber had run two errands* At noon Schreiber puchased two ventilated trunks, and he purchased an injectible sleeping drug at a Lisbon pharmacy. Heinig Report, January 6, 1947, KV 2/3568 (6b).

CHAPTER 25 D-DAY

221 *"Extreme caution in flip matters"* Intercept dated April 30, 1944, KV 2/860 (file 3).
221 *"As special machine cannot"* May 4, 1944, intercept, KV 2/860 (file 3).
221 *"FLIP taken by WALL"* Ibid.
222 *met with Dusko on May 7* Ian Wilson memo, May 8, 1944, KV 2/858 (p. 910b).
222 *"Dear Dusko"* KV 2/858 (p. 892b).
223 *"Effects of the Removal of ARTIST"* J. C. Masterman memo, May 9, 1944, KV 2/858 (p. 912).
223 *"was put into operation"* May 9, 1944, memo of Tomás Harris to Colonel Robertson and John Marriott, KV 2/858 (p. 912c).
224 *"DORA has arrived"* Intercept of May 9, 1944, KV 2/860 (file 3).
224 *notified Wilson the next day* Ian Wilson May 10, 1944, memo to Robertson, Masterman, and Marriott, KV 2/858 (p. 913b). Operation DORA identified also at KV 2/858 (p. 916).
225 *The dilemma that had to be decided* Ian Wilson May 10, 1944, "TRICYCLE" memo to Robertson, Masterman, and Marriott, KV 2/858 (p. 913c).
225 *Frank Foley notified him* Ian Wilson May 12, 1944, "TRICYCLE" memo, KV 2/858 (p. 914a).
225 *the Germans played their hand* Frank Foley memorandum to Colonel Robertson, May 12, 1944, KV 2/858 (p. 914b). Foley mentioned the "Lisbon International Police," which technically did not exist. The reference is to the PVDE secret police, which had an international section charged with control of immigrants, espionage, and counterespionage. Robertson's response is typed at the bottom of Foley's message.
225 *British or Russian agent* Frank Foley memorandum to Colonel Robertson, May 16, 1944, KV 2/858 (p. 915a).
225 *still free in Belgrade* Ian Wilson memorandum to file on May 17, 1944, KV 2/858 (p. 916).
226 *"accusations"* Ian Wilson May 19, 1944, "TRICYCLE and FREAK" memo, KV 2/858 (p. 920a).
226 *"no further evidence coming to light"* Correspondence of Colonel Wild to Colonel Robertson on May 25, 1944, KV 2/859 (p. 922c).
226 *"Said to be a lawyer"* Transmittal letter of Frank Fole to Colonel Robertson, May 28, 1944, accompanying translated report, KV 2/859 (p. 924a).
227 *"I am not in a position"* Correspondence of Colonel Robertson to Colonel Wild on May 29, 1944, KV 2/859 (p. 926a).
227 *"Artist has been arrested"* Popov, *Spy Counter-Spy*, 300; Miller, *Codename TRICYCLE*, 225.
227 *When Dr. Schreiber called Jebsen* Heinig Report, January 6, 1947, KV 2/3568 (6b).
227 *"He won't talk"* Popov, *Spy Counter-Spy*, 300–301.
228 *"urged with some vehemence"* Ian Wilson June 6, 1944, "TRICYCLE" memo, KV 2/859 (p. 929a).
228 *Hitler had warned* Führer Directive Number 51, quoted in Paul Carell, *Invasion! They're Coming!*, 6.
228 *"Today we are faced"* Ibid.
228 *Norway to Normandy Obergefreiter* Walter Sorge had claimed in a written report to the OKW in January 1944 that the Allies would invade at Normandy. Ibid., 14.
229 *the Somme, the Bay of Saint Malo, the Gironde estuary* Hans Speidel, *Invasion 1944*, 33–34. See also Albert Speer, *Inside the Third Reich (Memoirs)*, 422.
229 *coastal reconnaissance* Paul Leverkeuhn, *German Military Intelligence*, 199.

229 *Hitler had specifically included Normandy* Walter Warlimont, *Inside Hitler's Headquarters*, 409.
229 *May 18* Speidel, 32.
229 *sixty divisions west of the Rhine* Speidel, 43; Carell, 13.
229 *estimates of soldiers* Carell, 13.
229 *According to General Hans Speidel* Speidel, 41–42.
229 *GARBO, FREAK, and BRUTUS* J. C. Masterman, *The Double-Cross System*, 148–49, 169.
230 *If someone is lying* Joe Navarro, a retired FBI special agent who interrogated numerous spies and countless criminals, has written several books on the topic. See, e.g., John Schafer and Joe Navarro, *Advanced Interview Techniques*, 2010; Joe Navarro, *What Every Body Is Saying: An Ex-FBI Agent's Guide to Speed-Reading People* (New York: HarperCollins, 2008).
230 *First U.S. Army Group* Popov, *Spy Counter-Spy*, 273; Masterman, *The Double-Cross System*, 156.
230 *the weather at Normandy was abysmal* Carell, 18.
230 *"Then that means"* Ibid., 19.
230 *"There is no indication" . . . two Panzer divisions* Ibid., 20.
230 *Hans Speidel remembered* Speidel, 76–82, 86–87.
232 *"How many of those fine agents"* Albert Speer, *Inside the Third Reich (Memoirs)*, 422–23.
232 *"The enemy intelligence service" . . . "During the following days"* Ibid.
233 *twenty-five thousand sorties* Speidel, 80.
233 *"The reason for refusal"* Ibid., 81–82.
233 *"Sometimes we never knew"* Dusko Popov, interview with Jonathan Braun, "Superspy Dusko Popov: The Real-Life James Bond," *Parade*, 27. Popov's statement is confirmed by J. C. Masterman's 1945 postwar evaluation: "A German map of the British order of battle as on 15 May 1944 which was later captured in Italy showed how completely our imaginary order of battle had been accepted and was largely based on the information supplied by the double cross agents." J. C. Masterman, *The Double-Cross System*, 156.
234 *June 19 Robertson and Wilson met* Ian Wilson memo, June 19, 1944, KV 2/859 (p. 134a).
234 *FREAK, meanwhile, had been asked by King Peter* Ibid.
234 *had a mission for Dusko* Ian Wilson, June 26, 1944, "TRICYCLE and FREAK" memo, KV 2/859 (p. 938a).
234 *"The present position"* Ibid.
235 *"Had to stop"* Ian Wilson July 5, 1944, memo to Robertson, Masterman, and Marriott, KV 2/859 (p. 948a).
235 *"News of Jebsen"* Popov, *Spy Counter-Spy*, 303.
235 *"Yours thirtieth June" . . . "technical difficulties"* Ibid.

CHAPTER 26 NAKED AND SHAVED

237 For Ivo Popov arrest and escape, see numerous email interviews with Misha Popov (Ivo's son) from December 2014 to May 2015; Popov, *Spy Counter-Spy*, 303–306; Miller, *Codename TRICYCLE*, 232.
237 *radio signal from General Mihailovic* Ian Wilson August 2, 1944, "TRICYCLE & DREADNOUGHT" memo, KV 2/859 (p. 969a).
238 *"read and walk"* Popov, *Spy Counter-Spy*, 307.
238 *FBI had been pestering MI5 and BSC* Colonel Robertson's June 16, 1944, memo to Frank Foley, KV 2/859 (p. 933a).
238 *FBI had received a story* Ian Wilson June 16, 1944, memo to Robertson, Marriott, and Masterman, KV 2/859 (p. 933b).

238 *full report of Popov's last year* "TRICYCLE (April 1943–June 1944)" memo (p. 941g) and correspondence to M. J. Lynch of the American Embassy on June 29, 1944 (p. 944a), together at KV 2/859.

239 *Fisherman Inn* Popov, *Spy Counter-Spy*, 308.

239 *Kinlochbervie* J. H. Marriott August 11, 1944, "TRICYCLE & DREADNOUGHT" memo, KV 2/859 (p. 970a).

239 *Four days later* Ivo arrived in England on August 15, 1944. Ian Wilson memo, August 30, 1944, KV 2/859 (p. 973c). Popov doesn't mention Kinlochbervie in his memoirs, but it appears from Marriott's August 11, 1944, memo that the early morning message came here, rather than at Fisherman Inn near Tain. In addition, Marriott's memo indicates that Dusko was expecting John's call regarding Ivo's arrival in England, rather than being surprised by it as his memoir indicates.

239 *Savoy* Ibid. See also Popov, *Spy Counter-Spy*, 309.

239 *Jacqueline Blanc* Popov, *Spy Counter-Spy*, 310–13; Miller, 234–35.

CHAPTER 27 ULLA

241 *Hahn . . . Salzer* Popov, *Spy Counter-Spy*, 313; Miller, *Codename TRICYCLE*, 235.

241 *drafted a letter to Schmidtt* Popov, *Spy Counter-Spy*, 317.

241 *September 10, he asked Frank Foley* KV 2/859 (p. 978a).

242 *"Dear brother Dule"* Ian Wilson September 27, 1944, memo, KV 2/859 (p. 987a).

242 *"keener than ever"* Ibid.

242 *request to a Lieutenant Colonel Speir* Correspondence of Colonel Robertson on September 28, 1944, KV 2/859 (p. 988a).

242 *command and assignment from General Eisenhower* September 30, 1944, correspondence of Colonel Newman, Supreme Headquarters Allied Expeditionary Force, KV 2/859 (p. 989a).

243 *Dusko and Ian traveled to Paris* Ian Wilson's undated interoffice memo, KV 2/859 (p. 992a).

243 *gave Dusko the $10,000* Ian Wilson October 27, 1944, memo, KV 2/859 (p. 996a).

243 *Schmidtt . . . Oranienburg . . . Kammler* Popov, *Spy Counter-Spy*, 318.

243 *"Dressed in prison clothes"* Ibid.

244 *On November 11 Popov met with Wilson* Ian Wilson November 14, 1944, memo, KV 2/859 (p. 999a).

244 *"seek to do him harm" . . . Churchill* Ibid. (p. 1002a).

245 *"by excessive expenditure or otherwise"* Ibid.

245 *Dragica . . . George Vasic* Ian Wilson correspondence to Frank Foley on November 24, 1944, KV 2/859 (p. 1004a).

245 *"every deserter"* William Shirer, *The Rise and Fall of the Third Reich*, 1088.

245 *"Ulla"* Popov, *Spy Counter-Spy*, 319; Miller, 236.

245 *Ulla H. Moberg* Extract from Bermuda Censor Comment, December 17, 1941, KV 2/849 (p. 226j).

246 *"Give my love"* Correspondence of Dusko Popov to Ian Wilson, December 14, 1944, KV 2/859 (p. 1017B).

246 *He checked in at the Zum Storchen* The dates revealed in Popov's memoirs are slightly off. He mentions arriving in Zurich "exactly two weeks before Christmas," or on December 11. Popov, *Spy Counter-Spy*, 319. The letter to Ian Wilson on December 14, however, indicates a mailing from Paris. It appears that Popov arrived in Zurich, then, around December 15 or 16.

246 *"straight line-crossing agents"* Ian Wilson January 11, 1945, memo, KV 2/859 (p. 1023a). See also Wilson memo, February 2, 1945, KV 2/859 (p. 1034a).

246 *"as a question of foreign policy"* Ian Wilson February 2, 1945, memo, KV 2/859 (p. 1038a).

246 *Nazi collaborator, Dragica and Misha to be shot* Ian Wilson correspondence to Major Desmond Bristow, February 27, 1945, KV 2/859 (p. 1039a).

CHAPTER 28 PARTISAN POLITICS

247 *Dusko saw an old girlfriend in London* Ian Wilson correspondence to Major Desmond Bristow, February 27, 1945, KV 2/859 (p. 1039a). For background of Velebit, see Fitzroy Maclean, *Eastern Approaches*, 304–305.

247 *Churchill's personal representative* Maclean, introduction.

247 *"DREADNOUGHT's work"* Correspondence of L. H. Cohen to Ian Wilson, March 14, 1945, KV 2/860 (p. 1044a).

248 *Dragica dressed in a British uniform* Correspondence of Misha Popov to the author, February 14, 2015.

248 *April 6 he received word* Correspondence from Dusko Popov to Ian Wilson, April 6, 1945, KV 2/860 (p. 1048a).

248 *Wilson and Bristow told Duskow* Ian Wilson April 25, 1945, memo, KV 2/860 (p. 1054a).

248 *Banco Espirito . . . Schweizerische Bankverein* Dusko Popov telegram to Guy Deyris, April 27, 1945, KV 2/860 (p. 1057a).

248 *American source* Correspondence from Desmond Bristow to Ian Wilson, April 21, 1944, KV 2/860 (p. 1051A).

248 *left for England* Desmond Bristow correspondence to Ian Wilson on April 21, 1945, KV 2/860 (p. 1051).

249 *"and all my friends"* Dusko Popov letter to Ian Wilson, May 10, 1945, KV 2/860 (p. 1064B).

249 *"In spite and because"* Allied interrogation extract of Abwehr officer Waetjen on May 26, 1945, KV 2/860 (p. 1071B).

250 *"Hansen had to"* Allied interrogation extract of Abwehr officer Wilhelm Kuebart on June 6, 1945, KV 2/860 (p. 1074).

250 *Bear Hotel in Baden* Ian Wilson June 9, 1945, memo, KV 2/860 (p. 1074a).

250 *correspondence from Dusko to Ivo* Ibid.

250 *"You will remember"* Ian Wilson correspondence to Frank Foley, June 12, 1945, KV 2/860 (p. 1075a).

251 *"Johny Jebsen hun held"* SOE correspondence of June 11, 1945, KV 2/860 (p. 1077A).

251 *"Selection Trust"* Dusko operated a company in London called Selection Trust, and on August 21, 1945, a Madrid mining company sent him a letter soliciting business for the sale of iron ore, tin, lead, sulfate, and other metals. KV 2/861 (p. 1103).

251 *"Mrs. ARTIST"* Correspondence from Major R. M. Hamer to Ian Wilson, June 23, 1945, KV 2/860 (p. 1078H).

251 *"If you have luck"* Dusko Popov letter to Ian Wilson, June 25, 1945, KV 2/860 (p. 1079A). Popov spelled his name as "Quitting," but the correct spelling appears to be "Quetting." See November 30, 1945, correspondence from First Lieutenant Henry Hecksher to Major Forrest, KV 2/861 (p. 1120c).

251 *"In Berlin handed to Mueller"* June 29, 1944, telegram from SHEAF to Secret War Room, KV 2/860 (p. 1079B).

252 *"unofficially"* William Luke July 13, 1945, memo, KV 2/860 (p. 1082a).

252 *"even now, to suspect"* Ian Wilson July 28, 1944, memo to J. C. Masterman and William Luke, KV 2/860 (p. 1088B).

252 *"It is eminently satisfactory"* Ian Wilson July 31, 1944, memo to J. C. Masterman, William Luke, and Tomás Harris, KV 2/860 (p. 1088e).

252 *letters to the Army and the SOE* Ian Wilson August 2, 1945, letter to Major J. Delaforce, SOE, KV 2/860 (p. 1088E); Ian Wilson letter to Major S. H. Noakes, 21 Army Group, KV 2/860 (p. 1088F).

252 *"I am still concerned"* Extract of Ian Wilson August 18, 1945, note to William Luke, KV 2/860 (p. 1095a).

252 *OSTRO* Nigel West, *A Thread of Deceit*, 94-95; Ladislas Farago, *The Game of Foxes*, 603; David Kahn, *Hitler's Spies*, 356.

253 *he sent Ian a letter* Dusko Popov letter to Ian Wilson, August 27, 1945, KV 2/860 (p. 1099a).

CHAPTER 29 JOHNNY

254 *"You can imagine"* Dusko Popov letter to Ian Wilson, August 27, 1945, KV 2/860 (p. 1099a).

254 *"I had heard"* Major R. M. Hamer letter to Ian Wilson, September 6, 1945, KV 2/861 (p. 1102).

254 *General Velebit* Dragica Popov letter to General Velebit, August 29, 1945, KV 2/861 (p. 1104a).

254 *"only lived for her children"* Dragica Popov letter to Stojan Pribicevic, Esq., August 29, 1945, KV 2/861 (p. 1104).

255 *Americans had arrested* Correspondence from D. I. Vesey to Major William Luke, September 20, 1945, KV 2/861 (p. 1105a).

255 *"As we feel some sense"* William Luke letter to Major Forrest, September 27, 1945, KV 2/861 (p. 1106a).

255 *Vrnjačka Spa* Correspondence from Lieutenant Colonel Hamer to Major William Luke, October 17, 1945, KV 2/861 (p. 1115B).

255 *"As you know"* October 15, 1945, correspondence from Major Luke to Lieutenant Colonel Hamer, KV 2/861 (p. 1115a).

255 *Major Hope and Desmond Bristow* October 28, 1945, letter from Major Peter Hope to Major William Luke, KV 2/861 (p. 1118); October 31, 1945, letter from Desmond Bristow to Major Luke, KV 2/861 (p. 1119a).

255 *Major Jo Stephenson . . . Bruecher* November 6, 1945, correspondence from Major J. F. E. Stephenson to Major Luke and Major Hope, KV 2/861 (p. 1120B).

256 *"discuss the Jebsen case"* November 30, 1945, correspondence from First Lieutenant Henry Hecksher to Major Forrest, KV 2/861 (p. 1120c).

256 *"TRICYCLE is most anxious"* Colonel Robertson letter of April 3, 1946, to Lieutenant Colonel S. H. Noakes, KV 2/861 (p. 1150a).

256 *Jebsen assets* Dusko Popov "Belongings of J.J." memo, April 29, 1946, KV 2/861 (p. 1167c).

257 *letter to Lieutenant Colonel B. Melland* May 13, 1946, letter from Colonel Robertson to Melland, KV 2/861 (p. 1163a).

257 *"Getting Salzer"* Dusko Popov, interview with Frederick Bear, "Dusko [007] Popov: Exclusive Interview," *Genesis*, 48.

257 *"to put a bullet"* Ibid.

257 *"My superiors"* Popov, *Spy Counter-Spy*, 338–39.

257 *he smashed Salzer's face* Popov, *Genesis*, 48.

257 *"I vomited my sins"* Popov, *Spy Counter-Spy*, 339.

EPILOGUE

259 *"Spying is not a chivalrous business"* Dusko Popov, interview with Alan Road, "Double Agent Popov and the James Bond Affair," *Observer*, 29.

259 *"Killing a German"* Dusko Popov, interview with Frederick Bear, "Dusko [007] Popov: Exclusive Interview," *Genesis*, 48.

259 *Robertson told him of Johnny's death* Popov, *Spy Counter-Spy*, 320.

259 *as late as August 1947* See, e.g., August 13, 1947, internal memo of Allied HQ Intelligence Division at KV 2/861 (p. 1209a); M. Gunn memo dated April 9, 1947, for HQ Intelligence Division at KV 2/861 (p. 1205a); correspondence of M. Gunn on March 20, 1947 to Major A. F. Terry, War Crimes Investigation Unit, at KV 2/861 (p. 1203a); correspondence of J. Flinn to A. G. R. Brookland on February 24, 1947, at KV 2/861 (p. 1204); multiple letters between MI5's R. T. Reed and USN Lieutenant Commander Winston Scott, KV 2/861; correspondence from Reed to Scott on October 31, 1946, at KV 2/861 (p. 1190a).

259 *hunted Walter Salzer two years prior, 1945* Popov, *Genesis*, 48; Popov, *Spy Counter-Spy*, 334.

259 *"was tried and served several years"* Popov, *Genesis*, 48.

260 *Mrs. Petra Vermehren* See notes from J. Flinn interrogation of Petra Vermehren on February 24, 1947, at KV 2/861 (p. 1204).

260 *"Although Dusko never actually admitted"* Correspondence of Marco Popov to the author, November 27, 2014.

260 *Hofmeister "was responsible for everything"* Petra Vermehren interrogation, KV 2/861 (p. 1204).

260 *Quetting was the officer in charge of Johnny's investigation* Quetting was also the one Johnny expected to question him regarding his troubles with the Gestapo. April 27, 1944, memo at KV 2/858 (p. 907a).

261 *"If you have luck"* Dusko Popov letter to Ian Wilson, June 25, 1945, KV 2/860 (p. 1079A).

261 *looked after Johnny's widow after the war* Correspondence of Ian Wilson to Tar Robertson, October 1, 1947, KV 2/861 (p. 1210b).

261 *gave his entire Yugoslav army salary* Tar Robertson August 6, 1946, memo, KV 2/861 (p. 1179a).

261 *more operations* See Appendix 2.

261 *more actual sub-agents* See, e.g., Nigel West, *MI5*, 204. All of GARBO's sub-agents were notional.

261 *"Dusan POPOV is a Jugo-Slav"* Official MI5 application for Popov's recommendation for an OBE, September 22, 1945, KV 2/861 (p. 18a).

262 *"the most important and most successful"* Graham Greene, cited on the cover of Popov's *Spy Counter-Spy*.

262 *Tarlair, Ltd.* See, e.g., September 30, 1947, correspondence of Dickie Metcalfe to Tar Robertson, KV 2/861 (p. 1210a).

262 *significant business for the company in Krefeld* November 3, 1947, memo of A. F. Joslin, H.Q. Intelligence Division, KV2/862 (p. 1214); correspondence of Peter Hope to Tar Robertson on November 14, 1947, KV 2/862 (p. 1225).

262 *"I just want to thank"* Dusko Popov letter to Colonel Robertson, June 17, 1946, KV 2/861 (p. 1167c).

263 *King's Medal of Courage* Colonel Hinchley-Cooke delivered Ivo's KMC at Room 055, Friday, April 18, 1947, per file note by Colonel Robertson, April 21, 1947, KV 2/870 (p. 241B).

263 *naturalized as a British citizen* List of Naturalized Aliens, *London Gazette*, November 21, 1947, 5497 *et seq.*

263 *"Serving Officer in His Majesty's Forces"* Ibid.

263 *The Ritz bar* Colonel Robertson noted for the MI5 file on December 1, 1947: "I handed Popov his O.B.E., with apologies for the way in which I had to do it, in the Ritz Bar on 28th November, 1946." KV 2/862 (Table of Contents notation). See also Colonel Robertson letter to Montague Brown, March 3, 1948, KV 2/862 (p. 1237A).

263 *secretary-general of the European Movement* Miller, *Codename TRICYCLE*, 249.

263 *Château Castellaras* See http://www.chateaucastellaras.com.

263 *divorce in 1960* Correspondence of Marco Popov to the author, December 3, 2014.

263 *La Grande Bastide* Correspondence of Marco Popov to the author, December 3, 2014; Dusko Popov letter (letterhead) to Senator Hugh Scott, February 11, 1975, Record Group 65, Box 13, Part 19, 65-36994, NARA.

263 *"Dusko was such fun"* Miller, 250.

264 *"man of mystery"* Ibid., 251.

264 *"including his wife"* Correspondence of Marco Popov to the author, April 14, 2014.

265 *"In some ways"* Dusko Popov, interview with Jonathan Braun, "Superspy Dusko Popov: The Real-Life James Bond," *Parade*, 24.

265 *"That's a very foolish question"* Ibid., 27.

BIBLIOGRAPHY

ARCHIVES AND OFFICIAL DOCUMENTS

2.ª Conservatória do Registo Predial de Cascais, Portugal
American Historical Association, Washington, D.C.
Arquivo Municipal de Cascais, Portugal
Arquivo Municipal de Lisboa, Portugal
Arquivo Nacional, Torre do Tombo, Portugal
Arquivo Salazar, Biblioteca Nacional, Lisboa, Portugal
Bundesarchiv Berlin-Lichtenfelde, Germany
Bundesarchiv-Militärarchiv Freiburg, Germany
Calouste Gulbenkian Foundation, Portugal
Câmera Municipal de Cascais, Departmento de Cultura, Portugal
Casas das Historias Paula Rego, Cascais, Portugal
Central Intelligence Agency (OSS) Secret Control Intelligence Reports
Churchill Archives Centre, Cambridge University
Federal Bureau of Investigation Library and Vault
Franklin D. Roosevelt Library
Fundação Alexandre de Gusmão, Brasilia, Brazil
Geneva Convention: Laws and Customs of War on Land (Hague IV, October 18, 1907) and Convention Relative to the Treatment of Prisoners of War (Geneva, July 27, 1929)
Imperial War Museum, London
Liddell Hart Center for Military Archives, King's College, London
National Archives and Records Administration, College Park, Maryland (NARA)
National Archives of the UK
Polícia de Vigilância e Defesa Estado, Serviços de Informação, Biblioteca Nacional, Lisboa, Portugal
Records of the Reich Ministry for Public Enlightenment and Propaganda, NARA
The Ian Fleming Collection, Lilly Library, Indiana University, Bloomington
The Wiener Library, London
Trial of the Major War Criminals Before the International Military Tribunal, Official Text English Edition, Nuremberg
U.S. Holocaust Memorial Museum, Washington, D.C.
USS *Arizona* Memorial, National Park Service

BOOKS, PERIODICALS, AND NEWSPAPERS

Anderson, Jack. "Padding the Payroll." *Zanesville Times Recorder*, June 2, 1974, 4-A.
Andrew, Christopher. *Secret Service: The Making of the British Intelligence Community*. London: Heinemann, 1985.

———. *Defend the Realm: The Authorized History of MI5*. New York: Vintage, 2009.

Anjos, Maria Cristina de Carvalho dos. *O Turismo no Eixo Costeiro Estoril-Cascais (1929–1939): Equipamentos, Eventos e Promoção do Destino*. Universidade de Lisboa, Faculdade de Letras, Departmento de História, November 2012.

"A Politica e a Moda." *A Batalha*, Rio de Janeiro, April 15, 1939, 1.

Atkinson, Rick. *The Guns at Last Light: The War in Western Europe, 1944–1945*. New York: Picador, 2013.

Bassett, Richard. *Hitler's Spy Chief: The Story of Wilhelm Canaris*. New York: Pegasus, 2012.

Bayles, William D. "Lisbon: Europe's Bottleneck." *Life*, April 28, 1941, 77–86.

———. "Lisbon: The City of Refuge." *Picture Post*, June 28, 1941, 9–15.

Bear, Frederick. "Dusko [007] Popov: Exclusive Interview." *Genesis*, November 1974, 34–36, *et seq*.

Beesly, Patrick. *Very Special Admiral: The Life of Admiral J. H. Godfrey C. B.* London: Hamish Hamilton, 1980.

Beevor, Anthony. *D-Day: The Battle for Normandy*. New York: Viking, 2009.

Benton, Kenneth. "The ISOS Years: Madrid 1941–3." *Journal of Contemporary History* 30, no. 3 (July 1995), 359–410.

Berthold, Will. *Brandenburg Division*. Trans. Alan Neame. St Albans: Mayflower, 1973.

Bess, Demaree. "American Strategy Pains Portugal." *Saturday Evening Post*, August 30, 1941, 18–19, 36.

Bonhoeffer, Dietrich. *Letters & Papers from Prison*. Edited by Eberhard Bethge. 1953. Reprint, New York: Touchstone, 1997.

Bower, Tom. *Nazi Gold: The Full Story of the Fifty-Year Swiss-Nazi Conspiracy to Steal Billions from Europe's Jews and Holocaust Survivors*. New York: HarperCollins, 1997.

Bratzel, John F., and Leslie B. Rout, Jr. "Pearl Harbor, Microdots, and J. Edgar Hoover." *American Historical Review* 87, no. 5 (December 1982), 1342–51.

Braun, Jonathan. "Superspy Dusko Popov: The Real-Life James Bond." *Parade*, May 19, 1974, 24–27.

Breuer, William. *Hitler's Undercover War: The Espionage Invasion of the U.S.A.* New York: St. Martin's, 1989.

———. *Hoodwinking Hitler: The Normandy Deception*. Westport, CT: Praeger, 1993.

Bristow, Desmond. *A Game of Moles: The Deceptions of an MI6 Officer*. London: Little Brown, 1993.

Brown, Anthony Cave. *Bodyguard of Lies*. New York: HarperCollins, 1975.

———. *C: The Secret Life of Sir Stewart Graham Menzies, Spymaster to Winston Churchill*. New York: Macmillan, 1987.

———. *Wild Bill Donovan: The Last Hero*. New York: Times Books, 1982.

Busch, Noel F. "Juan Trippe: Pan American Airway's Young Chief Helps Run a Branch of U.S. Defense," *Life*, October 20, 1941, 110–24.

Campbell, John P. *Dieppe Revisited: A Documentary Investigation*. London: Frank Cass, 1993.

Carell, Paul (pseud., Paul Karl Schmidt). *Invasion! They're Coming!: The German Account of the D-Day Landings and the 80 Days Battle for France*. 1960. Trans. David Johnston. Reprint, Schiffer Military History, 1995.

Carter, Miranda. *Anthony Blunt: His Lives*. New York: Farrar, Straus & Giroux, 2001.

Carvalho, António, and João Miguel Henriques, eds. *O Estoril: e as Origens do Tourismo em Portugal (and the Origins of Tourism in Portugal)*, May 2011.

Carvalho, António, and Cristina Pacheco, eds. *Grande Hotel e Hotel Atlântico: boletins de alojamento de estrangeiros: boletins individuais e relação de hóspedes da Divisão Policial de Cascais: 1939–1944*. Cascais: Câmara Municipal, 2005.

Casey, William. *The Secret War Against Hitler*. Washington, D.C.: Regnery, 1988.

Chancellor, Henry. *James Bond, the Man and His World: The Official Companion to Ian Fleming's Creation*. London: John Murray, 2005.

Chapman, John W. M. "Tricycle Recycled: Collaboration Among the Secret Intelligence Services of the Axis States, 1940–41." *Intelligence & National Security*, Vol. 7, Issue 3, 268–99.

Churchill, Winston. *The Second World War: Volume Two, Their Finest Hour*. Boston: Houghton Mifflin, 1949.

———. *The Second World War: Volume Three: The Grand Alliance*. Boston: Houghton Mifflin, 1950.

Clausen, Henry C., and Bruce Lee. *Pearl Harbor: Final Judgment*. New York: Crown, 1992.

Colvin, Ian. *Admiral Canaris—Chief of Intelligence*. Colvin Press, 2007.

Crowdy, Terry. *Deceiving Hitler: Double-Cross and Deception*. Oxford: Osprey, 2008.

Dalzel-Job, Patrick. *From Artic Snow to Dust of Normandy*. 1991. Reprint, Oxford: ISIS, 2001.

Deacon, Richard (pseud., Donald McCormick). *Spyclopedia: The Comprehensive Handbook of Espionage*. New York: William Morrow, 1988.

Dear, I. C. B., and M. R. D. Foot. *The Oxford Companion to World War II*. Oxford: Oxford University Press, 1995.

Delmer, Sefton. *The Counterfeit Spy: The Untold Story of a Phantom Army That Deceived Hitler*. New York: Harper & Row, 1971.

Derrick, Michael. "Portugal Is Not Fascist." *O Estoril*, April 27, 1938, 3.

"Did Hoover Suspect an Attack on Pearl?" *Daily Herald*, April 1, 1983, 1.

Dillman, Grant. "Author Says Ex-F.B.I. Chief Sat on Pre-Pearl Harbor Report." *Santa Ana Register*, May 15, 1974, C6.

Doenitz, Karl. *Memoirs: Ten Years and Twenty Days*. Trans. R. H. Stevens. 1958. Reprint, New York: Da Capo Press, 1997.

Doerries, Reinhard. *Hitler's Last Chief of Foreign Intelligence: Allied Interrogations of Walter Schellenberg*. London: Frank Cass, 2003.

———. *Hitler's Intelligence Chief: Walter Schellenberg*. New York: Enigma, 2009.

Donne, John. *Devotions upon Emergent Occasions and Death's Duel*. Reprint, New York: Vintage, 1999.

Dorril, Stephen. *MI6: Inside the Covert World of Her Majesty's Secret Intelligence Service*. New York: Free Press, 2000.

Dostoyevsky, Fyodor. *The Gambler*. 1867. Trans. C. J. Hogarth. Reprint, London: Chancellor Press, 1994.

Dourlein, Pieter. *Inside North Pole: A Secret Agent's Story*. Trans. F. G. Renier and Anne Cliffe. London: William Kimber, 1953.

Dulles, Allen W. *Germany's Underground: The Anti-Nazi Resistance*. 1947. Reprint, Cambridge, MA: Da Capo Press, 2000.

"Dusko Popov, Ex-Spy, Dies: Aided British in World War II." *New York Times*, August 24, 1981.

Eccles, David. *By Safe Hand: The Letters of Sybil and David Eccles, 1939–1942*. London: Bodley Head, 1983.

Fairbairn, W. E. *Defendu: Scientific Self-Defense—The Official Text Book for the Shanghai Municipal Police, Hong Kong Police and Singapore Police*. Shanghai: North China Daily News & Herald, 1926. Reprint, Boulder: Paladin Press, 2007.

Farago, Ladislas. *The Game of Foxes: The Untold Story of German Espionage in the United States and Great Britain in World War II*. New York: David McKay Co., 1971.

———. "The Super Spies: Disaster at Dieppe." *Kingston Gleaner*, March 26, 1972, 47.

Farrington, Richard. "Super Spy Dusko Popov: He Lived the James Bond Legend." *True Action*, June 1975, 22–23, 74–78.

"Fascist Axis Emblems Torn from Clothing." Associated Press release, *The Independent*, St. Petersburg, Florida, April 18, 1939, 19.

Faye, Emmanuel. *Heidegger: The Introduction of Nazism into Philosophy.* New Haven: Yale University Press, 2009.

Federal Bureau of Investigation. Security Division's *Home Edition*, June 9, 1945.

Fleming, Ian. *Casino Royale.* 1953. Reprint, Las Vegas: Thomas & Mercer, 2012.

———. Foreword to *Room 3603*, by H. Montgomery Hyde. Farrar Straus & Co., 1962.

———. "James Bond" comic strip, *Casino Royale* series, drawings by John McLusky. *Daily Express*, September 29, 1958.

Foot, M. R. D. *S.O.E.: The Special Operations Executive, 1940–46.* 1984. Reprint, London: Mandarin, 1993.

Freud, Sigmund. *Dora: An Analysis of a Case of Hysteria.* Reprint, New York: Touchstone, 1997.

Gabler, Neil. *Winchell: Gossip, Power, and the Culture of Celebrity.* New York: Knopf, 1995.

Gardner, Ralph D. "The Age of Winchell," http://www.evesmag.com/winchell.htm (2001).

Gentry, Curt. *J. Edgar Hoover: The Man and the Secrets.* New York: Norton & Co., 1991.

Giles, Perrault. *The Secret of D-Day.* New York: Bantam, 1967.

Glenny, Misha. *The Balkans: Nationalism, War, and the Great Powers, 1804–1999.* New York: Penguin, 2000.

Godfrey, John H. *The Naval Memoirs of Admiral J. H. Godfrey*, Vol. V, 1939–1942. Naval Intelligence Division, Part I. Churchill Archives Centre, The Papers of Admiral John Henry Godfrey, GDFY 1/6.

Goebbels, Joseph. *The Goebbels Diaries, 1939–1941.* Trans. Fred Taylor. Reprint, New York: G. P. Putnam's Sons, 1983.

———. *The Goebbels Diaries, 1942-1943.* Trans. Louis P. Lochner. New York: Doubleday, 1948.

"Gold Tells the History of the 20th Century," SNBCHF.com, http://snbchf.com/gold-history/gold-tells-20th-century-history/.

Gorin, Julia. *PoliticalMavins.com.* "The Name Is Bond. James Dusan Popov Bond." March 28, 2011, http://politicalmavens.com/index.php/2011/03/28/the-name-is-bond-james-dusan-popov-bond/.

Grill, Johnpeter Horst. *The Nazi Movement in Baden, 1920–1945.* Chapel Hill: University of North Carolina Press, 1983.

Grossman, Ellie. "Pearl Harbor Is Another Matter: The Spy Who Couldn't Remember Names." *Dunkirk Evening Observer*, July 25, 1974, 3.

Hall, Adam. *The Quiller Memorandum.* New York: Simon & Schuster, 1965.

Hamilton, T. J. "Turbulent Gateway of a Europe on Fire." *New York* magazine, March 31, 1941, 13 et seq.

Handel, Michael. *Strategic and Operational Deception in the Second World War.* London: Frank Cass, 1987.

Hart, B. H. Liddell. *History of the Second World War.* New York: G. P. Putnam's Sons, 1971.

Hassell, Augustino von, and Sigrid MacRae. *Alliance of Enemies: The Untold Story of the Secret American and German Collaboration to End World War II.* New York: Thomas Dunne, 2006.

Haswell, Jock. *D-Day: Intelligence and Deception.* New York: Times Books, 1979.

Hemingway, Ernest. *Death in the Afternoon.* 1932. Reprint, New York: Touchstone, 1996.

Hesketh, Roger. *Fortitude: The D-Day Deception Campaign.* Woodstock, NY: Overlook, 2000.

Hilberg, Raul. *The Destruction of the European Jews, Vol. 2.* New Haven: Yale University Press, 2003.

Hills, Claire. *BBC News Online*, "The Name's Tricycle, Agent Tricycle," May 9, 2002, http://news.bbc.co.uk/2/hi/uk_news/1973962.stm.

Hilton, Stanley E. *Hitler's Secret War in South America, 1939–1945: German Military Espionage and Allied Counterespionage in Brazil.* Baton Rouge: Louisiana State University Press, 1999.

Hinsley, F. H. *British Intelligence in the Second World War.* Vol. 1. London: Her Majesty's Stationery Office, 1979.

————. *British Intelligence in the Second World War.* Vol. 3, Part 2. New York: Cambridge University Press, 1988.

————. *British Intelligence in the Second World War.* Vol. 4. New York: Cambridge University Press, 1990.

Hitler, Adolf. *Mein Kampf.* Trans. Ralph Manheim. Reprint, Boston: Houghton Mifflin, 1943.

"Hitler's Spying Sirens," *American*, December 1944, 40–41, 92–94.

Hoare, Marko Attila. *Genocide and Resistance in Hitler's Bosnia: The Partisans and the Chetniks, 1941–1943.* Oxford University Press, 2007.

————. *Hitler's Paper Weapon: How the Nazis Forged Millions of British Banknotes.* R. Hart-Davis, 1955.

Höhne, Heinz. *The Order of the Death's Head: The Story of Hitler's SS.* Originally published in 1966 in German as *Der Orden unter dem Totenkopf.* Trans. Richard Barry. Reprint, London: Penguin, 2000.

Holt, Thaddeus. *The Deceivers: Allied Military Deception in the Second World War.* New York: Scribner, 2004.

Hoover, J. Edgar. "Hitler's Spying Sirens," *American*, December 1944.

————. "The Enemy's Masterpiece of Espionage," *Reader's Digest*, vol. 48, April 1946, 1–6.

————. "War Begins at Home," *American*, September 1941, 28–29, 91–92.

Höttl, Wilhelm. *The Secret Front: Nazi Political Espionage, 1938–1945.* 1953. Reprint, New York: Enigma Books, 2003.

Howard, Michael. *Strategic Deception in the Second World War.* 1990. Reprint, New York: Norton, 1995.

Hoyt, Edwin. *The Invasion Before Normandy.* Lanham, MD: Cooper Square, 1999.

Hyde, H. Montgomery. *Room 3603: The Story of the British Intelligence Center in New York During World War II.* New York: Farrar, 1963.

————. *Secret Intelligence Agent: British Espionage in America and the Creaton of the OSS.* New York: St. Martin's, 1982.

Hynd, Alan. *Passport to Treason: The Inside Story of Spies in America.* 1943. Reprint, New York: Kessinger Publishing, 2010.

James, M. E. Clifton. *The Counterfeit General Montgomery.* New York: Avon, 1954.

Jeffery, Keith. *The Secret History of MI6, 1909–1949.* New York: Penguin, 2010.

Johnson, David Alan. *Betrayal: The True Story of J. Edgar Hoover and the Nazi Saboteurs Captured During WWII.* New York: Hippocrene, 2007.

Jones, R. V. *The Wizard War: British Scientific Intelligence, 1939–1945.* New York: Coward, McCann & Geoghegan, 1978.

Kahn, David. *Hitler's Spies: German Military Intelligence in World War II.* New York: Macmillan, 1978.

Kimmel, Husband E. *Admiral Kimmel's Story.* Chicago: Regnery, 1955.

Klemmer, Harvey. "Lisbon—Gateway to Warring Europe." *National Geographic*, August 1941, 259–76.

Klemperer, Klemens von. *German Resistance to Hitler: The Search for Allies Abroad, 1938–1945.* New York: Oxford University Press, 1992.

Klingaman, William K. *1941: Our Lives in a World on the Edge.* New York: Harper & Row, 1988.

Knightley, Phillip. *The Second Oldest Profession.* New York: Norton, 1987.

Kross, Peter. "Before Ian Fleming Created 007, He Was an Undercover Agent for the British During WWII." *Military Heritage*, Vol. 3, Issue 4, (February 2002), 24–27.

Kurapovna, Marcia. *Shadows on the Mountain: The Allies, the Resistance, and the Rivalries That Doomed WWII Yugoslavia.* Hoboken, NJ: Wiley & Sons, 2010.

Langelaan, George. *Knights of the Floating Silk.* London: Hutchinson, 1959.

Larson, Erik. *In the Garden of Beasts: Love, Terror, and an American Family in Hitler's Berlin.* New York: Crown, 2011.

Lawless, Jill. "Exhibit charts life of James Bond creator," *Lethbridge Herald*, April 19, 2008, E7.

Layton, Edwin T. *And I Was There: Pearl Harbor and Midway—Breaking the Secrets.* New York: William Morrow, 1985.

Le Bal de la Riviera. Under the patronage of Their Royal Highnesses Prince and Princess Michael of Kent and His Royal Highness Prince Charles-Philippe d'Orléans, Duc d'Anjou, tribute and gala to the Fleming Family in honor of the 50th anniversary of Ian Fleming's death, September 27, 1914. Estoril Casino and Palácio Hotel, official invitation.

Leverkeuhn, Paul. *German Military Intelligence.* Trans. R. H. Stevens and Constantine FritzGibbon. New York: Praeger, 1954.

Levine, Joshua. *Operation Fortitude: The Story of the Spy Operation That Saved D-Day.* London: HarperCollins, 2011.

Liddell, Guy. Liddell Diaries, Volumes 3–10. British Archives, KV 4/187–4/194.

———. *The Guy Liddell Diaries, 2 Volumes: 1939–1942: MI5's Director of Counter-Espionage in World War II.* Edited by Nigel West. New York: Routledge, 2005.

Lochery, Neill. *Lisbon: War in the Shadows of the City of Light, 1939–45.* New York: Public Affairs, 2011.

London Gazette. List of Naturalized Aliens. November 21, 1947.

Lord, Walter. *Day of Infamy.* New York: Henry Holt, 1957.

Lory, Jacques. "Tender Little Savage: France's Favorite Descends upon the Hollywood Scene." Screen & Radio Weekly, *Oakland Tribune*, December 29, 1935, 3.

Louça, António, and Ansgar Schafer. *Portugal and the Nazi Gold: The "Lisbon Connection" in the Sales of Looted Gold by the Third Reich.* CreateSpace, 2011.

Lycett, Andrew. *Ian Fleming: The Man Behind Bond.* 1995. Reprint, London: Phoenix, 2002.

MacDonald, Bill. *The True Intrepid: Sir William Stephenson.* 1998. Reprint, Vancouver: Raincoat, 2001.

Macintyre, Ben. *Agent Zigzag: A True Story of Nazi Espionage, Love and Betrayal.* New York: Crown, 2007.

———. *Double-Cross: The True Story of the D-Day Spies.* New York: Crown, 2012.

———. *For Your Eyes Only: Ian Fleming and James Bond.* New York: Bloomsbury, 2008.

———. *Operation Mincemeat: How a Dead Man and a Bizarre Plan Fooled the Nazis and Assured Allied Victory.* New York: Broadway, 2011.

———. "Was Ian Fleming the Real 007?" Times, April 5, 2008.

Mackenzie, William. *The Secret History of SOE: The Special Operations Executive, 1940–1946.* London: St. Ermin's Press, 2000.

Maclean, Fitzroy. *Eastern Approaches.* 1949. Reprint, London: Penguin, 1991.

Martinho, Mafalda, Cristina Neves, and Edite Sota, eds. *Cascais: 650 Anos de História, 1364–2014.* Câmara Municipal de Cascais, 2014.

Masterman, J. C. *Bits and Pieces.* London: Hodder & Stoughton, 1961.

———. *The Double-Cross System in the War of 1939 to 1945.* New Haven: Yale University Press, 1972.

———. *On the Chariot Wheel: An Autobiography.* Oxford, 1975.

McGlade, Fred. *The Diaries of Ronald Tritton, War Office Publicity Officer 1940–1945.* West Midlands: Helion, 2012.

McLachlan, Donald. *Room 39: A Study in Naval Intelligence.* New York: Atheneum, 1968.

McMillan, Penelope. "A James Bond Affair." *New York Daily News,* May 19, 1974.

———. "The Spy Who Came in from the Mold." *Stars and Stripes,* July 6, 1974, 14.

Meyers, Jeffrey. *Hemingway: A Biography.* New York: Da Capo Press, 1985.

Miller, Francis Trevelyan. *The Complete History of World War II.* Chicago: Readers' Service Bureau, 1947.

Miller, Russell. *Codename TRICYCLE: The True Story of the Second World War's Most Extraordinary Double Agent.* London: Secker & Warburg, 2004.

Monforte, Paulo de. "*O X aniversário da Posse do Sr. Dr. Oliveira Salazar da Pasta das Finanças,*" *O Estoril,* April 27, 1938, 6.

Montagu, Ewen. *The Man Who Never Was.* New York: Lippincott, 1953.

———. *Beyond Top Secret Ultra.* New York: Coward, McCann & Geoghegan, 1978.

Montgomery, Field Marshal Bernard. *Normandy to the Baltic.* Cambridge: Houghton Mifflin, 1948.

Moura, Gerson. *Brazilian Foreign Relations, 1939–1950: The Changing Nature of Brazil-United States Relations During and After the Second World War.* Fundação Alexandre de Gusmão, 2013.

Muggeridge, Malcolm. *Chronicles of Wasted Time: Vol. 1, The Green Stick.* New York: Morrow, 1973.

———. *Chronicles of Wasted Time: Vol. 2, The Infernal Grove.* New York: Morrow, 1974.

Murphy, Christopher J. *Security and Special Operations: SOE and MI5 During the Second World War.* New York: Palgrave Macmillan, 2006.

"Nazi Spies: The FBI Did a Superb Job of Smashing This Gang Before It Could Damage U.S. War Effort." *Life,* December 1941.

"*Notes a'un Passant.*" *L'Impartial, La Chaux-de-Fonds,* April 19, 1939, 1.

Orwell, George. *1984.* 1949. Reprint, New York: Signet Classics, 1977.

Pacheco, Cristina. "Cascais and Estoril During the Second World War." In *In Time of War: Portugal, Cascais, Estoril and the Refugees During the Second World War.* Antonio Carvalho and Cristina Pacheco, eds. Empresa Litografica do Sul, S.A., 2004.

———, ed. *Grand Hotel e Hotel Atlântico: Boletins de Alojamento de Estrangeiros/Boletins Individuais e Relação de Hóspedes da Divisão Policial de Cascais, 1939–1944.* Cascais: Camara Municipal, 2005.

———, ed. *Hotel Palácio: Estoril-Portugal: Boletins de Alojamento de Estrangeiros/Boletins Individuais,1939–1945.* Cascais: Camara Municipal, 2004.

Packer, Eleanor. "The Strange New Star in Hollywood's Heaven: They Wouldn't Give Simone Simon Her Chance, So She Stole It!" King Features Syndication, *Port Arthur News,* September 20, 1936.

Paine, Lauran. *German Military Intelligence in World War II: The Abwehr.* New York: Stein and Day, 1984.

Pascal, Blaise. *The Mind on Fire: An Anthology of the Writings of Blaise Pascal.* James M. Houston, ed. Portland: Multnomah Press, 1989.

Payne, Stanley G. *Franco and Hitler: Spain, Germany, and World War II.* New Haven: Yale University Press, 2008.

Pearson, John. *The Life of Ian Fleming.* New York: McGraw-Hill, 1966.

——————. "Alias James Bond: The Real Story of Ian Fleming," *Life*, October 7, 1966, 102–118.

Peis, Günter. *The Mirror of Deception: How Britain Turned the Nazi Spy Machine Against Itself.* New York: Pocket Books, 1977.

Perrault, Gilles. *The Secret of D-Day.* New York: Bantam, 1967.

Persico, Joseph E. *Roosevelt's Secret War: FDR and World War II Espionage.* New York: Random House, 2002.

Petropoulos, Jonathan. *Royals and the Reich: The Princes von Hessen in Nazi Germany.* New York: Oxford University Press, 2006.

Petrovic, Stevan. *Dzems Bond Se Zvao Dusko Popov* ("James Bond Named Dusko Popov"). DJuro salaj Bgd., 2001.

Philby, Kim. *My Silent War: The Autobiography of a Spy.* 1968. Reprint, New York: Modern Library, 2002.

Pimentel, Irene Flunser. *Judeus em Portugal durante a II Guerra Mundial: Em Fuga de Hitler e do Holocausto.* Lisboa: Esfera dos Livros, 2006.

——————. *Espiões em Portugal Durante a II Guerra Mundial.* Lisboa: Circle of Books, reprint, 2013.

Playfair, Major-General I.S.O. *The Mediterranean and Middle East, Volume 1, The Early Successes Against Italy (to May 1941), History of the Second World War, United Kingdom Military Series.* London: Her Majesty's Stationery Office, 1954.

Popov, Dusko. *Spy Counter-Spy.* New York: Grossett & Dunlap, 1974.

——————. Interview with Alan Road, "Double-Agent Popov and the James Bond Affair." *Observer*, May 13, 1973, 22 *et seq.*

——————. Interview with Frederick Bear, "Dusko [007] Popov: Exclusive Interview." *Genesis*, November 1974, 34–36, *et seq.*

——————. Interview with Jonathan Braun, "Superspy Dusko Popov: The Real-Life James Bond." *Parade*, May 19, 1974, 24–27.

——————. "A Spy's Spy Tells it All." *People*, June 17, 1974, 19–21.

——————. "Pearl Harbor: Did J. Edgar Hoover Blunder?" *True*, October 1973, 46–47, 107, 110, 113–114.

Popov, Ivan. *Stay Young: A Doctor's Total Program for Youthful Health and Vigor.* New York: Grossett & Dunlap, 1975.

Prange, Gordon. *At Dawn We Slept: The Untold Story of Pearl Harbor.* 1981. Reprint, New York: Penguin, 1991.

——————. *Pearl Harbor: The Verdict of History.* New York: McGraw Hill, 1986.

Pujol, Juan, with Nigel West. *Operation Garbo.* 1985. Reprint, New York: Pocket Books, 1987.

Queiroz, Mario de. "Will the Real James Bond Stand Up?" *Inter Press Service English News Wire*, December 1, 2005.

Quinn, Sally. "War-Time Spy Says He Warned About Pearl Harbor." *Winnipeg Free Press*, May 14, 1974, 49.

Ramalho, Margarida de Magalhães. *Lisboa: Uma Cidade em Tempo de Guerra.* Imprensa National da Moeda (n.d.).

Rickards, James. *The Death of Money: The Coming Collapse of the International Monetary System.* New York: Penguin, 2014.

Riebling, Mark. *Wedge: From Pearl Harbor to 9/11: How the Secret War Between the FBI and CIA Has Endangered National Security.* New York: Touchstone, 2002.

Rigden, Denis, intro. *How to Be a Spy: The World War II SOE Training Manual.* Toronto: Dundurn, 2004.

Road, Alan. "Double-Agent Popov and the James Bond Affair." *Observer*, May 13, 1973, 22–31.

Rothfels, Hans. *The German Opposition to Hitler*. 1947. Reprint, Chicago: Regnery, 1963.

Rout, Jr., Leslie B., and John F. Bratzel. *The Shadow War: German Espionage and United States Counterespionage in Latin America During World War II*. Frederick, MD: University Publications of America, 1986.

Rürup, Reinhard, ed. *Topography of Terror: Gestapo, SS and Reichssicherheitshauptamt on the "Prinz-Albrecht-Terrain": A Documentation*. Translated by Werner T. Angress. Berlin: Verlag Willmuth Arenhövel, 2006.

Schafer, John, and Joe Navarro. *Advanced Interview Techniques: Proven Strategies for Law Enforcement, Military, and Security Personnel*. Springfield, IL: Charles C. Thomas, 2010.

Schellenberg,Walter. *The Memoirs of Hitler's Spymaster*. 1956. Edited and translated by Louis Hagan. Reprint, London: Andre Deutsch, 2006.

Sears, Neil. "Agent Tricycle: That's What MI5 Called Its Three-in-a-Bed Spy Who Duped the Nazis and Seduced a Film Star." *Daily Mail*, May 9, 2002.

Sherry, Norman. *The Life of Graham Greene: Volume II, 1939–1955*. New York: Viking, 1995.

Shirer, William. *The Rise and Fall of the Third Reich*. New York: Simon & Schuster, 1960.

Smith, Michael. *Station X: The Codebreakers of Bletchley Park*. London: Pan Books, 2007.

Smithers, A. J. *Taranto 1940: Prelude to Pearl Harbor*. Annapolis: Naval Institute Press, 1995.

Soanes, Wood. "Pouting Lady from France." *Oakland Tribune*, November 29, 1936.

Speer, Albert. *Inside the Third Reich (Memoirs)*. New York: Macmillan, 1970.

Speidel, Hans. *Invasion 1944*. 1950. Reprint, New York: Paperback Library, 1972.

"*Spione: Popovs Erzählungen*." *Der Spiegel*, August 18, 1975.

Stafford, David. *Secret Agent: The True Story of the Covert War Against Hitler*. New York: Overlook Press, 2001.

———. *Ten Days to D-Day*. 2003. Reprint, Boston: Da Capo Press, 2005.

Stephens, Edward. "Just Like Bond, It's Suave and Sophisticated." *Birmingham Post*, June 7, 2012.

Stephenson, William Samuel. *British Security Coordination: The Secret History of British Intelligence in the Americas, 1940–45*. 1998. Reprint, New York: Fromm International, 1999.

Stevens, Donald G. "World War II Economic Warfare: The United States, Britain, and Portuguese Wolfram." *Historian* 61, no. 3 (1999), 539–55.

Stevenson, William. *A Man Called Intrepid: The Secret War*. New York: Harcourt Brace Jovanovich, 1976.

Stinnett, Robert B. *Day of Deceit: The Truth About FDR and Pearl Harbor*. New York: Free Press, 1999.

Summers, Anthony. *Official and Confidential: The Secret Life of J. Edgar Hoover*. New York: Putnam, 1993.

Talty, Stephen. *Agent Garbo: The Brilliant, Eccentric Secret Agent Who Tricked Hitler and Saved D-Day*. New York: Houghton Mifflin Harcourt, 2012.

Telo, Antonio Jose. "Portuguese Neutrality in the Second World War." In *In Time of War: Portugal, Cascais, Estoril and the Refugees During the Second World War*. Antonio Carvalho and Cristina Pacheco, eds. Empresa Litografica do Sul, S.A., 2004.

"The War in the Balkans: German Army Dismembers Yugoslavia." *Life*, April 28, 1941, 34–35.

Theoharis, Athan. *From the Secret Files of J. Edgar Hoover*. Chicago: Ivan R. Dee, 1991.

Thomas, Gordon. *Secret Wars: One Hundred Years of British Intelligence Inside MI5 and MI6*. New York: Thomas Dunne, 2009.

Thomas, Troy. "The British Assault on J. Edgar Hoover: The Tricycle Case." *Intelligence and Counter-intelligence* III, no. 3, 1989.

Thompson, Nigel. "Checking Out the James Bond Spy Society in Estoril." *Mirror*, January 7, 2012.

Todd, Tank, and James Webb. *Military Combat Masters of the 20th Century.* Dunedin, NZ: Todd Group, 2006.

Toland, John. *The Last 100 Days.* New York: Random House, 1966.

————. *Infamy: Pearl Harbor and Its Aftermath.* New York: Doubleday, 1982.

Tomaszewski, Irene, editor and translator. *I Am First a Human Being: The Prison Letters of Krystyna Wituska.* 1997. Reprint, Montreal: Vehicule Press, 1998.

Tortello, Dr. Rebecca. "Captivated by Jamaica: Ian Fleming (1908–1964)." *Kingston Gleaner,* August 26, 2002, A2.

Trefousse, Hans L. "Failure of German Intelligence in the United States, 1939–1945. *Mississippi Valley Historical Review* 42, no. 1 (June 1955), 84–100.

Trevor-Roper, Hugh. *The Wartime Journals.* Edited by Richard Davenport-Hines. London: I. B. Tauris, 2012.

Twain, Mark. *A Tramp Abroad.* CreateSpace Independent Publishing Platform, 2014.

Vandivert, William. "London: Life Staff There Reports on the War's Worst Air Raid." *Life,* April 28, 1941, 40–41.

Warlimont, Walter. *Inside Hitler's Headquarters.* 1962. Translated from German by R. H. Barry. Reprint, Novato, CA: Presidio Press, 1991.

Weber, Ronald. *The Lisbon Route: Entry and Escape in Nazi Europe.* Lanham, MD: Ivan Dee, 2011.

Weinraub, Bernard. "He Turned Gossip into Tawdry Power; Walter Winchell, Who Climbed High and Fell Far, Still Scintillates." *New York Times,* November 18, 1998. www.nytimes.com/1998/11/18.

West, Nigel. *MI5: The True Story of the Most Secret Counterespionage Organization in the World.* New York: Stein and Day, 1982.

————. *MI6: British Secret Intelligence Service Operations, 1909–45.* London: Weidenfeld and Nicholson, 1983.

————. *A Thread of Deceit: Espionage Myths of World War II.* New York: Random House, 1985.

————. *Seven Spies Who Changed the World.* London: Secker & Warburg, 1991.

————. *The A to Z of British Intelligence.* Lanham, MD: Scarecrow Press, 2005.

————. *Historical Dictionary of World War II Intelligence.* Plymouth: Scarecrow Press, 2008.

————. *Historical Dictionary of Ian Fleming's World of Intelligence: Fact and Fiction.* Lanham, MD: Scarecrow Press, 2009.

———— and Madoc Roberts. *Snow: The Double Life of a World War II Spy.* London: Biteback Publishing, 2011.

White, William. *The Microdot: History and Application.* Williamstown NJ: Phillips, 1992.

Wighton, Charles, and Günter Peis. *Hitler's Spies and Saboteurs.* New York: Holt, Rinehart & Winston, 1958.

Wilson, Earl. "It Happened Last Night." *Tucson Daily Citizen,* August 1, 1944, 5.

Winchell, Walter. "On Broadway." Syndicated column from *Daily Mirror.* Reprinted in: *High Point Enterprise,* July 16, 1942, A-4; *Panama City News-Herald,* July 19, 1942, 6; *Port Arthur News,* July 22, 1942, 4; *Wisconsin State Journal,* July 22, 1942, 6.

Winterbotham, F. W. *The Ultra Secret.* New York: Dell, 1974.

Wituska, Krystyna. *Inside a Gestapo Prison: The Letters of Krystyna Wituska, 1942–1944.* Edited and translated by Irene Tomaszewski. Detroit: Wayne State University Press, 2006.

Wohlstetter, Roberta. *Pearl Harbor: Warning and Decision.* Stanford, California: Stanford University Press, 1962.

Wragg, David. *Swordfish: The Story of the Taranto Raid.* Weidenfeld & Nicolson, 2003.

Wylie, Neville, ed. *European Neutrals and Non-Belligerents During the Second World War.* Cambridge: Cambridge University Press, 2002.

Young, Julian. *Heidegger, Philosophy, Nazism.* Cambridge: Cambridge University Press, 1997.

Young, Roger S., John F. Bratzel, Leslie B. Rout, Jr., Otto Pflanze, and John Toland. "Once More: Pearl Harbor, Microdots, and J. Edgar Hoover: Letters and Replies." *American Historical Review* 88, no. 4 (October 1983), 953–60.

Zimmerman, Dwight Jon. "Dusko Popov, Real Life James Bond, Ran Afoul of the FBI," *Defense Media Network*, September 1, 2011. http://www.defensemedianetwork.com/stories/when-%E2%80%9Cjames-bond%E2%80%9D-ran-afoul-of-the-fbi/

Zivanic, Andrej. *Britic: The British Serb Magazine.* Two-part series: "The Name Is Popov, Dusko Popov," December 13, 2009; "The Man with the Golden Gusle! Dusko Popov," May 13, 2010.

CORRESPONDENCE AND INTERVIEWS

Coleman, Mike, archivist and development manager of Ewell Castle (Dusko's London prep school). Email correspondence with the author June 21, 2013.

Fleming, Ian. Interview at Goldeneye, Jamaica for "Ian Fleming: The Brain Behind Bond," aired on Canadian Broadcasting Corporation, August 16, 1964. CBC digital archives (interviewer unnamed). http://www.cbc.ca/player/play/1856624190.

Fox, John F., Jr., FBI Historian. Email correspondence with author, March 2014.

Popov, Dusko. Guest on *To Tell the Truth*, hosted by Garry Moore, 1973. http://www.youtube.com/watch?v=jWi—54cctw.

———. Interviewed on *The Mike Douglas Show*, July 15, 1974, Season 12, Episode 221.

Popov, Marco. Multiple email interviews by author during 2014.

DOCUMENTARIES

Double Agent Dusko Popov—Inspiration for James Bond. Produced by Stephane Krausz and Barbara Necek. http://www.youtube.com/watch?v=fvZyy-_gXvE (minutes: 51:36).

Fantasia Lusitana. Produced by João Trabulo and João Canijo, distributed by Periferia Filmes, with archives from Arquivo National da Torre do Tombo, Arquivo RDP, Arquivo Histórico do Ministerio dos Negocios Estrangeiros, Yad Vashem, Steven Spielberg, United States Holocaust Memorial Museum, National Archives and Records Administration, the American Jewish Joint Distribution Committee, Prelinger Archives, Arquivo Histórico de Cascais, Espaçio Memória dos Exílios, Hemeroteca Municipal de Lisboa, Câmera Municipal de Lisboa, and Câmera Municipal de Cascais.

Secret War: Double Agent TRICYCLE. History Channel documentary published May 30, 2012. Executive producer Matthew Barrett, narrated by Alisdair Simpson. http://www.youtube.com/watch?v=Vtupvfr1m4I.

True Bond. Released June 22, 2007. Produced by Jane Armstrong and distributed by Starz Entertainment and CineNova Productions, Inc.

The Real Life James Bond: Dusan–Dusko Popov. Series of four videos in French, Serbian, and English (uploaded February 10, 2011). (1) http://www.youtube.com/watch?v=DxAnqRXUdlM (French/Serbian subtitles); (English version, 50 minutes) (2) http://www.youtube.com/watch?v=CzW3fLzbcmo (15 minutes) (3) http://www.youtube.com/watch?v=jM6w30TnxmU (15 minutes) (4) http://www.youtube.com/watch?v=YNvIgyUGIiE (6 minutes).

INDEX

Page numbers in **bold** indicate tables, those in *italics* indicate illustrations or photographs, and those followed by "n" indicate notes.

Ablege Kommandos, 193
Abwehr, xii, 16–17. *See also* Engels, Albrecht; espionage in WWII; Germany/Germans; Jebsen, Johann; Popov, Dusan Miladoroff "Dusko"; von Karsthoff, Albert
 Allied invasion of France, 230–231
 competing for power in Germany, 56
 Dusko and, 18–19, 23, 47, 57, 140–141, 153, 203, 222, 234, 235–236
 Gestapo vs., 200
 Ivo (Dusko's brother) and, 198
 Jebsen and, 16–17, 18, 19–20, 47, 69, 133, 180, 186, 187, 189, 190, 191, 192, 198, 204
 SD vs., 200, 202, 204–205, 213
 self-serving relationship of agents, 154
 structure given to MI6 by Dusko, 174, *175–177,* 177
 U.S. spy network, 58–60, 71, 72, 88, 91–92, 98, **277**
 Yugoslav Escape Route (Allied escape line), 157, 167, 201, **277**
Abwehr I (Foreign Intelligence), xii, 40, 150, 186, 199. *See also* Kammler, Hans; Munzinger, Ernst; Schreiber, Aloys
Abwehr III (Counterespionage), xii, 39, 40, 144, 213, 222
"academic fencing" (Mensur), 7–8
Air Ministry (British), 42, 139, 244
Alexander (King of Yugoslavia), 68
ALFREDO. *See* Engels, Albrecht
Allgemeine Elektrizitäts Gesellschaft (AEG), 118
Allied escape line (Yugoslav Escape Route), 52, 54, 167–168, 171, 172, 174, 193–194, 195, 200, 201, 211, 220, 236, 243, **277**
Allied invasion of France as decisive for war, 211, 228, 229. *See also* D-Day
Allied Supreme Headquarters, 242
American Export Line, 32
American Historical Review, 126
Americans. *See* United States of America
Ammann-Brass, Hans, 72
Anne (Queen of England), 46
Anzueto, 18. *See also* Munzinger, Ernst
Anzuweto, 25. *See also* von Karsthoff, Albert
Applegate, Rex, 82
ARABEL. *See* Pujol, Joan
Arisaig, Scotland, 161, 163, 164, 173, 209
Army Group B (German), 229, 231, 232, 233
ARTIST, 190, 192, 193, 199, 214, 223, 224, 227, 251, 252, 253, 255. *See also* Jebsen, Johann
art of silent killing, 163
Ashley, Gisela (Dusko's secretary), 262
assassination attempt on Dusko by FBI, 181–182, 185
assets (Jebsen's) and Dusko, 256–257, 261
Associated Press, 37
atomic bomb, 121, 132, 138–139, **277**
"auf" (good bye) from Jebsen, 214
Augustus (Emperor of Rome), 28
Aviz Hotel, Lisbon, *34,* 35, 38, 40, 41, 49, 196, 198, 199–200, 226

B1A, 42, 184, 223, 224, 225. *See also* Robertson, T. A.
baccarat battle, 81–82, 83n, 83–85, 87
Bacher, Mr., 151
Bailoni, Ljiljana (Dusko's girlfriend), 86, 143, 178–179, 181, 182, 226
Bailonis, 140, 143, 154, 178, 181, 226
bald-headed doctor, 121, 135–136, 184–185
"Balkan playboy," 110, 111. *See also* Popov, Dusan Miladoroff "Dusko"
Ball, Lucille, 133
BALLOON. *See* Metcalfe, Dickie
Banac, Bozo and Karlo, 14, 17
Banco Espirito Santo, 248
Banwedon, Peter, 200. *See also* de Bona, Marquis Frano
Barton, Susan (Gisela Ashley), 78
Battle of the Bulge, 249

Bazna, Elyesa (CICERO), 65, 260, **277,** 278
Beatty, Chester, 205, 205n
Beaumont-Nesbitt, F. C., 42
bee hive (Lisbon), 28, 31–38
Beesly, Patrick, 86
Belgrade, Serbia, *ix,* 14, 15, 22, 46, 57, 68, 90, 91, 98, 166, 179, 189, 195, 200, 212, 223, 228, 244, 248, 254, 255, 262
Beltrão, Luís Teixeira, 37
Benton, Kenneth (MI6), xi, 189–191, 193
Berghof retreat in Bavarian Alps, 230, 232
Berle, Adolf, 89, 110
Berlin, Germany, *ix,* 5, 6, 15, 23, 26, 30, 35, 55n, 56–59, 61, 62, 66, 69, 78, 79, 88, 97, 117, 121, 136, *137,* 138, 139, 143, 146, 151, 154–156, 166, 177, 179–181, 186–190, 195–196, 198, 202–210, 213–215, 219, 221–224, 227, 250, 251, 260
Best, S. Payne (MI6), 25–26, 252
Bevan, John, 149
Biarritz, France, 195, 221, 222, 227, 250
BICYCLE, 264. *See also* Popov, Dusan Miladoroff "Dusko"
Biddle, Francis, 104
Birlinger, Mrs., 6, 9
BISCUIT (McCarthy), 23
Bissell, J. T., 126
Black, George, 64
"Black Bag" jobs, 107
blackmail letter to Abwehr, Dusko, 234, 235
Blanc, Jacqueline, 239–240
Bletchley Park, 24, 26, 137, 224, 224n, 260
Blitz of 1940 (London), 46
Bloch, Lippmann or Albert, 83–84, 85, 87
blown cover of Dusko, 136–138, *137,* 137n, 139, *140,* 142–145, 146, 148, 262
Blunt, Anthony, 171, 171n
Bohlen (Major), 215, 218
Bohny, Hermann, 112, 119–120, 121
Bond and Dusko. *See also* Fleming, Ian; Popov, Dusan Miladoroff "Dusko"
  baccarat battle, 81–82, 83n, 83–85, 87
  inspiration for Bond, Dusko as, 265
  playboy lifestyle of, 85–86, 87
  potential models, 279, **280–284**
Bonhoeffer, Dietrich, 12
Boyle, Archie, 42
Bozidar (chauffeur), 19, 20–21, 22, 261
Brandes, Hans, 214, 223, 256
Bratzel, John F., 125–127, 128
Braun, Jonathan, 265
Bresson, Thomas, 125
Brimoes, Paulo, 51. *See also* von Karsthoff
Briscoe (Professor), 184
Bristow, Desmond (MI6), xi, 33, 246, 247, 248, 255
Britain/British. *See also* operations, Dusko; World War II
  Churchill, 40, 41, 43, 46, 88, 91, 219–220, 244, 247
  execution of spies by, 47
  Jebsen's ships sale negotiated by Dusko, 15–16, 47, 61–62
  Operation Sea Lion, 22, 24–25, 50
  Taranto, Italy raid by, 69–70, *71,* 76, 94, 96–97, 109, 124, 127
British commandos (SOE), xiii, 12, 160–165, 166, 173, 195, 250–251, 252
British Intelligence. *See also* espionage in WWII; MI5; MI6; operations, Dusko; Popov, Dusan Miladoroff "Dusko"
  blown cover of Dusko, 136–137, *137,* 137n, 139, *140*
  chicken feed (misinformation), 47, 48, 50–51
  Double-Cross Committee, xii, 42, 44–45, 46, 50, 65–66, 72, 77, 79, 88, 89, 95, 109, 149, 185–186, 203, 204, 224
  Dusko and, 17, 18, 19, 22
  ENIGMA code broken by, 24, 137
  Passport Control Office, 17, 19, 33, 171, 174, 200
  spies killed by SD, 32
  ULTRA intelligence, 24–25, 62, 137, 210, 214, 224
British Naval Intelligence, 42, 79, 85, 86. *See also* Fleming, Ian
British Official Secrets Act, 109, 114, 263
British Security Coordination (BSC), xii, 59–60, 88, 89, 92, 93, 95, 97, 98, 107, 108, 109, 110, 111, 112, 116, 134, 137, 139, 140, 164, 238, 245
British Weekly, 201
Brown, Foster, 47, 48
Bruecher, Max, 255, 256–257
BRUTUS, 144, 144n, 204, 229
BSC. *See* British Security Coordination
Buchan, John, 38
bullfighting, 60, 61, 145
Butler, Richard, 218
butterfly trays, 120, 123, *124, 129,* 129–130, *130, 131*

"C." *See* Menzies, Stewart "C"
Caio Diulio, 70
Cairo, Egypt, 160, 165, 166, 172, 201, 244
Calais, France, 200, 217, 228, 229, 231, 232, 233
Campiagni, Dr., 24, 27
Canaris, Wilhelm (Abwehr), xii, 16–17, 23, 56, 72, 202, 205, 235
Carmichael, Hoagy, 85

Caroli, Gösta (SUMMER), 23
Carson, C. H., 93, 113–114
Casablanca (movie), 33, 285
Cascais, Portugal, 35, 37, 48, 167, 179, 212
Casey, William, 128
Casino Estoril, Portugal, 31, 38, 63, *63, 64,* 79, 81, 83, 85, 87, 182, 214, 279, **283**
Casino Royale (movie), 81–82, 83, 85, 87, 265, 279
Cassini, Boris, 151
Castello, Martha (Dusko's girlfriend), 62, 63, 86
Cat People (movie), 147, 285
Cavendish-Bentinck, Victor, xiii, 148, 201
CELERY (Dicketts), 23
Cetniks, 68–69
Chambers (Lieutenant), 93
chicken feed (misinformation), 47, 48, 50–51
chocolates and nylons, Dusko, 159
Cholmondeley, Charles, 139
Churchill, Winston, 40, 41, 43, 46, 88, 91, 219–220, 244, 247
Churchill (killing for), spying for Hitler, 14–20
CICERO (Bazna), 65, 260, **277,** 278
Clauss, Adolf, 169
Clock House, London, 157, 166, 171, 183, 227, 235, 238
codes and clandestine meetings, 25
Cohen, L. H., 247–248
concentration camps, 5, 9, 13, 51, 227, 240, 243, 250, 251, 252, 260
Connelley, E. J. (FBI), xiii, *97. See also* FBI
  Dusko and, 93, 94, 108, 110–111, 115–116, 127
  Hoover and, 94n, 95–96, 103, 110–111, 273, *274–275*
  Pearl Harbor Questionnaire, 94, 95, *275,* **277**
Conti di Cavour, 70
Copperhead (Montgomery double), 278, **278**
counterfeit currency, 65, 184, 260
Counterfeit General Montgomery, The (James), 278
Counterfeit Spy, The (Delmer), 264
Country House, The (Galsworthy), 184
covers, Dusko, 14, 18, 19, 42, 51, 57, 64–65, 99, *101,* 143, 144, 151, 171, 172, 183
Cowgill, Felix (MI6), xi, 62
Croatians, 68, 90, 152, 194
Crosby, Bing, 133
Cumberledge (Lt. Commander), 250–251
Cummings, Sir Mansfield, 43
currency scheme, Jebsen, 212, 213, 223, 239, 240, 242, 243, 260

Daily Express, 85
Daily Mail, 63
Dancer, John, 71
danger and risk sought by Dusko, 166, 261
Danvers, John, 51. *See also* Popov, Dusan Miladoroff "Dusko"
D-Day, 223, 226, 227, 228, 228n, 229, 230–234, 238
death in afternoon (bullfight), Dusko, 60, 61
Death in the Afternoon (Hemingway), 60
de Bona, Marquis Frano (FREAK), xi, 200, 204, 209, 223, 226, 229, 234, 235, 236
Decker (Lieutenant), 151
Dekobra, Maurice, 51, 51n
Delmer, Sefton, 264
"demeanor evidence," 230
Dicketts, Walter (CELERY), 23
Diels, Rudolf, 7
diplomatic bags, 18, 172, 177–178, 183–184, 214, 219
Donne, John, 146
Donovan, William "Wild Bill" (OSS), xiii, 80, 82, 108, 109, 112, 128, 163–164
DORA, 224
Doran, D., 160
double-0 designation (003), 261
double agents, 19, 22–23, 25, 26, 46, 47, 52, 93, 95, 104. *See also* Popov, Dusan Miladoroff "Dusko"; *specific agents*
Double-Cross Committee, xii, 42, 44–45, 46, 50, 65–66, 72, 77, 79, 88, 89, 95, 109, 149, 185–186, 203, 204, 224. *See also* Masterman, J. C.; Montagu, Ewen; *specific members*
Double-Cross System, The (Masterman), 72, 72n, 109, 264
"double tap" by Fairbairn, 162
Dourlein, Pieter, 163
Dover, England, 202, 205, *217,* 229, 230, 233
Dr. No (movie), 285
DREADNOUGHT, xi, 198, 220, 228, 247. *See also* Popov, Ivo (Dusko's brother)
drunk American girl and a brawl, 63–64
Dubrovnik, Croatia, 14, 19, 46, 61, 68, 90, 200, 244, 254
Dusko. *See* Popov, Dusan Miladoroff

Eagle, 70
Eccles, David, 82, 83
Edinburgh, Scotland, *ix,* 51
Eighth Army (German), 16, 233
Eisenhower, Dwight, 202, 226, 242
Elera, Maria (Dusko's girlfriend), 62–63, 86
Ellis, C. H. "Dick," xii, 92, 93, 94, 106, 108, 109, 116
"Enemy's Masterpiece of Espionage, The" (Hoover), 109, 111–112, *112,* 113, 114, 121, 121n, 127

Engels, Albrecht (ALFREDO) (Abwehr), xii. *See also* Abwehr
atomic bomb research, 121, 138, **277**
Dusko and, 72, 112, 117–118, 118–119, 120–121, 121n, 123, 132
microdots, 72, 135
ENIGMA code broken by British, 24, 137
espionage in WWII. *See also* Abwehr; British Intelligence; FBI; Germany/Germans; operations, Dusko; Pearl Harbor; Popov, Dusan Miladoroff "Dusko"; TRICYCLE; United States of America/Americans; World War II
butterfly trays, 120, 123, *124, 129,* 129–130, *130, 131*
codes and clandestine meetings, 25
double agents, 19, 22–23, 25, 26, 46, 47, 52, 93, 95, 104
inks (secret), 19, 27, 40, 51, 91, 156, 184
Lisbon and, 31–38, 39
microdots, 71n, 71–72, 91, 94, 95, 96, *96,* 99, *100,* 101, *101, 102,* 103, *105,* 108, 109–110, 111, 112, 113, 121, 127, 132, 135, 138, 156, 245
paying agents on enemy soil, 62, 65–66
spies/spy advice, 3, 17, 19, 22, 25–27, 38, 55, 151, 168, 174, 259
triple agents, 22, 23, 46, 167
truth serum, 207, 208
Esquire, 149
Estoril, Portugal, 25, 33, 35, 37, 40, 41, 48, 49, 55, 61, 66, 83, 86, 90, 150, 156, 157, 167, 279, **284**
European Central Bank (ECB), 5
European Movement, 263
Ewell Castle, Dusko, 4, 47
exiting feet first, Dusko, 13
exit permit incident, Dusko, 136

Fairbairn, William Ewart "Shanghai Buster," 161–162, 162–163, 164, 165
Fairey Swordfish "Stringbag," 70
family concerns of Dusko, 57, 60, 68, 69, 90, 91, 133, 141, 148, 150, 157–158, 183, 234, 244, 245
Farago, Ladislas, 264
FBI, xiii. *See also* Connelley, E. J.; espionage in WWII; Foxworth, Percy; Hoover, J. Edgar; Lanman, Charles; operations, Dusko; Popov, Dusan Miladoroff "Dusko"
assassination attempt on Dusko, 181–182, 185
"Black Bag" jobs, 107
blown cover of Dusko, 136, 139, 145, 146
butterfly trays, *129,* 129–130, *130*
Dusko and, 91–92, 93–94, 94n, 96, 99, 101, 104, 108, 115–116, 134, 136, 139, 140, 143, 144, 145, 146–147, 148, 158, 159, 181–182, 185
German spy network in U.S., 58, 59–60, 88
"Konrad"/"Phil" report, 97
money borrowed by Dusko, 140, 158
Pearl Harbor cover-up, 109–110, 111–114, *112,* 125–128
re-engagement of Dusko, 146–147, 148
summary of Dusko's activities, MI5, 108–109
White-Slave Traffic Act (Mann Act) violation by Dusko, 104
Feldmann, Stefan Otto, 115–116
Felix (Gibraltar invasion), 30
Fidrmuc, Paul (OSTRO), 192, 192n, 214, 223, 252, 252n
Fifteenth Army (German), 202, 229, 231, 232, 233
Figueiredo, Fausto de, 35
financial troubles of Dusko, 135, 139, 140, 144, 151, 154, 155–156
First United States Army Group (FUSAG), 202, 206, 230, 233
Fitzgerald, Honorah, 187–188
5 Fingers (movie), 278
Flanders, David, 125
Fleming, Ian, 38. *See also* Bond and Dusko; British Naval Intelligence
baccarat battle, 81–82, 83n, 83–85, 87
British-American commando school in Canada, 164–165
Casino Royale (movie), 81–82, 83, 85, 87, 265, 279
Donovan and Colt revolver given to, 82
Dr. No (movie), 285
Dusko and, 79, 79n, 80, 83, 84, 85, 86–87, 265
Godfrey and, 80, 81, 82, 83, 86, 87, 90
Hoover and, 80, 89, 90
Menzies as "M." in Bond, 44
Midas (Germany funding MI5), 79, 79n, 80, 83, 86, 87, **277**
Palácio Hotel and, 80–81, *81,* 86–87
Fletcher, R. G., 126, 127
FLIP, 221–222, 260
Flynn, Errol, 133
flytrap (catching German spies) role of Dusko, 115, 133, 135, 143, 155
Fodor, Ilena, 39
Foley, Frank (MI6). *See also* MI6
Bailoni (Gordana) as AXIS spy, 143
Dusko and, 148, 149, 159, 174, 177, 246
Hyde Park Hotel dinner party, 218
Ivo (Dusko's brother) evacuation, 237
Jebsen and, 241–242, 250
Martins and, 196–197

Paris network support by Dusko, 246
quadruple-cross strategy, 192
questionnaires, 201
re-engagement of Dusko, 148, 149
forging the anvil, Dusko, 3–8, 11, 14–15, 23, 44, 46, 47
Forrest (Major), 255
Forscher (researcher) for Abwehr, 17, 190
Fortitude (Normandy invasion deception), 202–204, 205, 205n, 206, 209, 210, 211, 223, 224, 227, 228–230, 233–234, 252, 252n, **278**
For Whom the Bell Tolls (Hemingway), 133
Foster, H. G., 129–130
Foxworth, Percy "Sam" (FBI), xiii, *97,* 104n. *See also* FBI
butterfly trays, 130
Dusko and, 117–118, 130, 132, 133, 136–138, 182
Hoover and, 92–93, 103, 104
"stir up an idea," Hoover, 132, 133, 182
France/French, 29, 30, 32, 46, 85, 143, 167, 195, 205, 294
Franco, Francisco, 29, 31, 56, 193n, 194
FREAK. *See* de Bona, Marquis Frano
Frederick, Lothar, 59
"French popsie" incident, Dusko, 63
Freud, Sigmund, 151
FUSAG (First United States Army Group), 202, 206, 230, 233

Gable, Clark, 133
Gaertner, Friedl (Dusko's girlfriend) (GELATINE, IVONNE), xi, 52–53, *53,* 54, 55, 62, 66, 86, 87, 148, 196, 197, 200, 201, 204, 210, 214
Galsworthy, John, 184
gambling, Dusko, 81–82, 83n, 83–85, 87, 182–183, 214
Game of Foxes, The (Farago), 264
GARBO. *See* Pujol, Joan
Gardner, Nadya, 59
GELATINE. *See* Gaertner, Friedl
Geneva Convention, 19
Gentry, Curt, 89, 109
George V (King of England), 219
Germany/Germans. *See also* Abwehr; espionage in WWII; Gestapo; Hitler, Adolf; operations, Dusko; Popov, Dusan Miladoroff "Dusko"; SD
blown cover of Dusko, 136–138, *137,* 137n, 139, *140,* 142–145, 146, 148
competing for power in, 56
concentration camps, 5, 9, 13, 51, 227, 240, 243, 250, 251, 252, 260
economic hegemony, 4n, 4–5
education of Dusko, 4–5, 6, 8, 9, 14, 23, 44, 47
Jews and, 5, 6, 9, 28, 30, 51
kidnapping by, 25–26, 193, 252
Operation Felix (Gibraltar), 30
Operation Isabella (Portugal), 30–31, 68
Operation Normandy (invasion defense), 231
Operation Punishment (Belgrade), 57, 68
Operation Sea Lion (Britain), 22, 24–25, 50
Operation Willi (Duke of Windsor), 32
recruitment of Dusko, 14, 16, 17
rocket bombs developed by, 180
Sippenhaft protocol (exacting revenge on one's family), 180, 245
spy network in U.S., 58, 59–60, 88
unconditional surrender of, 249
Gestapo, xiii, 5. *See also* Germany/Germans; Reich Security Head Office (RSHA); SD
Abwehr vs., 200
bugging telephones, 58
competition for power, 56
Dusko vs., 9–10, 11, 13, 14, 15, 206
Ivo (Dusko's brother) vs., 237, 239
Jebsen vs., 180, 183, 187, 188, 189, 193, 198, 203, 204, 212, 213, 214, 223, 227, 235
Gibraltar, 30, 166, 167, 191, 200
Gillott, Miss, 189
Girls' Dormitory (movie), 134
"Girl You Like, The" *(Esquire),* 149
Glass, Eric, 78
"Glass" vs. "Sand" mistake, Dusko, 78
Glavnyaca prison, 237
Gledhill, Cecil (MI6), xi, 182, 207
Glusevic, Mihail, 241–242, 243
Godfrey, John, xii, 42, 80, 81, 82, 83, 86, 87, 89, 90
Goebbels, Joseph, 72
Goerdeler, Carl, 16, 17
Goering, Hermann, 15, 24, 56, 70
Goldberg, Emanual, 71n, 71–72
gold in Portugal, 31
Goudie, E., 168
Grasse, Bishop of, 263
Greene, Graham, 39, 262
Gregorio, 171. *See also* Popov, Dusan Miladoroff "Dusko"
Gubbins, Colin, 161, 162
Guggenheims, 28
Gulbenkian, Calouste, 34
GUTTMANN. *See* de Bona, Marquis Frano
Gwennie (Dusko's girlfriend), 86

Hahn, Frederick, 239, 240, 257
Hahn, Otto, 138

Halder, Franz, 25
Hammer, R. M., 254, 255
Hansen, Georg (Abwehr), xii, 199, 209, 210, 211, 227, 250
Harbottle, Miss, 256
Harriman, Averell, 133
Harris, Tomás, 204, 223–224, 252, 252n
Hart, Lorenz, 141
Hawaii, 72, 95, 97, 101, 103, 104, 126, 127, 151, 152, 153. *See also* Pearl Harbor
Heer, Eins, 204
Heidegger, Martin, 5
Hemingway, Ernest, 60, 133, 145
Henie, Sonja, 133
Hennecke (Admiral), 230
Henry VIII (King of England), 4
Henss, Wolfgang, 200–201, 218
"he's not dead" incident, Dusko, 64
Heydrich, Reinhard, 5, 43, 56
Himmler, Heinrich, 5, 9, 56, 59, 202, 220, 245
Histoire des Etats-Unis (Maurois), 201
Hitler, Adolf. *See also* Germany/Germans
  Allied invasion of France as decisive for war, 211, 228, 229
  Berghof retreat, Bavarian Alps, 230, 232
  Canaris fired by, 202, 205
  Franco and, 56
  Mensur ("academic fencing"), 7–8
  Nazi doctrine, spread of, 6, 9
  Normandy as a distraction, 232, 233
  "Ordinance for the Protection of the People and the State," 5
  Portugal and, 29–30
  spying for Hitler, killing for Churchill, 14–20
Hitler Youth, 30
HMS *Prince of Wales,* 91
HMS *Queen Elizabeth, 149*
HMS *Seraph,* 168–169
Hoare, Samuel, 58
Hoeflinger, 18. *See also* Munzinger, Ernst
Hofmeister *(Kriminalrat),* 222, 260, 261
Home Defense Executive, 42
Hoover, J. Edgar (FBI), xiii. *See also* FBI
  butterfly trays, *129,* 130
  Connelley and, 94n, 95–96, 103, 110–111, 273, *274–275*
  "Do Not File" system, 107
  Donovan vs., 111
  Dusko and, 88, 91–92, 93, 94n, 94–95, 95–96, 103, 104, 106–107, 109, 110–111, 113, 114, 115, 116, 132, 133, 134, 135, 143, 155
  "Enemy's Masterpiece of Espionage, The," 109, 111–112, *112,* 113, 114, 121, 121n, 127
  Fleming and, 80, 89, 90
  flytrap (catching German spies) role of Dusko, 115, 133, 135, 143, 155
  Foxworth and, 92–93, 103, 104
  Godfrey and, 89
  infighting, 89, 90, 96, 98, 107–108, 111
  Liddell and, 89
  microdots, 71n, 99, *100,* 101, *101, 102,* 103, 109–110, 111, 112, 113, 127
  Montagu and, 134
  Pearl Harbor cover-up, 109–110, 111–114, *112,* 125, 127
  Pearl Harbor questionnaire, 95, 99, 101, 103–104, 107–108, 125, 126, 128–129, 132, *275,* **277**
  Roosevelt and, 99, *100, 101, 102,* 103, *105,* 111, 112, 125, 127
  Stephenson vs., 89, 89n, 111
  Winchell and, 142
Hope, Peter (MI6), xi, 249, 250, 255
Horsfall, St. John "Jock," 41, 239
Höttl, Wilhelm, 260
How, Mr., 16, 46
Hull, Cordell, 103
Hyde, H. Montgomery (MI6), xii, 58, 60, 109, 264
Hyde Park Hotel dinner party, 218–219

"I'll kill her," Dusko, 116–117
Illustrious, 70
Impey, Edward, 44
import/export, Dusko, 14, 18, 19, 42, 57, 64–65, 99, *101,* 143, 262, 263, 264
incomplete canvas, Dusko's re-engagement, 146–147, 148–149, 151
inks (secret), 19, 27, 40, 51, 91, 156, 184
International Bible Research Association, 5
International Congress of Photography, 71, 71n
into the lion's mouth, 144–145, 146, 148–149, 149–150, 257–258, 262. *See also* Popov, Dusan Miladoroff "Dusko"
INTREPID. *See* Stephenson, William
Isham (Major), 52
IVAN, xi, 19, 49, 58, 66, 88, 117, 118, 119, 135, 136, 139, 140, 152, 167, 180, 186, 188, 195, 195n, 200, 201, 207, 210, 211, 215, 219, 224, 228, 233, 235, 241, 252, 264. *See also* Popov, Dusan Miladoroff "Dusko"
IVAN II. *See* Metcalfe, Dickie
Ivanovic, Predrag, 237. *See also* Popov, Ivo (Dusko's brother)
Ivanovitch, Mr., 17
Ivens (MI6 agent), 189
IVONNE. *See* Gaertner, Friedl

I Was Cicero (Bazna), 278
I Was Monty's Double (movie), 278

Jaksitch, Dr., 14
James, M. E. Clifton, 278
Japan/Japanese, 32, 72. *See also* Pearl Harbor
Jarvis, Ralph (MI6), xi, 171, 182
Jebsen, Johann "Johnny" (ARTIST), espionage, xi. *See also* Abwehr; Popov, Dusan Miladoroff "Dusko"; TRICYCLE
arrest of, 193, 220, 223–224, 225, 227, 227n, 235–236, 238, 250
bald-headed doctor and, 184
Benton and, 189–191, 193
Brandes and, 214, 223, 256
currency scheme, 212, 213, 223, 239, 240, 242, 243, 260
death of, 250–251, 260–261
de Bona and, 200
double-cross by, 189–191, 193, 194–195
Dusko and, 8, 10, 15–16, 17, 18, 19, 20, 22, 24, 25, 27, 36, 47, 55, 57–58, 61–62, 68, 141, 148, 157, 174, 177, 179–180, 186, 189, 190, 191, 195, 198, 206–207, 210, 213, 214, 218, 222, 223, 224–225, 227, 234, 239–240, 241–242, 243, 245–246, 248–250, 251–252, 253, 255–256, 256–257, 259, 260, 261, 262
FLIP, 221–222, 260
Foley and, 241–242, 250
Fortitude (Normandy invasion deception), 211, 223, 227, **278**
Gestapo vs., 180, 183, 187, 188, 189, 193, 198, 203, 204, 212, 213, 214, 223, 227, 235
Glusevic and, 241–242, 243
Hansen and, 250
Henss and, 200–201, 218
Ivo (Dusko's brother) and, 184, 190, 191, 198, 199, 212
Kammler and, 186, 187, 192, 199, 243
killing Johnny's killer? (by Dusko), 257–258, 259–261, 262
Kramer and, 213
Kuebart and, 215, 249n, 249–250, 252
KVK medal, 215, 215n, 218, 220, 222
Martins as informant for Abwehr, 196
Metcalfe and, 180–181, 185–186
MI5 and, 62, 187, 203, 223–224, 227, 227n, 228, 235–236
MI6 and, 62, 187, 189–191, 193, 194–195, 218, 249
Moldenhauer and, 187–188, 190–191, 221, 224, 224n, 227
Munzinger and, 198, 203
Pujol and, 204
pyramidon formula for spy ink, 27
quadruple-cross strategy, 191–192
questionnaires, 17–18, 21–22
release of, 239–240, 241, 242, 243
Robertson and, 62, 187, 191–192, 195, 220, 223, 224, 227, 227n, 235, 256, 257, 259, 261
Salzer as killer of, 257–258, 259–260
Schellenberg and, 251–252
Schreiber and, 195, 215, 215n, 218, 220, 222, 224, 227
SD vs., 183, 198, 204, 214, 218, 223, 250
ships sale negotiated by Dusko, 15–16, 47, 61–62
Sostaric and, 166–167
suicide note to Moldenhauer, 187–188, 190–191
Taranto, Italy investigation, 69, 70, 76, 96, 103, 109, 124, 127
Tripartite meetings, 69–70
truth serum, 207
Ulla and, 245, 246
"unconscious" source for MI6, 195, 196
Vermehren and, 260
von Gronau and, 69–70, 213, 255
Waetjen and, 249
warnings to Dusko, 25, 36, 55, 57–58, 174, 177, 206–207
Wilson and, 180–181, 191–192, 220, 222, 223, 224–225, 227–228, 236, 241–242, 243, 250, 251–252, 252–253
Yugoslav Escape Route (Allied escape line), 157, 167, 174, 193, 194, 195, 200, 211, **277**
Zeis and, 179
Jebsen, Johann "Johnny" (personal)
assets located by Dusko, 256–257, 261
"auf" (good bye) to Dusko, 214
background of, 10, 11, *12,* 15, 16, 189, 243
Jacob (Johnny's uncle), 10
Lore (Johnny's wife), 180, 249, 250, 251, 252, 253, 255, 256, 261
loyalty issue, 10, 19–20, 21
Michael, Jr. (Johnny's grandfather), 10
Nazi hatred of, 11, 15, 16, 17, 19, 179
unbreakable spirit of, 243–244
Vladan (brother) and, 212
wealth (shipping empire) of, 10, 16, 69
Jews, 5, 6, 9, 28, 30, 51, 68
Jigoro, Kano, 161
Jodl, Alfred, 228, 228n, 231, 249
Jonsson, Jill (Dusko's second wife), 263–264, *264,* 285
JUNIOR (Ruser), xi, 187, 192

Kadavergehorsam (zombie-like obedience Hitler demanded), 9
Kaltenbrunner, Ernst (RSHA), 7, 241, 241n, 260

Kammler, Hans (Abwehr), xii, 150n. *See also* Abwehr I
  background of, 150
  Dusko vs., 150, 150n, 151, 154, 155–157, 174–175, 186, 199
  Jebsen and, 186, 187, 192, 199, 243
  recalled to Berlin, 186, 187
  Salzer and, 260
  von Karsthoff vs., 186
Keitel, Wilhelm, 249n, 250
Kelley, Clarence, 107, 114
Kendrick (MI6 agent), 189
kidnapping by Germany, 25–26, 193, 252
killing Jebsen's killer?, Dusko, 257–258, 259–261, 262
Kimmel (Admiral), 97, 97n, 109–110
King's Medal of Courage in the Cause of Freedom (KMC), 263
Klemmer, Harvey, 30
"Konrad"/"Phil" report, 97
Kramer, Fritz (Abwehr), xii, 213
Kuebart, William, 215, 249n, 249–250, 252, 256, 260
Kuehn, Dr., 72
Kürer, Otto, 150n. *See also* Kammler, Hans
KVK medal, 215, 215n, 218, 220, 222

"Lady Is a Tramp, The" (Hart), 141
Langelaan, George, 163
Lanman, Charles (FBI), xiii, 97. *See also* FBI; Popov, Dusan Miladoroff "Dusko"
  bald-headed doctor and, 135–136
  Dusko and, 93, 94–95, 101, 104, 106, 108, 112, 115, 118, 121–122, 126, 127
  radio traffic (false) to Berlin, 117–121, 134, 135
  Richardson (Dusko's girlfriend) as spy, 116–117
Laub, Karl, 7–8
lawyer, Dusko, 14–15, 23, 49, 51, 58, 134
Layton, Edwin T., 128
Leisner, Wilhelm (Lenz), xii, 56n, 56–57
Lennox (Major), 49, 54
Lenz, Gustav "Papa" (Abwehr), xii, 56n, 56–57
Lethbridge, St. George (MI6), 17, 18, 22, 174
"Let's Fly Away" (Porter), 141
Leverkuehn, Paul, 229
Lewis (Sergeant), 49
Libeccio, 70
Liddell, Guy (MI5), xi, 23, 42, 65, 77, 89, 111, 218
Lido, Julio Lopez (Osten), 58–60, 97, 98
lion's mouth, 144–145, 146, 148–149, 149–150, 257–258, 262. *See also* Popov, Dusan Miladoroff "Dusko"
Lisbon, Portugal, *ix,* 24, 25, 28, 31–38, 39, 40, 48, 55, 62, 66–67, 86, 88, 135, 137, *137,* 139, 143, 144, 146, 149, 150, 154, 157, 167, 168, 170, 171, 172, 174, 179, 183, 187, 189, 194, 196, 200, 203, 209–211, 214, 215, 219, 220, 224–226, 235, 241, 248, 262
Littorio, 70
Lloyd, M., 218
London, England, *ix,* 46, 49, 52, 64–65, 86, 96, 107, 133, 134, 135, 147, 149, 157, 178, 179, 183, 185, 191, 193, 200, 201, 206, 214, 218, 225, 241, 248
Lourenço, Agostinho, 33, 34
Love and Hisses (movie), 135, 142
Ludwig, Kurt Frederick, 59–60
Luftwaffe, 24, 41, 57
Luger of Dusko, 1, 162, 172, 173
Luke, Mrs., 107
Luke, William (MI5), xi. *See also* MI5
  Dusko and, 46–47, 50, 51–52, 54, 65, 66, 253, 255
  Fortitude (Normandy invasion deception), 252, 252n, **278**
lying, art of, 151

"M." in James Bond (Menzies), 44
Machiavelli (fictional mines around Britain), 50–51, 57, **277**
Maclean, Fitzroy, 68, 69, 247, 248
Madrid, Spain, *ix,* 25, 29, 56–58, 57–58, 60, 61, 62, 86, 166, 168, 170–171, 172, 174, 179, 183, 187, 189, 194, 195, 200, 211, 212, 215, 222, 226, 227, 262
magic (secret inks), 19, 27, 40, 51, 91, 156, 184
Makins, Roger, 82
malefactors (opposing Nazi rule), 5–6
Man Who Never Was, The (movie), 278
Marcks (General), 231, 232
Marriott, John (MI5), xi. *See also* MI5; Robertson, T. A.
  Double-Cross Committee, 42
  Dusko and, 52, 148–149, 201, 235
  Fortitude (Normandy invasion deception), 223, **278**
  Hyde Park Hotel dinner party, 218
  Ivo (Dusko's brother) evacuation, 239
  Jebsen's arrest, 223, 224
  quadruple-cross strategy, 191–192
  questionnaires, 47–48
  re-engagement of Dusko, 148–149
  Wilson and, 180–181
"Martin, Major," 168–169, 179
Martins, 196–197
Mason, Fanny, 158

Mason, Miss, 184
Masterman, J. C. (Professor), xii, 42n. *See also* Double-Cross Committee
Double-Cross System, The, 72, 72n, 109–110, 264
Dusko and, 42, 49, 54–55, 134, 166
Fortitude (Normandy invasion deception), 223, 252, 252n, **278**
Hyde Park Hotel dinner party, 218
Jebsen's arrest, 223, 224
Midas (Germany funding MI5), 77, **277**
Pearl Harbor questionnaire, 95, 125, **277**
quadruple-cross strategy, 191–192
questionnaires, 201
Robertson and, 160
spy advice, 55, 151, 168
Wilson and, 180–181
Yugoslav Escape Route (Allied escape line), 54, **277**
Zeis and, 179
Matryoshka doll, Dusko as, 172
Matsuoka, Yosuke, 69
Matthews, William, 46. *See also* Luke, William
Maunsell (Colonel), 165–166
Maurois, Andre, 201
McCarthy, Sam (BISCUIT), 23
McClure, Robert, 148–149
McKenzie (Major), 205
Meier, Karl, 227
Melland, B., 257
Mendes, Aristides de Sousa, 30
Mensur ("academic fencing"), 7–8
Menzies, Stewart "C" (MI6), xii. *See also* MI6
assassination attempt on Dusko, 185
background of, 43, 44, 45
Canaris and, 23
Distinguished Service Order, 44
Double-Cross Committee, 42, 44–45
Dusko and, 23, 43, 44–45, 88
Gaertner and, 53
ideogram, 43
Military Cross, 44
"M." in James Bond, 44
Pearl Harbor cover-up, 109
power behind the throne, 43–44
secret passageway from workplace, 26
vetting Dusko by, 43, 44–45
"virtuoso," 44–45, 230
Wireless Board (W Board), 42
Yugoslav Escape Route (Allied escape line), 167–168, **277**
Metcalfe, Dickie (BALLOON, IVAN II), xi, 195n. *See also* TRICYCLE
Dusko and, 54, 55, 62, 139, 148, 185–186, 196
Jebsen and, 180–181, 185–186
Martins and, 197
von Karsthoff and, 66
METEOR (Sostaric), xi, 166–167, 200, 251
Meyer, Mr., 156
Miami, Florida, *ix,* 103–104, *106*
microdots, 71n, 71–72, 91, 94, 95, 96, *96,* 99, *100,* 101, *101, 102,* 103, *105,* 108, 109–110, 111, 112, 113, 121, 127, 132, 135, 138, 156, 245
microphones, Dusko's apartment, 115–116
Midas (Germany funding MI5), 66–67, 77–80, 79n, *80,* 83, 86, 87, 148, 152, **277**
MI5 (Security Intelligence Service), xi, 22. *See also* Luke, William; Marriott, John; Popov, Dusan Miladoroff "Dusko"; Robertson, T. A.; Wilson, Ian; *specific other agents*
Castello (Dusko's girlfriend) and, 63
decoration for Dusko, 261–262
Double-Cross Committee, 42, 46
Dusko and, 14, 42, 46, 62, 88, 157, 159, 165, 166, 261–262
FBI's summary of Dusko's activities, 108
Fortitude (Normandy invasion deception), 203, 224, **278**
Hyde Park Hotel dinner party, 218
Ivo (Dusko's brother) and, 199, 212
Jebsen and, 62, 187, 203, 223–224, 227, 227n, 228, 235–236
Midas (Germany funding MI5), 66, 78–79, 79n, 87, **277**
Owens (SNOW) and, 22–23
Pearl Harbor cover-up, 109, 112
questionnaires, 18, 22, 47–48, 50, *73–75*
vetting of Dusko by, 42, 46
warnings to Dusko, 165, 166
Wireless Board (W Board), 42, 204
Yugoslav Escape Route (Allied escape line), 167–168, **277**
Mihailovic, Draza, 68, 199, 212, 226, 234, 237, 246
Milanovic, Vladimir, 171
Milinovic, Branko, 242, 246
Military Intelligence Division (MID), 92, 93, 126, 127
Mincemeat (Sicily invasion deception), 168–169, 171, 172, 179, **277,** 278
MI6 (Secret Intelligence Service, SIS), xi–xii, 22. *See also* Foley, Frank; Menzies, Stewart "C"; *specific other agents*
Abwehr structure from Dusko, 174, *175–177,* 177
agents kidnapped by Germany, 25–26, 252
de Bona and, 200
Double-Cross Committee, 42, 72

MI6 (Secret Intelligence Service, SIS) (*cont.*)
Dusko and, 17, 18–19, 62, 88, 158, 174, *175–177*, 177, 205, 218, 246
Greene and, 39
Hyde Park Hotel dinner party, 218
Ivo (Dusko's brother) and, 211
Jebsen and, 62, 187, 189–191, 193, 194–195, 218, 249
Midas (Germany funding MI5), 79, **277**
Paris network support by Dusko, 246
Pearl Harbor cover-up, 109, 112
Pearl Harbor questionnaire, 95, **277**
questionnaires, 18, 201
S.S. *Uruguay* crew members interrogated by, 123, 130
transfer to U.S., Dusko, 88
Ulla and, 245
warnings to Dusko, 205
Wireless Board (W Board), 42
Mitchell, Hamish, 92
Moberg, Ulla H., 245–246
Moldenhauer (Abwehr), 187–188, 190–191, 220, 221, 224, 224n, 227
Monckton, Sir Walter, 95
monkey incident ("turn around slowly"), Dusko and von Karsthoff, 1, 173–174
"Monsieur Jean," 171. *See also* Popov, Dusan Miladoroff "Dusko"
Montagu, Ewen, xii. *See also* Double-Cross Committee
chicken feed (misinformation), 47, 48
Double-Cross Committee, 42, 46, 88
Dusko and, 46–47, 52, 88, 144–145, 149–150, 168, 262
Hoover and, 134
Machiavelli (fictional mines around Britain), 50–51, 57, **277**
Mincemeat (Sicily invasion deception), 168–169, 171, 172, 179, **277**
Pearl Harbor cover-up, 109
re-engagement of Dusko, 144–145, 149–150, 262
Montagu, Mrs., 108
Montgomery (General), 278, **278**
Most Secret Sources (MS.S), 224. *See also* ULTRA intelligence
Muggeridge, Malcolm, 43
Munzinger, Ernst (Abwehr), xii. *See also* Abwehr I
background of, 18
de Bona and, 200
Dusko and, 18–19, 23, 24, 27, 51, 205
ink (secret) given to Dusko, 19, 27
Ivo (Dusko's brother) and, 199
Jebsen and, 198, 203
questionnaires, 17–18, 21–22
replacement of, 205
Murray (Captain), 93
Mutiozobal, Don Augustin, 27

naked and shaved threat by Dusko, 240
Nani (Dusko's girlfriend), 86, 178
Nassenstein, Adolf (SD), xiii, 206
National Geographic, 30
navicerts, 50, 50n
Nazism, 5–6, 9. *See also* Germany/Germans; Hitler, Adolf
hatred of, 9, 11, 15, 16, 17, 19, 143, 148, 150, 172, 179
Newsweek, 169
New York, *ix*, 29, 32, 59, 60, 66, 72, 78, 79, 82, 86, 88, 90, 92, 93, 94, 96, 98, 99, 103, 104, 115, 117, 122, 134, 136, 140, 147, 159
New York Times, 28, 141, 142
Night and Day (Woolf), 91
Noakes, S. H., 256
Nobel Prize, 138
Nomura, Kichisaburo, 104
Normandy, France, 202, 226, 227, 228n, 231, 238
Normandy invasion deception (Fortitude), 202–204, 205, 205n, 206, 209, 210, 211, 223, 224, 227, 228–230, 233–234, 252, 252n, **278**
Nunes, Jose, 118. *See also* von Karsthoff
Nuremburg Trials, 6, 259, 260

OBE (Order of the British Empire), 261, 263
Office of Naval Intelligence (ONI), 86, 86n, 92, 93, 97, 126, 127
Office of Strategic Services (OSS), xiii, 80, 82, 89, 107–108, 111, 128, 164. *See also* Donovan, William "Wild Bill"
Ohnishi, Takijiro, 96–97
Oikawa, Koshiro, 96
O'Keefe, Gregory, 130
Oklahoma, 124
OKW (German Armed Forces Supreme Command), xiii, 206, 228, 228n, 229
Oliviera, Gaspar de, 225
Ollschlager (Major), 18
"On Broadway" (Winchell), 141
ONI (Office of Naval Intelligence), 86, 86n, 92, 93, 97, 126, 127
Operation Felix (Gibraltar), 30
Operation Isabella (Portugal), 30–31, 68
Operation Normandy (invasion defense), 231
Operation Punishment (Belgrade), 57, 68

operations, Dusko, *ix*, **277–278**. *See also* British Intelligence; espionage in WWII; FBI; Germany/Germans; Popov, Dusan Miladoroff "Dusko"
atomic bomb research, 121, 132, 138–139, **277**
CICERO (Bazna as German agent, notified MI6), 65, 260, **277,** 278
Copperhead (Montgomery double), 278, **278**
Fortitude (Normandy invasion deception), 202–204, 205, 205n, 206, 209, 210, 211, 223, 224, 227, 228–230, 233–234, 252, 252n, **278**
Machiavelli (fictional mines around Britain), 50–51, 57, **277**
Midas (Germany funding MI5), 66–67, 77–80, 79n, *80,* 83, 86, 87, 148, 152, **277**
Mincemeat (Sicily invasion deception), 168–169, 171, 172, 179, **277,** 278
Pearl Harbor Questionnaire, 71, 72, *73–75,* 76, 94, 94n, 95, *96,* 96–98, 99, 101, 103, 107–108, 109, 111, 123, 125, 126, 127, 128–129, 132, *275,* **277**
U.S. spy network, 58–60, 71, 72, 88, 91–92, 98, **277**
Yugoslav Escape Route (Allied escape line; trick Germans into sending double agents), 52, 54, 157, 167–168, 171, 172, 174, 193–194, 195, 200, 201, 211, 220, 236, 243, **277**
Operation Sea Lion (Britain), 22, 24–25, 50
Operation Willi (Duke of Windsor kidnapping), 32
Oranienburg camp, 13, 243, 250, 252, 260
Order of the British Empire (OBE), 261, 263
"Ordinance for the Protection of the People and the State" (Hitler), 5
OSS. *See* Office of Strategic Services
Osten, Ulrich von der, 58–60, 97, 98
OSTRO (Fidrmuc), 192, 192n, 214, 223, 252, 252n
Owens, Arthur (SNOW), 22–23
Oxford University, 42, 42n, 44, 46. *See also* Masterman, J. C.

Pacific Fleet, 97, 97n, 108, 128
Palácio Hotel, Estoril, 33, 35, 36, *36,* 37, 38, 40, 41, 49, 63, 64, *64,* 67, 79, 80–81, *81,* 83, *84,* 85, 86–87, 150, 172–173, 211, 226, 279
Pan American Airlines/Clipper, 29, 31, 82, 91, 119, 150
Parade magazine, 265
Paris, France, *ix,* 28, 134, 222, 239, 242–243, 245, 246, 248
Park Avenue New York, Dusko, 98, 134, 135
Parque Hotel, Estoril, 35, *64,* 85
Partisans, 61, 68–69, 244, 246, 247, 254
Pascal's Wager, 145
Passport Control Office, 17, 19, 33, 171, 174, 200
Patton, George S., 202, 230, 233, 249
Paul (Prince of Yugoslavia), 57
PAULA, xi, 195. *See also* Popov, Ivo (Dusko's brother)
Pavelic, Ante, 61, 68, 69
paying agents on enemy soil, 62, 65–66
Pearl Harbor. *See also* espionage in WWII
cover-up, 99–114, *112,* 125–128
Dusko's anger, intelligence failure, 1, 133
investigations into intelligence failure, 108
Japanese attack of, 123–125
Questionnaire, 71, 72, *73–75,* 76, 94, 94n, 95, *96,* 96–98, 99, 101, 103, 107–108, 109, 111, 123, 125, 126, 127, 128–129, 132, *275,* **277**
Taranto, Italy as blueprint, 69–70, *71,* 76, 94, 96–97, 109, 124, 127
Pearson, John, 81–82
Peter II (King of Yugoslavia), xiii, 200, 234–235, 244, 246, 255, 262
Petrie, Sir David, 218, 263
Philby, Kim, 89, 89n
Pieckenbrock, Hans (Abwehr), xii, 57, 199
playboy, Dusko, xiii, 6–7, 10, 36, 41, 51, 51n, 52–53, *53,* 62–64, 85–86, 87, 88, 103, 104, 106, 122, 133, 139, 140, 143, 170, 178, 182–183, 261, 263, 265
Polícia de Vigilância e Defesa do Estado (PVDE), 33, 34, 39–40, 49, 63, 99, 225, 238
Political Warfare Executive (PWE), 166
Politika, 9
Popitz, Johannes, 16
Popov, Dusan Miladoroff "Dusko" (IVAN, SKOOT, TRICYCLE), espionage. *See also* Abwehr; Bond and Dusko; espionage in WWII; FBI; Lanman, Charles; MI5; operations, Dusko; Popov, Ivo (Dusko's brother); von Karsthoff, Albert; Wilson, Ian; Yugoslavia, Serbia
Abwehr structure given to MI6, 174, *175–177,* 177
assassination attempt by FBI, 181–182, 185
bald-headed doctor, 121, 135–136, 184–185
bee hive (Lisbon), 28, 31–38
blown cover, 136–138, *137,* 137n, 139, *140,* 142–145, 146, 148, 262
Bozidar and, 19, 20–21, 22, 261
British Intelligence and, 17, 18, 19, 22
"British or Russian agent," 225, 226, 228
Campiagni and, 24, 27
Connelley and, 93, 94, 108, 110–111, 115–116, 127

Popov, Dusan Miladoroff "Dusko" (*cont.*)
covers, 14, 18, 19, 42, 51, 57, 64–65, 99, *101,* 143, 144, 151, 171, 172, 183
diplomatic bags, 18, 172, 177–178, 183–184, 214, 219
Double-Cross Committee, 42, 46
Engels and, 72, 112, 117–118, 118–119, 120–121, 121n, 123, 132
Feldmann trap and, 115–116
financial compensation for Allied invasion plans, 210, 215, 218, 219
Fodor and, 39
Foley and, 148, 149, 159, 174, 177, 246
Foxworth and, 117–118, 130, 132, 133, 136–138, 182
Gestapo vs., 9–10, 11, 13, 14, 15, 206
"Glass" vs. "Sand" mistake, 78
Hansen and, 211
Henss and, 200–201
Hoover and, 88, 91–92, 93, 94n, 94–95, 95–96, 103, 104, 106–107, 109, 110–111, 113, 114, 115, 116, 132, 133, 134, 135, 143, 155
Horsfall and, 41
How and, 16, 46
"I'll kill her," 116–117
import/export cover, 14, 18, 19, 42, 57, 64–65, 99, *101,* 143
incomplete canvas (re-engagement), 146–147, 148–149, 151
Kammler vs., 150, 150n, 151, 154, 155–157, 174–175, 186, 199
Lenz and, 56–57
Lethbridge and, 17, 18, 22, 174
lion's mouth survived by, 257–258
Louise and, 182–183
Luke and, 46–47, 50, 51–52, 52, 54, 65, 66, 253, 255
Marriott and, 52, 148–149, 201, 235
Masterman and, 42, 49, 54–55, 134, 166
Menzies and, 23, 43, 44–45, 88
Metcalfe and, 54, 55, 62, 139, 148, 185–186, 196
MI6 and, 17, 18–19, 62, 88, 158, 174, *175–177,* 177, 205, 218, 246
microphones in apartment, FBI, 115–116
Montagu and, 46–47, 52, 88, 144–145, 149–150, 168, 262
Munzinger and, 18–19, 23, 24, 27, 51, 205
Oliviera and, 225
Paris network support by, 246
Pearl Harbor cover-up, 109, 112, 113–114, 125
Pearl Harbor intelligence failure, 1, 133
Peter (King of Yugoslavia) and, 234–235, 238, 244, 246, 255
Pieckenbrock and, 57
questionnaires, 50, 55, 91, 93, 121, 132, 138–139, 156, 160, 169, 196, 200–201, 205, 206, 214, 216–217, *216–217,* **277, 278**
Quetting and, 251, 260–261
radio traffic (false) to Berlin, 1, 117–121, 134, 135, 144–145, 152
re-engaging in espionage after blown cover ("into the lion's mouth"), 144–145, 146, 148–149, 149–150, 262
Robertson and, 1, 46–47, 48, 49, 50, 52, 54, 62, 91, 108, 144–145, 148–149, 157, 160, 166, 171, 226, 235, 262
Sahrbach and, 36, 91
Schmidt and, 241, 243
Schreiber and, 196, 203, 206, 207, 208, 209, 210, 215, 218, 222
SD vs., 39–40, 202–203, 206, 225
Serb or Croat question, 61
serial numbers of bills checked at Customs, 62, 65
Special Operations Executive (SOE) training, 160, 163, 165, 173, 209
Spy Counter-Spy, 259, 262, 265
spying for Hitler, killing for Churchill, 14–20
success during WWII, 261–262
surveillance of, 6, 19, 22, 33, 39–40, 49, 50, 52, 58, 60, 62–63, 79, 79n, 83, 85, 86, 87, 92, 93, 103, 115–116, 129, 134, 151, 154, 157, 198
Terry and, 199–200
truth serum, 207, 208, 209
Ulla and, 245–246
VIPER and, 197, 198
von Stein recruitment of, 14, 16, 17
Warnecke and, 57, 58, 60
warnings to, 1, 25, 36, 55, 57–58, 144, 152, 165, 166, 168, 171, 172, 174, 177, 179, 180, 205, 206–207, 226
Wiegand and, 209–210
Winchell's exposure of, 142–143
Wren and, 122, 123
Zeis and, 179
Popov, Dusan Miladoroff "Dusko" (IVAN, SKOOT, TRICYCLE), Jebsen and. *See also* Jebsen, Johann
arrest of Jebsen, 222, 223, 224–225, 227, 234
assets of Jebsen found by, 256–257, 261
"auf" (good bye) from Jebsen, 214
blackmail letter to Abwehr, 234, 235
Blanc and, 239–240
Jebsen (Lore) looked after by, 261
killing Jebsen's killer?, 257–258, 259–261, 262
leave of absence, 243, 246
naked and shaved threat by, 240

release of Jebsen, 239–240, 241, 242, 243
Salzer vendetta, 257–258, 259–260
search for Jebsen, 239–240, 241–242, 243, 245–246, 248–250, 251–252, 253, 255–256, 257, 259, 260, 262
ships sale negotiation, 15–16, 47, 61–62
Popov, Dusan Miladoroff "Dusko" (personal), xi
appearance of, *11*, *43*, 52, 85, *264*
background (forging the anvil), 3–8, 11, 14–15, 23, 44, 46, 47
Bailoni, Ljiljana (girlfriend), 86, 143, 178–179, 181, 182, 226
Bata (aunt), 98
Birlinger café supported by, 6, 9
BMW, 10, 19, 21
Boris (Dusko's and Jill's son), 264
Castello (girlfriend), 62, 63, 86
Chen-Yen (manservant), 104
chocolates and nylons requested by, 159
danger and risk sought out by, 166, 261
Dean (Dusko's and Janine's son), 262, 263
death in the afternoon (bullfight), 60, 61
driver's license, 201–202
drunk American girl and a brawl, 63–64
dying vs. torture, 1, 172
Elera (girlfriend), 62–63, 86
English alien registration card, 43, *43*
Ewell Castle, 4, 47
exiting feet first, 13
exit permit incident, 136
family concerns of, 57, 60, 68, 69, 90, 91, 133, 141, 148, 150, 157–158, 183, 234, 244, 245
fear, 145
financial troubles of, 135, 139, 140, 144, 151, 154, 155–156
five lives lived by, 183
foreigner status as protection, 6, 8, 9
"French popsie" incident, 63
friendship with von Karsthoff, 25, 36, 55
Gaertner (girlfriend), xi, 52–53, *53*, 54, 55, 62, 66, 86, 87, 148, 196, 197, 200, 201, 204, 210, 214
gambling, 81–82, 83n, 83–85, 87, 182–183, 214
generosity of, 261
German education, 4–5, 6, 8, 9, 14, 23, 44, 47
Gwennie (girlfriend), 86
health, deteriorating, 183
Hyde Park Hotel dinner party, 218–219
import/export business, 262, 263, 264
incarceration by Nazis, 11–13
"Jackson, Mrs." and, 174
Janine (first wife), 262, 263
Jonsson (second wife), 263–264, *264*, 285
Jovan (uncle), 98
languages (5) spoken by, 10, 23
lawyer, 14–15, 23, 49, 51, 58, 134
"living expenses" funds, 158
loyalty issue, 10, 19–20, 21, 61–62
Luger of, 1, 162, 172, 173
Marco (Dusko's and Jill's son), 163, 260, 264
Matryoshka doll, Dusko, 172
Mensur ("academic fencing"), 7–8
Milorad (father), 3, 4, 15, 19, 44, 57, 60, 68, 90–91, 157–158, 183, 244, 245, 248–249, 250, 251, 252
Nani (girlfriend), 86, 178
naturalized British citizen, 262
Nazi hatred, 9, 11, 19, 143, 148, 150, 172
Nina (yacht) of, 15
Omar (Dusko's and Jill's son), 264
Omer (grandfather), 3, 44
Order of the British Empire (OBE), 261, 263
Park Avenue New York, 98, 134, 135
passion and addiction, 53
playboy, xiii, 6–7, 10, 36, 41, 51, 51n, 52–53, *53*, 62–64, 85–86, 87, 88, 103, 104, 106, 122, 133, 139, 140, 143, 170, 178, 182–183, 261, 263, 265
post WWII, 262, 263–264
publishing business, 248, 262
rescue of family, 90–91
reunion with Ivo (Dusko's brother), 239
Richardson (girlfriend), xiii, 86, 104, *106*, 116–117, 133
short-term photographic memory of, 10
Simon (girlfriend), xiii, 86, 106, 134–135, 136, 139–140, 142, *142*, 143, 147–148, 149, 151, 155, 157, 178, 285
too many devices (baggage), 45
"turn around slowly" (monkey), 1, 173–174
"Vivovdan and the September Constitution of Yugoslavia, The," 8, 9
Vladan (brother), 3–4, 91, 158, 179, 212, 241n, 241–242
war view of, 21
wealth of, 14–15
Zora (mother), 19, 57, 60, 68, 90–91, 158, 183, 244, 245, 253, 254–255
Popov, Ivo (Dusko's brother) (personal)
background of, 3, 4, 211, *238*
charm of, 198–199
Dragica (wife), 76, 90, 245, 246, 247–248, 254
Milorad (father) and, 158, 252
Milorad "Misha" (son), 76, 90, 246, 247, 248, 263
post WWII, 262–263

Popov, Ivo (Dusko's brother, DREADNOUGHT, PAULA), espionage, xi. *See also* TRICYCLE
  Abwehr and, 198
  arrest of, 236, 237
  bald-headed doctor, Ivo as, 121, 135–136, 184–185
  Bozidar and, 20
  currency deals and, 237
  de Bona and, 200
  Dusko and, 141, 148, 183, 211–212, 212–213, 225, 234, 236, 237–238, 239
  evacuation to U.K., 237–238, 239
  Foley and, 237
  Gestapo vs., 237, 239
  Jebsen and, 184, 190, 191, 198, 199, 212
  King's Medal of Courage in the Cause of Freedom (KMC), 263
  MI5 and, 199, 212
  MI6 and, 211
  Mihailovic and, 199, 237
  money problems of, 210
  Munzinger and, 199
  Sostaric and, 166–167
  Ustase vs., 68, 76, 90
  warnings to Dusko, 144
  Wilson and, 158, 199, 237–238, 239, 250
  Yugoslav Escape Route (Allied escape line), 52, 157, 167, 171, 193, 194, 195, 201, 220, **277**
  Zeis and, 179
Popovic, Sveta, 171, 212. *See also* Popov, Ivo (Dusko's brother)
Popper, Hans, 211, 263. *See also* Popov, Ivo (Dusko's brother)
Porter, Cole, 141
Portugal, 29–31, 49, 68, 167, 183, 245
"preventive arrest," 5–6
Prime (Colonel), 151
Prinz Albrechstrasse, 227, 240, 243, 251
Prussians, 16, 120
Pujol, Joan (ARABEL, GARBO), 144, 144n, 202, 204, 223, 224, 228, 229, 261

Quebec City, Canada, *ix,* 121, 135, 136
questionnaires, 50, 55, 91, 93, 121, 132, 138–139, 156, 160, 169, 196, 200–201, 205, 206, 214, 216–217, *216–217,* **277, 278**. *See also* Pearl Harbor
Quetting, Hermann, 221–222, 251, 256, 260–261

radio traffic (false) to Berlin, 1, 117–121, 134, 135, 144–145, 152
Rakic (General), 168, 171
Rantzau, Dr. (Nikolaus Ritter), 23
Reader's Digest, 109, 112–113, *112,* 113, 114, 121, 121n, 127, 169
Reich Security Head Office (RSHA), 7, 202, 241, 241n, 260. *See also* Gestapo; SD
Richardson, Terry (Dusko's girlfriend), xiii, 86, 103, 104, *106,* 116–117, 133
Richter, Gustav, 91
Rio de Janeiro, Brazil, *ix,* 72, 112, 117, 119, 130, 135, 136, *137*
Roberts, Owen J., 127
Robertson, T. A. "Tar" (MI5), xi. *See also* B1A; Marriott, John; MI5
  background of, 41–42
  Canaris interest of, 23
  chicken feed (misinformation), 48, 50
  diplomatic bags, 183
  Double-Cross Committee, 42
  Dusko and, 1, 46–47, 48, 49, 50, 52, 54, 62, 91, 107, 144–145, 148–149, 157, 160, 166, 171, 226, 235, 262
  Fortitude (Normandy invasion deception), 202, 203, 223, 228, **278**
  Gaertner and, 52–53
  Hoover-Dusko meeting, 108
  Hyde Park Hotel dinner party, 218
  Jebsen and, 62, 187, 191–192, 195, 220, 223, 224, 227, 227n, 235, 256, 257, 259, 261
  Martins and, 196–197
  Masterman and, 160
  Midas (Germany funding MI5), 66, **277**
  Owens and, 23
  Paris trip, 242
  quadruple-cross strategy, 191–192
  questionnaires, 47–48
  re-engagement of Dusko, 144–145, 148–149
  Special Operations Executive (SOE) training for Dusko, 160
  warnings to Dusko, 1, 171, 226
  Wild and, 226, 227
  Yugoslav Escape Route (Allied escape line), 54, 167, **277**
rocket bombs developed by Germany, 180
Röhm, Ernst (SA), 5, 7
Rome, Italy, *ix,* 23, 24, 41, 143, 262, 263
Rommel, Erwin, 3, 149, 202, 211, 229, 230, 231–232, 233
Room 3603 (Hyde), 80, 264
Roosevelt, Franklin D. *See also* United States of America
  Churchill and, 91
  Godfrey and, 82
  Hoover and, 99, *100, 101, 102,* 103, *105,* 111, 112, 125, 127

Portugal and, 29–30
Stephenson and, 106
Winchell and, 141
Rout, Leslie B., Jr., 125–127, 128
Royal Air Force (RAF), 23, 70, 167, 170
Royal Navy, 31, 47, 50, 70
Royal Victoria Patriotic Building in Wandsworth "London Reception Center," England, 166, 179
Ruser, Hans (JUNIOR), xi, 187, 192
Ryan, Cornelius, 82

Sahrbach, Elisabeth (von Karsthoff's mistress) (Abwehr), xii, 36, 48, 49, 55, 91, 150, 152, 154, 159, 174
Salazar, António de Oliveira, 29, 30, 31
Salzer, Walter, 241, 257–258, 259–260
"Sand, Mr.", 78, 79, 148
Savoy, London, 41, 46, 47, 52, 91, 239
Savska Bank of Belgrade, 14, 41, 65, 143
Schachno, Joseph, 6
Schacht, Hjalmar, 243–244
Schaffgotsch, Felix, 133
Schellenberg, Walter (SD), xiii. *See also* SD
blackmail letter to Abwehr, 235
competition for power, 56
counterfeiting currency, 65
cyanide capsules carried by, 26
Hansen and, 211
Jebsen and, 251–252
Madrid agents, 58
MI6 agents kidnapped by, 25–26
office and desk (armed) of, 26
"reporter" for SD, 6, 7
Salzer and, 260
Schmidt, Karl, 25
Schmidt, Wulf (TATE), 65, 79
Schmidtt, Dr., 241, 243
Schmissen ("smite"), Mensur scars, 7, 14
Schmitz *(Sturmbannführer)*, 260, 261
Schoeps, Hans, 16
Schreiber, Aloys (Abwehr), xii. *See also* Abwehr I
background of, 186
Dusko and, 196, 203, 206, 207, 208, 209, 210, 215, 218, 222
Jebsen and, 195, 215, 215n, 218, 220, 222, 224, 227
Salzer and, 260
Schroeder, Erich (SD), xiii, 66, 192, 208, 260
Schutzhaft, 12
Schweizerische Bankverein, 248
Scotland, *ix*, 51, 52, 161, 163, 164, 173, 180, 209, 238–239
SD *(Sicherheitsdienst)*, xiii, 5. *See also* Gestapo; Reich Security Head Office (RSHA); Schellenberg, Walter
Abwehr vs., 200, 202, 204–205, 213
blown cover of Dusko, 144
British spies killed by, 32
competing for power in Germany, 56
counterfeit currency, 260
Dusko vs., 39–40, 202–203, 206, 225
German aristocrats joining, 16
Jebsen vs., 183, 198, 204, 214, 218, 223, 250
selling war assets to Allied country, 15
"Working Associations" at universities, 6
Sea Lion (Britain), 22, 24–25, 50
Second Army (British), 233
Secret Intelligence Service (SIS). *See* MI6
Secret War Against Hitler, The (Casey), 128
Security Intelligence, Middle East (S.I.M.E.), 160
Security Intelligence Service. *See* MI5
Serbia/Serbs, 68, 69, 195, 211, 237, 247. *See also* Yugoslavia
Serb or Croat question, Dusko, 61
Seventh Heaven (movie), 135
Severn, 149
Sharp, Frederick (Colonel), 93
ships (Jebsen) sale negotiated by Dusko, 15–16, 47, 61–62
"shots rang out," 193
Sicily invasion deception (Mincemeat), 168–169, 171, 172, 179, **277**, 278
Simic, Mrs. Ruza, 184
Simon, Madame (Monique Ciorcelli), 136
Simon, Simone (Dusko's girlfriend), xiii, 86, 107, 134–135, 136, 139–140, 142, *142*, 143, 147–148, 149, 151, 155, 157, 178, 285
Sinclair, Hugh (Admiral), 43
Sippenhaft protocol (exacting revenge on one's family), 180, 245
SIS (Secret Intelligence Service). *See* MI6
SKOOT, xi, 23, 46, 47, 48, 49, 50, 51, 54, 54n. *See also* Popov, Dusan Miladoroff "Dusko"
Skorzeny, Otto, 7
Slaatten (Captain), 151
SNOW (Owens), 22–23
Socialist Appeal, 201
sodium pentothal, 207, 208, 209
SOE (Special Operations Executive), xiii, 12, 160–165, 166, 173, 195, 250–251, 252
Sonderbehandlung ("special treatment") execution, 13
Sostaric, Eugen (METEOR), xi, 166–167, 200, 251
Soucy, E. A., 93
Sousa, Alves de, 112–113, 113–114

Spain, *ix,* 30, 31, 167, 168, 169, 174, 183, 193, 193n, 213, 221, 248, 294
Special Operations Executive (SOE), xiii, 12, 160–165, 166, 173, 195, 250–251, 252
Speer, Albert, 232
Speidel, Hans, 229, 230–232, 233
Speir (Lt. Colonel), 242
spies/spy advice, 3, 17, 19, 22, 25–27, 38, 55, 151, 168, 174, 259. *See also* espionage in WWII
Spy Counter-Spy (Dusko), 259, 262, 265
spying for Hitler, killing for Churchill, 14–20
S.S. *Uruguay,* 122, 123, *124, 128,* 129, 130
Station X, 136n, 136–137, *137,* 139, *140,* 219, 221–222, 224, 260
Steimle, Eugen (SS), 256
Stephenson, Jo, 255
Stephenson, William (INTREPID), xii, 59, 89, 89n, 107, 108, 109, 111, 112, 163–164, 165
Stevens, Richard (MI6), 25–26
Stewart, Jimmy, 135
"stir up an idea" (Foxworth), 132, 133, 182
Stott, William, 93, 137–138, 139
Sturmabteilung (Storm Battalion, SA), 5
Sturrock, H. N., 16
suicide note (Jebsen), 187–188, 190–191
SUMMER (Caroli), 23
Summers, Anthony, 108
Sunday Times (Johannesburg), 264
Sun Valley, Idaho, *ix,* 133, 134
Sun Valley Serenade (movie), 133
Supreme Headquarters Allied Expeditionary Force (SHEAF), 226, 251
surveillance of Dusko, 6, 19, 22, 33, 39–40, 49, 50, 52, 58, 60, 62–63, 79, 79n, 83, 85, 86, 87, 92, 93, 103, 115–116, 129, 134, 151, 154, 157, 198
Sweden, 29, 245
Switzerland, *ix,* 29, 141, 157, 167, 168, 195, 212, 241, 244, 245, 246, 248, 249, 250, 251
Sykes, Eric Anthony, 161, 162, 164, 165

TALLYRAND, 264. *See also* Popov, Dusan Miladoroff "Dusko"
Taranto, Italy (first aerial assault against a defended port) raid by British, 69–70, *71,* 76, 94, 96–97, 109, 124, 127
TATE (Schmidt), 65, 79
Technical High School, Dresden, 71n, 110, 111
"tells," 230
Terry, Beatrice, 199–200
Thurston, Arthur, 126, 127, 182, 185
ticking (assassination attempt on Dusko by FBI), 181–182, 185
Times (London), 31
Tirpitzufer, 55n, 55–56, 121, 186, 187
Tito, Josip, 61, 68, 234, 244, 247, 255
Toki-Ona, Lisbon, 35, 36–37, 38
Toland, John, 125, 127
too many devices (baggage), Dusko, 45
Topete, Margot Seco de, 37–38
Töppen, Martin (Abwehr), xii, 77–78
Tourjansky, Viktor, 134
Tovey, Sir John, 40, 47
Trento, 70
TRICYCLE, xi, 54, 54n, 55, 62, 77, 88, 92, 108, 128, 138, 139, 143, 146, 160, 165, 166, 167, 169, 170, 179, 181, 187, 195, 198, 200, 203, 204–205, 205, 210, 212, 220, 223, 224, 225, 228, 235, 236, 243, 245, 247, 252, 255, 256, 262, 264. *See also* espionage in WWII; Jebsen, Johann; Metcalfe, Dickie; Popov, Dusan Miladoroff "Dusko"; Popov, Ivo (Dusko's brother); *specific other agents*
Tripartite Pact, 69–70
triple agents, 22, 23, 46, 167. *See also* Popov, Dusan Miladoroff "Dusko"; *specific agents*
truth serum, 207, 208, 209
tungsten (wolfram), 31
"turn around slowly" (monkey incident), Dusko and von Karsthoff, 1, 173–174
Twain, Mark, 7
Twenty Committee (XX). *See* Double-Cross Committee

Ucovic, Mirko, 90
ULTRA intelligence, 24–25, 62, 137, 210, 214, 224
United States of America/Americans. *See also* espionage in WWII; FBI; Pearl Harbor; Roosevelt, Franklin D.
  atomic bomb, 121, 132, 138–139, **277**
  King Peter of Yugoslavia mission for Dusko, 234–235, 238
  spy network, 58–60, 71, 72, 88, 91–92, 98, **277**
U.S. Forces European Theater Office (USFET), 256
Ustase, 61, 68, 69, 76, 90, 98, 141, 246
Ustinov, Jona von, 33, 33n

Vasic, George (Dragica's father), 245
VE Day (Victory in Europe), 249, 249n
Velebit, Vlatko, 247, 254
Venlo, Netherlands incident, 25–26, 252
Vermehren, Erich, 213
Vermehren, Petra, 260
"Views on Preparation for War" (Yamamoto), 96
VIPER, 197, 198, 199
"virtuoso," 44–45, 230. *See also* Popov, Dusan Miladoroff "Dusko"

"Vivovdan and the September Constitution of Yugoslavia, The" (Dusko), 8, 9
von Auenrode, Kremer, 25. *See also* von Karsthoff, Albert
von Braun, Werner, 180
von Choltitz, Dietrich, 16
von Gronau, Baron Wolfgang, 69–70, 96, 109, 124, 127, 213, 255
von Harnack, Ernst, 16
von Hassell, Ulrich, 16
von Helldorf, Wolf-Heinrich Graf, 16
von Kageneck, Alfred "Freddy" Graf, 6, 10, 187–188
von Karsthoff, Albert "Ludovico" (Abwehr), xii. *See also* Abwehr
  background of, 25, 35–36, 36
  blown cover of Dusko, 137, 139, *140*
  counterfeit currency, 184
  covers used by, 40, 51
  Dusko and, 1, 25, 35–37, 38, 39, 40–41, 48–49, 50, 51, 54, 55–56, 61, 62, 65, 66–67, 71, 72, 88, 137, 139, *140,* 150–154, 155–156, 168, 169, 172, 173–174, 198, 199–200, 205, 206, 209–210, 210, 219
  Kammler vs., 186
  Lenz and, 56, 56n
  Metcalfe and, 66
  microdots, 71, 72, 138
  Midas (Germany funding MI5), 66–67, 77–78, 79, **277**
  questionnaires, 40, 49, 50, 55, 71, 72, *73–75,* 76
  radio traffic (false) to Berlin, 117, 118–119, 152
  replaced, 202, 205, 208, 210
  skimming money sent for IVAN, 66
  Terry and, 199–200
  Topete and, 37–38
  "turn around slowly" (monkey), 1, 173–174
  U.S. spy network, 71, **277**
  Wiegand vs., 219
  Yugoslav Escape Route (Allied escape line), 167, 174, 193–194, 195, **277**
von Kleist, Paul Ludwig, 16
von Moltke, Helmuth Graf, 16
von Rundstedt, Gerd, 211, 229, 231
von Tresckow, Henning, 16
von Trott zu Solzm, Adam, 16
von Wartenburg, Peter Yorck, 16

Waetjen (General), 249
Waldron (Commander), 151
Warlimont, Walter (General), 229
Warnecke, Dr. (Gestapo), xiii, 57, 58, 60
warnings to Dusko, 1, 25, 36, 55, 57–58, 144, 152, 165, 166, 168, 171, 172, 174, 177, 179, 180, 205, 206–207, 226
War Office, 42, 168, 201, 239
Watson, Edwin (Major General), 99, *100, 101, 102,* 103, *105*
Wavell, Sir Archibald, 88
Wehrmacht, 16, 30, 211, 232, 239
White, William, 111, 160, 165
White-Slave Traffic Act (Mann Act), 104
Whitman, Walt, 88
Wiegand, Helmut (Abwehr), xii, 200, 201, 205, 209–210, 218, 219, 249
Wild, H. N. H., 226, 227
Wilde, Oscar, 134
Willi (Duke of Windsor kidnapping), 32
Wilson, Ian (MI5), xi. *See also* MI5; Popov, Dusan Miladoroff "Dusko"
  assassination attempt on Dusko, 185
  Bailoni (Gordana) as Axis spy, 143
  D-Day and, 226
  diplomatic bags, 177–178, 183–184, 214
  Dusko and, 144, 146–147, 148, 152, 158, 159, 160, 166, 168, 169–170, 172, 177, 222, 238, 239, 243, 246, 249
  Fortitude (Normandy invasion deception), 203–204, 209, 223, 228, 252, 252n, **278**
  Hyde Park Hotel dinner party, 218–219
  information security lacking in Yugoslavia, 247–248
  Ivo (Dusko's brother) and, 158, 199, 237–238, 239, 250
  Jebsen and, 180–181, 191–192, 220, 222, 223, 224–225, 227–228, 236, 241–242, 243, 250, 251–252, 252–253
  Marriott and, 180–181
  Martins and, 196–197
  Masterman and, 180–181
  Metcalfe and, 180–181, 185–186
  Peter (King of Yugoslavia) and, 234–235, 244
  protecting families of agents, 244, 245, 248, 250, 251–252, 254
  quadruple-cross strategy, 191–192
  Quetting and, 251, 260–261
  re-engagement of Dusko, 144, 146–147, 148
  restlessness of Dusko, 160
  Schreiber's positive views of Dusko, 196
  VE Day party, 249
  warnings to Dusko, 1, 152, 168, 172
  Yugoslav Escape Route (Allied escape line), 201, 236, **277**
  Zeis and, 179
Wilson, Trevor, 252
Winchell, Walter, 135, 141–142, 142–143

Wireless Board (W Board), 42, 204
Woolf, Virginia, 91
World War I (First World War), 29, 44
World War II (Second World War), 87. *See also* Britain/British; espionage in WWII; Germany/Germans; United States of America/Americans; Yugoslavia, Serbia
WORM, THE (Zeis), xi, 171, 179, 228
Wren, Walter (MI6), xii, 122, 123, 159

Yamamoto, Isoroku, 96–97
Young, Roger S., 126n, 126–127, 128
Yugoslav Escape Route (Allied escape line; trick Germans into sending double agents), 52, 54, 167–168, 171, 172, 174, 193–194, 195, 200, 201, 211, 220, 236, 243, **277**
Yugoslavia, Serbia. *See also* Popov, Dusan Miladoroff "Dusko"; World War II
  atrocities across, 68, 69, 91, 93, 98
  bureaucracy in, 27
  economy destruction, 212
  Franco and, 194
  information security lacking in, 247–248
  officers in Switzerland, 167, 168
  Serb or Croat question to Dusko, 61
Yugoslav Legation stamp and seal, *215*

Zapp (Professor), 71n, 110, 111
Zeis, Stefan (THE WORM), xi, 171, 179, 228
Zhukov (General), 249n
Zurich, Switzerland, *ix*, 141, 157, 245, 246, 248